Veteran Care and Serv

Veteran Care and Services

*Essays and Case Studies on Practices,
Innovations and Challenges*

Edited by JOAQUIN JAY GONZALEZ III,
MICKEY P. MCGEE *and* ROGER L. KEMP

*May the Force
be with you!
Enjoy—
Jay Gonzalez
1-18-20*

*Violence, be forgotten!
lest they McGee
1-21-20*

McFarland & Company, Inc., Publishers
Jefferson, North Carolina

ALSO OF INTEREST AND FROM McFARLAND

Legal Marijuana: Perspectives on Public Benefits, Risks and Policy Approaches,
edited by Joaquin Jay Gonzalez III and Mickey P. McGee (2019)

Cybersecurity: Current Writings on Threats and Protection,
edited by Joaquin Jay Gonzalez III and Roger L. Kemp (2019)

*Eminent Domain and Economic Growth: Perspectives on Benefits, Harms
and New Trends,* edited by Joaquin Jay Gonzalez III, Roger L. Kemp
and Jonathan Rosenthal (2018)

Small Town Economic Development: Reports on Growth Strategies in Practice,
edited by Joaquin Jay Gonzalez III, Roger L. Kemp and Jonathan Rosenthal (2017)

*Privatization in Practice: Reports on Trends, Cases and Debates in Public Service
by Business and Nonprofits,* edited by Joaquin Jay Gonzalez III and
Roger L. Kemp (2016)

Immigration and America's Cities: A Handbook on Evolving Services,
edited by Joaquin Jay Gonzalez III and Roger L. Kemp (2016)

*Corruption and American Cities: Essays and Case Studies in Ethical
Accountability,* edited by Joaquin Jay Gonzalez III and Roger L. Kemp (2016)

ISBN (print) 978-1-4766-7326-4
ISBN (ebook) 978-1-4766-3857-7

LIBRARY OF CONGRESS AND BRITISH LIBRARY
CATALOGUING DATA ARE AVAILABLE

© 2020 Joaquin Jay Gonzalez III, Mickey P. McGee
and Roger L. Kemp. All rights reserved

*No part of this book may be reproduced or transmitted in any form
or by any means, electronic or mechanical, including photocopying
or recording, or by any information storage and retrieval system,
without permission in writing from the publisher.*

Front cover photograph by Ivan Chudakov (Shutterstock)

Printed in the United States of America

*McFarland & Company, Inc., Publishers
Box 611, Jefferson, North Carolina 28640
www.mcfarlandpub.com*

Jay dedicates this book to the Filipino American
World War II veterans, their families and supporters,
particularly his grandfathers, Federico M. Lucero and Antonio C. Castrillo,
U.S. Commonwealth Army of the Philippines under General Douglas MacArthur

Mick dedicates this book to his Father, Clyde E. McGee,
veteran of World War II, 584th Bombardment Group (H),
8th Air Force, Grafton Underwood, England

Roger dedicates this book to his granddaughter, Anika,
the best and the brightest

Jay, Mick, and Roger also dedicate this book to the late veteran
Dr. Paul Mico, PFC, 29th Infantry Division, U.S. Army,
Omaha Beach, June 6, 1944

Acknowledgments

We are grateful for the support of the Mayor George Christopher Professorship at Golden Gate University and GGU's Pi Alpha Alpha Chapter. We appreciate the encouragement from Deans Gordon Swartz and Marianne Koch and our wonderful colleagues at the Edward S. Ageno School of Business, the Department of Public Administration, and the Executive MPA Program.

Our heartfelt "Thanks!" goes to the contributors listed in the back section and the individuals, organizations, and publishers below for granting permission to reprint the material in this volume and the research assistance. They all expressed support for practical research and information sharing that benefits our citizens, communities, and cities.

Alan Roper
Alexandra Logsdon
American Legion
American Society for Public Administration
Barbara Ward
Bataan Legacy Historical Society
Benedict Serafica
Beth Payne
Cecilia I. Gaerlan
Center for Children and Family Futures
City of New York
City of Vallejo, California
City of Worcester, Massachusetts
Elise B. Gonzalez
Daniel Devoy
Elisha Harig-Blaine
Gabby Moraleda
Ginger Miller
Glenn J. Galman
Golden Gate University Library
Grant Rissler
Idelfonso "Tatang Floro" Bagasala
International City/County Management Association
Jeanne DeLaney
Jeffrey R. Zimmerman
Kaiser Health News
Karen Garrett

Kayla M. Williams
Kira Serna
Kurt Schake
Larisa Owen
Lichao Zhang
Luisa M. Antonio
Makati Chiropractic Center
Michelle Hong-Gonzalez
Monterey County Veterans Transition Center
National League of Cities
Nestor Aliga
PA Times
Pilipino Senior Resource Center
PM Magazine
Ronald Mitchell
Rachel Robinson
Ruth Astle Samas
Shelley McGee
Sidney Gardner
Silvana Giacalone
State of Nevada
Terry Curl
theconversation.com
U.S. Department of Defense
U.S. Department of Veterans Affairs
University of San Francisco Library
William Bare
Willie L. Britt

Table of Contents

Part II. Services, Innovations and Challenges
A. *Education, Employment and Entrepreneurship*

B. *Health and Wellness*

C. Housing and Homelessness

Appendices

Preface

There are close to 20 million veterans in the United States. Thus, it's not a surprise that the U.S. Department of Veterans Affairs (VA) has the second highest budget allocation after the U.S. Department of Defense. For 2020, the VA requested an appropriation of more than $220 billion. But even with this staggering amount, quality care and service still seem so elusive as we see homeless veterans panhandling on our city sidewalks and hear many complaining of the long waits at VA hospitals.

This public awareness of our military veterans and their families' needs and challenges has evolved into a critical area of study and practical innovation, particularly in public administration and urban affairs. As our contribution to their cause, we decided to create a first of its kind, state-of-the art best practices and narratives compilation. We gathered contributions from veterans and their allies as well as observers. The result is *Veteran Care and Services: Essays and Case Studies on Practices, Innovations and Challenges*, which is the first book to inform citizens what care and services are available to veterans not only from the federal, state, county, and city governments but also innovative alternatives from nonprofits, businesses, and public-private partnerships. And, it is the first book to share veterans' success stories alongside the sad reports on homelessness, forgotten recognition for minorities and immigrants, women's abuse, Military Sexual Trauma (MST), as well as those on veterans seeking ways to address PTSD through marijuana.

Veteran Care and Services brings together 74 chapters in three parts and five appendices. Parts I through III include an introduction to this important subject and the primary care and service providers; the services, innovations, and challenges that are available to our veteran population; and future trends and concerns. The appendices contain important documentation related to understanding this field, including a comprehensive glossary of terms and acronyms, samples of city veteran commissions, veteran departments, as well as common veteran services being administered by our state governments.

Part I: Introduction

Section A: Governments. This section includes five chapters on government organizations and highlights The GI Bill of Rights, information on the formation of the U.S. Department of Veterans Affairs, an example of one city's comprehensive provision of veterans' services to their respective veteran population, and information on how cities can help their veterans and how veterans can help their cities. In her chapter, International

City/County Management Association manager Samantha Wagner tackles the biggest concern of veterans when returning home from a war zone—applying their military training and skills to their civilian workplace. Wagner describes how cities and veteran organizations are creating innovative ways of connecting veterans and their spouses to careers in many fields.

Section B: Nonprofits. Five chapters are included in this section delving into nonprofit organizations and veterans. The American Legion chapter includes a listing of ways that a community can help its veteran population, a summary of community clinics delivering veteran health care and medical services, and information about how these veteran services are presently being provided to a city's veteran citizens and their families. In her contribution, journalist Laurie Udesky describes how valuable a health clinic is to a community, with a chapter tracing the almost psychedelic journey of the 1960s San Francisco district of Haight-Asbury free health clinic. It has morphed to today's unhippie name of HealthRIGHT360 and continues to support community and veteran health care needs.

Part II: Services, Innovations and Challenges

Section A: Education, Employment and Entrepreneurship. Eleven chapters elucidate the types of veterans seeking services; the various organizations, from both public and private sectors; information on the personal life of our veterans; the various college and university veteran services; how local governments hire veterans; and how businesses opens up career opportunities to our nation's veteran population; and lastly, how our federal government mandates hiring preferences to our nation's veterans. In one of the chapters, veteran-turned-city manager Roger L. Kemp offers an amazing chronology of his flights of military and public service adventures and landings of opportunities to do good work. Typical of many veterans who have taken advantage of the education benefits of the GI Bill, Kemp's combination of personal fortitude and use of attainable resources forged a record of service to our nation, counties, and cities.

Section B: Health and Wellness. Eleven chapters in this section are on health care and medical services accessible to our nation's veterans. These services are available from individual doctors' offices, local health care centers, and regional medical facilities like hospitals and medical centers. Additionally, information is provided on the medical and health care services granted by states, as well as our federal government. In one of his chapters, retired army veteran Willie L. Britt reminds veterans and the public, "Many of our needs are similar to the civilian sector but there are other needs that are unique to military service." A successful health care entrepreneur, Britt also penned a piece on "Veterans and Chiropractic Care."

Section C: Housing and Homelessness. Included in this section are twelve chapters which examine and highlight housing and homeless services provided by all levels of government, including the nonprofit sector, to our nation's veteran population. These services include health and medical services, homeless centers and facilities, as well as case studies on how individual cities, counties, and state governments are making services available to their respective veteran populations. These services also include "aid-in-dying" individual veteran service programs. In his chapter, veteran-turned-scholar Mickey P. McGee shares the innovative actions he discovered at an award-winning community-based organization in Monterey County which has synchronized funding streams, operates a homeless center and connects veterans with employment and job training, housing and secure additional social services for thousands of veterans, homeless veterans, and their families.

Section D: Women, Minorities and Immigrants. This section has eleven chapters that reveal gripping real-life situations, the outreach, and care options that are available to veterans who are female, a minority, and/or a member of our nation's immigrant population. Citizens throughout our nation will be made aware of the critical outreach and actions toward our nation's women, minority, and immigrant veteran populations. Ginger Miller shared her own experience being a homeless minority woman veteran: "Where do you go with a husband suffering from PTSD, being a young mother, and having a young toddler, no formal training and an associate's degree? I was afraid to ask for help and we ultimately became homeless. My world as I had known it and the one that I imagined were all gone in the blink of an eye!"

Section E: PTSD and Marijuana. The eleven chapters in this section discuss and debate the most talked about four letters in veteran care and services—PTSD. It delves into the use of controlled substances, including legal marijuana, to enhance the health and wellness and improve the level of patient care to our nation's veteran population. Many of these chapters represent innovative patient care technologies that are now accessible to many segments of our nation's veteran population. *Kaiser Health News* columnist Michelle Andrews reports on the growing interest on the value of medicinal marijuana to alleviating PTSD and writes: "'Don't ask, don't tell' is how many veterans have approached health care conversations about marijuana use with the doctors they see from the Department of Veterans Affairs."

Part III: The Future

Part III offers eight chapters on the future of veteran care and services. What about the social workers and mental health providers who care for our veterans? Do they ever get burned out? Kira Serna and Mickey P. McGee team up to answer these questions in a brilliant chapter. Chapters also delve into veterans who are now protesting wars, their moral injuries, the controversies of VA privatization, veteran treatment courts, and the inclusion of World War II in the Philippines into California's history curriculum.

Appendices

The appendices contain what we feel are innovative practical documentations for better veteran care and service. Lost in the many new terms and acronyms? That is why we produced a comprehensive glossary, since this is a very specialized field, with complex terms and acronyms of which citizens, advocates, and veterans should be aware. We also include "boilerplates" for the: (1) formation of a city veteran advisory commission; (2) establishment of a city veteran services department; (3) provision of essential state veteran benefits and discounts; and (4) commemoration of significant historical events connecting veterans, cities, and citizens.

For the most part, care and services budgeted for our millions of veterans are being delivered by public, private, and nonprofit organizations. But all is not perfect. *Veteran Care and Services* compiles the many issues, debates, and challenges requiring practical and innovative solutions in this rapidly evolving critical public and urban affairs field. It is important to codify the innovative best practices and solutions for the sake of veterans, their families, and advocates. It is also critical for public officials, at all levels of our government—local, state, and federal—to know the nature of the multiple and overlapping services now being provided to our veteran population, as well as to their families.

We appreciate the opportunity to document and share information on what is working and what is not as well as the outreach to the vulnerable, marginalized, and forgotten veterans. Efficient and effective government, business, and nonprofit services will make their personal and family lives much better for the future. It is an honor for us to serve our nation's veteran population.

We hope that you have a "good read" on these important and timely topics. We also hope that the knowledge contained in this volume will lead to more innovative improvements to the level of care services for veterans and their families in cities and states throughout our nation.

PART I

Introduction

1. The GI Bill of Rights: History and Timeline*

U.S. Department of Veterans Affairs

It has been heralded as one of the most significant pieces of legislation ever produced by the federal government—one that impacted the United States socially, economically and politically. But it almost never came to pass.

The Servicemen's Readjustment Act of 1944—commonly known as the GI Bill of Rights—nearly stalled in Congress as members of the House and Senate debated provisions of the controversial bill.

Some shunned the idea of paying unemployed Veterans $20 a week because they thought it diminished their incentive to look for work. Others questioned the concept of sending battle-hardened Veterans to colleges and universities, a privilege then reserved for the rich.

Despite their differences, all agreed something must be done to help Veterans assimilate into civilian life.

Much of the urgency stemmed from a desire to avoid the missteps following World War I, when discharged Veterans got little more than a $60 allowance and a train ticket home.

During the Great Depression, some Veterans found it difficult to make a living. Congress tried to intervene by passing the World War Adjusted Act of 1924, commonly known as the Bonus Act. The law provided a bonus based on the number of days served. But there was a catch: most Veterans wouldn't see a dime for 20 years.

A group of Veterans marched on Washington, D.C., in the summer of 1932 to demand full payment of their bonuses. When they didn't get it, most went home. But some decided to stick around until they got paid. They were later kicked out of town following a bitter standoff with U.S. troops. The incident marked one of the greatest periods of unrest our nation's capital had ever known.

The return of millions of Veterans from World War II gave Congress a chance at redemption. But the GI Bill had far greater implications. It was seen as a genuine attempt to thwart a looming social and economic crisis. Some saw inaction as an invitation to another depression.

---

*Public document originally published as U.S. Department of Veterans Affairs, "The GI Bill of Rights: History and Timeline," https://www.benefits.va.gov/gibill/history.asp (August 6, 2018).

Harry W. Colmery, a former national commander of the American Legion and former Republican National Chairman, is credited with drawing up the first draft of the GI Bill. It was introduced in the House on Jan. 10, 1944, and in the Senate the following day. Both chambers approved their own versions of the bill.

But the struggle was just heating up. The bill almost died when Senate and House members came together to debate their versions. Both groups agreed on the education and home loan benefits, but were deadlocked on the unemployment provision.

Ultimately, Rep. John Gibson of Georgia was rushed in to cast the tie-breaking vote. The Senate approved the final form of the bill on June 12, and the House followed on June 13. President Franklin D. Roosevelt signed it into law on June 22, 1944.

The Veterans Administration (VA) was responsible for carrying out the law's key provisions: education and training, loan guaranty for homes, farms or businesses, and unemployment pay.

Before the war, college and homeownership were, for the most part, unreachable dreams for the average American. Thanks to the GI Bill, millions who would have flooded the job market instead opted for education. In the peak year of 1947, Veterans accounted for 49 percent of college admissions. By the time the original GI Bill ended on July 25, 1956, 7.8 million of 16 million World War II Veterans had participated in an education or training program.

Millions also took advantage of the GI Bill's home loan guaranty. From 1944 to 1952, VA backed nearly 2.4 million home loans for World War II Veterans.

While Veterans embraced the education and home loan benefits, few collected on one of the bill's most controversial provisions—the unemployment pay. Less than 20 percent of funds set aside for this were used.

In 1984, former Mississippi Congressman Gillespie V. "Sonny" Montgomery revamped the GI Bill, which has been known as the "Montgomery GI Bill" ever since, assuring that the legacy of the original GI Bill lives on, as VA home loan guaranty and education programs continue to work for our newest generation of combat Veterans.

In 2008, the GI Bill was updated once again. The new law gives Veterans with active duty service on, or after, Sept. 11, 2001, enhanced educational benefits that cover more educational expenses, provide a living allowance, money for books and the ability to transfer unused educational benefits to spouses or children.

President Franklin D. Roosevelt signs the GI Bill into law.

President Franklin D. Roosevelt's Statement on Signing the GI Bill June 22, 1944

This bill, which I have signed today, substantially carries out most of the recommendations made by me in a speech on July 28, 1943, and more specifically in messages to the Congress dated October 27, 1943, and November 23, 1943:

It gives servicemen and women the opportunity of resuming their education or technical training after discharge, or of taking a refresher or retrainer course, not only without tuition charge up to $500 per school year, but with the right to receive a monthly living allowance while pursuing their studies.

It makes provision for the guarantee by the Federal Government of not to exceed 50 percent of certain loans made to veterans for the purchase or construction of homes, farms, and business properties.

It provides for reasonable unemployment allowances payable each week up to a maximum period of one year, to those veterans who are unable to find a job.

It establishes improved machinery for effective job counseling for veterans and for finding jobs for returning soldiers and sailors.

It authorizes the construction of all necessary additional hospital facilities.

It strengthens the authority of the Veterans Administration to enable it to discharge its existing and added responsibilities with promptness and efficiency.

With the signing of this bill a well-rounded program of special veterans' benefits is nearly completed. It gives emphatic notice to the men and women in our armed forces that the American people do not intend to let them down.

By prior legislation, the Federal Government has already provided for the armed forces of this war: adequate dependency allowances; mustering-out pay; generous hospitalization, medical care, and vocational rehabilitation and training; liberal pensions in case of death or disability in military service; substantial war risk life insurance, and guaranty of premiums on commercial policies during service; protection of civil rights and suspension of enforcement of certain civil liabilities during service; emergency maternal care for wives of enlisted men; and reemployment rights for returning veterans.

This bill therefore and the former legislation provide the special benefits which are due to the members of our armed forces—for they "have been compelled to make greater economic sacrifice and every other kind of sacrifice than the rest of us, and are entitled to definite action to help take care of their special problems." While further study and experience may suggest some changes and improvements, the Congress is to be congratulated on the prompt action it has taken.

2. Mission and History of the U.S. Department of Veterans Affairs*

U.S. Department of Veterans Affairs

Mission Statement: To fulfill President Lincoln's promise "To care for him who shall have borne the battle, and for his widow, and his orphan" by serving and honoring the men and women who are America's veterans.

Vision: To provide veterans the world-class benefits and services they have earned—and to do so by adhering to the highest standards of compassion, commitment, excellence, professionalism, integrity, accountability, and stewardship.

Core Values

- Integrity: Act with high moral principle. Adhere to the highest professional standards. Maintain the trust and confidence of all with whom I engage.
- Commitment: Work diligently to serve Veterans and other beneficiaries. Be driven by an earnest belief in VA's mission. Fulfill my individual responsibilities and organizational responsibilities.
- Advocacy: Be truly Veteran-centric by identifying, fully considering, and appropriately advancing the interests of Veterans and other beneficiaries.
- Respect: Treat all those I serve and with whom I work with dignity and respect. Show respect to earn it.
- Excellence: Strive for the highest quality and continuous improvement. Be thoughtful and decisive in leadership, accountable for my actions, willing to admit mistakes, and rigorous in correcting them.

---

*Public document originally published as U.S. Department of Veterans Affairs, "Mission and History of the U.S. Department of Veterans Affairs," https://www.va.gov/about_va/vahistory.asp (August 6, 2018).

History of the Department of Veterans Affairs (VA)

The United States has the most comprehensive system of assistance for Veterans of any nation in the world, with roots that can be traced back to 1636, when the Pilgrims of Plymouth Colony were at war with the Pequot Indians. The Pilgrims passed a law that stated that disabled soldiers would be supported by the colony.

Later, the Continental Congress of 1776 encouraged enlistments during the Revolutionary War, providing pensions to disabled soldiers. In the early days of the Republic, individual states and communities provided direct medical and hospital care to Veterans. In 1811, the federal government authorized the first domiciliary and medical facility for Veterans. Also in the 19th century, the nation's Veterans assistance program was expanded to include benefits and pensions not only for Veterans, but for their widows and dependents.

Following the Civil War, many state Veterans homes were established. Since domiciliary care was available at all state Veterans homes, incidental medical and hospital treatment was provided for all injuries and diseases, whether or not of service origin. Indigent and disabled Veterans of the Civil War, Indian Wars, Spanish-American War, and Mexican Border period, as well as the discharged regular members of the Armed Forces, received care at these homes.

As the U.S. entered World War I in 1917, Congress established a new system of Veterans benefits, including programs for disability compensation, insurance for service personnel and Veterans, and vocational rehabilitation for the disabled. By the 1920s, three different federal agencies administered the various benefits: the Veterans Bureau, the Bureau of Pensions of the Interior Department, and the National Home for Disabled Volunteer Soldiers.

The first consolidation of federal Veterans programs took place August 9, 1921, when Congress combined all World War I Veterans programs to create the Veterans Bureau. Public Health Service Veterans' hospitals were transferred to the bureau, and an ambitious hospital construction program for World War I Veterans commenced.

World War I was the first fully mechanized war, and as a result, soldiers who were exposed to mustard gas, other chemicals and fumes required specialized care after the war. Tuberculosis and neuro-psychiatric hospitals opened to accommodate Veterans with respiratory or mental health problems. A majority of existing VA hospitals and medical centers began as National Home, Public Health Service, or Veterans Bureau hospitals. In 1924, Veterans benefits were liberalized to cover disabilities that were not service-related. In 1928, admission to the National Homes was extended to women, National Guard and militia Veterans.

The second consolidation of federal Veterans programs took place July 21, 1930, when President Herbert Hoover signed Executive Order 5398 and elevated the Veterans Bureau to a federal administration—creating the Veterans Administration—to "consolidate and coordinate Government activities affecting war veterans." At that time, the National Homes and Pension Bureau also joined the VA.

The three component agencies became bureaus within the Veterans Administration. Brig. Gen. Frank T. Hines, who had directed the Veterans Bureau for seven years, was named the first Administrator of Veterans Affairs, a job he held until 1945.

Dr. Charles Griffith, VA's second Medical Director, came from the Public Health Service and Veterans Bureau. Both he and Hines were the longest serving executives in VA's history.

Following World War II, there was a vast increase in the Veteran population, and Congress enacted large numbers of new benefits for war Veterans—the most significant of which was the World War II GI Bill, signed into law June 22, 1944. It is said the GI Bill had more impact on the American way of life than any law since the Homestead Act of 1862.

The GI Bill placed VA second to the War and Navy Departments in funding and personnel priorities. Modernizing the VA for a new generation of Veterans was crucial, and replacement of the "Old Guard" World War I leadership became a necessity.

Veterans Benefits Administration (VBA)

The VA Home Loan Guaranty Program is the only provision of the original GI Bill that is still in force. Between the end of World War II and 1966, one-fifth of all single-family residences built were financed by the GI Bill for either World War II or Korean War Veterans. From 1944 through December 1993, VA guaranteed 13.9 million home loans valued at more than $433.1 billion.

Eligible loan guaranty users are now able to negotiate loan terms, including the interest rate, which helps VA loan participants to compete better in the housing market. The loan guaranty program no longer has a terminating date and can be used by any Veteran who served after Sept. 16, 1940, as well as men and women on active duty, surviving spouses and reservists.

To assist the Veteran between discharge and reemployment, the 1944 GI Bill also provided unemployment benefits of $20 per week, for a maximum of 52 weeks. It was a lesser amount than the unemployment benefits available to non-veterans. This assistance avoided a repetition of the World War I demobilization, when unemployed Veterans were reduced to relying on charities for food and shelter.

Critics dubbed the benefit the "52–20 Club" and predicted most Veterans would avoid jobs for the 52 weeks that the checks were available.

But only a portion of Veterans were paid the maximum amount available. Less than one-fifth of the potential benefits were claimed, and only one out of 19 Veterans exhausted the full 52 weeks of checks.

In 1945, General Omar Bradley took the reins at VA and steered its transformation into a modern organization.

In 1946, Public Law 293 established the Department of Medicine and Surgery within VA, along with numerous other programs like the VA Voluntary Service. The law enabled VA to recruit and retain top medical personnel by modifying the civil service system. When Bradley left in 1948, there were 125 VA hospitals.

The VA was elevated to a cabinet-level executive department by President Ronald Reagan in October 1988. The change took effect March 15, 1989, and administrative changes occurred at all levels. President George H.W. Bush hailed the creation of the new Department, saying, "There is only one place for the Veterans of America, in the Cabinet Room, at the table with the President of the United States of America." The Veterans Administration was then renamed the Department of Veterans Affairs, and continued to be known as VA.

VA's Department of Medicine and Surgery, established in 1946, was re-designated as the Veterans Health Services and Research Administration at that time, though on May 7, 1991, the name was changed to the Veterans Health Administration (VHA).

Veterans Health Administration (VHA)

VHA evolved from the first federal soldiers' facility established for Civil War Veterans of the Union Army. On March 3, 1865—a month before the Civil War ended and the day before his second inauguration—President Abraham Lincoln signed a law to establish a national soldiers and sailors asylum. Renamed as the National Home for Disabled Volunteer Soldiers in 1873, it was the first-ever government institution created specifically for honorably discharged volunteer soldiers. The first national home opened November 1, 1866, near Augusta, Maine. The national homes were often called "soldiers' homes" or "military homes," and only soldiers who fought for the Union Army—including U.S. Colored Troops—were eligible for admittance. These sprawling campuses became the template for succeeding generations of federal Veterans' hospitals.

By 1929, the federal system of national homes had grown to 11 institutions that spanned the country and accepted Veterans of all American wars.

But it was World War I that brought about the establishment of the second largest system of Veterans' hospitals. In 1918, Congress tasked two Treasury agencies—the Bureau of War Risk Insurance and Public Health Service—with operating hospitals specifically for returning World War I Veterans. They leased hundreds of private hospitals and hotels for the rush of returning injured war Veterans and began a program of building new hospitals.

Today's VHA—the largest of the three administrations that comprise VA—continues to meet Veterans' changing medical, surgical and quality-of-life needs. New programs provide treatment for traumatic brain injuries, post-traumatic stress, suicide prevention, women Veterans and more. VA has opened outpatient clinics, and established telemedicine and other services to accommodate a diverse Veteran population, and continues to cultivate ongoing medical research and innovation to improve the lives of America's patriots.

VHA operates one of the largest health care systems in the world and provides training for a majority of America's medical, nursing and allied health professionals. Roughly 60 percent of all medical residents obtain a portion of their training at VA hospitals; and VA medical research programs benefit society at-large.

The VA health care system has grown from 54 hospitals in 1930 to 1,600 health care facilities today, including 144 VA Medical Centers and 1,232 outpatient sites of care of varying complexity.

National Cemetery Administration (NCA)

On July 17, 1862, Congress enacted legislation that authorized the president to purchase "cemetery grounds" to be used as national cemeteries "for soldiers who shall have died in the service of the country." That first year, 14 cemeteries were established, including one in the sleepy Maryland town of Sharpsburg, where 4,476 Union soldiers were laid to rest following the bloody Battle of Antietam.

By 1870, the remains of nearly 300,000 Union dead from the Civil War had been buried in 73 national cemeteries. Most of the cemeteries were located in the Southeast, near the battlefields and campgrounds of the Civil War. After the war, Army crews scoured the countryside to locate the remains of soldiers who had died in battle. They were buried with honor in the new national cemeteries. However, the identities are unknown for nearly half of those who died in service to the Union and are buried in national cemeteries.

The national cemetery system has evolved slowly since the initial period of great challenge associated with the Civil War. All honorably discharged Veterans became eligible for burial in 1873.

In the 1930s, new national cemeteries were established to serve Veterans living in major metropolitan areas such as New York, Baltimore, Minneapolis, San Diego, San Francisco and San Antonio. Several of them, closely associated with battlefields such as Gettysburg, were transferred to the National Park Service because of the value of their use in interpreting the historical significance of the battles.

In 1973, Public Law 93-43 authorized the transfer of 82 national cemeteries from the Department of the Army to the Veterans Administration, now the Department of Veterans Affairs. Joining with 21 VA Veterans cemeteries located at hospitals and nursing homes, the National Cemetery System comprised 103 cemeteries after the transfer. On November 11, 1998, the President signed the Veterans Programs Enhancement Act of 1998, changing the name of the National Cemetery System to the National Cemetery Administration (NCA).

Today, there are 135 national cemeteries in all, with new cemeteries in development. Through NCA, VA administers 131 of them. Two national cemeteries—Arlington and the United States Soldiers' and Airmen's Home National Cemetery—are still maintained by the Department of the Army. Fourteen national cemeteries are maintained by the Department of the Interior. More than 3.5 million people, including Veterans of every war and conflict—from the Revolutionary War to the wars in Iraq and Afghanistan—are honored by burial in VA's national cemeteries. Today there are more than 22 million living Veterans who have earned the honor of burial in a national cemetery, including the more than 350 Medal of Honor recipients buried in VA's national cemeteries. More than 21,400 acres of land are devoted to the memorialization of those who served this nation.

3. City Veteran Services[*]

Department of Veterans' Services, City of Cambridge, Massachusetts

The Department of Veterans' Services (DVS) serves as an advocate for all Cambridge veterans and their dependents. DVS advises clients as to the availability of benefits, services, and provides financial assistance to those veterans/dependents who are in need. The department assists veterans and their families in processing applications for federal Veterans' Affairs claims for pensions, disability and death benefits, burial plots, grave markers, home loans, educational benefits, medical services, and life insurance benefits.

The Department assists its veterans in applying for the following services that are available to veterans

Chapter 115 Veterans' Benefits: Veterans and dependents whose income is below 200 percent of the Federal Poverty Level, and whose assets do not exceed $5,000 if single or $9,800 if married, may be eligible for Chapter 115 benefits.

If a veteran or dependent qualifies, the veterans' agent will provide a monthly cash benefit to help defray the costs of housing, food, and clothing.

In order to apply for these benefits the following documentation must be provided to the Veterans' Department:

- Military Discharge (DD214)
- Marriage Certificate (if married)
- Veteran's Death Certificate (if widow is applying for benefits)
- Birth Certificate for children under 19 years old
- Rent receipt signed by landlord, or current lease
- 3 Months of bank statements
- Document all monthly income (Social Security Award Letter, VA Award Letter, 4 weeks of pay stubs)

VA Aid and Attendance: Wartime Veterans who are more seriously disabled may qualify for Aid and Attendance or Housebound benefits. These are benefits that are paid in addition to the basic pension rate. This benefit may also be applied for by those with service-connected compensation provided that the compensable injury is causing the

---

[*]Public document originally published as Department of Veterans' Services, City of Cambridge, Massachusetts, "Veteran Services," www.cambridgema.gov/Departments/veteransservices (2019).

need for the Aid and Attendance. If not service-connected, this benefit may not be paid without eligibility to pension.

Widows of wartime veterans may also file for Aid and Attendance if they meet the criteria. If the widow remarries and the second marriage ends, she may apply for VAP and A+A.

Medical premiums and expenses will be counted by VA to offset some of the incomes Combined annual income and assets (not counting primary home) must not exceed $80,000.

To complete an application, the following documentation is needed:

- Military Discharge (DD214)
- Marriage Certificate (If Married)
- Veterans' Death Certificate (If widow applying)
- Proof of medical expenses
- Letter of medical necessity
- Direct deposit information

VA Disability Compensation: For veterans who were injured on active duty or during a drill period. The injury, condition, effects or scarring must continue to exist and be a problem. Pre-existing conditions (those which existed before the veteran began active duty) may be claimed if the veteran can show that the condition was worsened by active duty or by drill periods. If a service-connected rating has been previously granted and the condition has worsened, the veteran may file for an increase.

Compensation claims are filed through the nearest VA Regional Office. The VA may deny the claim or may find in the veteran's favor at a level of 0 percent to 100 percent. Note: A 0 percent finding is not a denial. It is an acknowledgment that the injury is service-connected but not serious enough to warrant a monthly payment.

To complete and application the following documentation is needed:

- Military Discharge (DD214)
- Marriage Certificate (If Married)
- Birth Certificate (Children under 19)
- All private medical documentation for conditions being claimed.
- Direct deposit information

VA Health Care: Available to all veterans who were granted an other than dishonorable discharge, provided that they meet other requirements listed under Considerations below.

Veterans who are admitted to the VA Medical system may receive all of their medical care through the system if they wish including prescriptions.

If the desire to use an outside care provider, they must be seen once per year in the VA system to maintain their eligibility. The VA will fill prescriptions from outside care providers.

To complete and application the following documentation is needed:

- Military Discharge (DD214)

VA Non-Service Pension: Pension is a benefit paid to wartime veterans who have limited or no income, and who are age 65 or older, or, if under 65, who are permanently and totally disabled, not due to their own willful misconduct. This is a low income benefit.

Pays approximately $1,074/month minus offsets for all other incomes. The VA will add approximately $177/month for each dependent child. Medical premiums and expenses will be counted by VA to offset some of the incomes. Net worth rule of thumb is that gross income plus gross assets (excluding primary home) should not exceed $80,000.

To complete an application, the following documentation is needed:

- Military Discharge (DD214)
- Marriage Certificate (If Married)
- Birth Certificate (Children under 19)
- All private medical documentation for conditions being claimed.
- Direct deposit information

Veterans' Exemption: To qualify, all veterans (and spouses where applicable) must:

- be legal residents of Massachusetts.
- be occupying the property as his/her domicile on July 1 in the year of application.
- have lived in Massachusetts for at least six months prior to entering the service (spouses exempted) or,
- have lived in Massachusetts for five consecutive years immediately prior to filing for a property tax exemption.

In most cases a surviving spouse receives the exemption if s/he was receiving it before the veteran passed away. However, surviving spouses receiving exemption under Clauses 22 and 22D lose the exemption upon remarriage.

M.G.L. ch. 59, s.5, clause 22: Clause 22 allows for a $400.00 tax exemption for the following persons:

- 10 percent (or more) service-connected disabled veteran;
- Purple Heart recipient;
- Gold Star mothers and fathers;
- Spouse of veteran entitled under Clause 22;
- Surviving spouses who do not remarry.

M.G.L. ch. 59, s.5, clause 22A: Clause 22A allows for a tax exemption of $750.00 if the veteran meets the following:

- Loss or loss of use of one hand above the wrist, or one foot above the ankle or one eye.
- Congressional Medal of Honor
- Distinguished Service Cross
- Navy Cross or Air Force Cross

M.G.L. ch. 59, s.5, clause 22B: Clause 22B allows for tax exemption of $1,250.00 if the veteran meets the following:

- Loss or loss of use of both hands or both feet
- Loss or loss of use of one hand and one foot as described above
- Loss or loss of use of both eyes (blind)

M.G.L. ch. 59, s.5, clause 22C: Clause 22C allows for tax exemption of $1,500.00 if the veteran:

- Is rated by the VA to be permanent and totally disabled and has specially adapted housing.

M.G.L. ch. 59, s.5, clause 22D: Clause 22D is for surviving spouses (who do not remarry) of soldiers, sailors, or members of the Guard whose death occurred as a proximate result of an injury sustained or disease contracted in a combat zone, or who are missing in action with a presumptive finding of death, as a result of combat as members of the armed forces of the United States.

- Total exemption so long as the spouse does not remarry.

M.G.L. ch. 59, s.5, clause 22E: Clause 22nd E allows for $1,000.00 for veterans that are 100 percent disabled by the VA.

M.G.L. ch. 58, s.8A: Paraplegic veterans, those with service-related injuries as determined by the VA, or their surviving spouses are eligible for total exemption on their property taxes.

Veterans' State Annuity Benefit: The Commonwealth of Massachusetts and the Department of Veterans' Services provide an annuity in the amount of $2000 to 100 percent service-connected disabled veterans. This annuity is payable biannually on August 1st and February 1st in two installments of $1000 each. It is granted to 100 percent service-connected disabled veterans, to the surviving parents (Gold Star Parents) and the un-remarried spouses (Gold Star Wives or Husbands) of certain deceased veterans who gave their lives in the service of their country during wartime. Each has a separate application form.

Eligibility for Annuity Benefit by Veteran: An applicant veteran who satisfies the following prerequisites shall be eligible to receive a special benefit payment of $2000 in the form of an annuity:

- Meets one of the service time requirements set forth in M.G.L. ch. 115, s.6A, 6B, and 6C;
- Has received an honorable discharge from military service;
- Any person who served on active duty in the armed forces of the United States for a period of at least 180 days and whose last discharge was under honorable conditions and continues to be a resident of the Commonwealth;
- Meets the requirements for blindness, paraplegia, double amputation or other disability set forth in M.G.L. ch. 115, s.6B and is so certified by the Department of Veterans Affairs. Proof of service and disability shall be furnished to the Secretary of DVS as per M.G.L. ch. 115, s.6CH.

Application Procedure for Annuity Benefit by Surviving Parents or Un-remarried Spouse: The annuity applicant must be a resident of the Commonwealth at the time of filing and also continue to reside in Massachusetts. Payments shall be due and payable from the date of the application. To receive the annuity, the applicant must complete the application, submit a copy of discharge (DD Form 214), a recent VA award letter, and a W-9 form (for address verification). Applications may be obtained by visiting Veterans' Services or by visiting http://www.mass.gov/veterans/benefits-and-services/bonus/annuity.html.

Veterans' Welcome Home Bonus: The Commonwealth of Massachusetts provides a bonus to veterans of certain designated campaigns who were domiciled in Massachusetts immediately prior to entry in the armed forces. In case of the death of a veteran, the spouse and children, mother or father, brother or sister or other dependents of the deceased veteran (in that order) are eligible for a bonus.

For more information, or for assistance in applying for this benefit, please contact the Veterans' Service department.

Public Events and Dedications: The department also coordinates public events on Patriots, Veterans, and Memorial Days, including the City's annual Memorial Day Parade. On Memorial Day, citizens place over 9,000 flags on the graves of veterans interred in the City of Cambridge cemeteries. In addition, the Department of Veterans Services, throughout the year, coordinates the dedication of streets, squares and parks named after veterans who were killed in action.

Veterans Services Contact: (617) 349-4760; 51 Inman Street; Cambridge, MA 02139.

4. The Local Government Community Supports Veterans[*]

SAMANTHA WAGNER

According to the U.S. Census Bureau's 2015 American Community Survey, there are more than 18.8 million veterans living in our communities today. While the majority of these men and women are 65 and older, there are still 1.6 million veterans that are younger than age 35 who are looking for jobs post-military.

Their biggest concerns when returning home? A survey conducted by the Center for Research and Public Policy found that veterans are concerned about applying military training to the workplace, job placement, and career counseling. Some local governments have successfully found ways to become involved with veterans in their communities and finding them a career. Here are several great examples.

City of Fayetteville puts veterans to work: Located in Fayetteville, NC, Fort Bragg is the largest military installation in the U.S., so it only made sense for the city to help the thousands of service members who leave the base each year to find a job. The city created a new federal partnership with the U.S. Department of Veterans Affairs—where eligible veterans have the opportunity to interview with the city and be placed into temporary jobs where there are openings.

Veterans Watchmaker Initiative: In the county of New Castle, Delaware, the doors just opened on November 7 for its newest program, the Veterans Watchmaker Initiative, the nation's only school dedicated to teaching the watchmaking trade to veterans—especially those with disabilities—for free. In a recent Smyrna-Clayton *Sun-Times* article, it mentions that county executive, Tom Gordon, was a huge reason for the new program as the county agreed to lease the program a vacant building in Odessa, with a 10-year lease at $1 a year and option for renewal.

Sam Cannan, a longtime master watchmaker who cofounded the Initiative and chairs its board, also told the Smyrna-Clayton *Sun-Times*, "Veterans who complete training will have 'instant employment,'" citing a massive need for watchmakers. There are fewer than 3,000 nationwide and more than 4,000 more needed just to meet current demand created by a global revival of mechanical watches.

---

*Samantha Wagner, "The Local Government Community Supports Veterans," November 10, 2016, https://icma.org/articles/article/local-government-community-supports-veterans. Originally published in *Leadership Matters*, November 10, 2016, by ICMA, the International City/County Management Association (icma.org); reprinted with permission.

"These jobs can start at about $85,000 a year," Cannan added, and veterans will not be charged any fees for training. "They don't pay anything and the VA doesn't pay anything and all the instructors are unpaid volunteers."

City of Dallas creates healing space for veterans with FARM: The city of Dallas agreed to lease a paved-over city-owned parcel for the next decade to the nonprofit organization, FARM (Farmers Assisting Returning Military), a place where returning veterans can learn to work with earth and receive support from fellow veterans.

In an interview with Next City, founders Steve Smith and James Jeffers explain that the six-month program trains veterans to become farmers. Afterward, interns can stay at the organization's farm or move on to partnering ones as farmers or educators. After two years of farming experience—a year less than civilians under the new Farm Bill— veterans are eligible for the federal loans that would help them buy their own farm.

Arlington County, VA, participates in regional partnership to connect veterans to high demand jobs: The Arlington County Board accepted a $150,000 state grant to train military veterans and connect them with careers in the high-growth, high-demand Information Technology (IT) field. The County is working with the City of Alexandria and others in a regional partnership for the new initiative, called IT Jobs for Veterans.

The partnership is funded by a $150,000 Virginia Workforce Investment Act Rapid Response Assistance grant from Gov. Bob McDonnell and Virginia's Community College System. The Alexandria/Arlington Workforce Investment Board received the funding for this partnership between Alexandria City, Arlington County, the Virginia Employment Commission, Northern Virginia Community College, and Acentia. Acentia, a private employer, is representing the local IT industry and will assist in coordinating the hiring of this program's graduates.

This innovative partnership is expected to serve more than 50 veterans over an 18-month period. The grant covers all the program's education, certification, and job training activities.

"Hiring Red, White & You": In Arlington, Texas, Workforce Solutions, the Texas Veterans Commission and Texas Workforce Commission (TWC) hosts the annual Hiring Red, White & You! Job Fair. This event aims to connect Texas veterans and their spouses with Texas employers who value the skills, experience, discipline and other exceptional qualities inherent with a military background. The job fair has more than 150 employers on site, as well as resource agencies, and workshops.

5. Helping Veterans Helps Communities*

Jonn Melrose

After years of military campaigns, our communities are seeing an influx of returning military service members. These men and women have access to various benefits that support them and the communities in which they live.

Gaining access to these benefits, however, can be a daunting process. Returning military need to contend with one of the largest bureaucratic systems in the U.S. government as they attempt to gain access to their benefits. The Department of Veterans Affairs (VA) sometimes doesn't have the best reputation when it comes to dealing with its clients.

After completing my own military service and college, I went to work at the Veteran Benefits Administration (VBA). I was employed at the pension management center located in Milwaukee, Wisconsin, and then at the regional office in Reno, Nevada.

I know firsthand the pressure that the VA service representatives are under for production, along with the extremely cumbersome quality control process every case goes through. I worked for more than six years before I decided that the frustrating delays and bureaucratic requirements limited my ability to serve veterans. Eventually, I was hired as veteran service officer (VSO) for Placer County, California. As VSO, I can make use of the lessons I learned while working for the VA.

County staff are responsible for working with a claimant to ensure his or her forms are completed and submitted in a timely manner. We also develop and maintain relationships with the VA to ensure the progress of submitted claims can be tracked. It is also routine for us to explain the complex workings of VA's system to people who simply want to make use of their benefits.

Understanding Benefits

The three main benefits that former military members make use of are home loan guarantees, education benefits, and health care. There are two other under-used benefits: service-connected compensation and non-service-connected pension.

---

*Jonn Melrose, "Helping Veterans Helps Communities," *Public Management (PM)* magazine, May 1, 2017, https://icma.org/articles/pm-magazine/helping-veterans-helps-communities. Originally published in the May 2017 issue of *Public Management (PM)* magazine and copyright by ICMA, the International City/County Management Association (icma.org); reprinted with permission.

The non-service-connected pension is a little-known benefit, primarily because the claimant must have little income or net worth. The service-connected benefit is more well-known; however, quite a few claimants do not want to make a claim. They have the mentality that there are other members of the military who need the benefits more than they do.

Service-connected compensation benefits are paid directly to the veteran for an injury or illness that was caused or aggravated by service. There is no income threshold or means test required for this benefit.

Non-service-connected pension is a needs-based benefit that provides for a basic quality of life. This benefit requires a means test, as it is income and net-worth dependent. It is for low-income, former military members who served during a wartime period. Non-service-connected pension should not be confused with an individual's military retirement.

Service-connected benefits are the most advantageous to a veteran. If a service member is injured while on active duty and there isn't willful misconduct associated with it, he or she may be entitled to direct federal financial aid.

These amounts can range from about $130 monthly for a 10 percent service connection, to more than $4,000 per month for a 100 percent service connection with significant medical needs.

Local Government Support

The first step is finding out what VSO resources already exist in your community. Depending on the area, a VSO can be a state or county position.

Still others are employed by such national service organizations as the American Legion, Disabled American Veterans, and AMVETS (see Resources list).

Current times require that county executives make tough budgetary decisions. As an appointed department head, I understand budget constraints. A VSO, however, is unique in that the employee can help produce direct federal financial aid to a former military member, which then can be spent and contributed to a community as a whole.

When a former military member is granted a VA rating, he or she can receive cash each month. This rating is the method by which VA determines the percentage of disability. Then, the money probably is spent in the community fueling the local economy, so the community receives the benefit in the form of tax revenue.

Placer County, for example, is currently serving some 5,300 of its known 30,000 veteran residents. According to VA data, 400 are in receipt of non-service connected pensions, and 4,900 are on service-connected compensation. Pension payments can range from $100 per month to as high as $2,100 per month.

Non-service-connected pension payments can average $1,300 per month; service-connected compensation amounts can range from $130 to just over $3,000. Service-connected payments average some $1,600 per month.

In 2016, my office of four completed more than 1,700 claims. Of this amount, 300 were denied or granted without a monetary benefit, and when this article was written, we still had more than 400 pending with the VA. The claims that were granted totaled $3 million in retroactive payments and $3.2 million in new monthly benefits. In all, during calendar year 2016, we generated more than $6.2 million in benefits.

On average, the Placer County office continues to draw $4.5 million to $5 million each month. This is a combination of the new benefits and the running benefits realized. VA data show Placer County receives closer to $7 million per month; however, I can prove the receipt of only $4.5 to $5 million. While some of this money is saved, I suspect that most of it is spent in Placer County, again helping to drive the local economy.

Reaching Out

As mentioned earlier, it makes sense for local government managers to learn more about VSOs in their communities. Find out more about their work and how the community might be able to provide support. Not only could a small motivated local department be able to return a tangible monetary benefit to the community, allowing local leadership to develop such a program clearly shows support for returning military service men and women.

We find in our department that returning members generally feel they did nothing extraordinary. They simply did their duty. My office, and others like it all over the country, do our best to ensure that people realize the benefits they have earned. Remarkably, a lot of time is spent convincing men and women to make use of the benefits. When they do, however, all of us benefit.

Take a closer look at what services are being provided in your community. Also find out how service members are continuing to contribute where they live. There is an opportunity here to help not only military service members, but also communities as a whole.

REFERENCES

www.data.gov. FY 2015 Compensation and Pension Payments by County.

RESOURCES

To learn more about veteran service officers, check out the information provided by these organizations:

- National Association of County Veterans Service Officers: https://www.nacvso. org
- The American Legion: https://www.legion.org/serviceofficers
- National Veterans Foundation: http://nvf.org/veteran-service-officers

6. Veterans, Youth, Defense, Americanism, Communities*

THE AMERICAN LEGION

Mission

The American Legion was chartered and incorporated by Congress in 1919 as a patriotic veterans organization devoted to mutual helpfulness. It is the nation's largest wartime veterans service organization, committed to mentoring youth and sponsorship of wholesome programs in our communities, advocating patriotism and honor, promoting strong national security, and continued devotion to our fellow service members and veterans.

Hundreds of local American Legion programs and activities strengthen the nation one community at a time. American Legion Baseball is one of the nation's most successful amateur athletic programs, educating young people about the importance of sportsmanship, citizenship and fitness. The Operation Comfort Warriors program supports recovering wounded warriors and their families, providing them with "comfort items" and the kind of support that makes a hospital feel a little bit more like home. The Legion also raises millions of dollars in donations at the local, state and national levels to help veterans and their families during times of need and to provide college scholarship opportunities.

The American Legion is a nonpartisan, not-for-profit organization with great political influence perpetuated by its grass-roots involvement in the legislation process from local districts to Capitol Hill. Legionnaires' sense of obligation to community, state and nation drives an honest advocacy for veterans in Washington. The Legion stands behind the issues most important to the nation's veterans community, backed by resolutions passed by volunteer leadership.

The American Legion's success depends entirely on active membership, participation and volunteerism. The organization belongs to the people it serves and the communities in which it thrives.

The American Legion was chartered by Congress in 1919 as a patriotic veterans organization. Focusing on service to veterans, service members and communities, the Legion evolved from a group of war-weary veterans of World War I into one of the most

---

*Published with permission of the author.

influential nonprofit groups in the United States. Membership swiftly grew to over 1 million, and local posts sprang up across the country. Today, membership stands at over 2 million in more than 13,000 posts worldwide. The posts are organized into 55 departments: one each for the 50 states, along with the District of Columbia, Puerto Rico, France, Mexico and the Philippines.

Over the years, the Legion has influenced considerable social change in America, won hundreds of benefits for veterans and produced many important programs for children and youth.

The American Legion Is the Largest Veterans Service Organization

Working and volunteering in communities, states and around the world, The American Legion has been dedicated to veterans, troops, national security, youth and patriotism since its founding nearly a century ago.

More than 2.1 million wartime veterans of the U.S. Armed Forces are members of The American Legion. Joining them are nearly 1 million members of the American Legion Auxiliary, the nation's largest patriotic women's association, and more than 360,000 Sons of The American Legion, male descendants of U.S. wartime veterans. They work as one great American Legion Family of shared values, at more than 13,500 local posts worldwide, in all 50 states, the District of Columbia, the Caribbean, Europe, Latin America and Asia.

As a federally chartered organization, The American Legion upholds a sacred duty to provide free expert assistance for all who have served our country in the U.S. Armed Forces, as well as their families.

The American Legion is at work today in rural towns, urban neighborhoods, military installations and college campuses everywhere.

Each local post has its own unique identity, but they are all connected by common core values. A post in Puerto Vallarta, Mexico, for instance, provides care for children with cerebral palsy, Down Syndrome and other serious diseases. The American Legion in Wyoming coordinates the state high school rodeo championships. An American Legion post in central California operates a multi-county ambulance service. Another, in Alabama, offers after-school mentorship for students seeking direction. A post in Connecticut built, owns and operates a housing facility to help homeless veterans restart their lives. Local examples of The American Legion's highest values are found worldwide, where differences are made daily for individuals, communities, states and the nation.

The Legion's fastest-growing membership segment is the post–9/11 generation. More than 100,000 strong and increasing, these young veterans help lead the organization in every way, alongside those who served in Desert Storm/Desert Shield, Grenada, Panama, Lebanon, Vietnam, Korea and World War II. No matter the war era, our members are indelibly connected through love of country, hope for the future, remembrance of the fallen and duty before self.

- The Constitution.
- Law and order.
- Americanism.

- Memories of the Great Wars.
- Individual obligation.
- Peace, good will, prosperity, justice, freedom and devotion to mutual helpfulness.

Such values are embedded in the language of the Preamble to The American Legion Constitution. Generation after generation, one century to the next, the words have come to define a purpose as meaningful today as ever before.

A Legacy of American Legion Accomplishments and Impact

- Consolidation of multiple disconnected federal offices, agencies and bureaus into one Veterans Administration in 1930
- Formulating, drafting and fighting for passage of the GI Bill of Rights in 1944, which educated millions, triggered a half-century of U.S. prosperity, revolutionized higher education and made home ownership possible for average Americans
- Establishment of a U.S. Flag Code and standard rules of respect and display
- Collaborated with Columbia University to prove that exposure to the defoliant
- Agent Orange caused deadly diseases and adverse health conditions among veterans
- Introduction, growth and continued administration of unparalleled youth programs in government (Boys State and Boys Nation); constitutional understanding and public speaking (American Legion Oratorical Contests); healthy competition (American Legion Baseball and Junior Shooting Sports); and more
- National leadership to help reform the Department of Veterans Affairs to improve health-care accessibility, accelerate benefits processing, update education assistance, and improve employee and management accountability
- Leadership in veteran career services, including employer-applicant networking, a successful business task force, and representation in Washington to improve the military-to-civilian career transition

Services That Make Differences

- Representing at no cost more than 700,000 veterans and their families seeking VA disability and medical benefits every day.
- Participating in more than 1,000 job fairs and other career events for veterans and their families every year nationwide.
- Fighting for fair conversion of military experience into credit hours for civilian careers in specialized fields such as emergency medicine, commercial driving, civil engineering and hazardous materials handling.
- Providing comfort items for hospitalized military personnel recovering from wounds and illnesses.
- Supporting and helping homeless veterans

- Spending millions of volunteer hours at VA medical facilities at an estimated annual value of $20 million.
- Supporting veterans suffering from post-traumatic stress disorder and traumatic brain injury.
- Addressing and lobbying Congress and the White House to provide timely VA health care, efficient benefits processing, effective GI Bill education provisions, a decent quality of life for active-duty military personnel and other issues important to Americans.
- Assisting during natural disasters, from converting local posts into clinics after hurricanes and tornadoes, to providing food, relief items and other needs to displaced citizens.
- Providing financial assistance to needy military and veteran families with young children at home.
- Awarding grants to organizations that provide support for children in need.
- Awarding college scholarships to children of U.S. service members killed while on active duty since the terrorist attacks of Sept. 11, 2001.
- Mentoring youth through American Legion Boys State and Boys Nation, as well as local, state and national American Legion Oratorical Contests.
- Running hundreds of youth programs, including more than 3,000 Scouting units, nearly 4,000 American Legion Baseball teams, dozens of Junior Shooting Sports clubs, Junior ROTC and Junior Law Cadet programs.
- Providing citizenship and naturalization education and support for legal immigrants seeking to become Americans.
- Serving as the nation's foremost authority on U.S. flag respect, procedures and code.
- Educating school children on such topics as flag respect, military service, history and patriotism.
- Providing and distributing U.S. flags for the graves of American military personnel laid to rest at overseas cemeteries.
- Demanding full accounting and repatriation, when possible, of all U.S. military personnel listed as prisoners of war or missing in action.
- Participating at thousands of patriotic observances and events around the world each year at the local, state, national and international levels.
- Handling honor guard services and memorial tributes for fallen military personnel and veterans, from individual funerals to memorial dedications.

For Veterans

- Free assistance for veterans and families applying for VA benefits
- Relentless advocacy for a strong VA health-care system
- Free representation for veterans appealing claims decisions
- More than 1,000 job fairs and career events
- Support and assistance for homeless veterans

For America's Youth

- American Legion Baseball
- Scholarships
- Flag education programs
- Oratorical competitions
- American Legion Junior Shooting Sports
- Youth Cadet Law Enforcement program
- Boys State and Boys Nation
- Junior ROTC
- Scouting

Defense

- Cash grants for military families who have temporary financial needs
- Comfort items for hospitalized military personnel
- Advocacy for fair military retirement benefits
- Family Support Network of volunteers to help military families
- Representation in Washington to support proper DoD funding
- Assistance in cases before military discharge review boards

Americanism

- National leadership in U.S. flag protection and respect
- Services to help legal immigrants become U.S. citizens
- Support for public expression of the Pledge of Allegiance and the national anthem

Community

- Honor and remembrance of those who served and sacrificed
- Emergency relief in times of natural disaster
- Leadership at patriotic ceremonies and special events
- Connections with local schools and home-school students
- Numerous local programs and initiatives, tailored to each community's needs

7. Want to Support Veterans?
Four Tips for Finding Good Charities*

Brian Mittendorf

Many Americans donate to charities that help military veterans as a way to honor them for their service to the country. It can, however, be daunting to choose from the more than 8,000 such groups operating nationwide.

Donor trepidation is magnified by the scandals that have embroiled vets' groups. In fact, more than 10 percent of the charities tagged as "America's Worst Charities" by the *Tampa Bay Times* and the Center for Investigative Reporting in 2013 focus on veterans.

As a professor who researches nonprofit organizations and teaches about their finances, I have observed that while some veterans' charities do squander donors' dollars, others make the most of donations in meeting their mission. Fortunately, a little research goes a long way toward spotting the difference between a good cause and a lost cause.

The following four tips will help you vet these charities.

1. Learn what exactly the charities do

Be wary of vague statements about a group's activities. While language indicating that a charity "supports" or "honors" veterans does not always signal a problem, it does mean you should seek more specific information. Many of the veterans' charities that have faced criticism, such as Paralyzed Veterans of America and National Veterans Services Fund, have had vague mandates to educate the public about what veterans need.

A detailed description of a group's mission and activities can instill confidence that veterans truly benefit from its work. An exemplary charity is the Honor Flight Network, which flies veterans to Washington, D.C., to visit military monuments and honor fallen colleagues. The benefits are self-evident, as I've seen firsthand as a flight volunteer. Fisher House Foundation, which provides temporary housing to families of veterans receiving treatment at VA facilities, is another good example. There are many ways that organizations can and do directly serve veterans. To find them, look for clear-cut programs you find meaningful and significant.

2. Find out what share of the money raised for organizations actually supports them

Another common pitfall: for-hire fundraisers that siphon too much of the donated funds.

*Originally published as Brian Mittendorf, "Want to Support Veterans? 4 Tips for Finding Good Charities," *The Conversation*, May 22, 2017. Reprinted with permission of the publisher.

Michigan's attorney general determined that only 39 percent of funds raised by professional solicitors for charity in the state in 2016 actually supported those groups. The fundraising contractors kept the rest of the money. The picture is even more lopsided for veterans' charities in the state, with only 23 percent of donations making it into their coffers. The track record in Michigan is no anomaly—New York, Massachusetts and other states have found similar patterns.

Operation Homefront, which *Consumer Reports* named as one of the best veterans' charities last year, clearly states on its website how much it spends supporting its mission.

Professional solicitation is not inherently problematic—but outsourced fundraisers keeping most of the money raised for a charity is a real concern. The federal government does not track this information but most offices of state attorneys general maintain databases that indicate how the organizations raising funds in their states stack up.

Since national campaigns also show up in these databases, even if your own state doesn't make all the details easily accessible, you can use the online tools other states offer to evaluate different charities. New York's database is especially user-friendly.

3. Check out IRS 990 forms

OK. I know perusing IRS forms is not everyone's favorite activity. But it's the best way to discover how donor dollars are actually spent. Finding a charity's tax form is easy, even if groups don't post them on their own websites, thanks to databases like Propublica's Nonprofit Explorer and the Foundation Center's 990 Finder.

The Semper Fi Fund 990 form from its 2016 fiscal year suggests that the group does not spend an excessive amount of money on fundraising and administration. Semper Fi Fund.

If you do check out a 990 form, be sure to go to page 10. That's where nonprofits classify their expenses, both by function and type. There, you can see where donated money primarily goes. If the organization has a stated focus on providing financial assistance to veterans, for example, you should see lots of grants to individuals on line 2, and not so much in the way of advertising, travel and postage listed on the other lines.

Consider how the Semper Fi Fund, a group that provides financial and other aid to injured and ill post–9/11 veterans and their families, stated its functional expenses for its 2016 fiscal year. The numbers indicate that the group spends over 90 percent of its funds on its mission. Three-fourths of that mission spending is direct grants to individuals— a good sign.

4. Inquire about donor privacy policies

When you make charitable donations, you give away both money and personal information. What charities do with your personal data is part of the picture and how they handle this information varies widely.

Consider how the Wounded Warrior Project, among the nation's most visible veterans' organizations, has handled donor data. The group came under fire in 2015 and 2016 for alleged waste, as well as routinely selling personal information culled from its donors to other nonprofits and defending this practice. The controversy resulted in a shakeup at the top.

Other groups do a better job of protecting donor privacy. Fisher House Foundation, which clearly states a policy of not sharing or selling donor lists, offers a good example of how to do this. If an organization doesn't state its privacy policy on its website, take the time to ask.

When it comes to vetting charities, a little work goes a long way. These four steps should help you find veterans' charities with goals that match your own and that you can trust to make the most of the money you give away.

8. From Its Counterculture Roots, Haight Ashbury Free Clinic Morphs*

LAURIE UDESKY

Since it opened 50 years ago, San Francisco's Haight Ashbury Free Medical Clinic has been a refuge for everyone from flower children to famous rock stars to Vietnam War veterans returning home addicted to heroin.

Strolling through the clinic, one of the first of its kind in the nation, founder Dr. David Smith points to a large collage that decorates a wall of an exam room affectionately referred to as the Psychedelic Wall of Fame. The 1967 relic shows a kaleidoscope of images of Jefferson Airplane and other legendary counterculture bands, floating in a dreamscape of creatures, nude goddesses, peace symbols and large loopy letters.

"That was made by a woman who had just taken LSD. She stayed here for a very long time and put all that up. It lasted as long as her LSD trip," Smith said moving on to what was once called the "bad trip" room, where clinic staff would talk down clients during acid trips gone awry.

Fundamentally, Smith and others say, the organization has remained true to its counterculture roots, still offering free care in a deliberately nonjudgmental atmosphere.

But it is also drastically different: It is now the Haight Ashbury Free Clinics—plural—and part of a multi-million-dollar conglomerate with the decidedly un-hippie name of HealthRIGHT360.

All told, HealthRIGHT 360 serves approximately 40,000 patients each year in a wide range of programs, including "reentry" services to formerly incarcerated adults and teens, residential and outpatient drug treatment, mental health care and medical and dental care. In 2014, it purchased a 50,000 square foot building at 1563 Mission Street in San Francisco as additional space to offer all of these services under one roof. The organization also serves patients in San Mateo and Santa Clara counties.

It's been a long journey from Smith's early days running a standalone clinic.

When the clinic first opened, it operated 24 hours a day with an army of volunteer physicians from the University of California–San Francisco and Stanford. The one paid staffer was a nurse. The first year's budget was her salary: $25,000.

*Originally published as Laurie Udesky, "From Its Counterculture Roots, Haight Ashbury Free Clinic Morphs Into Health Care Conglomerate," *Kaiser Health News*, January 25, 2017. This story was produced by Kaiser Health News, which publishes California Healthline, an editorially independent service of the California Health Care Foundation.

It had a "guerrilla" pharmacy, Smith said. Pharmaceutical representatives would load up their trunks with medication samples and drop them off at the clinic, where a team of UCSF volunteer pharmacists bottled up the medication and shelved it, according to Smith, who noted wryly that the illegal activity long ago reached its "statute of limitations."

"Our first exam table was my kitchen table," he recalls. Decisions were made by consensus, and even the janitor weighed in, Smith said.

Benefit rock concerts organized by the iconic music promoter Bill Graham, featuring performances by George Harrison and Janis Joplin, helped the clinic stay afloat financially.

Smith remembers when Joplin overdosed on heroin, and the clinic rushed over an "overdose team" armed with the anti-opioid medication naloxone: "We zipped out there and reversed her overdose," recalls Smith.

As Smith tells it, many Vietnam veterans returned from the war in the early 1970s addicted to heroin. They felt ostracized by what was then called the Veterans Administration and headed to Haight Ashbury and its clinic, which by then offered comprehensive medical cares and a drug detox program.

The influx of veterans led to federal grants from Special Action Office on Drug Abuse Prevention. "That began the government funding era in the 1970s and ensured our survival," said Smith.

In the 1980s, a young woman named Vitka Eisen learned firsthand the value of the personal attention the clinic offered. She came to the Haight Ashbury clinic struggling with heroin addiction. "I went there for detox at least nine times," she said. "I never felt shamed or judged. They always acted like they were glad to see me."

Her trust in the staff led her to kick her heroin habit and return to school, where she eventually earned a doctorate in education from Harvard.

Eisen took the helm as CEO of HealthRIGHT360 in 2010.

The clinic's business model began to change dramatically in 2007, when it added another site at 1735 Mission Street, San Francisco.

But by 2011, like many recession-era nonprofits, the clinics were deeply in debt, Smith said. So they merged with the renowned San Francisco–based addiction and mental health treatment program, Walden House, which wanted to offer comprehensive medical care to its patients. The two nonprofits merged, and adopted the name HealthRIGHT360.

By joining forces in 2011, Walden House and the Haight Ashbury Free Clinics were able to weather the extraordinary financial expense of shifting their organizations to electronic health records, a requirement of the Affordable Care Act, said Eisen.

With the system in place, she said, it's easy enough to train and add on new providers as HealthRight360 has expanded. The merger also allowed the Haight Ashbury Free Clinics to erase its debt in a year.

Between then and its latest merger in July with Prototypes, a Southern California women's drug treatment center, HealthRIGHT360 has acquired five other community clinics in Northern California and offers treatment at 40 sites up and down the state, according to its former Vice President of Development Michelle Hudson.

Ben Avey, assistant director for external affairs at the California Primary Care Association, said such mergers aren't new, but they have accelerated under the now-imperiled ACA.

At the individual clinics that comprise health systems like HealthRIGHT360, "they speak your language, know your culture, understand the situation you're coming from," Avey added.

As CEO, Eisen led the consolidation that streamlined HealthRIGHT 360. "We have one board, one human resources department, one finance department, one payroll department and one executive." The annual revenue, said Eisen, is $110 million. Medi-Cal, the city, county, state and federal governments reimburse HealthRIGHT 360 for providing patient services, as do commercial health insurers.

But ties to the early days remain. The early treatment of concertgoers evolved into San Francisco–based Rock Medicine, which is now part of HealthRight360 and sets up on site at rock concerts, circuses and fairs in the San Francisco Bay Area and Los Angeles garnering $1,038,000 annually from the venues.

And the non-judgmental reception by the Haight Ashbury Free Clinics' staff continues to this day, according to 61-year-old David Smith (no relation to the clinic founder), who has been coming to the clinic since the 1980s and has always felt welcomed and accepted.

This was true even when Smith was homeless in the early 2000s.

"It didn't matter if I was dirty," he says. "I didn't have to feel like I couldn't come in here because I wasn't in the proper state of cleanliness, which was unfortunately the case for a quite bit of the time."

9. Sometimes the Best Medicine for a Veteran Is the Company of Another Veteran[*]

Elisa Borah

Many take time on Memorial Day to remember the Americans who have given their lives in service to our country.

For veterans and their families, that sentiment of remembrance is felt year-round. Many veterans suffer lifelong anguish over the loss of their brothers and sisters in arms. For them, Memorial Day is a day like every other day—a day they remember those who died at war.

This shared grief is just one way some veterans are affected by their military service. Veterans are also molded by military culture—a unique set of values, traditions, language and even humor. Military culture has unique subcultures, but it has enough consistency across different branches, ranks and time periods to make most veterans feel a kinship.

Recognizing this kinship has led veteran service and health care organizations to encourage veterans to build trusting relationships and support each other. Researchers have learned that veterans are more likely to share personal information and ask advice about many things, including health care, from fellow veterans. That's why the VA offers employment to veterans as peer specialists.

I'm a mental health services researcher at the University of Texas at Austin School of Social Work. I focus on increasing the availability of social supports and improving the efficacy of mental health treatment options for veterans and their families. Last year I had the opportunity to study the Texas-funded Military Veteran Peer Network, a statewide program that provides peer-to-peer support in 37 communities.

My research supports the idea that veterans are an important resource who can be trained to support fellow veterans in need. What's more, I've learned that civilian care for veterans can be improved when civilians are trained in military culture. The MVPN offers military-informed care training to civilian providers and law enforcement personnel throughout the state.

---

*Originally published as Elisa Borah, "Sometimes the Best Medicine for a Veteran Is the Company of Another Veteran," *The Conversation*, May 29, 2016. Reprinted with permission of the publisher.

Understanding the Need

The bond that soldiers share can help them stay mentally strong. Mental health issues are acute for a significant number of veterans.

As many as 25 percent experience some form of mental health concern, such as depression. The VA reports that veterans have a higher risk of suicide compared to the U.S. population.

Post-traumatic stress disorder (PTSD) is another well-known concern. Estimates of the prevalence of PTSD vary widely due to the variety of study samples and assessment tools. A conservative measure suggests PTSD affects eight percent of service members returning from Afghanistan and Iraq.

Veteran peer support shows promise in addressing these common mental health issues. An example is the Vet to Vet program, a VA program developed by Moe Armstrong, a decorated Vietnam War veteran, in 2002. Research has shown that veterans who receive peer support have greater levels of empowerment and confidence, improved functioning and reduced alcohol use compared to those who didn't receive peer support.

Researchers are increasingly understanding the value of incorporating veteran peers into health care teams. Given the large numbers of veterans returning from prolonged combat, the documented shortage of trained behavioral health providers to treat mental health problems, overly long wait times for treatment and stigma felt by veterans regarding seeking help, veteran peer support offers great promise in improving treatment outcomes.

While peer counseling is not new—it was formally recognized in the 1970s—its value in treating veterans has gained recognition since President George W. Bush's New Freedom Commission on Mental Health, which was released in 2003.

President Barack Obama has also seen the value of peer support. His Executive Order 13625 of 2012 sought to improve access to mental health services for veterans, service members and military families by including the hiring of peer specialists. As of 2015, the hiring of peer specialists has exceeded the goal set in the executive order. In 2015, President Obama renewed his support by calling for more peer support as part of the Clay Hunt Suicide Prevention for American Veterans Act.

Research on the role of veteran peers has shown their positive impact in assisting homeless veterans to transition to housing.

There is early evidence that veterans charged with misdemeanors and arraigned in Veteran Treatment Courts receive invaluable support from veteran peers throughout their probation and treatment for mental health, substance use problems and receive help with housing, transportation and employment.

These are two among many other areas that veteran peers are providing effective supports.

Getting Civilians into the Act

The mental health care provided by civilians for veterans can also benefit from lessons learned from these veteran-driven programs.

Understanding the unique culture shared by military members and their families can be a daunting task for Americans who have not experienced the military lifestyle.

Given the volunteer nature of our armed services and the historically small size of our current force, this culture is familiar to only a small proportion of American citizens. Instead of assuming this cultural gap cannot be breached, we are learning the powerful impact that civilian health care professionals can make when they become trained in military culture and practice military-informed care.

Research efforts are underway to understand how to best train practitioners to better understand the clinical impact of this cultural competency. Research can assess, for example, whether this knowledge can help improve veterans' engagement in care, increase their treatment completion and improve their clinical outcomes.

The VA has hired 800 peers as of 2013 with 100 more planned annually. In addition to Texas, New York, Michigan and California, as well as Canada and the United Kingdom, have veteran peer support programs.

Although most of us can never truly understand what war is like, we can honor all veterans, including those who didn't make it home, by valuing the special knowledge and connection that veterans bring to bear in therapeutic care settings. By prioritizing veterans' experiences and knowledge, we can build a society that promotes real healing and a respectful homecoming.

10. Collaborating at the Local Level to Serve Veterans and Their Families[*]

SIDNEY GARDNER *and* LARISA OWEN

In another chapter, we reviewed the case for serving veterans and their family members through community-based agencies. These agencies can go well beyond what the Department of Veterans Affairs (VA) is able to do to provide services and supports to the 40 percent of discharged veterans with children. The VA focuses on veterans, but state, local and community agencies can help their families.

But how can these agencies and those that serve veterans directly work together to achieve better results and wider funding? There are three critical ingredients to such an effort by local agencies working in collaboration: The numbers: how many children and veterans live here? The need: what services and supports do they need? The networks: which agencies can provide those services, working across agency boundaries and how can they be held accountable for results?

Each of these steps, undertaken by a group of agencies and organizations working as a coalition, can make a big difference for the 30 percent to 35 percent of veteran families affected by a returning veteran's trauma and substance use problems.

The Numbers

What we currently know is over 2.4 million active duty service members were soldier-deployed to Iraq and Afghanistan since 2001. An estimated 40 percent of them are now veterans separated from service, living in their communities. Roughly one third of those separated veterans are married, over half have children, averaging two each. Most recently, the VA has published data for the total number of children of veterans of recent conflicts.

Based on the VA data on the percentage of children of veterans affected by family disorders such as PTSD and substance abuse, we can estimate the total number affected in your area.

You can't coordinate what you can't count. Knowing the total number of veterans

*Originally published as Sidney Gardner and Larisa Owen, "Collaborating at the Local Level to Serve Veterans and Their Families," *PA Times*, August 25, 2017. Reprinted with permission of the publisher.

in your county or state and the estimated annual increase in those veterans is a vital set of facts. Just as important are the number of veterans served by the local and regional VA health facilities, total homeless veterans, total unemployed veterans, and the total veterans attending college. All of this data is available through local agencies.

The Need

Approximately 30 percent to 35 percent of separated veterans exhibit symptoms of PTSD and/or substance abuse. These are problems which affect the entire family, with an impact on children's cognitive learning, emotional stability and risky behaviors. Some of these children need early identification and screening, substance abuse prevention services and mental health services aimed at social and emotional stability.

Veteran-serving agencies don't always understand that when they serve the veteran, they are also serving the family. Employment agencies serve veterans' families, because child care, child support, health coverage, transportation—all of these affect veterans' ability to get and keep a job. Housing agencies serve veterans' families. Are housing units for single veterans—or for families?

The essential component of needs is the missing box on the form: How many veterans are in our caseload? We know from the literature that what affects one member of the family affects all of them. In veteran agencies that work with veterans every day, front-line staff can learn about what is needed and available to families by asking about their children, spouses and partners.

Once you have completed your intake and you are aware that the client has kids, spouses, or partners, you can refer that family to agencies that work with children and families. Their case management can keep your agency informed while working with the family on other referrals, linkages and possibly counseling.

The Networks

Several cities, counties and regions have formed veteran and military family collaboratives, made up of both veteran-serving agencies and their civilian children and family-serving counterparts. These networks can do their own resource inventories, and gradually, as they build up information about services and needs, they can develop an annual report card that tracks not only who is being served—but how they number compares with total needs in the area. That results in a network that is not just a bunch of meetings, but a coalition of shared accountability fort results.

Conclusion

Putting these pieces together is a kind of services integration—a phrase which reminds us that the military services have been working since 1947 to develop a unified response to our nation's adversaries. The same kind of unified response is needed to respond to the needs of veterans and their families. We can't count on the VA to do that job—they have their hands full serving veterans. It's up to the rest of us, guided by our answer to the central question: should any child or family member be worse off because his or her parent served their country?

The answer, of course, is NO. That's where our mission begins.

PART II

Services, Innovations and Challenges

• *A. Education, Employment*
and Entrepreneurship •

11. Military Transitioning: U.S. Coast Guard Service Member Preparation for Civilian Employment[*]

Glenn J. Galman

Every military service member knows that they will eventually leave their service. How they prepare for the transition is often a chaotic and personal journey. The U.S. Department of Veterans Affairs (VA) estimated that, between 2011–2016, more than 1 million service members would separate from the military and transition into civilian life (VA, 2015). In 2012, researchers at Prudential Financial surveyed more than 2,400 veterans and, not surprisingly, concluded that veterans worried about finding employment in a post-transition environment. For example, significant percentages of veterans expressed concerns about finding a meaningful job (80 percent), how their military skills translated to the civilian sector (58 percent), and cultural barriers (45 percent) in the civilian sector (Prudential Financial, 2012).

What Our Service Members Can Expect in the Civilian Employment Sector: Today's current job market can be characterized by high volatility which can directly lead to high levels of unemployment. As a result, "the single lifelong employment relationship with one employer tends to be rare, with people tending to have multiple career transitions" (Vigoda-Gadot et al., 2010, p. 379). The reason or impetus is typically influenced by external (i.e., economy), internal (personal decision) or combination of the two factors (Robertson & Brott, 2014; Vigoda-Gadot et al., 2010). Research has shown that cultural differences exist between military and private organizations and military service members historically underestimate the vast changes resulting from transition from the military (Edwards, 2015; King, 2011; Morin, 2011). The VA (2018) summarized the common challenges military service members face during transitioning. The challenges include:

- Relating to people who do not know or understand military culture and life
- Reconnecting with family and re-establishing a role in the family
- Joining or creating a community

---

*Published with permission of the author.

- Preparing to enter the work force
- Returning to a job
- Creating structure
- Adjusting to providing basic necessities (food, clothing, housing, etc.)
- Adjusting to a different pace of life and work
- Establishing services (medical, dental, insurance, etc.)

How Our Service Members Can Prepare for Their Transition to Civilian Employment Sector: A fundamental mandate of each branch of the U.S. Armed Forces is to man, train, and equip its forces in order to effectively accomplish its statutory missions. As such, each service expends tremendous resources (e.g., career development plans/guides, initial training, specialty/advanced training, etc.) to ensure that each military member is mission ready throughout the course of their military career. Compared to mission readiness, traditionally, very few federal resources have been afforded to military members and/or their families to ensure they are ready for life as a civilian member of society. This situation changed in 1990. Through Congressional legislation, all military branches are required to provide separating service members with pre-separation counseling. This counseling offers members a minimal level of training and education to prepare them for transition to life outside of the military.

How Military Branches Fulfill Their Transition Service Additional Responsibilities: While the U.S. Coast Guard (USCG) is a branch of the military, it functions substantially differently from the other branches (Edwards, 2015). The USCG established transition assistance for its personnel in October 1994 which provided "all separating and retiring service members with access to transition assistance services"; the program also offered members involuntarily separated (IVS) with specific benefits (USCG, 2003, p. 1). "The diverse complement of individual programs, services, and benefits can be classified into four categories: pre-separation counseling, employment assistance, relocation assistance for separating members stationed overseas, and benefits for IVS members" (USCG, 2003, p. 2). The program's primary goal "is to provide information and assistance to all separating and retiring members to help them make an effective transition from military to civilian life; this ensures that separating members are made aware of, and have access to, the numerous programs and services (military, government, nonprofit, and commercial) available to assist them in the transition process" (USCG, 2003, p. 2). Since inception of the Transition Assistance Program (TAP), the program has morphed and changed to address socio-economic changes within the country (Vow, 2011; GAO, 2005 and 2018). The current TAP focuses on the pre-separation readiness of service members through three- to five-day workshops involving a core curriculum focused on financial planning, career planning, resume building, interviewing skills, networking, and veterans benefits (DoD, 2016; Edwards, 2015).

How Does the Transition Assistance Program Work? A significant amount of research has been performed "to understand the success of ongoing initiatives and identify possible barriers to Veterans' economic mobility" (VA, 2015, p. 8). These studies have identified the most current veteran employment trends, gaps, barriers and opportunities (Prudential Financial, 2012; VA, 2015). Remarkably, two-thirds of DoD veterans indicated TAP as their primary tool for pre-separation assistance (Prudential Financial, 2012). According to Prudential (2012), 60 percent of respondents indicated the translation of "military skills to civilian work as a roadblock to finding a job" (Prudential Financial,

2012, p. 4). In addition, of the services offered under TAP, pre-separation counseling with a focus on developing a detailed and clear career transition plan, educational benefits, and access to mental health professionals was the most valuable to a service member preparing for life as a civilian (Morin, 2011). However, according to Buzzetta et al. (2015), these services truly gain relevancy and value when individualized (and supported by career transition specialists) to each transitioning service member. The results of these studies supported evidence-based strategies aimed at increasing the economic competitiveness of U.S. military veterans, many of which were incorporated in the update to the current version of TAP (VA, 2015).

While USCG TAP usage data was absent from previous research, recent academic analysis of the USCG TAP program suggests parity between USCG and DoD veteran employment challenges. For example, 49 percent of DoD veterans indicated that TAP was effective in preparing them for military transition (Prudential Financial, 2012). Similarly, 51 percent of USCG retirees indicated support of TAP's effectiveness (Galman, 2019). In contrast to these lukewarm opinions of TAP's effectiveness, a small sampling of career transition specialists indicated an overwhelming indictment of TAP's effectiveness to prepare service members for civilian employment (Galman, 2019). These results imply room for improvement of TAP to address the job hunting needs of transitioning service members.

According to the academic analysis of USCG TAP's effectiveness, while the overall program was mildly effective, the TAP services that were directly related to tangible career development and planning outcomes were particularly valuable (Galman, 2019). These services included development of an individual transition plan and job application package, employment and non-medical VA benefits counseling, and resume building. In addition, the analysis emphasized the need for individualized assistance that is specific to the service member's unique needs (Galman, 2019). This is consistent with DoD veteran research where "interest is high for new transition programs or services customized for veterans, which close to three-quarters (of surveyed DoD veterans) view as being important to their success" (Prudential Financial, 2012, p. 3).

In addition, the analysis results indicated strong interest in TAP devoting more time to explaining VA health care and disability benefits. These results are consistent with DoD research that indicate nearly two-thirds of DoD veterans with a health challenge experience a difficult transition from the military (Prudential Financial, 2012; Morin, 2011). Morin (2011) explained that over 40 percent of post 9–11 veterans had a military-related experience that they characterized as "emotionally traumatic or distressing" and 16 percent suffered a serious injury (Morin, 2011, p. 3).

Additionally, the analysis suggested the need to shift to a case management approach for transition assistance (e.g., positive hand-off of service members to organizations that address individualized needs), updating career transition curriculum and delivery methods to match current requirements and trends (e.g., training available accessible 24/7 through public electronic media [YouTube], increased practical interviewing activities, and current resume writing techniques for different employment sectors/categories), and adding resources to the military budget to improve TAP. Lastly, the analysis indicated, while only a slight majority of USCG retirees felt TAP was effective in preparing them for civilian employment, 92 percent of those surveyed were able to obtain civilian employment within 18 months of service-separation (Galman, 2019).

How Successful Are Service Members in Finding Employment? While chance and luck are undeniable factors, successful employment transitions are shown to be influenced more by the experiences and characteristics of the veteran. For example, the Pew Research Center (2011) identified that being an officer, having a consistently clear understanding of the missions while in the service, being a college graduate, and, for post–9/11 veterans, attending religious services frequently were all characteristics that positively influenced civilian employment opportunities (Morin, 2011). The Pew Research Center (2011) identified the factors of "having a traumatic experience, being seriously injured, serving in the post–9/11 era, serving in a combat zone, serving with someone who was killed or injured, and being married while in the service" as having a moderating impact on a successful military transition (Morin, 2011, p. 3). In addition, Schmit et al. (1993) determined that assertive job-seeking behavior did not have a significant correlation to successful employment outcomes. More remarkably, individuals with a type-A personality, internal locus of control, self-efficacy, and positive self-esteem were more likely to experience successful employment outcomes (Schmit et al., 1993). Once armed with life enhancing information and given the task of successfully transitioning from the military, most service members will find the right fit for their unique needs. Simply put, the warrior spirit of service members does not entertain failure as an option, especially when it comes to their personal well-being or that of their family.

How the Service Member's Transition Burden Is Reduced. Improvements to the USCG's TAP require changes at the macro and micro levels. Programmatically, the service needs to address the findings and conclusions of a 2018 U.S. Government Accountability Office (GAO) report on the USCG TAP. Conventional organizational performance management principles can offer the formula for program improvement through establishment of agency goals and priorities consistent with USCG culture and leadership, inform agency policies and resource (funding and staffing) decisions, etc.. For example, USCG TAP officials should immediately define program success and establish a performance goal for program effectiveness (e.g., 70 percent overall effectiveness rating). Following USCG doctrine, this recommendation is directly linked to the USCG's commitment to its workforce through the USCG Human Capital Strategy (2016).

While a plethora of research exists regarding the transition experiences of DoD veterans, it is highly recommended that the attitudes and experiences of all USCG veterans regarding USCG TAP's effectiveness in preparing USCG service members for military transitioning be examined. Used as a standalone or part of a USCG TAP improvement plan, the new research should focus on examining the homogenous pre- and postseparation needs of the various age or service experience groups within the service; especially with emerging needs from the new Blended Retirement System. In addition, to inform existing human resource management concerns for retaining talented women in the workforce, new research should be conducted specific to experiences and needs of female service members. All of this new evidence could highlight demographic specific military transitioning requirements and enlighten officials with additional factors that influence USCG strategic human resource management.

Every journey begins with a single step. While the previous recommendations offer ideas for macro-level, long-term solutions, micro-level, near-term solutions can begin to address the current needs of service members preparing for military transitioning. Recent research suggests that the greatest return (benefit to service members) on the USCGs investment (resources) are TAP services that offer tangible career development outcomes (e.g., resume building, interview preparation, individual transition plan, etc.).

In addition, research proposes these services are especially effective when tailored and delivered to meet the specific needs of the service member. Almost immediately, USCG officials should examine the improved use of the existing network of federal, state, local, and non-profit organizations as (relatively) resource-neutral, force multipliers to the limited USCG career transition staff and resources. For example, the United Service Organizations (USO) offers active service members (active duty, reserves, guard, and their dependents) free, individualized career transition services through the USO PATH-FINDER program. This program offers participants personalized support within a case management framework. Formal incorporation of a USO PATHFINDER representative into a USCG TAP workshop could yield immediate, positive dividends to the service member, USCG, and USO.

References

Buzzetta, M., Hayden, S.C.W., & Ledwith, K. (2017). Creating Hope: Assisting Veterans with Job Search Strategies Using Cognitive Information Processing Theory. *Journal of Employment Counseling*, 54(2), 63–74. https://doi.org/10.1002/joec.12054.

Edwards, G.J. (2015). *Exploring Critical Success Factors of the Redesigned Military Transitioning Program* (Doctoral dissertation). Retrieved from Walden Dissertations and Doctoral Studies. (Accession No. 1689).

Galman, G.J. (2019). *Military Transitioning: Assessing the Effectiveness of the U.S. Coast Guard Transition Assistance Program* (Master's capstone). Golden Gate University, San Francisco, California.

King, E. (2011). *Field Tested: Recruiting, Managing, and Retaining Veterans.* New York: American Management Association.

Morin, R. (2011). *The Difficult Transition from Military to Civilian Life.* Retrieved from http://www.pewsocial trends.org/2011/12/08/the-difficult-transition-from-militaryto-civilian-life/.

Prudential Financial. (2012). *Veterans' Employment Challenges.* Retrieved from http://www.prudential.com/documents/public/VeteransEmploymentChallenges.pdf.

Robertson, H.C., & Brott, P.E. (2014). Military Veterans' Midlife Career Transition and Life Satisfaction. *The Professional Counselor*, 4(2), 139–149. doi:10.15241/hcr.4.2.139.

Schmit, M.J., Amel, E.L., & Ryan, A.M. (1993). Self-Reported Assertive Job-Seeking Behaviors of Minimally Educated Job Hunters. *Personnel Psychology*, 46(1), 105–124. Retrieved from http://0-search.ebscohost.com.library.ggu.edu/login.aspx?direct=true&db=bth&AN=9609192385&site=eds-live&scope=site

U.S. Coast Guard [USCG]. (2003). *Commandant Instruction (COMDTINST) 1900.2A—Transition Assistance Program.* Retrieved from https://media.defense.gov/2017/Mar/06/2001707840/-1/-1/0/CI_1900_2A.PDF.

U.S. Coast Guard [USCG]. (2016). *U.S. Department of Homeland Security Component Review: Coast Guard.* Retrieved from https://www.uscg.mil/Portals/0/documents/PTT_USCG1.pdf?ver=2016-09-06-163615-050.

U.S. Department of Defense [DoD]. (2016). *U.S. Department of Defense Instruction (DoDI) 1332.35–Transition Assistance Program (TAP) for Military Personnel.* Retrieved from https://www.esd.whs.mil/Portals/54/Documents/DD/issuances/dodi/133235p.pd

U.S. Department of Veterans Affairs [VA]. (2015). *Economic Opportunities for Veterans: Understanding Economic Competitiveness in Relation to Their Non-Veteran Counterparts.* Retrieved from https://www.data.va.gov/story/economic-opportunities-veterans.

U.S. Department of Veterans Affairs [VA]. (2018). *Veterans Employment Toolkit: Common Challenges During Re-Adjustment to Civilian Life.* Retrieved from https://www.va.gov/VETSINWORKPLACE/docs/em_challengesReadjust.asp.

U.S. Government Accountability Office [GAO]. (2005). *Military and Veteran's Benefits: Improvements Needed in Transition Assistance for Reserves and National Guard*, GAO-05-844T: Published: June 29, 2005, Retrieved from https://www.gao.gov/products/GAO-05-844T.

U.S. Government Accountability Office [GAO]. (2018). *Transitioning Veterans: USCG Needs to Improve Data Quality and Monitoring of Its Transition Assistance Program*, GAO-18–135: Published: April 19, 2018, Retrieved from https://www.gao.gov/products/GAO-18-135.

Vigoda-Gadot, E., Baruch, Y., & Grimland, S. (2010). Career Transitions: An Empirical Examination of Second Career of Military Retirees. *Public Personnel Management*, 39(4), 379–404. https://doi.org/10.1177/009102 601003900405.

Vow to Hire Heroes Act of 2011 [VOW], Pub. L. No. 112–56, 125 Stat. 711–735 (2011). Retrieved from https://www.gpo.gov/fdsys/pkg/PLAW-112publ56/pdf/PLAW-112publ56.pdf.

12. Military Friendly Universities and Helping Veterans Succeed Academically[*]

SILVANA GIACALONE *and* MICKEY P. MCGEE

The basis for this chapter was a study completed at Golden Gate University in 2016. The main research question asked in this study was whether universities have implemented effective veteran services that help student veterans succeed academically. The study focused on services available to student veterans at selected universities in the San Francisco Bay Area. Data was collected to determine which services contribute the most to student veterans' success. Primary data was collected using survey questionnaires, focus groups and individual interviews. Sources of data included: (1) veteran students currently attending local colleges, have recently attended, or are looking to attend in the Northern California area; (2) current and prospective students currently in the military; and (3) VA School Certifying Officials in San Francisco Bay Area colleges. The student veterans offered insights on their transition from military to civilian life, their needs and concerns, as well as what they consider a military friendly university to be. VA Certifying Officials are generally the first contacts for the student veteran population and have insight on the needs and concerns of this population.

The Department of Veterans Affairs (VA) has been helping veterans pursue their educational goals since 1944, when the Servicemen's Readjustment Act commonly known as the GI Bill was signed into law. This act has been noted as being "one of the most significant pieces of legislation ever produced by the federal government" (www.benefits.va.gov) and one that has significantly impacted the millions of men and women that have served our country. This Act provided grants for school, funding for college tuition, low interest mortgage rates, job training, business loans, unemployment payments and more. Its original purpose was to help veterans transition to civilian life soon after coming back from deployment. Since then there have been many additions and variations to the original GI Bill; however, the goal has always been to assist veterans readjust into civilian life and provide these veterans educational opportunities that they may have missed due to their military commitments.

The most commonly utilized GI Bill benefit is the post–9/11 Veterans Educational

---

*Published with permission of the authors.

Assistance Act of 2008. Since its implementation, it has "provided educational benefits to 773,000 veterans and their families, amounting to over $20 billion in benefits" (www. va.gov) in just 7 short years. The Act provides financial support for tuition and housing for individuals whom have at least served for 90 days of service, service must have occurred after September 11, 2001. Today the majority of student veterans utilize the post–9/11 benefits at their college. The post–9/11 alone has been the most utilized VA Educational Benefit since 2010; in addition to the other programs within the GI Bill over 1 million veterans have utilized the benefits.

The GI Bill educational benefits are utilized by veterans in colleges all over the United States, and although the benefits do assist with the educational costs associated with getting a degree, they do not help with any other expenses nor do they assist with the needs that many veterans require in order to succeed academically. Therefore, colleges must have services readily available for veterans to utilize and assist with their educational needs. Additionally, should also have a competent and highly trained staff that is aware of the needs and challenge of this unique population. Unfortunately, many schools are not staffed with enough knowledge of veteran service needs. Because the Department of Veterans Affairs does not provide schools with guidance, many schools must create services on their own, complete staff training, and compensate for financial burdens that the benefits do not cover.

It is important to understand what exactly constitutes a Military Friendly University because it is more than just a label placed by outside sources and/or the media. Many universities offer services geared towards veterans but identifying whether these services are enough to help veterans and service members returning from deployment succeed academically is a major concern within higher education. Ideally a Military Friendly University is generally an academic environment where student veterans feel safe, where there are services available not only on campus but online as well, and where there are highly trained staff and faculty that have a full scope of knowledge on VA related matters, including the needs and challenges of this population. Services can include a veterans club, priority scheduling, discounts and scholarships, accepting military training for credits, policies for withdrawing due to deployment, special accommodations, counseling, and so forth. Military Friendly Universities can vary depending on the needs of Veterans and service members however it's important to create a sense of community for these veterans and have services available geared to help them transition to civilian life but also to help them succeed academically. As service members return to the U.S. from combat area deployments, many are starting or re-entering college and universities and utilizing their available services. A Military Friendly University can make or break a veteran's transition to the civilian world. Veterans need support services from a knowledgeable and qualified staff prepared to address the needs and concerns they bring onto the campus.

Understanding veteran student needs is crucial because every veteran has a unique need depending on their experiences in the military. For example, a veteran may need counseling, additional time to complete an exam, or maybe help in job searching, etc. Mental and physical challenges and barriers are extremely common for combat veterans, so it's important to have services available that cater to all challenges regardless whether it is a wheelchair accessible classroom or even one-on-one psychological counseling, barriers are not just physical but mental as well. Veteran student programs in universities and colleges are crucial because having these services can be the difference between a student veteran succeeding or failing academically, graduating or not, and transitioning smoothly or roughly into civilian life.

Given the increasing number of veterans returning to college and utilizing the GI Bill benefits, "higher education must find ways to address the needs of this population and decrease the risk that they will leave college before achieving their goals" (Renn & Reason, 2013, p. 14). Schools must be aware of and understand the needs and challenges of each individual student veteran. These needs are unique and can vary depending on age, gender, and individual military experiences. There are many levels of concerns and needs of each individual veteran, ranging from mental to physical disabilities. It is important that schools understand these needs and provide proper training to staff and faculty. Challenges can be mental or physical; some veterans may have visible wounds while others may have hidden wounds. Nonetheless, given the increasing number of veterans returning to college and utilizing the GI Bill benefits, higher education must find ways to address the needs and challenges of this population and decrease the risk that they will leave college before achieving their goals.

Lack of services is a big contributor to the failure of veterans in higher education, especially because the GI Bill offers so many promises (financially) and veterans are not generally prepared for the realities. Many veteran students need support and more than what they were accustomed to in the military. Many "student veterans face challenges that range from lack of disability accommodations to difficulty interacting with a younger body that represents a sharp contrast to someone transitioning from the demands of the military" (Hamrick & Rumann, 2013, p. 6); many veterans need help adapting and navigating within the college environment, so services do need to be geared towards this so that there are no barriers present for veterans.

Because the effects of deployment are different for each individual, some of the most common would include mental and physical concerns such as PTSD (Post Traumatic Stress Disorder), TBI (Traumatic Brain Injury) and physical impairments. Overcoming barriers is a struggle for returning veterans; generally, a sense of feeling lost or lonely because there is no micromanagement or sense of brotherhood in college as there is in the military, feelings of being different because of the physical impairments, or shame because of the mental disorders.

Many universities have services geared towards their student veteran population; they may include career and vocational support, counseling services, legal support, financial planning, and academic accommodations. Veterans must complete their degree within 36 months, the amount of time allowed to utilize VA Educational Benefits. To succeed academically, a student must maintain satisfactory academic progress. At Golden Gate University a "C" average must be maintained as an undergraduate, and a "B" average must be maintained as a graduate student. Generally, if a student does not maintain satisfactory academic progress they are at risk of being disqualified from the University.

The conclusions and recommendations of this study are:

Conclusion 1: With the rising costs in the San Francisco Bay Area, financial assistance is needed for veteran students. Although the GI Bill benefits offers generous assistance towards tuition and living expenses, student veterans do still need assistance with additional costs that may not be covered fully by the benefits. Although the Bay Area has some of the top housing allowance benefits in the country, with the rising costs it is still not enough for many veterans and military members that have a family, or have unforeseen expenses such as medical or child care costs. More and more student veterans decide to attend school full time in order to maximize their benefits, which means they generally do not work.

Conclusion 2: The majority of veterans and military members in this study that are utilizing VA Educational Benefits find that this is their primary motivation for succeeding academically in their current and/or past institution. Ironically, a benefit that was meant to help veterans be successful in life after coming back from deployment is doing just that in current times. The Post 9/11 GI Bill which offers 36 months worth of benefits has been an essential part of student veteran success; in fact in the survey 65 percent of respondents stated that the fear of losing or wasting their educational benefits was the reason they succeeded academically.

Conclusion 3: A military friendly university provides services specifically geared towards veterans such as academic and counseling. However, academic and counseling services are not well-utilized possibly because many on-line students are not physically present on campus to utilize the services and many students are unaware of the available services.

Conclusion 4: There is a lack of connection and collaboration between the VA and schools. VA policies create barriers for school certifying officials. School Certifying Officials are very limited as to how much information is provided to them by the VA. However other issues such as any student veteran debts must be handled directly by the student themselves. These veteran students may not know how to resolve these issues. The veteran student may seek the advice and assistance of the school's VA representatives who might also not know how to resolve it because of lack of training and lack of knowledge.

Recommendation 1: Expand on discounts/scholarships on the university level. The goal here is to help veterans and military members financially with expenses that the GI Bill does not cover. Veteran students' main concern is to be able to afford college. The majority of veterans today quit their jobs to attend school full time, resulting in financial stress which some hope that schools can alleviate. Potential remedies to this problem include seeking donors, veteran and military associations and alumni veterans willing to donate funds for this population. Another action might be to allocate money in a school's budget to provide scholarships/grants for this population.

Recommendation 2: Partner with Community Based Organizations like Swords to Plowshares who share similar goals to help veterans and military members succeed academically. Schools support veteran students to ensure they succeed academically. CBOs provide support to ensure veteran needs are met (whether that means housing, legal representation, counseling, etc.). The partnership can include staff training and workshops to veteran students.

Recommendation 3: The VA should create a VA School Certifying Official Academy where VA reps are trained and certified by the VA, especially on VA changes to educational/tuition assistance benefits, tuition payments, and housing allowances. A sustaining training partnership agreement should be established to ensure that university and college staff and faculty are aware of and updated on VA and military related issues/needs/concerns. Knowledgeable experts from the Department of VA, local CBO subject matter experts, county VA Services offices should be encouraged to provide workshops and webinars to train school staff on VA related topics as well as provide information pamphlets and current reference guides. The VA Education Liaison and the California State Approving Agency should be asked to facilitate this partnership and collaboration.

13. From Military Service to Public Service Through GI Bill

ROGER L. KEMP

My Military Service Time

My active duty military time gave me an appreciation for public service, and the opportunity to get the education that I wanted after I was discharged from the U.S. Coast Guard. My memberships in national professional associations let me network with fellow professionals, both from the municipal and academic communities, and provided me with a knowledge of possible available internships, and information on possible employment opportunities in my field of study—public administration. Some of these professionals even let me use them as references during my job searches. I welcomed this opportunity.

The first time I flew on an airplane in my life was when I joined the U.S. Coast Guard at nineteen years old, and I flew from San Diego, in southern California, to Alameda, in the San Francisco Bay Area, the home of the U.S. Coast Guard training center. I was there eight weeks for my initial military service training. Upon the completion of this training, I was transferred to the 11th Coast Guard District Office headquarters in Long Beach. I worked in our district office with a 9 to 5 o'clock office job that I held for nearly four years. This position, and its hours, allowed me to attend night school at Long Beach City College and earn an AA degree, making me the first person in my family ever to attend and graduate from college. This was done prior to my discharge from the military service in the evening while I was on active duty.

The military taught me the value of public service and the need to have a good education to serve the citizens. In the military service I learned on-the-job skills that made a significant difference in my life. I was honored to serve our nation during my military service. It made me want to continue to serve the public in future years. When I returned to civilian life, I went to night school on the GI Bill for nearly 15 years—and never missed a semester! During my public service career, I served for nearly three decades as a city manager in cities on both coasts of the United States—in California, Connecticut, and New Jersey. I was also an adjunct professor at leading public and private universities, teaching night courses, during my city management career.

---

*Published with permission of the author.

My Educational Benefits

After completing my B.S. degree and a Master of Public Administration degree at San Diego State University, I found a job in the office of city manager in Oakland, California. I still had time left on the GI Bill, so I set my sights on a Ph.D. degree program in public administration in California and looked for a nighttime program, since I had to work full-time during the day. There were only two nighttime doctoral programs in public administration in California at the time. I chose the one at Golden Gate University, in San Francisco, across the bay from Oakland. The other nighttime doctoral program in public administration was at the University of Southern California, which is in Los Angeles. I preferred the San Francisco Bay Area, so I chose to relocate from San Diego to Oakland, right next to the San Francisco Bay, and not far from the City of San Francisco, the home of Golden Gate University.

It took me five years to complete the doctoral degree's program requirements, one night class per semester while working full-time in Oakland. The same month that I received my Ph.D., I went from being an assistant to the city manager in Oakland to becoming a city manager in Seaside, California. And I have served as a city manager ever since that time—in Southern California, New Jersey, Connecticut, and then back in Northern California. Every place where I served as a city manager, I taught courses in MPA programs at night at primarily local public and private universities. It was easy to get a teaching assignment as an adjunct professor at a local university with my MPA from San Diego State University, my Ph.D. in public administration from Golden Gate University, and my experience as a seasoned career city manager.

Other Military Service Benefits

While the GI Bill was a major benefit of my having been a veteran, there are various other veteran benefits available from other levels of government too, like states, their counties, and their municipal governments. Many public officials approve benefits for veterans that include reductions of taxes and user fees and various discounts. Nowadays, even many businesses in the private sector offer discounts to veterans, including goods and services from national commercial retail establishments, and from national restaurants. Benefits to veterans include all branches of the military service and continue to evolve and expand. As years go by, the types of benefits for veterans and the level of cost reductions available have been increasing.

This is a trend that will continue in future years. It is great for the private sector to honor our citizens that have served in our military service, in all branches of military service—the U.S. Army, the U.S. Navy, the U.S. Air Force, the U.S. Marine Corps, and the U.S. Coast Guard.

Other Lifetime Accomplishments

Over the years I have published, or have been a contributing author to, nearly 50 books on various topics related to public management, including strategic planning in local governments, homeland security practices, and the preservation/restoration of natural resources in our communities. My book on the best practices in homeland security was made available to every city manager in America, since it was published by the International City/County Management Association. These accomplishments are based on my military service, and my ability to go to school in the years that followed on the GI Bill.

Getting college degrees on the GI Bill changed my life. It greatly enhanced my public service career and provided me with the opportunity to teach night courses at some of the leading public and private universities throughout the nation. The first book that I had published was my doctoral dissertation at Golden Gate University.

I have also given speeches, based on the research for my books, all over the world, as well as in states throughout the United States of America. Over the years, I gave presentations to members of professional associations in dozens of states in America, as well as many countries throughout the world, such as Australia, Canada, England, Italy, Germany, and Puerto Rico. I've also worked in and been a career city manager in the largest council-manager cities across the nation, on both coasts of the United States, including Oakland, California; Clifton, New Jersey; and Meriden, Connecticut. It has been a wonderful experience to live on both coasts of this great nation. All of my educational and professional accomplishments, including the ability to live on both coasts of our nation, were based on my active duty military service, and receiving the benefits of the GI Bill afterwards to attend college to receive undergraduate, graduate, and advanced graduate degrees. I used all of my educational entitlements under the GI Bill, and went to night-school for nearly 15 years without ever missing a semester. If not for the GI Bill, I would not have gone to college, since I would not have been able to afford it.

Later during my city management career, I applied to and was accepted into the Senior Executives in State and Local Government Program at the John F. Kennedy School of Government at Harvard University. They had government leaders from throughout the world in this program that was designed for senior executives in state and local governments. I also attended the Graduate Finance Institute at the Graduate School of Business at the University of Wisconsin, Madison. This was, and still is, the only program of its type in our nation, and is sponsored by the Government Finance Officers Association (GFOA). My acceptance into these programs was based on my previous educational experience and my professional accomplishments, all of which were based on my ability to utilize the GI Bill to attend college because of my prior active duty military service.

The Future

I encourage young people throughout America to serve in one of the branches of our military service and to receive the subsequent benefits provided to them under the GI Bill. It will help them achieve their personal and career goals in cities and states throughout America, which many citizens call "the land of opportunity." The GI Bill paid for my entire education, which has served me well, both personally and professionally, throughout my lifetime.

Students, especially graduate students, should join national professional associations too. Such groups have regular local and regional meetings, hold workshops, and help their members network with other professionals in their field. It also provides an excellent opportunity for young people to acquire a knowledge of possible internships and employment opportunities in many professional fields. Students receive discounts from their membership fees in these national professional associations.

Memberships in such associations will also enhance a person's resume. Much as the GI Bill helps you achieve your educational goals, your membership in national professional associations will help you achieve your desired professional employment goals in the field that you were educated in. Networking with professionals also helps young citizens put their education to good use, and facilitates their local, regional, and national job-seeking opportunities.

Lastly, I recently heard a young person say, when asked if he was going to college, that "my mom and dad can't afford to send me to college, so therefore I won't be going to college." I also heard a parent say, when asked if his daughter was going to college, that "she applied and was accepted into a good school, but she failed to get her scholarship and, therefore, she won't be attending college." I would like to say, in closing, that a young person's education is not dependent upon the wealth of the parents or his ability to receive a scholarship to pay for his educational expenses.

All young people nowadays have the opportunity to join the military after high school, serve their active-duty time, and then attend college on the GI Bill afterwards, as I did, after they are discharged from their military service. All it takes is having a knowledge of this educational opportunity, being dedicated to your country, and being willing to serve your time in the military service, then going to school, either full-time or part-time, based on the payments that they receive from the U.S. government for their active duty military service. Such opportunities, and the accomplishments that you receive from them, will change your life, as you will have higher career goals, and will have received a good education to help you achieve them.

14. Military Lessons Applied to Private Sector Consultancy Work[*]

Terry Curl

This chapter presents 11 areas of key military lessons that I learned during my 23 years in the U.S. Army Corps of Engineers. I applied these lessons to my private port and marine consultant organizational work after retirement from the military service.

In every military assignment of my career, I learned the importance of leadership, teamwork, having a balance in your life, and taking care of your staff. My 23 years in U.S. Army were very rewarding. In every assignment as a military officer, you really are a teacher to soldiers, sailors, airmen or marines as well as civilians. I had assignments in Vietnam, Korea, Panama, Europe, and the United States (Pentagon). My military education included: basic and advanced officer engineer courses, Armed Forces Staff College, and the U.S. Army War College. I attended the U.S. Naval Postgraduate School, Monterey, California, and earned a master's degree in applied mathematics.

After retiring from the U.S. Army, I worked in a small California city government and with small and large global engineering and construction companies for 12 years. The engineering companies ranged in size from 50 employees with local projects and simple organizational structure to large engineering companies with 100,000 employees with a very complex structure. I also became registered as a professional engineer in California and Virginia. I graduated from the University of Southern California with master's and doctorate degrees in public administration. The focus of this chapter is on my private port and marine assignments.

Since 2007, I worked as a senior port and marine consultant for four large global engineering companies with over 10,000 employees. My responsibilities included design and construction for the major U.S. West Coast ports (Los Angeles, Long Beach, San Diego, Seattle, Tacoma, Anchorage, Honolulu and Korea). I oversaw over 200 employees spread out in those port locations.

Based on my military experience, what are the military lessons that I have applied to both the public (ports) and private organizations (global large engineering companies) to improve the services to those clients and citizens? This chapter addresses the top 11 lessons learned in the military and in public and private organizations.

---

[*]Published with permission of the author.

1. Leadership

John Gardner defines leadership as "the process of persuasion or example by which an individual (or leadership team) induces a group to pursue objectives held by the leader or shared by the leader and his or her followers" (Gardner, 1990, p. 1). In his 40 years of observing public and private leaders, he found there are very few good ones. There are very few true leaders in the military and even fewer in the private sector. I was fortunate to have worked for a few outstanding military and private leaders and learned a lot from them.

My first assignment as a new second lieutenant, U.S. Army Corps of Engineers, was as a construction project officer in Germany. My company commander was a seasoned military officer. I learned important lessons, the value of delegation and proper care of direct reports/non-commissioned officers. He held monthly company town hall meetings. He reviewed the status of projects, changes in personnel, and answered questions. I have used town hall meetings many times to communicate to employees during my Army assignments and in my private consulting career. The town hall meeting is a great way to communicate to employees.

In mid–1987 a new commanding general (CG) arrived at South Pacific Division (SPD), Corps of Engineers Headquarters in San Francisco. SPD was responsible for civil and military construction in the Western U.S. with a construction value of over $3 billion. After 90 days on the job, the general made major and radical organizational structure changes. He discussed my role as chief of staff in detail and told me "you run the staff, and I will focus on meeting our employees, meeting with congressional leaders, and stockholders." I learned a great deal about how best to delegate; make prompt decisions; promote teamwork, communications and trust; and get support from the boss. I made mistakes but he always supported me.

Leaders must communicate regularly with their employees. Employees that don't know what is going on will assume the worst. Many large engineering companies focus almost all their efforts on making a profit and often neglect treatment of employees. If well treated by the company leadership, employees will help create a good profit. In a private company, managers must care for their employees while completely satisfying client requirements.

2. Communications

Almost every year, the *Harvard Business Review* bi-monthly publication has an article that covers the biggest error senior managers make—"they don't communicate." I had town hall meetings monthly but also biweekly one-hour senior staff meetings. I learned to run effective focused meetings. The importance of knowing details about your employees is critical. I always gave a personal hand-written note to each employee on their birthday. Also, I spent time with each employee once every three months visiting with them and discussing the details of their work, their career plans and family life. Every Friday I required my key staff to provide me a very short one-half page report. The report included what they accomplished for the week and what their key actions were for the following week. I also provided my own report to each of my direct reports and my boss.

3. Delegation

Blanchard discusses in his book that delegation is a manager and leader's number one management tool, and the inability to delegate well is the leading cause of management failure (Blanchard, 2007). The delegating authority must trust the delegated employee and must be able to let the employee execute the authority and responsibility that they have been given and not micromanage them.

As Chief of Staff for South Pacific Division, I shared responsibility for day to day operations with the Commander. I delegated a lot. The key for delegating was to be clear what you are delegating. The worst thing you can do is to delegate and then micromanage the person. Managers and leaders must delegate to be successful, especially as they move up in an organization. When you delegate, many times mistakes will be made but the ones to whom you delegate responsibilities will learn and grow.

4. Organizations

Military organizations are "lean and mean": everyone is clear on one another's role and responsibilities, and there are only a few layers to the top. The focus is on completing the assigned mission and supporting the front-line staff.

Large global engineering companies' organizational structure is very heavily layered and top heavy with too many managers. With this large complex organization, it takes a lot of time to get anything approved. Maintaining the many layers of management is very expensive. Large engineering companies should minimize the management levels and use the money saved by reduction in managers for use by front line managers to meet the needs of clients.

I have pushed my bosses very hard to reduce the management layers. In my Golden Gate University "Organizational Development and Leadership" course, I emphasize to keep organizational structure flat, and make roles and responsibilities clear for all. I simply make decisions based upon my experience and many times I did not wait for the cumbersome layers of management approval.

5. Employee Performance Evaluations

Most managers do not do a satisfactory job on employee performance appraisals. They do not take time to develop realistic, measurable goals at the start of the year, periodically review those goals and provide feedback during the year. In the U.S. Army, the efficiency report is the basis for assignment and promotions. At the beginning of the period and within the first 30 days, the rater and ratee must meet and develop specific, measurable, realistic and attainable goals. The key in the final evaluation meeting is to review all the accomplishments and then discuss the goals that were not totally accomplished.

6. Culture

My military career provided exceptional opportunities to understand different cultures and the importance of culture from both the individual and from an organizational perspective. Schein defines "culture as a pattern of shared basic assumptions that was learned by a group as it solved it problems of external adaption and internal integration, that has worked well enough to be considered valid and, therefore, to be taught to new members as the correct way to perceive, think, and feel in relation to problems" (Schein, 2004, p. 17). Leaders and managers must clearly understand the culture within as well as outside of the organization. My different cultural experiences were:

- Combined Forces Command, Korea, is a command of U.S. and Korean personnel responsible for the defense of Korea. I had two assignments in the Command. My boss in both assignments was a Korean General. I was very successful in the assignments because I learned the Korean culture and customs.
- U.S. Southern Command, Panama (SouthCom), was a U.S. Unified Command in Panama. I was responsible for DOD construction and then the closeout of facilities and returning them to the Republic of Panama. There were a lot of hard negotiations since the Panamanian Government wanted facilities to meet higher standards than were required. The negotiations were difficult but with patience, listening, and following DOD guidance both sides were satisfied. As the Area Engineer, U.S. Army Corps of Engineers, Panama, I had fourteen Panamanians working for me on the U.S. Base Construction Program. We were very successful because we learned to have patience and listen to each other, and had many social family functions to help in better understanding our cultural differences.

7. Teamwork

My high school baseball coach kept a sign outside his door: "Team work is essential for success—Some of us are not as good as all of us working together." I agree totally with the contents of that sign. The U.S. Army Corps of Engineers is a large Federal engineering and construction organization with over 50,000 employees. Over 95 percent of the employees are civilian. As chief of staff, South Pacific Division, I interacted with three district commanders. The most successful district commander was from Sacramento District. He considered the civilians as critical team members and always listened to their advice.

John Wooden, former UCLA Hall of Fame basketball coach, created a learning video named *The Pyramid of Success (POS)* (Wooden, 2010). The POS covered many topics for success. The one topic I focused on was his concept of team work. Wooden always identified each player's strengths and weaknesses. He then built the team based upon a combination of players' individual strengths, always in context of team strength. He never discussed winning but always asked his players to do their best. His teams won 10 of 12 NCAA championship using the pyramid concepts. The pyramid provided his players the key concepts to be applied for success in life. I take considerable time understanding each of my employees, especially their strengths, and help them improve on their weakness.

8. Mentor

I wish I had mentors throughout my military career to help guide my career, provide advice and just be a "sounding board" for my ideas. As a Panama senior manager for DoD Construction, I was fortunate to work for a great leader, the district engineer, located in Mobile, Alabama. He was very supportive and visited my office in Panama at least once every three months. We developed great respect for each other and communicated frequently. He moved to new assignments and eventually was promoted to major general. This experience really demonstrated to me the importance of having mentors to discuss ideas and give guidance. They can help in not only your professional work but also in your personal life.

9. Balance in Your Life—Don't Be a Workaholic

I had two tours in Vietnam. In each tour, the normal work day was 18 hours a day. Everyone was exhausted for the long work day. During my second tour, the battalion chaplain came to me one day and said that I looked exhausted. He asked, "What do you do besides work?" In a combat zone, there are very few things to do but eat, sleep, and fight. He suggested a few things that helped relax me: take short walks around the compound; pray; do yoga; learn the Vietnamize language. He discussed the importance of creating balance in your life and avoiding being a workaholic. He suggested continuing to learn languages, practicing yoga and other important activities. I have followed his advice and my life is very well balanced. I take two Hawaiian vacations each year, go to the gym, walk my dog daily, and attend my grandchildren's activities. I continue to serve as a port and marine consultant, advisor to a Korean Drone Survey Company, and California notary public, and I teach two courses per quarter at three universities (Golden Gate, JFKU and Brandman).

10. Network

I have developed a large network of key contacts (fellows, peers and bosses) and maintained those contacts. As I approached retirement, I applied for civilian jobs. My boss at that time was a two star general. He emphasized the importance of a solid network of individuals to maintain contact and get their advice and counsel. I used my key contacts as references. I applied for and was selected as assistant city manager in Eureka. The city manager said he talked to my key references, and he received exceptionally positive comments.

Today, over 20 years since I left the Army, I maintain a strong network with 20 military peers and bosses. Furthermore, I have developed a strong network from key engineering companies since leaving the Army. I have used both networks extensively for advice and references. I could not have done as well without an active network.

11. Praise in Public; Counsel in Private

Many times, in my military career as well in the civilian world, I have seen leaders yell and talk down to subordinates in front of a large audience. As a senior analyst for the Engineer Studies Center in Washington, D.C., I was required to attend the annual town hall presentation by the Army chief of engineers, a three-star general officer. At the end of the general's presentation, a very senior civil service manager asked a question related to the construction work in Honduras. The general exploded and said, "That is the dumbest question that I have ever heard." This discussion was in front of 600 employees. Many people left right after that blow-up. The civilian who asked the question was a top employee. The general later apologized for his actions but it was too late. The employees in the entire organization lost respect for him and within months, he left the organization. The lesson learned: Praise in public and counsel in private.

REFERENCES

Blanchard, Ken (2007). *Leading at a Higher Level.* Upper Saddle River, NJ: Prentice Hall.
Gardner, J.W. (1990). *On Leadership.* New York: Free Press.
Schein, E.H. (2004). *Organizational Culture and Leadership.* San Francisco: Jossey-Bass.
Wooden, John (2010). *The Wisdom of Wooden.* New York: McGraw Hill.

15. The Emotional Challenges of Student Veterans on Campus*

ANN CHENEY

On Veterans Day, Americans will honor the heroism and sacrifice of the nearly 22 million men and women who have served in the U.S. military. Among them will be student veterans. Since 2009, nearly one million veterans have benefited from the post–9/11 GI Bill, which has allowed them to pay for educational expenses such as tuition, textbooks and housing.

There is no doubt this federal policy does exactly what it was designed to do—facilitate access to higher education and provide training benefits. This bill offers substantial financial assistance, but as my research shows, an important benefit is missing: What the post–9/11 GI Bill does not prepare veterans for is the emotional and psychological stress linked to transitioning from military to student life.

The Challenges of a New Role

When servicemen and servicewomen leave the military and enter higher education, they exit one institution, with its set of values, norms and expectations—"the military"—and enter into a new one—"the university." Social scientists refer to this as "role exit."

These servicemen and women replace their physical training uniforms with jeans and sweatshirts boasting the university's logo. They replace their rank—as corporal, for instance—with their year in college, such as freshman. In other words, they say goodbye to the world they know, including their comrades, and step foot on their college or university campus alone. In this transition, their identity shifts from warrior to student.

Through my work on projects funded by the Department of Defense and VA Office of Rural Health, I have closely examined this transition. And I can tell you it is anything but easy.

---

*Originally published as Ann Cheney, "The Emotional Challenges of Student Veterans on Campus," *The Conversation*, November 8, 2017. Reprinted with permission of the publisher.

Campus and Classroom Experiences

In my conversations with student veterans, I found them struggling with their new identity. Many realize they are no longer a service member, but they do not, at the same time, feel like a student. As one student veteran told me, he had a "disjointed" identity. He was trying to figure out who he was in his new identity.

In the military, service members felt a sense of brotherhood, became leaders and found a life of meaning and purpose. In higher education, however, many student veterans experience isolation rather than belonging. Even when they find success, it is individual rather than team-based. Some find little to no life meaning. As one veteran said, "You go from being somewhat important in the military, to having a purpose every day, to go home and, 'Well there goes the wife to work.' I should be going to work too but I'm gonna sit here and do school work."

As they struggle to balance the demands of marriage, parenthood and school, many live from paycheck to paycheck. Some feel, as one veteran so clearly articulated to me, "just a drain on society."

Common classroom experiences could trigger memories of combat in students. Add to this the fact that many returning student veterans have witnessed, been subjected to and experienced combat violence. Students told me how their experience of violence follows them, shadowlike, on campus and in classrooms. Sounds that might be familiar or normal to other students can evoke vivid memories of combat for student veterans.

One veteran, for example, shared with me that the sound of flip flops in a corridor triggered memories of fire fights in Iraq. Another student said classroom discussion brought up combat memories. Instead of focusing on class material, he found himself "zoned off in deep thought" about flashbacks from the past.

Afraid of Reaching Out

The campus community can do much to support student veterans. Indeed, there are tools to minimize these adverse campus and classroom experiences and help veterans achieve academic success.

The VA Campus Toolkit, for example, offers tips on how higher administration can address invisible wounds like depression, anxiety and PTSD. Faculty can alert students to unsettling images, text or discussions. As my research found, veteran-led services such as peer advisors for Veterans connect veterans to needed resources and offer veterans a sense of community. Such programs have great potential to increase retention rates and academic success.

But the issue is that some veterans may be afraid to disclose their veteran identity to professors or classmates because they fear the stigma they may experience as a result of being a former member of the military. There is a popular perception that veterans returning from the wars in Iraq and Afghanistan pose a security risk to others. My colleagues and I have found student veterans perceive public stigma as a significant barrier to accessing mental health care services.

How Can They Find Support?

Faculty, staff and students might want to remember that there is a very strong likelihood that one of the students in their classes is a veteran. And as Americans come together to honor veterans' military service and their valor in defending our nation, let us also acknowledge the commitment of these men and women to higher education.

16. Veterans Legal Advocacy and Law Schools[*]

Daniel Devoy

In the last ten years law schools throughout the country have opened legal clinics devoted to addressing the unmet legal needs of military veterans. At present there are nearly seventy such clinics in American law schools. Law school clinics devoted to military veterans have a far-reaching impact on both the student clinician and the veteran client. Through these programs, clinics provide pro bono legal services to an underserved and valued community while at the same time law students engage with real cases and are provided with valuable hands-on legal experience. Many law students are even inspired to pursue a career in public interest law after completing their clinical work.

Every clinic has the ability to focus on a specific area of law. Almost all are based within a law school, but many travel to different locations to meet with their clients. Some hold walk-in hours at a local VA office or hospital, and some even have drop-in clinics at local coffee shops. Many are even able to represent their clients without being limited by geographical distance between the clinic and the client. Eligibility for most programs is very consistent. Clients must be veterans of the military, and a variety of discharge levels are accepted. Generally, there is a priority for low-income veterans, and some programs even offer services to family members of the client. The following is a non-exhaustive list of legal services offered by law school clinics throughout the county.

- VA service-connected disability benefits
- Military discharge upgrades
- Access to VA healthcare
- VA pensions
- Representation in Veterans Treatment Court (VTC)
- Bankruptcy and consumer debt
- Probate and estates
- Housing and landlord/tenant disputes
- Family law and immigration law
- Policy promotion and regulatory and legislative reform

---

*Published with permission of the author.

Military veterans can potentially be confronted with numerous unforeseen legal issues when they leave the military and again many years after military service. While serving in the military, one is provided housing, employment, food, and physical and mental health treatment. All of these disappear once a service member transitions into civilian life. Additionally, veterans who separate without an honorable discharge may have more difficulty adjusting to civilian life, and may suffer from homelessness, unemployment, and physical health difficulties.

While some of these issues are the same issues many in the general population face, many are unique issues that require a trained legal advisor. Veteran-specific legal issues such as discharge upgrades and access to state and federal veteran benefits are unique to veterans. Veterans may also require access to social and mental health services to deal with issues unique to them including post-traumatic stress disorder (PTSD) and military sexual trauma (MST). Oftentimes, veterans who did not receive an honorable discharge face additional problems because they are ineligible for services and benefits. Many practicing attorneys do not focus on these unique issues, and thus a substantial gap between services available and those requiring legal services has emerged. Accordingly, law school clinics devoted to assisting military veterans provide the perfect solution.

For nearly five years I have been the director of one such law school clinic. The Golden Gate University School of Law Veterans' Legal Advocacy Center opened in the fall of 2014. Our clients are low-income military veterans and we primarily focus on two legal areas: (1) change of discharge status to those that received a less than honorable discharge due to PTSD, MST, or discrimination; and (2) initial and appellate matters for those seeking service-connected disability compensation. Our clinic represents clients nationwide and argues before administrative and judicial bodies in the San Francisco Bay Area, and the Board of Veterans' Appeals and Court of Appeals for Veterans Claims in Washington, D.C. We also provide a variety of legal services to incarcerated veterans participating in the San Francisco Veterans Treatment Court rehabilitation program.

Our clinic, like all clinics, is able to promote two essential functions necessary in the legal system. First, we represent those that may not otherwise be able to retain an advocate to protect their rights. Second, we train the next generation of practitioners to aspire to a career in public interest. A recent success story of our clinic illustrates these values.

Our client was a decorated combat U.S. Marine veteran who served in the Iraq War and fought in the Battle of Ramadi in 2006. He served as a medic and treated numerous casualties during combat and was highly decorated. Unfortunately, our client had difficulty adjusting to life outside an active combat environment. While still serving in the Marines and back in the United States, our client began to suffer from severe mental health injuries and began to self-medicate with drugs and alcohol. At his lowest point he disappeared from duty for several days and was punished for being absent without leave (AWOL). After a positive drug test, he was discharged "under other than honorable conditions." Upon returning home our client was unable to access mental health treatment due to his discharge status and was unemployed. These problems were made even more difficult because our client was the primary income earner for his spouse and children.

When our students first began to work on the case they interviewed the client for nearly two hours and allowed him to bring his spouse and children to the meeting. Very few attorneys or pro bono organizations would conduct an initial two-hour meeting with a potential client and their family without knowing if they would be retained. This is an inherent advantage of a law school clinic, because even if the client is not retained our students gain a valuable experience by way of conducting a client interview and engaging in a strategic analysis of the case. Similarly, the client gains a valuable experience because they are given an informed legal opinion of their matter by a trained advocate. Accordingly, both the pedagogical mission of a law school clinic and the objectives of the client are met.

Next our students began to analyze the case. They reviewed over a thousand pages of documents and spoke with medical providers that could provide expert opinion testimony and lay witnesses that could collaborate the sequence of events in question. After compiling all the evidence and conducting legal research, we were able to draft a legal brief that was submitted to the Board of Corrections for Military Records. Ultimately, we were able to establish that our client's post-traumatic stress disorder combined with his laudable military service mitigated any alleged negative conduct committed, and in addition the proper discharge procedures were not followed in accordance with the law. As a result, our client's military service was officially upgraded to honorable, and he was eligible for VA services.

We used his newly documented honorable service to remove the previously imposed statutory bar to benefits, and successfully advocated for our client to be awarded a 100 percent service-connected compensation rating from the Department of Veteran Affairs. Our client received nearly $25,000 in a one-time lump sum payment from the VA, a continuous monthly payment of approximately $3,500, and free health care for all his medical needs. The result was life changing for our client and his family.

Challenges for providing quality pro bono legal services to veterans will continue to exist, but with every challenge comes an opportunity. There are numerous clinical programs at law schools throughout the country that focus on the needs of veterans, and through their efforts our nation's military veterans are able to gain access to legal services.

17. Veterans Guide to Finding a Job in Local Government: An Excerpt*

MEMBERS OF THE ICMA VETERANS TASK FORCE

You've been in the military for six, 12, or even 20 years, but now a transition to civilian employment is upon you. The job you performed in the military will always be important and helped mold you into the stellar soldier and future asset to any local government organization. The challenges you face during your transition period to civilian employment are something you can overcome by keeping the following in mind.

First, be aware of tunnel vision. The more important the goal, the more likely you are to focus too much on it. Don't allow your military job, or your rank, to define your civilian career path. Trying jobs that are identical to your military career is never bad, but don't eliminate those that are different. Make a list of 10 to 12 local government careers you think you might enjoy and draw additional skills sets from those. Local government employers are always looking for great leadership; teach yourself how to fit the bill and stay motivated.

Second, approach your transition with an open mind. Many former military members leave active duty with very high expectations only to find their dream job wasn't waiting for them on the other end. Don't feel defeated and never ever give up; you weren't trained to quit! Start charting your course! Some local government positions may require you to start one level below what you're capable of doing. Don't take offense to working your way up to a job more commensurate with your age and experience level. This provides an opportunity to build on your experiences just as you did in the military. Take the risk, while it may hurt financially at first, seeing your goal and achieving it will be worth it in the end. When you initially interview with a local government agency, inform them of your willingness to accept a lower star ng salary with the intention of working hard, proving yourself, and your desire to be promoted after obtaining the skills and training necessary.

Third, it will be uncomfortable, and at times very overwhelming. We're all aware the transition itself isn't that difficult; lots of paperwork, medical appointments, clear-

*Members of the ICMA Veterans Task Force, "Veterans Guide to Finding a Job in Local Government: Excerpts," November 2018, pp. 4–10, 45–47 only. https://icma.org/documents/veterans-guide-finding-job-local-government. Originally published as the 2018 report "Veterans Guide to Finding a Job in Local Government: Excerpts," by ICMA, the International City/County Management Association (icma.org); reprinted with permission.

ances, etc. The overwhelming part is all of the transitioning happening at once. This is why preparation is a priority. Start early, complete your education, and continue learning throughout your military career. The transition process begins months—even years— before you are ready to separate. Always invest in your future self; attend a trade school, take the extra leadership course in the military, ask your command staff to support your training requests.

Fourth, tell your individual military story because it's one of the most important things about you. Don't be afraid; pay attention to what your audience (prospective employer) wants and provide pointed details that make you shine. The opportunity to relate your military career to the position you're applying for will present itself, and when it does, don't shy away. Provide prospective employers with those important job-related connections, capitalize on your strengths, as they relate to the position your applying for, and never omit the leadership qualities that have been so valuable to you throughout your extensive career. Your military experiences are individual to you. Be able to effectively communicate and prove to the prospective employer that your skills are topnotch.

In closing, you can successfully maneuver the transition from military life to a career in local government. Remember to be aware of tunnel vision and try not to focus on only one career path; branch out and take some risks. Always approach your transition with an open mind and be prepared to take one step back to eventually move two steps forward. Prepare to be overwhelmed; but know it will pass. Education and job-related training is the best investment you can make in yourself. Lastly, tell your story, make it relatable, and provide those valuable connections. Take this information and go forth, like the Army slogan says, "Be all you can be."

What Is Your Level of Experience as a Veteran?

- Early Career Veterans. Your military skill sets are most common with 1 to 10 years of service. You've been given immense responsibility in austere and politically sensitive environments at a young age. You've managed budgets and cross-functional teams that are larger than an entire local government staff. You are great under pressure and rarely intimidated by complex problems or issues. You are the perfect fit for a local government job.
- Mid-career Veterans. Your military skill sets are most common with 10 to 16 years of service. As a mid-career veteran, you know what it's like to run cross-functional teams, like those in local government organizations: human resources, fleet and facilities maintenance, budget and procurement, logistics, operations management, information technology, and civil affairs. Your experience and maturity make you an incredible asset for conflict management with a demonstrated ability to solve complex local government problems. You will succeed in any local government role offered to you.
- Senior Veterans. As a senior veteran, you may have a myriad of city- and county-manager level leadership experience in strategic planning, operations, budgeting, logistics, transportation, and city/base operations. You have excelled in leading a diverse team of talented people that involved significant interaction on a daily basis with the local city and county governments, school boards and chambers of commerce, as well as businesses and the general public. Further,

you worked with the state and federal levels of government during state and national emergencies. Let's get started.

Why Should You Consider a Career in Local Government?

While many who are transitioning out of the military naturally gravitate to careers in law enforcement or choose to return to school to learn a new profession, there are actually many options within local government that might be appealing to veterans. For some, having a lower-stress job, or one where you're not on-call all of the time, is one of the greatest pulls toward some government jobs. According to Chris Taylor, assistant director of transportation in Abilene, Texas, he was looking for "a little or no stress career" when he was transitioning out of a nearly 27-year career in the U.S. Marine Corps. Initially, he says he wanted "a career where I would look at my watch at 5:00 p.m. and could go home for the day. A career that would enable me to have weekends with my friends and family." Ultimately, Chris says he "didn't go into that career. Instead I went into airports," but there are lots of other options for folks who are looking for a slower-paced, less stressful environment within local government, especially within many entry-level positions. Fortunately, the diverse training that most in the armed services receive can help them have the needed skills for a variety of jobs. As Perry Tucker, a 24-year veteran of the U.S. Air Force and a member of Abilene's traffic signals department, relates, "It was easy for me because I had been tasked in so many different positions [i.e., aircraft maintenance, safety, logistics, management, etc.] throughout my military career that I could apply for many different jobs." While it can be hard to "translate" those military skills over to civilian jobs, the wealth of experience and training military folks receive opens them up to lots of job options.

Trouble with "translating" skills. While you know things will change once you leave the military, being able to successfully navigate that transition by getting the credit you deserve for all of the work you've done can be particularly challenging. Because the military uses such specialized vocabulary (and lots of acronyms) for many of its jobs and skills, it can be difficult to know the equivalents in "civilian-speak." According to John Hardy, a 21-year veteran of the U.S. Air Force and a code compliance officer in the stormwater division of Abilene, "I found it extremely difficult to articulate the levels of responsibility I had during my service to individuals with limited or no knowledge of military structure. I also had some trouble explaining the correlation between the jobs I had in the military and the position I was trying to get."

To make the translation easier, be sure to take advantage of the transition services on your installation.

Launching the civilian job search. As you get ready to leave your post for the last time, there are several things you can do to help make your civilian-life job search successful. Be sure to take full advantage of the transition resources your installation offers, but also do some of the thing civilians do every day when looking for a new job. Search the Internet, network with your friends "on the outside," take advantage of local workforce centers, and attend local job fairs. Just be aware that you're starting over in many ways, and don't be frustrated with how new and strange that may feel. John Hardy of Abilene shares, "I really didn't know what to expect with any job outside the military; it was scary and exciting at the same time. I would compare it to my first job search as a young adult." Many veterans want to continue a career in service in some way, and that's often why work in local government can seem so attractive. Be sure to check out your local government's webpages and job postings to see if a career in a highly structured, service-oriented local organization might make you feel right at home.

Slow down, soldier. You know on some level that your working life is going to be very different once you get out of the service, but what exactly that's going to look like is hard to tell. One thing that has frustrated more than one veteran is the much different pace within local government. According to Perry Tucker of Abilene, things in local government "move very slowly, unlike the military, where things happen as you speak." While the differences in speed of execution can be jarring at first, local governments often have many more hoops and hurdles to jump through and over when implementing new projects and initiatives. To help provide a context for that seemingly glacial pace of government change in the public sector, you can get educated on your local government and its structure. Learning more about how your government works and the different roles the council or board, mayor, city or county manager, and others have can help you understand their decision-making and reporting structures and the timelines they often operate within.

There's no crying in baseball (or in the military). One of the toughest things for many veterans to navigate when entering the civilian workforce is the "really thin skin" civilians have, according to Adam Esquivel of Abilene's streets division and a 20-year veteran of the U.S. Marine Corps. Many veterans have noted that others view them as particularly abrupt, callous, and sharp when they are new to the workforce because the tone and expectations within the military are much different. In order to adjust your tone and vocabulary and to develop your more sympathetic side, spend a little time each day as you transition out of the military talking with and listening to other people. While you need to speak to other adults as adults, slowing down your pace, warming up your tone, and finding kinder, gentler words will help others receive your messages more easily.

A job in local government is not about the money … right now. Like the military, most local governments do not offer the best pay, but try to make up for it with a good benefits package. For those transitioning out of the military after a few years of service, having access to these benefits can be a real benefit to your family. And for those who have transitioned to the reserves, you will often find that local governments are very understanding of the commitment this will entail. Perry Tucker put it well when he said, "If someone is looking for a job with security and benefits that will offer a secure future in retirement, then the city [or county] may be where you want to be. But, if you are more interested in short-term financial gain, then you should look somewhere else for employment." Because budgets are limited, jobs within the public sector often don't pay as much as similar jobs in the private sector.

A perk for most civilian employees is the package of benefits—medical insurance, life insurance, and such. If you've left the service before retirement, these benefits will provide help and support to your family. However, if you've re red from the military, your retirement benefits cover many of the same things the local government may offer at no cost to you, so hearing about a robust benefits package in your new job might be a bit grating. However, there may be some supplementary products your organization offers that your family may want, and remember, medical insurance "on the outside" will cover dependent children un l they are 26 years of age. Also, whatever isn't being deducted for benefits from your paycheck goes straight to you, so maybe that can take some of the s ng out of the whole "less money" thing earlier.

There is a trade-off for those who aren't rolling in dough right now that occurs down the road. One of the best things about working for a local government is that most organizations have really good retirement plans. Even for those who remain in the reserves hoping to one day earn a pension, or have already qualified for a military pension, the additional retirement funds that will be available when you re re from your local government job will provide a wonderful safety net for you and your family. And, for many organizations, your years in the military may count toward your vestment with the new organization's retirement, helping you get more credit and money more quickly.

18. Veteran Profile: Clint Holmes[*]

Samantha Wagner

Prior to his appointment as city manager in 1998, Clint Holmes, city manager of Brown City, Michigan, served three years in the Headquarters and Headquarters Company (HHC), 2nd Brigade, 82nd Airborne Division in the U.S. Army and another 17 plus years as a naval intelligence officer. He also serves as executive director of the Brown City Downtown Development Authority and advisor to the Planning Commission, Park Board, Cemetery Board, and Festival Commission. He is a member of the Michigan Local Government Management Association.

After serving in the military, what interested you in having a career in local government?

I developed an interest in local government while serving on active duty in the Navy and attending Auburn University to obtain an MPA. My interest was confirmed by a brief internship in Layton, Utah (pop. 67,311). Shortly thereafter, I read a letter to the editor in *PM* magazine about an individual who had followed the standard career path and had transitioned from a department in a larger organization to city manager of a small community, only to be surprised at how his previous experience had not fully prepared him for his new role. After reading the article, I decided that I wanted to start work in a smaller community, rather than trying to move up through a larger organization. Accordingly, upon my retirement from the Navy, I conducted a six-week job search for a management position in a small community, which resulted in to my appointment in Brown City. Then, as now, I believed municipal management would be an optimal way for me to make a difference.

What skills/knowledge/background from your military career have you been able to apply to your local government career?

I believe my military background helped distinguish me from other job applicants since it had provided me with the necessary skills—including the ability to take charge of situations, prioritize, and focus on the mission—necessary to transition into a management role in a smaller community.

The military also trains its people to research and analyze a situation, coordinate a reasonable response, and then resolve the issue in response to the demands of the situation

---

*Samantha Wagner, "Veteran Profile: Clint Holmes," November 9, 2015, https://icma.org/articles/article/veteran-profile-clint-holmes. Originally published in *Leadership Matters*, November 9, 2015, by ICMA, the International City/County Management Association (icma.org); reprinted with permission.

and to very quickly gain a level of expertise on a very wide range of issues and concerns. Which is, after all, an excellent city manager job description.

While acclimating to the local government profession, however, I did experience challenges in identifying the informal chain of command (also known as figuring out who really runs the department and who is the actual subject matter expert), determining the competency and reliability of contractors and engineers, and adapting to the governmental budgeting process, which initially demanded many very long days. Since my military career consisted almost exclusively of staff work and situation analysis in multiple organizations, my transition from military to civilian was relatively smooth. Military service also provides the opportunity to work with and for highly diverse groups of people and thus aids in the rapid assimilation of the local municipal culture.

One big difference, however, is that projects tend to move much faster in the military. But the slower speed of progress in municipal government is counterbalanced by the fact that few other occupations have results that are potentially as long lasting, such as street and bridge projects.

Also, military experience provides the requisite skills to serve as a facilitator of communication between interest groups and stakeholders in a government environment in which building relationships can be easier than fostering long-lasting relationships in the military. These communication skills are critical to responding to elected officials and residents, who can be adamant and vocal in their concerns. Finally, it turns out that the forms and procedures for acquiring a satellite photo are very similar to applying for a grant.

Do you have any tips/advice for active duty personnel or veterans who are interested in a career in local government?

Notwithstanding the differences between military service and municipal management, I believe that the fit for prior military in local government is a good one, and that any individual with military experience who is considering the local government profession should do the necessary due diligence and then give it a try.

For example, staff work is staff work and both professions consist of similar core challenges: responding to complex challenges in visible roles in condensed spans of time; determining and supporting the overall needs of the organization based on the mission; and contributing to the betterment of society in a lasting, tangible manner.

Ultimately, however, I would encourage any individual with a military background to consider local government, since being a city manager is like being a unit commander, the goal of virtually every officer and senior NCO.

However, as with any profession, the military has its own language and buzzwords. Whenever transitioning from a military career to a civilian one, it is necessary to translate cover letters, résumés or applications listing job history, skills, and experience into language readily understood by a prospective employer. I also found it most helpful to have taken some vacation time while still on active duty to do a short internship with a municipal government. This provided both an introduction to the type of work and skills actually required, as well as initial access to mentors in the profession. Overall, I was amazed at the amount of overlap between the military and municipal management. However, there will always be those "they didn't mention this in graduate school" moments.

With veterans returning home to a weak and challenging labor market, have you implemented any sort of veteran's program in your community, such as: employment, health, housing, education, and the transition to civilian life?

In order to reach individuals with a military background, I feel that ICMA and the state-based organizations should focus on providing educational materials to individuals with military experience who are nearing separation or retirement and entering transition training, a final stage of service that occurs prior to reentry to civilian life.

In reaching out to such individuals in the same manner that ICMA may reach out to students or young professionals, I think that program coordinators for these military transition resources would welcome the opportunity to receive and implement the use of such materials.

In doing so, ICMA and the local government profession may further strengthen our ranks by recruiting individuals who have already contributed to a service ethic rooted in the American ideal of providing a brighter future for those who will inherent our work product.

Are there any educational/professional development programs that you would recommend to veterans who are transitioning from a career in the military to a career in local government?

Obviously, a graduate degree in public administration is increasingly mandatory; however, many very small communities still require little or no college if an applicable work history exists. But at a minimum, anyone seriously thinking about local government should attend the ICMA Annual Conference and/or the state-level equivalent. This is particularly important to meet those who can serve as mentors and those who can provide background and expertise in the profession.

19. Breaking Down Their Own Stereotypes to Give Veterans More Career Opportunities[*]

Eileen Trauth

Military veterans have a higher unemployment rate than nonveterans, according to federal statistics. One reason may be that when veterans seek civilian jobs, they often face stereotypes from hiring managers. But another set of stereotypes may come into play as well: Veterans fall prey to their own preconceptions about certain types of jobs and miss out on promising opportunities.

Research I conducted with K.D. Joshi from Washington State University found that many veterans are well-qualified for work in the information technology sector—a wide and diverse range of computer- and communications-related jobs. But large numbers of veterans hold stereotypes that discourage them from seeking IT employment, depriving companies of skilled employees and veterans of meaningful and rewarding work.

Fortunately, this problem can be corrected, and relatively easily, if veterans and those who serve them work together.

Veterans Have the Skills

We wanted to understand what influenced the decisions of military veterans with various types of disabilities about whether to pursue IT careers in civilian life after their time in uniform. To begin, with the help of retired Marine lieutenant colonel Kimberly Graham, now a job-training consultant, and veterans affairs offices at four universities, we asked 297 military service members and veterans, all with disabilities, a series of open-ended questions about post-military careers. Some of them were searching for work, while others were either still in the service or in college—but would be looking for jobs upon completion.

Our questions included whether they had ever considered a career in information

*Originally published as Eileen Trauth, "Breaking Down Their Own Stereotypes to Give Veterans More Career Opportunities," *The Conversation*, May 21, 2017. Reprinted with permission of the publisher.

technology, and their thoughts about how their disabilities affect their interest in pursuing an IT career. We also asked them how they thought their military training and experiences might help or hinder their success if they did get an IT-related job.

We learned that these veterans had many skills and abilities that would serve them well in various IT fields. The military is good at teaching people about leadership, management, problem solving, teamwork and handling stressful situations.

Some Positive Views

But we also found that they had stereotypes about what kinds of jobs were available. Some of the respondents were interested in IT work, either since their youth or as a result of their military experience. For example, one told us, "I am currently working in military intelligence. I plan to work in cyber intelligence after leaving the military."

Still others had begun to consider a career in IT as a result of their disabilities, telling us, "It is a good field for people with hearing disability," "I suffer from generalized anxiety disorder with panic. It is easier to interact with a computer than with people," and "It is less strenuous than [my former job of] being a construction electrician."

Many Negative Views

Many of the people we questioned revealed stereotypes about IT work. "I would rather work with people," one respondent told us. This reflects the misconception that IT professionals sit in front of computer screens all day and do not interact with people. That is true of some jobs, but not all of them.

Many IT workers interact with customers to understand their needs, help people with research questions and technology malfunctions, or design systems to enhance user experiences.

Another respondent told us, "It is not something I consider myself gifted enough at to pursue." This represents a common theme running through research about groups of people who are underrepresented in IT fields, like women, African-Americans and people with disabilities. Many people told us they thought they needed to have a lot of formal education or be a technical whiz or possess some other sort of superstar qualities to work in IT. That simply isn't true. The wide variety of IT jobs means there's work for people of almost any interest and ability.

Others told us they thought IT work required long hours or skills with complex computer-programming languages—or even that they worried IT jobs would be outsourced or sent overseas, putting American workers back on the job search. Those are real concerns, but neither exclusive to IT work nor applicable to all jobs in the field.

Other Misconceptions

Several respondents didn't know they could have IT careers in the business world. One told us, for example, "I worked in supply chain for 10 years and have business courses; I would have to get a different education to enter the IT field."

My own university, Penn State, among many others, offers courses in project management and enterprise architecture. Those are IT-related subjects that respondents didn't identify with IT work. Many American business schools, again including Penn State's, have information systems departments that teach supply chain management.

Beyond their stereotypes and misconceptions, some of the people we interviewed did not recognize that much of their knowledge and experience from military service would transfer well to IT. "I would enjoy an IT career, but I have too much experience in leadership and management to switch a career to IT," one person told us, apparently not realizing almost every field needs people who can lead and manage others.

What to Do Now?

For more than 30 years, I've been studying what effects technological advances have on the skills and knowledge needed by IT workers. It pains me to see stereotypes standing in the way of rewarding careers in IT. Fortunately, this problem is relatively easy to address, if different units in a university work together.

Veterans and disabilities offices need to make sure that military service members and veterans with disabilities are aware of the range of career opportunities available to them, including in IT. University career counselors need to help these students identify their transferable skills. Of course, that assumes the advisers and counselors know enough about the IT field themselves.

That is where academics come in. Information technology professors need to educate their students, but also their colleagues across their universities. In particular, faculty need to share their knowledge of marketable skills and career opportunities as widely as they can. Through a coordinated effort, we can break down barriers to IT careers one stereotype at a time.

20. The Preferred Class?
Veterans in the Workforce*

JEFFREY R. ZIMMERMAN

The number of military members separating from the military has increased. This is due to several factors, including the unpopularity of the wars in Iraq and Afghanistan and President Obama's decisions to withdraw troops from these conflicts. These veterans are now looking for employment opportunities in the civilian sector, whether it is in the private business world or in the government sector.

According to a report from the North Carolina General Assembly, the state has a veteran population of around 800,000 as of the 2012–2013 fiscal year. The total population of North Carolina is around 10 million people, so the veteran population is a significant class of individuals who choose to live in the state after their service contract ends.

When it comes to employing veterans, several questions must be asked and answered by organizations in both the public and private sectors. First, are veterans the preferred employee for private companies and government organizations? If so, do they possess skills outside of their military training that are transferrable to the civilian world and will allow them to prosper? Do veterans require additional education and job training after leaving the service but before they are hired?

I would opine that military veterans are a preferred class of employees because of the myriad skillsets they learn and acquire during their time of service. These skills include, but are not limited to, discipline, teamwork, critical thinking, organizational skills and determination. These skills can serve organizations outside the military very well.

There are employment opportunities that are similar to a military organization, such as law enforcement or security firms. However, most organizations do not operate in a military fashion. As a result, veterans must adjust their approach and demeanor when seeking employment in these organizations.

There are a number of veterans who obtain undergraduate, graduate and even professional degrees while serving in the armed forces. They enter the civilian workforce as attractive candidates compared to other veterans who do not possess college degrees. However, the lack of a degree should not deter a veteran from seeking employment, as

---

*Originally published as Jeffrey Zimmerman, "The Preferred Class? Veterans in the Workforce," *PA Times,* November 3, 2015. Reprinted with permission of the publisher.

the skills acquired during their military service cannot be obtained in college classrooms. They simply have to find the right fit unless they choose to go to college or a trade school.

Veterans are afforded a preference when applying for jobs, particularly with government entities in North Carolina. This preference usually guarantees veterans an opportunity to interview for a position but does not guarantees them a job. I am a hiring manager for a state agency in North Carolina and have interviewed and hired many veterans into state government positions. By and large, these veterans have transitioned very well into the civilian world. There have been a few that did not work, mostly because they were not a good fit for the organization. While I would argue that veterans are a preferred class, I would be remiss if I did not mention that the fit of the potential employee and organization is a crucial part of the process.

As a society, we should continue to grant preference to our veterans. This preference can come in the form of higher education, job or trade training, interview skills and resume writing. There are many veterans who learn trade skills in the military that are easily transferrable to the civilian world such as welding, mechanical work, culinary arts, etc. More apprenticeships could be awarded to veterans to assist them in finding long-term employment based on the training they acquired during their service. I would further advocate that governments could make it easier for veterans with certain qualifications to obtain similar civilian qualifications for skills learned in the military. This could be achieved by reducing testing standards or restrictions and awarding these qualifications based on equivalent military training.

Veterans should not be awarded a job they do not deserve or if they are less than qualified. Using their veteran status alone could become a detriment to the organization, both in the short and long term. However, society can do a much better job in assisting our veterans to make a successful transition into the workforce after their military service ends.

21. U.S. Civil Service's Preference for Hiring Military Vets Comes at a Hidden Cost[*]

Gregory B. Lewis

An important way the U.S. shows its gratitude to veterans who have fought America's wars is by giving them a leg up in getting a job with the federal government.

The policy, known as "veterans' preference," became law after the Civil War, was strengthened following World War I and grew even more entrenched after World War II and in the wake of the wars in Iraq and Afghanistan.

While it's good that the nation thanks its troops, the strong preference for veterans has had some negative effects as well, particularly in terms of lessening the civil service's diversity, as my research into this policy shows.

How Veterans' Preference Works

Congress gave disabled veterans preference in hiring for some federal jobs after the Civil War.

Lawmakers greatly expanded it after World War I, allowing able-bodied, honorably discharged veterans to receive a hiring preference in most civilian federal jobs, as well as widows of deceased veterans and wives of severely disabled ones. More recently, the Obama administration strengthened veterans' preference by directing agencies to establish hiring goals and making other changes.

As a result, one-third of new federal hires are veterans.

Here's how it worked up to 2010. The civil service rated job applicants for almost all nonpolitical jobs on a 100-point scale, typically by having them take a test or evaluating their education and experience. Disabled veterans got an extra 10 points added to that score, while other former soldiers received 5 points.

The federal personnel agency ranked applicants based on this score and, when the final score was a tie, placed veterans ahead of nonveterans. Thus, disabled veterans with

*Originally published as Gregory B. Lewis, "U.S. Civil Service's Preference for Hiring Military Vets Comes at a Hidden Cost," *The Conversation*, May 21, 2017. Reprinted with permission of the publisher.

scores of 90 and other veterans with scores of 95 ranked higher than nonveterans with scores of 100. In addition, veterans with more serious service-related disabilities "floated" to the top of the list as long as they scored above a passing grade of 70.

Typically, hiring officials had to choose one of the three candidates with the top scores. If the final three included both veterans and nonveterans, the hiring official needed written permission from the federal personnel agency to "pass over" a veteran to hire a nonveteran lower on the list.

That's how the vast majority of current federal employees were hired. Since 2010, hiring officials set bars in advance to divide qualified applicants into two or more levels. They can consider anyone in the most-qualified category.

Veterans no longer get extra points, but they do get placed at the top of whichever category they qualify for, and veterans with compensable disabilities go to the very top if they meet minimum qualifications. Hiring officials cannot pass over veterans in the top category to hire more qualified nonveterans.

The evidence is not all in, but the new system probably strengthens veterans' preference.

The Policy's Impact

This preference dramatically increases one's chances of getting a federal job. Even though veterans have decreased as a share of the federal workforce—as World War II and Vietnam War veterans have retired—their odds of getting government jobs have actually increased.

In 1980, census data show that veterans were about twice as likely as nonveterans to hold federal jobs (9 percent of veterans were federal employees, compared with 4 percent of Americans without military service). By 2015, the share of veterans working for the feds soared to 18 percent, while less than 3 percent of nonveterans held federal jobs— mostly thanks to the changes initiated during the Obama years. (The percentages are estimates based on a sampling of data from census years.)

The pattern is especially strong among younger veterans, those born since 1980, who are about 15 times as likely as nonveterans of the same age to hold federal jobs. Nearly 10 percent of veterans born from 1920 to 1950 held federal jobs when they appeared in the census data. That rose to about 15 percent for those born in the 1950s and 1960s. Veterans born since 1970 are even more likely to be federal employees, and nearly half of those born in 1990 had a federal job by 2015.

Every state also gives veterans some hiring preference for government jobs. Four— Massachusetts, New Jersey, Pennsylvania and South Dakota—even provide "absolute" preference, that is they hire veterans with a passing score ahead of all nonveterans. These programs have had much less impact on state government workforces, however, perhaps because veterans have less desire for state than for federal jobs.

How This Affects Diversity

This very strong preference for veterans ends up hurting groups that are less likely to have military service.

Strongly preferring a group that is so male necessarily disadvantages women. Even today, 89 percent of veterans are men, yet only 53 percent of nonvets in the work force are. White men make up 69 percent of vets but only 37 percent of nonveterans. And most minority groups apart from black men are under represented among veterans, particularly women. White women, for instance, make up only 7 percent of veterans, even though they make up 32 percent of the rest of the workforce.

My research finds that the civil service would be more diverse in the absence of veterans' preference, in which case the male-female split in the federal service would be 50–50 rather than its current 57–43 breakdown. And the employment of Latinos, Asians and gay men would probably all increase by 20 percent.

The Costs of Preferring Vets

Clearly veterans' preference has had a powerful and growing impact on who gets federal jobs.

Although it only directly benefited about one-tenth of veterans in the past, nearly one-third of recent veterans have federal jobs, many more than would have them in the absence of preferential hiring. This makes it an effective policy to express the nation's thanks for veterans' sacrifices.

Yet all policies come with costs. Applicants without military service pay some of them by having a lower chance to get these jobs, and nonveterans are concentrated among women and, to a lesser extent, Hispanic, Asian and gay men.

The nation loses, in my opinion, from a less diverse federal service.

22. Veterans and Medical Care*

WILLIE L. BRITT

As a retired veteran, I can appreciate the medical needs of other veterans who have served and are currently serving on active duty or in the United States Army Reserve or National Guard. I have received services from a Veterans Affairs (VA) medical facility. Many of our needs are similar to the civilian sector but there are other needs that are unique to military service. As part of any vision or mission statements, we must recognize the care that is needed in a combat zone and care that is needed in support locations in theater but not directly involved in combat.

We must also address the varied needs of those who have medical conditions associated with physical or emotional injuries from combat. As a lower priority but in the spirit of thanking all honorably discharged veterans for their service, we must be able to provide medical and chiropractic services to all veterans who have served in any branch of the armed services. Some of these veterans may lack economic resources.

Our goals and objectives must focus on providing high quality accessible, affordable, patient friendly and patient satisfaction health care that is equivalent to that provided in other developed nations. One of the weaknesses of the U.S. health care system is over-priced services and charges for pharmaceuticals and medical supplies. Many services are "emergency room" or near that status which is more expensive rather than maintenance and prevention. Most policymakers and public discussions do not focus on substantive ways to reduce costs, without reducing services and the quality of those services.

Given the size and scope of the VA, it is imperative to use that clout to engineer lower cost services and payments for drugs and supplies/supports. Services for veterans must not be driven by profits incentives, but rather care and respect for these individuals who have sacrificed so much in service of this country. Although the numbers and cost may appear substantial, veterans are a small percentage of the overall U.S. population. Those services must be sufficient to address varying needs. Treatment should include a multi-disciplinary team.

Veteran Care Since the Revolutionary War

Health care in America, like most other operations, was very primitive from the founding of the country until after the Civil War. After the Civil War, the National Asylum

---

*Published with permission of the author.

for Disabled Volunteer Soldiers was established. Within three years after the Civil War, three branches were established initially for Union veterans who had suffered economic distress from disabilities incurred during the war. A fourth branch was founded in 1870. In 1873 the name was changed from asylum to home. In 1887, veterans suffering economic distress from disabilities not incurred in military service became eligible for admission.

At the beginning, medical care was only incidental. The number of branches increased. Further, after the Civil War, a number of states established state homes for disabled soldiers and sailors. This was occurring during the industrial revolution and the transformation of the country to scientific management. With this period came improvements in health care. The military established a network of hospitals, other health care facilities and outreach to address the needs of those who had provided service in the name of the United States.

This has continued through World Wars I and II, the Korean conflict, Vietnam, the Gulf wars (Iraq and Afghanistan) and for smaller conflicts along the way. Starting with World War I, there was a significant increase in medical and hospital care for those veterans suffering from wounds or disease incurred in service. Medical care was initially provided by the Public Health Service or by contract with civilian hospitals. After 1920, the hospitals of the Army, Navy, and National Home were also used. In 1922, 57 Public Service Hospitals were transferred to the Bureau of Veterans. In 1930, 47 of these 57 Public Service Hospitals, the National Home for Disabled Volunteer Soldiers and a sanitarium were consolidated to form the Veterans Administration (VA). During World War II, 72 new hospitals were authorized.

It is significant to note that the current VA provides care for veterans from World War II, Korea, Vietnam, Iraq and Afghanistan. Due to improved medical care on the battlefield and acute care from battlefield to initial inpatient care, many veterans survived that would have otherwise been casualties in earlier times. Therefore, this has placed additional demands upon the VA because there are more veterans to treat and some have conditions that require lifelong care.

https://doi.org/10.1111/j.1532-5415.1986.tb04307

Stateside and Overseas Base Facilities: The primary network in the United States, its territories and foreign countries consists of base hospitals and selected treatment facilities in the United States and strategically around the world to accommodate combat operations and other veterans who have served.

Field Units/Medical Teams: All military branches have established detailed standard operating procedures that are constantly updated based on field exercises, training and evaluations. This is significant because we have developed "Best Practices" and "Milestones" that have universal application.

Public-Private Sector Relations: The Department of Veterans Affairs (VA) and colleges and universities have had a very successful and productive relationship collaborating to provide medical doctors' services to veterans. This can also be an avenue for chiropractors. Institutions of higher learning require students to participate in training outside of the classroom. This usually means internships at medical facilities. The VA has needed low to no cost providers and this aided in reducing VA costs. Further, some interns could later be hired as staff if it was deemed that they had performed satisfactorily and were interested in continuing this service.

VAMC Fort Miley and UCSF: The San Francisco Veterans Affairs Medical Center (SFVAMC) is closely affiliated with the University of California San Francisco (UCSF).

That relationship is especially evident in the VA Medical Service, the academic partner with the UCSF Department of Medicine. In fact, the concept of a close, mutually beneficial and formal affiliation between a medical university and a VA medical center was created in the 1960s at UCSF, later spreading to other parts of the VA system as its substantial rewards became clear.

UCSF medical students, residents and fellows rotate through the VA which provides nearly one third of all of the University's medical training. The SFVAMC has no free-standing training programs of its own; every aspect is fully integrated with UCSF. In addition, each VA staff physician in the Medical Service is a full UCSF Department of Medicine faculty member, following the same process for appointment and promotion as those based in other campus sites.

The VA Medical Service Chief serves as the Vice Chair of the Department of Medicine, coordinating academic affairs at the VA with those across the broader Department."
https://medicine.ucsf.edu/campuses/vamc.html
https://www.sanfrancisco.va.gov/

Veterans Choice Program (VCP)

The Veterans Choice Program is one of several programs through which a veteran can receive care from a community provider, paid for by VA. For example, if a veteran needs an appointment for a specific type of care, and the VA cannot provide the care in a timely manner or the nearest VA medical facility is too far away or too difficult to get to, then a veteran may be eligible for care through the Veterans Choice Program.

To use the Veterans Choice Program, veterans must receive prior authorization from VA to receive care from a provider that is part of VA's VCP network of community providers. The authorization is based on specific eligibility requirements and discussions with the veteran's VA provider. VA must authorize care that is needed beyond the scope of the first authorization.

Veterans Affairs Patient-Centered Community Care (PC3). Patient-Centered Community Care is a Veterans Health Administration (VHA) nationwide program that utilizes health care contracts to provide eligible veterans access to primary care, inpatient/outpatient specialty care, mental health care, limited emergency care, and limited newborn care for enrolled female veterans following birth of a child.

In instances where veterans require primary and specialty care that is not readily available through the VA Health Care Facility (HCF), the HCF may use a Patient-Centered Community Care (PC3) contract to purchase care for the veteran. The HCF's clinical and Non-VA care teams coordinate to determine if the care is available at the HCF, a nearby HCF or another health care partner. If not, they will look to the PC3 contract to buy the care. If the veteran needs care, the veteran should always start with the VA health care provider at the local facility.

Traditional VAMC model versus privatization. There has been a long running tension between maintaining and improving the traditional VAMC model and some degree of privatization. The recent terminations of the VA Secretary and his predecessor suggest that the VA is incapable of "policing its own" and improving care for veterans, that somehow this could be done better by the private sector. Which is perceived as a better approach to modernizing and providing veterans quality health care in the future?

Any analysis of this difference of strategical approach must consider that the VA is the second largest government entity, second only to the Department of Defense. It commands a large budget (approximately 200 billion dollars annually) for human (approximately 377,000 personnel) and capital resources (hospitals, clinics, veterans' cemeteries, and other veteran benefits).

As a reminder, the VA administers both veteran medical/health care and veterans benefits. The VA medical structure has a long history and embedded culture. Any policy formulation is substantive and symbolic offerings will further exacerbate the problems that currently exist. It would appear that the current structure that exists on active and reserve military bases should be a key component. A second component would examine military facilities in separate communities and apply a process similar to the Base Realignment and Closure (BRAC) in 1988, 1991, 1993, 1995 and 2005. This was a process by a United States federal government commission to increase United States Department of Defense efficiency by planning the end of the Cold War realignment and closure of military installations. More than 350 installations have been closed in those five BRAC rounds. Similar to the BRAC rounds, some medical facilities closely located can be combined and have joint operations.

Others within close proximity may have to be eliminated, modified or utilize privatization. The reorganization and realignment have to be careful to offer greater access (reasonable commuting distances) rather than making it more difficult to get appointments and then commute to them. These were some of the primary deficiencies that the Arizona investigation revealed. A third component would be an expansion of the "choice" programs the VA has been testing and some implemented to provide more private practitioners outside of military facilities. This affords greater opportunities for chiropractors and other practitioners as discussed herein.

A majority of organizations that represent veterans prefer that the VA continue to have the primary role in actually proving medical services. They are open to some privatization. A majority of veterans who were surveyed indicated satisfaction with the services provided, once they are able to get an appointment and see a provider. Most of my personal experiences with the VA have been positive. Many feel VA medical facilities have a sense of awareness and sensitivity to veterans' needs. The main reason to request authorization to go outside of the VA system is to get an appointment faster or in a location more convenient for commuting.

Therefore, based on my personal experiences and the research I have done, I conclude that the current VA medical structure should be improved upon for greater appointment and location access. Privatization can be added, but it should be a secondary provider. Also, private contracts may be utilized to improve technology within the VA structure, not supplant the VA in providing these services. During World War I, there was contracting with civilian hospitals. Since that time, it has been deemed necessary that the federal government should retain the primary responsibility and only augment some services through contracting out.

A historical review of medical services provided in the United States reveals that the private sector will always attempt to maximize profits unless there are legislative controls or other incentives to lower costs. In the private sector, the cost of health care has been on an upward spiral over the past 50+ years. If we compare that to two programs that are government run, we may find that the costs have not risen as fast. Medicare, which was founded in 1964 as one of several programs under the "Great Society" of President Lyndon Johnson, has provided reasonable access and care at reasonable prices. The federal government has been able to leverage its clout through the number of participants and its purchasing power. The second example is the VA that many want to convert to private contracts. It appears that appointment scheduling and access arguments against the current structure have more symbolic than substantive implications. With modern technology, it would appear very feasible to upgrade the current scheduling system and to develop a nationwide grid that provides more access and care that would be more patient focused than process driven.

Summary, Recommendations, Future Research

When discussing modernization of VA practices, we must conduct evaluations that do not allow political bias to color the outcomes. All evaluations are political. However, we must use performance measurements determined by "metaevaluations" that can be objectively assessed to guide future policy decision-making and legislation. Most of the major complaints are tied to waiting times for a veteran to get an appointment and a location that is within a reasonable commuting distance. These are substantive issues but "symbolic fixes" are often attached. New Public Management's five tenants of alertness, agility, adaptability, alignment and accountability should be employed to take advantage of the latest technology to make VA personnel and equipment more efficient, effective, equitable and accessible. Once a veteran is able to get an appointment and to get treatment within the existing system, there are limited complaints. In fact, a majority are satisfied with the care they receive. Therefore, it appears that the current VA model of utilizing existing medical facilities on military bases and VAMC's is creditable.

The UCSF SFVAMC model is successful. Chiropractors can be integrated into more care, both in existing military facilities and as private contractors as part of the Veterans Choice Program (VCP) and Veterans Affairs Patient-Centered Community Care (PC3). The existing military facilities can be augmented with private contracting out but privatization of a majority of the services should not supplant the current structure. Although the current model may have some challenges, we cannot leave something as vital as veterans' health care to the "free market" that may not be free of political influence and unlimited money lobbyists are able to utilize to influence actions that may not be in the best interest of veterans. Decisions must not be profit driven under the disguise of providing better services to veterans and reducing costs. Current data does not support such an argument. Through the years, Medicare and the VA have provided health care that has been less costly than the private sector. It should be improved upon, not eliminated.

REFERENCES

"Base Realignment and Closure." https://en.wikipedia.org/wiki/Base_Realignment_and_Closure.
"A Coup at Veterans Affairs." (2018, March 29). The Editorial Board of *The New York Times*. Retrieved from http://www.nytimes.com/interactive/opinion/editorialboard.html.
Mather, John H., MD, & Abel, Robert W. (1986). Medical Care of Veterans: A Brief History. *Journal of the American Geriatrics Society*. Retrieved from https://dol.org/10.1111/j.1532-5415, 1986.tb04307.
Patient-Centered Community Care (PC3)—VHA Office of Community. (2017, May 11) https://www.va.gov/COMMUNITYCARE/programs/veterans/pccc/index.asp.
Shulkin, David J. (2018, March 28). Privatizing the V.A. Will Hurt Veterans. *The New York Times*. Retrieved from https://www.nytimes.com.

"Timeline: The Story Behind the VA Scandal." (2014, May 21). *USA Today*. https://www.usatoday.com/story/news/politics/2014/05/21/...scandal.../9373227/

U.S. Department of Veterans Affairs. "About VA, History—VA History." Retrieved from https://www.va.gov/about_vahistory.asp.

U.S. Department of Veterans Affairs. "Roots of VA Health Care Started 150 Years Ago." Retrieved from https://www.va.gov/HEALTH/NewsFeatures/2015/March Roots-of-Health-Care-Started-150-Years-Ago/.

Veterans Choice Program (VCP). VHA Office of Community Care. (2018, March 15). https://www.va.gov/opa/choiceact/.

23. Veterans and Chiropractic Care*

WILLIE L. BRITT

Given their service to protect and promote freedom around the world, veterans are deserving of quality, accessible and affordable care that should be second to none. Chiropractors are in a unique position to supplement this care. Chiropractors are designated as physician-level providers and provide effective, affordable and safe services to the private and public sectors.

In addition to the private sector, chiropractors provide public services for Medicare, Medicaid, the U.S. Departments of Veterans Affairs and Defense, Federal Employees Health Benefits Program, Federal Workers' Compensation, and all state workers' compensation programs. It is imperative that multi-disciplinary services are readily accessible in sufficient quality and quantity to address varying needs.

The participation of chiropractors should be greatly increased. Given that chiropractors provide non-invasive and drugfree care, this promotes conservative care to address conditions before attempting treatment procedures that may be unnecessary and can be expensive. Chiropractors emphasis on a holistic approach that includes diet and nutrition, and exercise has been proven to promote healthier lifestyles and lower medical costs.

With current and projected drug addiction increases and associated risks with doctor prescribed medications, it is advantageous that chiropractors provide health care and do not promote the use of drugs. This can further reduce the risk of addiction from drugs and provide an opportunity for a vital health care role by chiropractors who provide non-invasive and drugfree care at fees that are considered "usual, customary and geographically appropriate."

Chiropractic can be "high tech" but it can also be "low tech" with a simple adjustment (manipulation) using human hands to relieve short and long-term neuro-muscular-skeletal disorders. Yes, veterans are very deserving of our best approaches at finding and implementing the best service outcomes. Chiropractors can help with that implementation and continuing assessment and reevaluation.

Chiropractic is a natural approach to health care, the largest drugless healing discipline in the world. Doctors of chiropractic are the acknowledged specialists in the treatment of back and neck pain. Chiropractors, however, are concerned with overall health. How do they do what they do? The brain and the nervous system control and

---

*Published with permission of the author.

92

monitor all functions throughout the body. The nerves which pass between the vertebrae in the spine are a vital part of the nervous system. The major focus for the chiropractor is to locate misaligned vertebrae in the spine which create nerve irritation. Then the chiropractor corrects these misalignments through gentle, skillful manipulation, called "adjustments." A misaligned vertebra causing nerve irritation is called a "subluxation." Therefore, it is apparent how other areas of the body, not just the back and neck, are affected.

Based on my personal experiences working in the daily operations of chiropractic clinics for more than 25 years and the applicable research, the history and philosophy of chiropractic can be examined through the vision and mission statements offered by four prominent representatives of the profession. From a global to a local perspective, we can examine the vision and mission statements of the International Chiropractic Association (ICA), World Federation of Chiropractic (WFC), American Chiropractic Association (ACA), and California Chiropractic Association (CCA).

International Chiropractic Association (ICA)

Vision. To empower humanity in the expression of maximum health, wellness and human potential through universal chiropractic expression and utilization.

Mission. To advance chiropractic throughout the world as a distinct health care profession predicated upon its unique philosophy, science, and art.

Objectives:

- Maintain and promote chiropractic's unique identity as a non-therapeutic, drugless and surgical-free health science, based on its fundamental principles and philosophy. Provide leadership in the establishment of chiropractic licensure regulation in every nation and promote the quality and authenticity of chiropractic education.
- Foster the professional and technical development of the Doctor of Chiropractic through programs of continuing education, research, political, and social action.
- Encourage the highest professional, technical, and ethical standards for the doctor of chiropractic while safeguarding the professional welfare of its members.
- Champion the principle that every citizen in the world has the right to freedom of choice in health care and be able to choose unhampered the doctor and the healing art of his/her choice.
- Work harmoniously with other health care organizations and governments in a global humanitarian effort to foster chiropractic and spinal hygiene in the fields of family health (including children, women, and the elderly), and occupational health.
- Work for full inclusion of chiropractic in all public and private health care delivery programs [http://www.chiropractic.org/; https://en.wikipedia.org/wiki/International_Chiropractors_Association].

World Federation of Chiropractic (WFC)

The original World Federation of Chiropractic was established at the World Chiropractic Congress in Sydney, Australia in 1988.

The voting members of the World Federation of Chiropractic (WFC) are national associations of chiropractors in 88 countries. The WFC represents them and the chiropractic profession in the international community. Its goals, found in section 6 of the WFC Articles and Bylaws, include:

- Acting with national and international organizations to provide information and other assistance in the fields of chiropractic and world health;
- Promoting uniform high standards of chiropractic education, research and practice;
- Developing an informed public opinion among all peoples with respect to chiropractic; and
- Uniting members of the chiropractic profession and protecting the character and status of the profession [https://www.wfc.org/].

American Chiropractic Association (ACA)

The American Chiropractic Association (ACA) is the largest professional chiropractic organization in the United States. The ACA prides itself on leading by working hand in hand with other health care professionals, by lobbying for pro-chiropractic legislation and policies, by supporting meaningful research and by using that research to inform our treatment practices.

The ACA also provides professional and educational opportunities for all its members and is committed to being a positive and unifying force for the practice of modern chiropractic.

Mission. To inspire and empower our members to elevate the health and wellness of their communities.

Vision. The American Chiropractic Association is leading a modern movement of chiropractic care based on higher standards and a focus on patient outcomes.

Values

- We model excellence in patient-centered, evidence-based care.
- We serve our patients in the interest of public health.
- We participate in the health care community through collaboration and integration.
- We hold each other to higher standards.

Promise

To make accountability, to members and to the public, a priority. To abide by standards that provide higher quality care and consistency for patients. To embrace a collaborative approach and inclusive attitude that moves the organization, and the profession, forward (https://www.acatoday.org/About).

California Chiropractic Association

The mission of CCA is positioning doctors of chiropractic to improve the quality of life of all Californians, such that all Californians have a chiropractic doctor on their health care team (http://www.calchiro.org/).

Chiropractic's Effective Role in the Future of Health Care for Veterans

The Department of Veterans Affairs (VA) has been challenged to provide more accessible and timely health care to veterans. Part of this challenge is to provide these services as near as possible to the veteran's home of record. Further, a major concern has been the extended wait periods for veterans to get an appointment. This was much publicized in the Phoenix, Arizona, investigation and findings relative to the Veterans Health Administration scandal in 2014.

As a result of the changes the VA has implemented, there are now two programs that will be addressed and chiropractic's inclusion. Those programs are Veterans Choice Program (VCP) and Veterans Affairs Patient-Centered Community Care (PC3). As the Business Manager for a chiropractic clinic, I have personally spoken with representatives of the VA to discuss and schedule veterans for chiropractic appointments.

Veterans Choice Program (VCP)

The Veterans Choice Program is one of several programs through which a veteran can receive care from a community provider, paid for by VA. For example, if a veteran needs an appointment for a specific type of care, and the VA cannot provide the care in a timely manner or the nearest VA medical facility is too far away or too difficult to get to, then a veteran may be eligible for care through the Veterans Choice Program.

To use the Veterans Choice Program, veterans must receive prior authorization from the VA to receive care from a provider that is part of the VA's VCP network of community providers. The authorization is based on specific eligibility requirements and discussions with the veteran's VA provider. VA must authorize care that is needed beyond the scope of the first authorization.

Veterans Affairs Patient-Centered Community Care (PC3)

Patient-Centered Community Care is a Veterans Health Administration (VHA) nationwide program that utilizes health care contracts to provide eligible Veterans access to primary care, inpatient/outpatient specialty care, mental health care, limited emergency care, and limited newborn care for enrolled female veterans following birth of a child.

In instances where veterans require primary and specialty care that is not readily available through the VA Health Care Facility (HCF), the HCF may use a Patient-Centered Community Care (PC3) contract to purchase care for the veteran. The HCF's clinical and Non-VA care teams coordinate to determine if the care is available at the HCF, a nearby HCF or another health care partner. If not, they will look to the PC3 contract to buy the care. If the veteran needs care, the veteran should always start with the VA health care provider at the local facility.

Veterans and Chiropractic—History and Treatment Locations

In 2002, President George W. Bush signed Public Law 107-135, which guarantees chiropractic treatment for all eligible VA patients. However, many veterans do not know this service is available to them, even though it has been included in their Medical Benefits Package since 2004.

Furthermore, the VA is still in the process of making this service accessible to all veterans in need. According to the American Chiropractic Association (ACA), in 2015, only 48 of 152 VA Medical Centers offered chiropractic care for their patients. In 2018, the ACA reported that number had grown to 70.

Both articles further state if you're a veteran suffering from a musculoskeletal disorder, or pain in the muscles, joints and bones, chiropractic care may be a treatment option worth pursuing.

Here's what you need to know about chiropractic care and how to receive it:

First, contact your VA primary care provider (PCP) and see if they provide this service on site. If they do, ask to begin the process for approval.

Second, if your PCP does not offer chiropractic care, the VA can send you to a private chiropractic clinic through the "Choice Program" and cover the bill for you. This option is called "fee-basis" and will also require approval from your PCP.

Personal Testimonial

As previously mentioned herein, I have personally answered telephone calls from VA representatives checking for the availability of chiropractic appointments for veterans who were requesting care near their homes of record. As a veteran myself, needless to say, we welcomed/welcome fellow veterans and ensure timely and complete services based on their needs. The chiropractor who provided/provides the services was a former military officer whose father had been a Command Sergeant Major. That further added a comfort level due to the military familiarity.

Palmer College of Chiropractic

Palmer's Department of Defense/Veterans Affairs (DoD/VA) student rotation opportunities give students the opportunity to serve our nation's military members and veterans while gaining valuable clinical experience in a multi-disciplinary environment. These rotations are available to senior-level students on all Palmer campuses.

The basis of this program has some similarities to the SFVAMC UCSF relationship discussed herein.

Vignette: Face of Defense: Chiropractor Treats Troops' Aches, Pains

By Navy Petty Officer 2nd Class Zulema Sotelo DoD News, Defense Media Activity:

SILVERDALE, Wash., April 6, 2015—Aches and pains, whether from age or accident, have a tendency to be a byproduct for many sailors and Marines in their duties. To help ease the hurt, active-duty personnel have the option of seeking help from a chiropractor.

Spring Aragon, the resident chiropractor at Branch Health Clinic Bangor, ensures service members get the best care for muscular pain and physical discomfort.

Aragon said she supports the mission of Naval Hospital Bremerton to enable readiness, wellness and health care by the accurate diagnosis of spinal, neuromusculoskeletal injuries and conditions, providing corrective and rehabilitative adjustments and treatments for those conditions listed, and performing prevention therapy.

VAMC Fort Miley and UCSF

The San Francisco Veterans Affairs Medical Center (SFVAMC) is closely affiliated with the University of California San Francisco (UCSF). That relationship is especially evident in the VA Medical Service, the academic partner with the UCSF Department of Medicine. In fact, the concept of a close, mutually beneficial and formal affiliation between a medical university and a VA medical center was created in the 1960s at UCSF, later spreading to other parts of the VA system as its substantial rewards became clear.

UCSF medical students, residents and fellows rotate through the VA which provides nearly one third of all of the University's medical training. The SFVAMC has no freestanding training programs of its own; every aspect is fully integrated with UCSF. In addition, each VA staff physician in the Medical Service is a full UCSF Department of Medicine faculty member, following the same process for appointment and promotion as those based in other campus sites. The VA Medical Service Chief serves as the Vice Chair of the Department of Medicine, coordinating academic affairs at the VA with those across the broader Department."

https://medicine.ucsf.edu/campuses/vamc.html
https://www.sanfrancisco.va.gov/

Summary, Recommendations, Future Research

It appears that the current VA model of utilizing existing medical facilities on military bases and VAMC's is creditable. The UCSF SFVAMC medical model created in the 1960s continues to be very successful. The SFVAMC has no free-standing training programs of its own; every aspect is fully integrated with UCSF. Similarly, Palmer and Life Chiropractic Colleges and the SFVAMC should explore similar integration. Chiropractors can be integrated into more care, both in existing military facilities and as private contractors as part of the Veterans Choice Program (VCP) and Veterans Affairs Patient-Centered Community Care (PC3).

The existing military facilities can be augmented with private contracting out but privatization of a majority of the services should not supplant a structure that has a mix based on outcome successes proven to be veteran centered high quality accessible, affordable, patient friendly and patient satisfaction health care that is equivalent or better than that provided in other developed nations.

REFERENCES

"Chiropractic Care Available Through the VA." Retrieved from https://www.military.com/benfits/veterans.va-to-provide chiropractic-care.html

"Chiropractic Practice in Military and Veterans Health Care: The State of the Literature." (2009, August). *The Journal of the Canadian Chiropractic Association.* Retrieved from https://ncbi.nlm.nih.gov/pmc/articles/PMC2732257

"Chiropractic Services—Rehabilitation and Prosthetic Services." (2016, August 9). Retrieved from https://www.rehab.va.gov/chiro/.

"Does VA Provide Chiropractic Care?" (2017, December 20). *Veterans Anonymous.* Retrieved from https://va.org/faq-items/does-va-provide-chiropractic-care/.

"Fact Sheet for Chiropractic Services. Rehabilitation and Prosthetic Services." (2017, April). Retrieved from www.rehab.va.gov/chiro.

"Free Chiropractic Care Available for Eligible Vets—Military Veterans." (2015, February 19). milvetsrc.org/free-chiropractic-care-available-eligible-vets/.

"Patient-Centered Community Care (PC3)—VHA Office of Community." (2017, May 11). https://www.va.gov/COMMUNITYCARE/programs/veterans/pccc/index.asp.

Veterans Choice Program (VCP) –VHA Office of Community Care. (2018, March 15). https://www.va.gov/opa/choiceact/.

"Veterans—How to Receive Services Provided by a Doctor of Chiropractic." (2018). American Chiropractic Association. https://www.acatoday.org/Patients/Access-Coverage/Veterans.

www.defense.gov/News/Article/Article/604412/face-of-defense-chiropractor-treats-troops-aches-pains/.

www.gpo.gov/fdsys/pkg/GAOREPORTS-GAO-05-890R/pdf/GAOREPORTS-GAO-05-890R.pdf.

24. A VA Hospital You May Not Know[*]

SANJAY SAINT

Death is never easy. Even when expected, a person's death leaves a void for those who remain. As a physician, it is especially difficult for me when one of my patients dies.

I practice medicine at one of America's approximately 160 Veterans Affairs hospitals, so my patients are all veterans. The VA system—the largest integrated health care system in the United States—cares for approximately 9 million veterans, men and women who were willing to sacrifice greatly for our country.

News about transitions at the very top of the VA put me in a reflective mode, thinking about the core reason that we do what we do at VA health care facilities around the nation. As a VA doctor, it is sometimes difficult to read the frequent criticism about the VA and its hospitals without getting dejected, but, fortunately, most of us are inspired by those who entrust us with their care and their lives.

Abraham Lincoln, in his second inaugural address on March 4, 1865, gave the VA its mission: "To care for him who shall have borne the battle and for his widow, and his orphan."

I've been involved in caring for veterans since my first days in medicine, through many changes. As a medical student and resident, I cared for World War I veterans. They are now all gone.

I am now always honored to care for World War II veterans, most of whom have also passed.

Next will be veterans of the Korean War (like my father-in-law), Vietnam, Iraq and Afghanistan. It was these men and women who bravely served this country and who kept it free and open to people like me and my family—immigrants who were looking for better lives.

I did not sit in the foxhole with them or parachute into jungles, but I still have a duty. My duty is to provide America's veterans with superb medical care, delivered in a humane, compassionate and high-quality manner.

---

*Originally published as Sanjay Saint, "A VA Hospital You May Not Know: The Final Salute, and How Much We Doctors Care," *The Conversation*, March 30, 2018. Reprinted with permission of the publisher.

The Final Salute

When a veteran dies at our VA hospital, we all feel the loss. Even though I have been caring for veterans for over two decades in four different VA hospitals—as a medical student, resident, fellow and now as an attending physician—I only recently witnessed a ceremony that is both beautiful and heart-wrenching.

It is known as the Final Salute, and it is done for veterans who die under our care.

After pronouncing death, the patient's family is called and comes in to see their loved one. The body is placed on a gurney and is draped with Old Glory, the symbol of our freedom. As the body and family are led out of the hospital room to the exit, "Taps" is played—the signal for the health care workers, and, especially, their fellow soldiers, to come to the doors of their rooms.

Civilians stand with their hands on their hearts. Veterans give the military salute, standing if they are able.

For me as a civilian, I am reminded of how lucky others and I are that we get to care for these men and women, who all too often are forgotten and are struggling with demons. Rituals and ceremonies are important links to the past, and they are reminders of what it takes to improve tomorrow. Being a VA doctor gives me pride, no more so than when I watch how our VA honors those veterans who have died.

Veterans Deserve Top Priority

As the headlines point out, however, the VA should strive to provide the best care anywhere. Even though studies have found that overall VA care is comparable to and often better than non–VA care, the VA needs to do much more to make the VA a model system for not just this country but the entire world.

I think that President Donald Trump's call to increase the VA budget for fiscal year 2019 is a step in the right direction. Not only will extra resources provide veterans more choices for care, but they also will help prevent veteran suicides, reduce opioid use, and expand cutting-edge VA research on prosthetics and veteran safety.

Support for veterans has, fortunately, remained bipartisan. Despite the change of leadership currently happening in the VA secretary's office—and the continued controversy the role of the private sector could and should have in providing care to veterans—my plea from the field is that our elected leaders continue to do right by veterans.

My colleagues and I—the men and women who have the privilege to care for America's heroes in VA health care facilities around the country—are honored to provide the high-quality and compassionate care veterans deserve from the moment they leave the service to the time of their Final Salute.

25. Caring for Veterans: A Privilege and a Duty*

SANJAY SAINT

Veterans Day had its start as Armistice Day, marking the end of World War I hostilities. The holiday serves as an occasion to both honor those who have served in our armed forces and to ask whether we, as a nation, are doing right by them.

In recent years, that question has been directed most urgently at Veterans Affairs hospitals. Some critics are even calling for the dismantling of the whole huge system of hospitals and outpatient clinics.

President Obama signed a $16 billion bill to reduce wait times in 2014 to do things like hire more medical staff and open more facilities. And while progress has been made, much remains to be done. The system needs to improve access and timeliness of care, reduce often challenging bureaucratic hurdles and pay more attention to what front-line clinicians need to perform their duties well. There is no question that the VA health care system has to change, and it already has begun this process.

Over the past 25 years, I have been a medical student, chief resident, research fellow and practicing physician at four different VA hospitals. My research has led me to spend time in more than a dozen additional VA medical centers.

I know how VA hospitals work, and often have a hard time recognizing them as portrayed in today's political and media environment. My experience is that the VA hospitals I know provide high-quality, compassionate care.

Treating Nine Million Veterans a Year

I don't think most people have any sense of the size and scope of the VA system. Its 168 medical centers and more than one thousand outpatient clinics and other facilities serve almost nine million veterans a year, making it the largest integrated health care system in the country.

And many Americans may not know the role VA hospitals play in medical education. Two out of three medical doctors in practice in the U.S. today received some part of their training at a VA hospital.

---

*Originally published as Sanjay Saint, "Caring for Veterans: A Privilege and a Duty," *The Conversation*, November 10, 2016. Reprinted with permission of the publisher.

The reason dates to the end of World War II. The VA faced a physician shortage, as almost 16 million Americans returned from war, many needing health care.

At the same time, many doctors returned from World War II and needed to complete their residency training. The VA and the nation's medical schools thus became partners. In fact, the VA is the largest provider of health care training in the country, which increases the likelihood that trainees will consider working for the VA once they finish.

Specialized Care for Veterans

The VA network specializes in the treatment of such war-related problems as post-traumatic stress disorder and suicide prevention. It has, for example, pioneered the integration of primary care with mental health.

Many veterans live in rural parts of the U.S., are of advanced age and have chronic medical conditions that make travel challenging. So the VA is a national leader in telemedicine, with notable success in mental health care.

The VA's research programs have made major breakthroughs in areas such as cardiac care, prosthetics and infection prevention.

I can vouch for the VA's nationwide electronic medical records system, which for many years was at the cutting edge.

A case in point: Several years ago a veteran, in the middle of a cross-country trip, was driving through Michigan when he began feeling sick. Within minutes of his arrival at our VA hospital, we were able to access his records from a VA medical center over a thousand miles away, learn that he had a history of Addison disease, a rare condition, and provide prompt treatment.

I am therefore not surprised that the studies that have compared VA with non–VA care have found that the VA is, overall, as good as or better than the private sector. In fact, a recently published systematic review of 69 studies performed by RAND investigators concluded: "the available data indicate overall comparable health care quality in VA facilities compared to non–VA facilities with regard to safety and effectiveness."

The VA Offers Veterans More Than Health Care

The most remarkable aspect of VA hospitals, though, is the patient population, the men and women who have sacrificed for their country. They have a common bond. A patient explained it this way: "The VA is different because everyone has done something similar, whether you were in World War II or Korea or Nam, like me. You're not thrown into a pot with other people, which would happen at another kind of hospital."

The people who work at VA hospitals have a special attitude toward their patients. It takes the form of respect and gratitude, of empathy, of a level of caring that is nothing short of love. You can see it in the extra services provided for patients who are often alone in the world, or too far from home to be visited.

Take a familiar scene: a medical student taking a patient for a walk or wheelchair ride on the hospital grounds. It is common for nurses to say "our veteran" when discussing a patient's care with me.

Volunteers and chaplains rotate through VA hospitals on a regular basis, to a degree unknown in most community hospitals. The social work department is also more active. The patients are not always so patient, but these visitors persevere. "They're a good bunch of people," one veteran said of the staff. "I know because I'm irritable most of the time and they all get along with me."

Physicians everywhere are under heavy pressure these days, in part because of the increase in the number of complex patients they care for. Yet I have spent hours observing doctors in VA hospitals around the country as they sit with patients, inquiring about their families and their military service, treating the veterans with respect and without haste.

Earlier this year, I cared for a veteran in his 50s, a house painter, whom we diagnosed with cancer that had metastasized widely. We offered him chemotherapy, which could have given him an extra few months, but he chose hospice. He told me he wanted to go home to be with his wife and play the guitar. One of the songs he wanted to sing was "Knocking on Heaven's Door."

I was deeply moved. I liked and admired the man, and I was disturbed that we had been unable to save him. My medical student had the same feelings. Before the patient left, the student told me, "He shook my hand, looked me in the eyes, and said, 'Thanks for being a warrior for me.'"

That's the special kind of patient who shows up at a VA hospital. Every single one of them should have the special kind of care they deserve. And we must ensure that the care is superb on this and every day.

26. Military Veterans Battling Substance Abuse Helped by Addressing Addictions Together[*]

KATHERINE ALBERTSON

Each year, roughly 15,000 people leave the British armed forces. The vast majority make a successful transition into civilian society, having had their lives enriched by their service experience.

But a small and increasing number of ex-forces personnel face difficulties making that successful transition. They can struggle alone for long periods of time with problems such as alcohol misuse, mental health issues, unemployment, homelessness and prison. It has been estimated that the symptoms of poor transition from military service cost the UK tax payer £98m in 2015.

New research that my colleagues and I have just published highlights of one project that is making a difference. The project we evaluated, Right Turn, was designed for military veterans with alcohol and drug addictions and is run by the charity Addaction in 20 locations across the UK. For those taking part, it involves weekly peer support meetings with fellow veterans, supplemented by social activities and mentor training. The main point of the project was to foster friendships so group members would support each other out side of formal meetings.

We found that compared to a different intervention run by Addaction that wasn't aimed specifically at veterans, the project had a marked difference in veterans' transition to civilian life and recovery from addictions.

Tough Times on Civvy Street

The task of becoming a civilian after time in the forces can prove one of the toughest changes that service personnel face. One ex-forces member in recovery from addiction,

*Originally published as Katherine Albertson, "Military Veterans Battling Substance Abuse Helped by Addressing Addictions Together," *The Conversation*, June 23, 2017. Reprinted with permission of the publisher.

Gillie (not his real name), explained to me: "Being able to go out in to the world and not 'tolerate' civilians, but sort of realize 'Well, I am a civilian now,' and have that like change in thinking of being like 'I'm not going to get very far if I think that every civilian is an alien,' if you like."

Many veterans can struggle with this sense of separation from the civilian population—and some veterans need more help than others. Substance misuse problems may arise from a sense of loss of a veteran's military identity and confidence. Veterans often find themselves at the end of their military career without having the inclination or the emotional and social resources to adopt a civilian identity.

Some non-veteran-specific services may not adequately address veterans' distinct transitional and ongoing challenges.

The veterans we interviewed in the Right Turn project told us that they had previous experience of support services that were designed for civilians. But they said these services did not acknowledge the unique experience of those who have served in the military and how this is linked to other aspects of their lives.

Help Back on the "Straight and Narrow"

The Right Turn model looks at a person's issues in the context of their whole life, rather than focusing on their substance use in isolation. We found this reduced the likelihood of contact with the criminal justice system and continued substance misuse. It also helped to avoid further deterioration in mental and physical health, as well as helping participants address practical day-to-day issues, such as the social exclusion that many veterans experience on leaving service.

Some of the veterans had come into contact with criminal justice services before joining the project. Since the Right Turn intervention all the 23 veterans we interviewed and surveyed throughout the project had stayed on the straight and narrow. They all also gained and maintained recovery status—meaning they had achieved their goal of managing their addiction.

When we compared this with an equivalent group of veterans who accessed a separate service run by Addaction that wasn't aimed specifically at veterans, the Right Turn participants achieved improved physical and psychological health outcomes. In contrast, the majority of the veterans in the comparison sample experienced a significant deterioration in their physical and psychological health.

Using Military Camaraderie

Rather than ignoring veterans' military identity, the Right Turn project builds upon it to create a new military-veteran citizenship in the civilian world. Right Turn redirects the comradeship and mutual resilience that underpinned veterans' military life to support them in establishing a new identity. This then helps them to sustain their recovery from alcohol and drug addiction.

Our research illustrated that the greatest asset veterans have is their membership of the wider armed forces community—with a shared sense of belonging and purpose. Two ex-forces personnel meeting on the street for the first time instantly know they have more in common with each other than their work colleagues, their neighbors and other civilians living around them. They are still "in it" together.

We found that engaging in this project resulted in significant behavior change. Veterans reported a greater sense of security and confidence in their capacity to manage practical, day-to-day matters, such as accommodation and finances.

As Gillie told me: "I've got to conform, but you've got that safety net from the Right Turn that helps you make that transition"

Veterans told us that they had accessed Right Turn because it was only for military veterans. This also meant they were motivated to keep attending because they did not want to let down the group. If military identity is valued these veterans can recognize their individual strengths and play a full and valued part in civilian life—a part enhanced by their proud acceptance of their status as ex-forces.

27. Fix for VA Health Snarls Veterans and Doctors in New Bureaucracy[*]

QUIL LAWRENCE, ERIC WHITNEY *and* MICHAEL TOMSIC

Veterans are still waiting to see a doctor. Two years ago, vets were waiting a long time for care at Veterans Affairs clinics. At one facility in Phoenix, for example, veterans waited on average 115 days for an appointment. Adding insult to injury, some VA schedulers were told to falsify data to make it looks like the waits weren't that bad. The whole scandal ended up forcing the resignation of the VA secretary at the time, Eric Shinseki.

Congress and the VA came up with a fix: Veterans Choice, a $10 billion program. Veterans received a card that was supposed to allow them to see a non–VA doctor if they were either more than 40 miles away from a VA facility or they were going to have to wait longer than 30 days for a VA provider to see them.

The problem was, Congress gave them only 90 days to set up the system. Facing that deadline, the VA turned to two private companies to administer the program—helping veterans get an appointment with a doctor and then working with the VA to pay that doctor.

It sounds like a simple idea but it's not working. Wait times have gotten worse. Compared to this time last year, there are 70,000 more appointments where it took vets at least a month to be seen, according to the VA's own audit.

The VA claims there has been a massive increase in demand for care, but the problem has more to do with the way Veterans Choice was set up. It is confusing and complicated. Vets don't understand it, doctors don't understand it and even VA administrators admit they can't always figure it out.

Veterans Face Delays and Worry

This is playing out in a big way in Montana. That state has more veterans per capita than any state besides Alaska. This winter Montana Sen. Jon Tester sent his staff to meet with veterans across the state. Bobby Wilson showed up to a meeting in Superior. He's a

*Originally published as Quil Lawrence, Eric Whitney and Michael Tomsic, "Fix for VA Health Snarls Veterans and Doctors in New Bureaucracy," *Kaiser Health News*, May 16, 2016. This story is part of a partnership that includes Montana Public Radio, WFAE, NPR's Back at Base project and Kaiser Health News.

Navy vet who served in Vietnam and is trying to get his hearing aids fixed. Wilson is mired in bureaucracy.

"The VA can't do it in seven months, eight months? Something's wrong," he said. "Three hours on the phone," trying to make an appointment. "Not waiting," he said, "talking for three hours trying to get this thing set up for my new hearing aids."

Tony Lapinski, a former aircraft mechanic, has also spent his time on the phone, with Health Net, one of the two contractors the VA selected to help Veterans Choice patients.

"You guys all know the Health Net piano?" he said. "They haven't changed the damn elevator music in over a year!" That elicits knowing chuckles from the audience. Later during an interview, he said when he gets through to a person, "They are the nicest boiler room telemarketers you have ever spoken to. But that doesn't get your medical procedure taken care of."

Lapinski has an undiagnosed spinal growth and he's worried. "Some days I wake up and go, 'Am I wasting time, when I could be on chemotherapy or getting a surgery?'" he said. "Or six months from now when I still haven't gotten it looked at and I start having weird symptoms and they say, 'Boy, that's cancer! If you had come in here six months ago, we probably could have done something for ya, but it's too late now!'"

Lapinski finally got to a neurosurgeon, but he didn't exactly feel like his Choice card was carte blanche. Doctors, it turns out, are waiting, too—for payment, he said.

"You get your procedure done, and you find out that two months later the people haven't been paid. They have got $10 billion that they have to spend, and they are stiffing doctors for 90 days, 180 days, maybe a year!" said Lapinski. "No wonder I can't get anyone to take me seriously on this program."

He said he gets it. He used to do part-time work fixing cars, and he would still take jobs from people who had taken more than 90 days to pay him or bounced a check. But he did so reluctantly.

"I had a list of slow-pay customers," he said. "I might work for them again, but everybody else came before them. So why would it be any different with these health care professionals?"

Hospitals, clinics and doctors across the country have complained about not getting paid, or only paid very slowly. Some have just stopped taking Veterans Choice patients altogether, and Montana's largest health care network, Billings Clinic, doesn't accept any VA Choice patients.

Not cool, said Montana Sen. Jon Tester, of Health Net and other contractors.

"The payment to the providers is just laziness," Tester said. "I'm telling you, it's just flat laziness. These folks turn in their bills, and if they're not paid in a timely manner, that's a business model that'll cause you to go broke pretty quick."

The VA now admits the rushed timeframe led to decisions that resulted in a nightmare for some patients.

Health Net declined to be interviewed for this story. But in a statement, the company said that VA has recently made some beneficial changes that are helping streamline Veterans Choice. For example, the VA no longer demands a patient's medical records be returned to VA before they pay.

Meanwhile, though, veterans continue to wait. "If I knew half of what I knew now back then when I was just a kid, I would've never went in the military," said Bobby Wilson. "I see how they treat their veterans when they come home."

Scheduling Lags Also Irk the Doctors' Offices and the VA

And there's another whole side to the coin. Doctors are frustrated in dealing with another government health care bureaucracy.

In Gastonia, North Carolina, Kelly Coward dials yet another veteran with bad news.

"I'm just calling to let you know that I still have not received your authorization for Health Net federal. As soon as I get it, I will give you a call and let you know that we have it and we can go over some surgery dates," she told a veteran.

Coward works at Carolina Orthopaedic & Sports Medicine Center, a practice that sees about 200 veterans. Dealing with Health Net has become a consuming part of her job.

"I have to fax and re-fax, and call and re-call. And they tell us that they don't receive the notes. And that's just every day. And I'm not the only one here that deals with it," she said.

Carolina Orthopaedic's business operations manager, Toscha Willis, is used to administrative headaches—that's part of the deal with health care—but she's never seen something like this.

She said it takes, "multiple phone calls, multiple re-faxing of documentation, being on hold one to two hours at a time to be told we don't have anything on file. But the last time we called about it they had it, but it was in review. You know, that's the frustration."

It can take three to four months just to line up an office visit.

The delays have become a frustration within the VA, too. Tymalyn James is a nurse care manager at the VA clinic in Wilmington, North Carolina. She said Choice has made the original problem worse. When she and her colleagues are swamped and refer someone outside the VA, it's supposed to help the veteran get care more quickly. But James said the opposite is happening.

"The fact is that people are waiting months and months, and it's like a, we call it the black hole," she said. "As long as the Choice program has gone on, we've had progressively longer and longer wait times for Choice to provide the service, and we've had progressively less and less follow through on the Choice end with what was supposed to be their managing of the steps."

The follow-through is lacking in two ways. The first is the lengthy delay in approving care. And after that's finally resolved, there's a long delay in getting paid for the care.

At least 30 doctors' offices across North Carolina are dealing with payment problems, some that have lasted more than a year.

Carolina Orthopaedic's CEO Chad Ghorley said his practice is getting paid after it provides the care. It's the lengthy delay on the front end that burdens his staff and, he worries, puts veterans at risk. He's a veteran himself.

"The federal government has put the Band-Aid on it when there's such a public outcry to how the veterans are taking care of, all right?" he said. "Well, they've got the Band-Aid on it to get the national media off their backs. But the wound is still open, the wound is still there."

Those experiences for both veterans and providers are typical. Congress is now working on a solution to the original solution, a bill is expected to clear Congress by the end of the month.

28. Health Care Battle on Hill Has Veterans Defending Obamacare Benefits*

STEPHANIE O'NEILL

Air Force veteran Billy Ramos, from Simi Valley, Calif., is 53 and gets health insurance for himself and for his family from Medicaid—the government insurance program for low-income people. He says he counts on the coverage, especially because of his physically demanding work as a self-employed contractor in the heating and air conditioning business.

"If I were to get hurt on the job or something, I'd have to run to the doctor's, and if I don't have any coverage they're going to charge me an arm and a leg," he said. "I'd have to work five times as hard just to make the payment on one bill."

There are about 22 million veterans in the U.S. But fewer than half get their health care through the Veterans Affairs system; some don't qualify for various reasons or may live too far from a VA facility to easily get primary health care there.

Many vets instead rely on Medicaid for their health insurance. Thirty-one states and the District of Columbia chose to expand Medicaid to cover more people—and many of those who gained coverage are veterans.

The GOP health care bill working its way through the Senate would dramatically reduce federal funding for Medicaid, including rolling back the expansion funding entirely between 2021 and 2024.

Medicaid coverage recently has become especially important to Ramos—a routine checkup and blood test this year showed he's infected with hepatitis C. California was one of the states that chose to expand Medicaid, and the program covers Ramos' costly treatment to eliminate the virus.

"Right now, I'm just grateful that I do have [coverage]," he said. "If they take it away, I don't know what I'm going to end up doing."

The Senate health plan—which proposes deep cuts to federal spending on Medicaid—has veterans and advocates worried. Will Fischer, a Marine who served in Iraq, is with VoteVets.org, a political action group that opposes the Republican health plan.

---

*Originally published as Stephanie O'Neill, "Health Care Battle on Hill Has Veterans Defending Obamacare Benefits," *Kaiser Health News*, June 30, 2017. This story is part of NPR's reporting partnership with Kaiser Health News.

"If it were to be passed into law, Medicaid would be gutted. And as a result, hundreds of thousands of veterans would lose health insurance," Fischer said.

It's too early to know just how many veterans might lose coverage as a result of the Medicaid reductions. First, states would have to make some tough decisions: whether to make up the lost federal funding, to limit benefits or to restrict who would get coverage.

But Dan Caldwell thinks those concerns are overblown. He's a Marine who served in Iraq and is now policy director for the group Concerned Veterans for America.

"The people who are saying that this is going to harm millions of veterans are not being entirely truthful," Caldwell said. "They're leaving out the fact that many of these veterans qualify for VA health care or in some cases already are using VA health care."

About a half-million veterans today are enrolled in the VA's health care program as well as in some other source of coverage, such as Medicaid or Medicare. Andrea Callow, with the non-profit group Families USA, wrote a recent report showing that nearly 1 in 10 veterans are enrolled in Medicaid.

"Oftentimes veterans will use their Medicaid coverage to get primary care," Callow said. "If, for example, they live in an area that doesn't have a VA facility, they can use their Medicaid coverage to see a doctor in their area."

Whether a particular veteran qualifies for coverage through the VA depends on a host of variables that she said leaves many with Medicaid as their only option.

But, Caldwell said, rather than fighting to preserve Medicaid access, veterans would be better served by efforts to reform the care the VA provides to those who qualify.

"We believe that giving veterans more health care choice and restructuring the VA so that it can act more like a private health care system will ultimately lead to veterans who use the VA receiving better health care," he said.

The Urban Institute found that the first two years after the enactment of the Affordable Care Act saw a nearly 44 percent drop in the number of uninsured veterans under age 65—the total went from 980,000 to 552,000. In large part, that was the result of the law's expansion of Medicaid.

29. McCain's Complicated Health Care Legacy: He Hated the ACA. He Also Saved It*

Emmarie Huetteman

There are many lawmakers who made their names in health care, seeking to usher through historic changes to a broken system.

John McCain was not one of them.

And yet, the six-term senator from Arizona and decorated military veteran leaves behind his own health care legacy, seemingly driven less by his interest in health care policy than his disdain for bullies trampling the "little guy."

He was not always successful. While McCain was instrumental in the passage of the Americans with Disabilities Act in 1990, most of the health initiatives he undertook failed after running afoul of traditional Republican priorities. His prescriptions often involved more government regulation and increased taxes.

In 2008, as the Republican nominee for president, he ran on a health care platform that dumbfounded many in his party who worried it would raise taxes on top of overhauling the U.S. tradition of workplace insurance.

Many will remember McCain as the incidental savior of the Affordable Care Act, whose late-night thumbs-down vote halted his party's most promising effort to overturn a major Democratic achievement—the signature achievement, in fact, of the Democrat who beat him to become president. It was a vote that earned him regular—and biting—admonishments from President Donald Trump.

McCain died in 2018, following a battle with brain cancer. He was 81. Coincidentally, his Senate colleague and good friend Ted Kennedy died on the same date, Aug. 25, nine years earlier, succumbing to the same type of rare brain tumor.

Whether indulging in conspiracy theories or wishful thinking, some have attributed McCain's vote on the ACA in July 2017 to a change of heart shortly after his terminal cancer diagnosis.

But McCain spent much of his 35 years in Congress fighting a never-ending supply of goliaths, among them health insurance companies, the tobacco industry and, in his

---

*Originally published as Emmarie Huetteman, "McCain's Complicated Health Care Legacy: He Hated the ACA. He Also Saved It," *Kaiser Health News*, August 25, 2018.

estimation, the Affordable Care Act, a law that extended insurance coverage to millions of Americans but did not solve the system's ballooning costs.

His prey were the sort of boogeymen that made for compelling campaign ads in a career stacked with campaigns. But McCain was "always for the little guy," said Douglas Holtz-Eakin, the chief domestic policy adviser on McCain's 2008 presidential campaign.

"John's idea of empathy is saying to you, 'I'll punch the bully for you,'" he said in an interview before McCain's death.

McCain's distaste for President Barack Obama's health care law was no secret. While he agreed that the health care system was broken, he did not think more government involvement would fix it. Like most Republicans, he campaigned in his last Senate race on a promise to repeal and replace the law with something better.

After Republicans spent months bickering amongst themselves about what was better, McCain was disappointed in the option presented to senators hours before their vote: hobble the ACA and trust that a handful of lawmakers would be able to craft an alternative behind closed doors, despite failing to accomplish that very thing after years of trying.

What bothered McCain more, though, was his party's strategy to pass their so-called skinny repeal measure, skipping committee consideration and delivering it straight to the floor. They also rejected any input from the opposing party, a tactic for which he had slammed Democrats when the ACA passed in 2010 without a single GOP vote. He lamented that Republican leaders had cast aside compromise-nurturing Senate procedures in pursuit of political victory.

In his 2018 memoirs, *The Restless Wave*, McCain said even Obama called to express gratitude for McCain's vote against the Republican repeal bill.

"I was thanked for my vote by Democratic friends more profusely than I should have been for helping save Obamacare," McCain wrote. "That had not been my goal."

Better known for his work on campaign finance reform and the military, McCain did have a hand in one landmark health bill—the Americans with Disabilities Act of 1990, the country's first comprehensive civil rights law that addressed the needs of those with disabilities. An early co-sponsor of the legislation, he championed the rights of the disabled, speaking of the service members and civilians he met in his travels who had become disabled during military conflict.

McCain himself had limited use of his arms due to injuries inflicted while he was a prisoner of war in Vietnam, though he was quicker to talk about the troubles of others than his own when advocating policy.

Yet two of his biggest bills on health care ended in defeat.

In 1998, McCain introduced a sweeping bill that would regulate the tobacco industry and increase taxes on cigarettes, hoping to discourage teenagers from smoking and raise money for research and related health care costs. It faltered under opposition from his fellow Republicans.

McCain also joined an effort with two Democratic senators, Kennedy of Massachusetts and John Edwards of North Carolina, to pass a patients' bill of rights in 2001. He resisted at first, concerned in particular about the right it gave patients to sue health care companies, said Sonya Elling, who served as a health care aide in McCain's office for about a decade. But he came around.

"It was the human, the personal aspect of it, basically," said Elling, now senior director of federal affairs at Eli Lilly. "It was providing him some of the real stories about how people were being hurt and some of the barriers that existed for people in the current system."

The legislation would have granted patients with private insurance the right to emergency and specialist care in addition to the right to seek redress for being wrongly denied care. But President George W. Bush threatened to veto the measure, claiming it would fuel frivolous lawsuits. The bill failed.

McCain's health care efforts bolstered his reputation as a lawmaker willing to work across the aisle. Sen. Chuck Schumer of New York, now the Senate's Democratic leader, sought his help on legislation in 2001 to expand access to generic drugs. In 2015, McCain led a bipartisan coalition to pass a law that would strengthen mental health and suicide prevention programs for veterans, among other veterans' care measures he undertook.

It was McCain's relationship with Kennedy that stood out, inspiring eerie comparisons when McCain was diagnosed last year with glioblastoma—a form of brain cancer—shortly before his vote saved the Affordable Care Act.

That same aggressive brain cancer killed Kennedy in 2009, months before the passage of the law that helped realize his work to secure better access for Americans to health care.

"I had strenuously opposed it, but I was very sorry that Ted had not lived to see his long crusade come to a successful end," McCain wrote in his 2018 book.

While some of his biggest health care measures failed, the experiences helped burnish McCain's résumé for his 2000 and 2008 presidential campaigns.

In 2007, trailing other favored Republicans, such as former New York City mayor Rudy Giuliani in early polling and fundraising, McCain asked his advisers to craft a health care proposal, said Holtz-Eakin. It was an unusual move for a Republican presidential primary.

The result was a remarkable plan that would eliminate the tax break employers get for providing health benefits to workers, known as the employer exclusion, and replace it with refundable tax credits to help people—not just those working in firms that supplied coverage—buy insurance individually. He argued employer-provided plans were driving up costs, as well as keeping salaries lower.

The plan was controversial, triggering "a total freakout" when McCain gained more prominence and scrutiny, Holtz-Eakin said. But McCain stood by it.

"He might not have been a health guy, but he knew how important that was," he said. "And he was relentless about getting it done."

30. VA Adding Opioid Antidote to Defibrillator Cabinets for Quicker Overdose Response[*]

Martha Bebinger

It took more than 10 minutes for paramedics to arrive after a housekeeper found a man collapsed on the floor of a bathroom in a Boston Veteran Affairs building.

The paramedics immediately administered naloxone, often known by its brand name Narcan, to successfully reverse the man's opioid overdose. But it takes only a few minutes without oxygen for brain damage to begin.

Pam Bellino, patient safety manager for the Boston VA, read that incident report in December 2015 with alarm. "That was the tipping point for us to say, 'We need to get this naloxone immediately available, without locking it up,'" she said.

The easiest way to do it quickly, Bellino reasoned, would be to add the drug to the automated external defibrillator, or AED, cabinets already in place. Those metal boxes on the walls of VA cafeterias, gyms, warehouses, clinic waiting rooms and some rehab housing were installed to hold equipment for a fast response to heart attacks.

Now the VA, building on the project started in Boston, is moving to add naloxone kits to the AED cabinets in its buildings across the country, an initiative that could become a model for other health care organizations.

Equipping police with nasal spray naloxone is becoming more common across the country, but there has been some resistance to making the drug available in public.

Bellino has heard from critics who say easy access to naloxone gives drug users a false sense of safety. She disagrees.

"Think of this as you would a seat belt or an air bag," she said. "It by no means fixes the problem, but what it does is save a life."

Giving naloxone to someone who hasn't overdosed isn't harmful, but it is a prescription drug. So, Bellino said, the VA had to persuade the accrediting agency, The Joint Commission, to approve guidelines for the AED naloxone project.

The cabinets must be sealed and alarmed so staff can tell if they've been opened. They must be checked daily and refilled when the naloxone kits expire.

*Originally published as Martha Bebinger, "VA Adding Opioid Antidote to Defibrillator Cabinets for Quicker Overdose Response," *Kaiser Health News*, October 3, 2018. This story is part of a reporting partnership that includes WBUR, NPR and Kaiser Health News.

The commission didn't agree to let the VA put the words "naloxone" or "Narcan" on the cabinet doors to alert the public that the drug is inside, but did allow the VA to affix the letter "N."

In December, the project will expand nationwide, as VA hospitals across the country will add naloxone to their AED cabinets.

"The overwhelming evidence is that it just saves lives," said Dr. Ryan Vega with the VA's Center for Innovation. "We're hopeful that other health systems take notice and think about doing the same."

Vets have nearly twice the risk of overdose, compared with civilians, said Amy Bohnert, an investigator with the VA Ann Arbor Healthcare System, citing 2005 death data. She said it isn't clear why veterans are more likely to OD, but many do have complex medical conditions.

"Some of that's related to combat exposure," Bohnert said. "They've got mental health treatment needs. They may have injuries that result in them being more likely to be prescribed opioids than your average person. And all of these things can impact their risk of overdose."

A smattering of schools, airports, churches and employers around the country have added naloxone to their AED cabinets.

Some stock other lifesaving tools as well: tourniquets to stop bleeding after a shooting; EpiPens to keep airways open; and even injectors to treat diabetic shock.

Dr. Jeremy Cushman leads a project at the University of Rochester that has placed both tourniquets and naloxone in 80 AED cabinets across that campus as of July.

"This system is already in place," Cushman said. "The question is, how can we leverage it to save more lives?"

Turning AED cabinets into miniature emergency medical stations presents challenges, Cushman said. Medicines can't be left outside during extreme temperatures. They are expensive and expire.

Dr. Scott Weiner, president of the Massachusetts College of Emergency Physicians, said he has dealt with those issues while developing street-level dispensing stations for naloxone.

And then there's the belief among some critics that naloxone enables drug use by offering an assurance of life after an overdose. Weiner said that attitude is waning and, as it does, the public may be more open to other controversial, lifesaving measures.

"Naloxone is kind of the lowest barrier for people to understand, where someone has already overdosed and we're going to give them the antidote," Weiner said. "The leap to giving them needles [through a needle exchange] or allowing them to inject in a safe space, that's just another level of acceptance that people will have to get to."

The Boston VA's Bellino said she hopes that AED manufacturers will start selling cabinets that meet the new hospital accreditation standards. So far, the Boston VA counts 132 lives saved through all three parts of its naloxone project: training high-risk veterans, equipping police and the AED cabinets.

31. VA Shifts to Clinical Pharmacists to Help Ease Patients' Long Waits[*]

Phil Galewitz

Something astonishing has happened in the past year to outpatient treatment at the Veterans Affairs hospital in Madison, Wisconsin.

Vets regularly get next-day and even same-day appointments for primary care now, no longer waiting a month or more to see a doctor as many once did.

The reason is they don't all see doctors. Clinical pharmacists—whose special training permits them to prescribe drugs, order lab tests, make referrals to specialists and do physical examinations—are handling more patients' chronic care needs. That frees physicians to concentrate on new patients and others with complex needs.

A quarter of primary care appointments at the Madison hospital are now handled by clinical pharmacists since they were integrated in patient care teams in 2015. Several VA hospitals—in El Paso, Texas, and Kansas City, Mo., among them—have followed Madison's approach and more than 36 others are considering it, according to hospital officials.

"It's made a tremendous positive impact in improving access," said Dr. Jean Montgomery, chief of primary care services at the Madison hospital.

That's critical for the VA, the focus of a national scandal in 2014 after news reports revealed the Phoenix VA hospital had booked primary care appointments months in advance, schedulers falsified wait times to make them look shorter and dozens had died awaiting care. Further investigations uncovered similar problems at other VA facilities. More than two years later, tens of thousands of vets are still waiting a month or two for an appointment, according to the latest data from the VA.

The Obama administration has allowed some veterans to seek care in the private sector if they choose, but VA wait times remain long and more action is needed, the General Accountability Office reported in April.

Expanding clinical pharmacists' role is a solution.

They receive two more years of education than regular pharmacists and they can handle many primary care needs for patients, particularly after physicians have diagnosed their conditions.

---

*Originally published as Phil Galewitz, "VA Shifts to Clinical Pharmacists to Help Ease Patients' Long Waits," *Kaiser Health News*, October 25, 2016.

The VA has had them for more than 20 years, but their growing involvement in patient care is more recent. This year it employs 3,185 clinical pharmacists with authority to prescribe medications, order lab tests and perform physical assessments—nearly a 50 percent increase since 2011.

"It's having a significant impact on reducing wait times and our office is trying to expand more of them nationally to increase access," said Heather Ourth, national clinical program manager for VA Pharmacy Benefits Management Services.

In 2015, VA clinical pharmacists wrote 1.9 million prescriptions for chronic diseases, according to a report co-authored by Ourth and published in September in the American Journal of Health-System Pharmacy.

A goal is to increase the use of clinical pharmacists to help patients with mental health needs and pain management.

"This helps open up appointment slots for physicians to meet patients with acute care needs," Ourth said.

Clinical pharmacists' authority is determined at each VA hospital based on their training and knowledge.

The Madison VA allowed clinical pharmacists to take over management of patients with chronic diseases such as diabetes and high blood pressure, participate in weekly meetings with doctors and other members of patients' care teams and handle patients' calls about medications.

They typically see five patients in their office each day, usually for 30 minutes each, and they talk to another 10 by telephone, said Ellina Seckel, the clinical pharmacist who led the changes at the hospital.

Many issues involve adjusting medication dosages such as insulin, which do not require a face-to-face visit. When Seckel sees patients, she often helps them lower the number of drugs they take because they may cause unnecessary complications.

Expanding clinical pharmacists' role in primary care has cut readmission rates and helped more patients keep their diabetes under control, Seckel said.

VA hospital officials in both Madison and El Paso said they faced challenges initially in persuading doctors to delegate some duties to qualified pharmacists.

"Some physicians feel like it's a turf war and don't want to refer their patients because they feel the clinical pharmacist is trying to practice medicine," said Lanre' Obisesan, a clinical pharmacist and assistant chief of pharmacy at the El Paso VA.

Even so, the El Paso VA's average wait time fell from two months to two weeks, he said, after it added several clinical pharmacists and gave them independence to help patients. About 30 percent of the VA patients in El Paso have used clinical pharmacists, Obisesan said.

That share will rise. The hospital now has one clinical pharmacist for every six physicians, but it aims to add more pharmacists to reduce the ratio to 1 to 3.

The Madison VA is close to that ratio now after adding four clinical pharmacist positions in the past year.

Patients there can choose whether to see a doctor or a pharmacist. With approval from primary care physicians, pharmacists took over 27 percent of the follow-up appointments for patients with chronic illnesses, Seckel said.

That shift yields benefits for both doctors and patients, said Montgomery, the head of primary care services at the Madison VA.

Many VA doctors only have time to deal with patients' acute care issues, such as knee or back pain, with little time to focus on a patient's multiple chronic illnesses and often a dozen or more medications they may be taking for them.

"The more we can have members of the team to do routine things that do not require a physician's time the better the quality of the visit and the better patient outcomes," he said.

Patients seem to like what the hospital is doing.

Stephen Howard Foster saw a clinical pharmacist recently who told him he could stop taking one heartburn medication and switched him to another medicine to reduce side effects. He said he was comfortable with the pharmacist advising him without first consulting his physician and he saved time.

"This is a good idea rather than put up with normal delays," said Foster, 51.

Another Madison VA patient, Mike Fonger, 71, saw clinical pharmacist Anita Kashyap recently to get a blood pressure check, lab test results, a review of his medications and to change an ointment he was taking for back and shoulder pain. Kashyap also helped him ease the side effects from the cholesterol-lowering drug he takes by cutting his dosage in half.

"I like the extra attention I get here," Fonger said.

32. Vietnam Veteran Who Died of Hepatitis Added to Memorial Wall[*]

MICHELLE ANDREWS

The Vietnam War ended more than 40 years ago, but it continues to claim soldiers' lives. Nearly every spring new names are etched into the black granite walls of the Vietnam Veterans Memorial in Washington, D.C., that pays tribute to the more than 58,000 service members who lost their lives.

Jim McGough is one of them. As a 19-year-old infantry soldier, McGough was with his unit near the Laotian border in 1971 when they came under fire. A grenade exploded nearby, tearing up his feet and lower legs. McGough was taken by medevac to Okinawa, where he underwent surgery, including a transfusion to replace the blood he had lost. Unable to wear army boots after the injury, he was shipped back to the States, where he married his high school sweetheart, Sheryl Isaacson, and they settled down near their hometown of Fort Dodge, Iowa.

Twenty years passed before McGough, who worked in magazine advertising sales, learned that he had hepatitis C, a blood-borne viral infection that attacks the liver and can cause scarring called cirrhosis and liver cancer. The virus only was discovered in 1989, and routine testing of the blood supply began shortly afterward. It was about that time that McGough, a regular Red Cross blood donor, learned he had been infected. He'd never been an intravenous drug user or gotten tattoos, common routes of infection, so the McGoughs figured he must have contracted the virus when he had the blood transfusion in Japan.

Veterans are more than twice as likely to have hepatitis C as members of the general population, studies have found. The virus is significantly more common among Vietnam era veterans than those of any other service era.

McGough went to a liver specialist, who found no damage. The standard treatment at the time, a combination of the drugs interferon and ribavirin, had debilitating side effects. So Jim and Sheryl, who had two daughters, decided not to do anything.

"We were having a great time," said Sheryl, now 62. "We're going, 'No big deal.' When you're young, you're invincible."

In his late 40s, Jim started to show signs of liver damage. About that time, he and

---

*Originally published as Michelle Andrews, "Vietnam Veteran Who Died of Hepatitis Added to Memorial Wall," *Kaiser Health News*, November 8, 2016.

Sheryl took a trip to the nation's capital, and visited the Vietnam Memorial. He thought it was magnificent, Sheryl remembers, and told her, "If this thing kills me, I want to get my name added."

In January 2014, the virus did kill him. Jim had gone through the interferon treatment but couldn't shake the disease and finally succumbed to liver cancer.

In order to have their names added to "The Wall," Vietnam veterans have to meet criteria established by the Department of Defense. Many of the 376 names that have been added since the memorial was completed in 1982 are people who died during the war or shortly afterward but whose records were misplaced, for example, or who were overlooked for other reasons. Their deaths generally must be the result of injuries sustained during the war in Vietnam or a defined combat zone. A number of causes of death don't qualify, including exposure to the defoliant Agent Orange or similar chemicals, illness or suicide related to post-traumatic stress disorder, diabetes, cancer and heart attack.

"They reject far more than they accept," said Tim Tetz, director of outreach for the Vietnam Veterans Memorial Fund, which founded the memorial and is responsible for adding new names to it.

In McGough's case, at the bottom of a box in their basement he and Sheryl found a handwritten note from a nurse in Okinawa ordering a blood transfusion for Jim the day after he was wounded. That was the documentation they needed to prove his disease was service related so he could qualify for veteran's disability benefits. Later, after his death and a lengthy application and evaluation, adding McGough's name to the memorial also was approved.

In addition to Jim McGough, seven names were inscribed in 2016. There's not much room left to add more names, Tetz said, at least not long ones. There's space for one more long name, he said, fewer than 20 medium-length names and a basically unlimited number of short ones. It's an issue that the National Park Service is wrestling with, according to Tetz.

In 2013, the first of a number of pricey new drugs was approved by the Food and Drug Administration that cure hepatitis C in as little as eight weeks with few side effects. Yet the price tags for a course of treatment, which can exceed $84,000, created financial challenges for programs like the Veterans Health Administration. But with additional financial support from Congress, the VHA has reduced the number of vets who are eligible for treatment from 145,000 to 71,000, said Dr. David Ross, director of the HIV, Hepatitis, and Public Health Pathogens Programs at Department of Veterans Affairs.

It was too late for McGough, though, who died just weeks before the drug came on the market.

"I can hardly bear to watch those commercials," said Sheryl. "It's just heartbreaking."

33. Ensuring All Veterans Have Safe Housing Requires All Hands on Deck[*]

ELISHA HARIG-BLAINE

In recent years, dramatic progress has been made across the nation in the effort to reduce Veteran homelessness thanks to strategic planning, bold leadership, and unprecedented community collaboration. These elements are being paired with data-driven strategies that have resulted in a nationwide decline of 33 percent since 2010. This progress is paving the way for success in other sub-groups of the homeless population.

While headway on Veteran homelessness is notable by itself, the efforts also offer insight about how city leaders can ensure all Veterans have a safe place to call home.

The Anatomy of Success: Strategic Planning

Beginning in 2010, the federal government's response to homelessness became guided by the Opening Doors strategic plan. For the first time, the plan broke the nation's work on homelessness into specific sub-populations. The first sub-population was Veterans. Bringing focus to a specific sub-population is one approach to make progress on municipal challenges.

Another way to make progress, is by bringing focus to a specific issue. In nearly every city across the country, access to safe, affordable housing is a challenge. This year's State of the Cities report found housing as one of the top ten issues receiving significant coverage in mayoral addresses.

Like homelessness, progress on addressing housing overall can be made with a focus on Veterans. Realizing this progress comes when cities use the dual lenses of Veterans and housing to guide how existing programs and municipal networks are utilized.

---

*Originally published Elisha Harig-Blaine, "Ensuring All Veterans Have Safe Housing Requires All Hands on Deck," https://citiesspeak.org/2015/09/01/ensuring-all-veterans-have-safe-housing-requires-all-hands-on-deck/#_ga=2.185492330.29049585.1553888189–259213687.1553888189 (September 1, 2015). Reprinted with permission of the publisher and author.

Bold Leadership and Community Collaboration

In Los Angeles, Mayor Eric Garcetti used his State of the Cities address to announce that in the past year, the city had decreased Veteran homelessness by 50 percent. Across the city and county of Los Angeles, community stakeholders have housed 6,538 Veterans since June 2014.

To continue this progress, access to housing is key. A first step taken by city leaders and federal partners is to engage property owners and managers of existing market-rate housing. In June, Secretary of Veterans Affairs, Bob McDonald joined the Mayor and others in calling on landlords to join local efforts.

In addition to increasing access to existing market-rate housing, there is the need to increase the supply of affordable housing and preserve existing affordable housing. To support these goals, the Mayor Garcetti has proposed an additional $10 million for the city's Affordable Housing Trust Fund (AHTF). Recognizing the need to tie the emerging sharing economy to the pragmatic needs of residents with lower-incomes, the Mayor proposed generating $5 million for the AHTF from taxes collected for the first time from Airbnb.

These resources are particularly needed in the face of past and proposed cuts to the Community Development Block Grant (CDBG) and the HOME Investment Partnerships program (HOME). In addition to program cuts, the demand for affordable housing is exacerbated as the affordability restrictions on thousands of housing units are ending. In the next five years, in California alone, at least 1,380 properties will have a subsidy expire, impacting the affordability of at least 100,181 units of housing.

To meet these challenges, cities are increasingly building collaborative partnerships beyond their existing relationships with non-profits and the federal and state government. Recognizing the unique role foundations can play in bridging the gap in services, cities are turning to the philanthropic sector to help meet the housing needs of Veterans.

Using Data to Drive Decision-making

Tragically, Veterans are over-represented among the homeless.

Nationwide, Veterans comprise 8.1 percent of the general population. However, with the homeless population, 8.6 percent are Veterans. This over-representation is particularly seen in the unsheltered homeless population, where 10 percent are Veterans. In Los Angeles city and county, these numbers are even starker. Veterans comprise only 3.6 percent of the overall population, but are 10.8 percent of the overall homeless population and 11.3 percent of the unsheltered homeless population.

In addition to being over-represented in the homeless population, the percentage of Veterans who are seniors is significantly greater than the general population. Nationwide, 47.3 percent of Veterans are over the age of 65, compared to 15.9 percent of non–Veterans. In Los Angeles city and county, the numbers are again striking. In Los Angeles city and county, 53.2 percent of Veterans are over the age of 65, compared to 13.6 percent of non–Veterans.

These facts show that by using the lenses of housing and Veterans, city officials and their partners can not only make progress in these areas, but also position the community to better address the housing needs of other sub-populations, such as seniors.

One illustration of a housing development at this intersection is the Guy Gabaldon project. Developed by the East Los Angeles Community Corporation (ELACC), the 33-unit facility is operated by New Directions for Veterans and exclusively serves Veterans aged 55 and older.

Finished in September 2014, the project was fully leased in less than three months as a result of being part of Los Angeles' coordinated entry system developed as part of the Home for Good campaign. Staff from the U.S. Department of Veterans Affairs work with New Directions to provide on-site supportive services to clients. Amenities include a community garden, a community room with gym equipment and on-site laundry facilities. All units are furnished and as they moved in, Veterans were provided a "move-in" kit with paper products, toiletries and other essentials.

To allow the units to be affordable for homeless senior Veterans, ELACC used Los Angeles' AHTF, Low Income Housing Tax Credits (LIHTCs) as well as project-based HUD-VASH vouchers. Additional funding came from the Federal Reserve's Affordable Housing Program (AHP) and The Home Depot Foundation. Similar support for housing developments serving Veterans from The Home Depot Foundation has helped cities build or preserve more than 17,000 units of housing. Over the past three years, the Foundation has invested more than $90 million in projects supporting Veterans and their families.

In addition, volunteer groups of Home Depot associates known as Team Depots have worked on more than 3,780 projects building or improving homes for Veterans. Just in California, The Home Depot Foundation has supported 622 projects impacting 2,520 units of housing benefitting Veterans with either financial or volunteer support.

While the role of philanthropies is critical, in the face of declining resources for affordable housing, cities are increasingly making systems changes to use the funds more efficiently. In 2013, Los Angeles began developing a "managed pipeline" to guide the distribution of LIHTCs, as well as support the coordination of allocations from the various state programs.

The "managed pipeline" has evolved to support 24 projects every 24 months. Every six months, six projects are moved forward and six new projects enter the pipeline. The result has been more certainty for developers, providing them the confidence to move forward with pre-development outlays and stronger applications for additional support from financial institutions, philanthropies, housing authorities and others. By initially focusing on the housing needs of homeless Veterans and gradually expanding the community coordination efforts to ensure all Veterans have access safe housing solutions, cities lay the groundwork for all community members to be housed.

Despite consistently encouraging news about the growth of city workforces, it is likely that support for affordable housing programs will continue to face fiscal constraints. For cities to create and grow relationships with committed philanthropic partners, local leaders must be strategic in how existing resources are used. Focusing on a specific population, such as Veterans, and a specific issue, such as housing, is one way cities can help ensure meaningful investments benefit all community members in the long-term.

34. VA National Center
on Homelessness Among Veterans[*]

U.S. DEPARTMENT OF VETERANS AFFAIRS

The mission of the National Center on Homelessness among Veterans is to promote recovery-oriented care for Veterans who are homeless or at risk of homelessness. The center is designed to improve the lives and treatment services of veterans who are homeless and who have mental health, substance use disorders, medical illness, cognitive impairment or other psychosocial treatment needs.

The primary goal of the National Center on Homelessness Among Veterans is to develop, promote, and enhance policy, clinical care research, and education to improve and integrate homeless services so that Veterans may live as independently and self-sufficiently as possible in a community of their choosing.

The Department of Veterans Affairs has been providing direct and specialized services for homeless veterans for over 20 years. Beginning in 1987 with 43 pilot programs, which provided street outreach and residential community services, VA Homeless Programs have developed and expanded to be the largest integrated provider of homeless services in the country.

VA has enhanced these efforts by committing to the Five-Year Plan to End Homelessness among Veterans by 2015, part of the larger Federal Strategic Plan to Prevent and End Homelessness, "Opening Doors." Strategies for achieving the plan's goal are to increase leadership, collaboration and civic engagement; increase access to stable and affordable housing; increase economic security; improve health and stability; and improve homeless crisis response. The center has been a significant contributor to this federal goal.

The center works in collaboration with VHA's Homeless Programs Office, network directors, network homeless coordinators, national professional associations, and community partners as well as with their academic partners from the University of Massachusetts Medical School, University of Pennsylvania, and the University of South Florida to: The center will support the development of a network of excellence with the scope and vision that will enable it to have substantial impact within the host VAMCs, the

---

*Public document originally published as U.S. Department of Veterans Affairs, "VA National Center on Homelessness Among Veterans," https://www.va.gov/homeless/nchav/about-us/about-us.asp (May 18, 2018).

VISNs, and across the nation. In coordination with the national office and host-site academic affiliates, the University of Pennsylvania and the University of South Florida, Louis de la Parte Florida Mental Health Institute, the Center will have an impact along several dimensions of the delivery of care for Veterans who are homeless. These include but are not limited to:

- Develop of new empirical knowledge and policy that can be directly applied to improve services for Veterans who are homeless;
- Develop of quality management strategies that promote timely access to evidence-based services and/or emerging best practices;
- Develop education for a broad target audience of providers with the ultimate goal of enhancing the delivery of high quality services to homeless Veterans and their dependents.
- Serve as a national resource for policy development, program implementation, education, research and the care of Veterans who are homeless; and
- Establish ongoing efforts to identify potential areas for federal, state and local as well as non-profit and faith-based collaboration in service integration and training.

The center embraces and practices ICARE, the core values of the U.S. Department of Veterans Affairs.

- Integrity: Act with high moral principle. Adhere to the highest professional standards. Maintain the trust and confidence of all with whom I engage.
- Commitment: Work diligently to serve Veterans and other beneficiaries. Be driven by an earnest belief in VA mission. Fulfill my individual responsibilities and organizational responsibilities.
- Advocacy: Be truly Veteran-centric by identifying, fully considering, and appropriately advancing the interests of Veterans and other beneficiaries.
- Respect: Treat all those I serve and with whom I work with dignity and respect. Show respect to earn it.
- Excellence: Strive for the highest quality and continuous improvement. Be thoughtful and decisive in leadership, accountable for my actions, willing to admit mistakes, and rigorous in correcting them.

These core values are the basic elements of how we go about our work. They define "who we are" and form the underlying principles we use every day in our service to Veterans.

Rural Veterans and Homelessness: When the initiative to eradicate Veteran homelessness was launched in 2009, efforts and resources were focused in urban areas, where the problem was most visible. But poverty and housing problems are also major issues in rural settings. On June 22 the Center hosted its fifth Homeless Evidence and Research Synthesis virtual symposium where researchers, clinicians, service providers, and advocates discussed what homelessness and risk look like in rural areas, the particular needs and challenges of Veterans, and how the VA is addressing them. Go to the Center website for links to the webinar online and a list of questions and answers posted in the chatroom during the presentations. Written proceedings from the event will be available on the Center website in August.

Center Research Affiliates: The Center affiliated researcher group was established in 2016 to expand the scope and breadth of the Center's research portfolio and place it in greater alignment with the priorities and needs of field staff and leadership within the Homeless Programs Office. This is a secondary affiliation that provides an opportunity to collaborate with like-minded investigators within VA and the Center on homeless-related projects, apply for intramural funding for operations focused rapid response analyses, and participate in ongoing cyber-seminars, research-in-progress presentations, and hosted conferences. You can find more information about the research group on the Center website.

Recent Publications: The special issue in *Psychological Services* (Vol. 14, Issue 2), "Homelessness Among Veterans, Other Adults, and Youth," features many authors affiliated with the National Center on Homelessness among Veterans and is guest edited by Jack Tsai, Ph.D., Center Research Affiliate, and Thomas O'Toole, M.D., center director. For a list of these and other recently published articles, go to the center website.

35. Ending Veteran Homelessness*

U.S. Department of Veterans Affairs

VA is committed to ending Veteran homelessness, community by community. Our work in collaboration with large and small localities proves that—through their leadership, cooperation and evidence-based practices—it's possible to ensure that every Veteran has a home.

Here's what national, state and local leaders are saying about these successes:

Little Rock, AR, Mayor Mark Stodola, Dec. 14, 2018

"We've re-tooled programs and systems to be more coordinated and overall more effective at finding our most vulnerable Veterans, triaging their needs, and then navigating them to the most appropriate housing resources and supportive services."

Miami–Dade County, FL, Mayor Carlos A. Gimenez, Aug. 2, 2018

"Today, we say with certainty that Miami-Dade is treating its Veterans with the respect they deserve."

Norman, OK, Mayor Lynne Miller, Feb. 27, 2018

"It is because of this relentless community-wide effort that we have reached such a significant and immeasurably impactful goal."

Beckley, WV, Mayor Rob Rappold, Feb. 8, 2018

"It's certainly an accomplishment that we don't take lightly. It's something that certainly puts our local VA and its great staff on the map nationally. It also is a real compliment to the City of Beckley."

Pittsburgh, PA, Mayor Bill Peduto, Nov. 21, 2017

"Five hundred eighty-seven individuals and their families are in a much better position because of the work that was done between federal, state, county and city government together with those that were on the ground carrying out the mission."

Kansas City, KS, Mayor Mark Holland, Nov. 20, 2017

"One of the things we recently did was we took the opportunity to combine the Coordinated Council for Homelessness so there could be one single voice. We need to

---

*Public document originally published as U.S. Department of Veterans Affairs, "Ending Veteran Homelessness," https://www.va.gov/HOMELESS/endingVetshomelessness.asp (January 22, 2019).

do a better job of tracking and caring for people and not caring what side of the state line they are on."

Atlanta, GA, Mayor Kasim Reed, Nov. 6, 2017

"I want to express my sincere thanks to all of our partners and the providers who made this possible. It means so much to me to know that we have been able to help the women and men who risked it all in service to their country."

Kent County, MI, Board Commissioner Tom Antor, Sept. 26, 2017

"The County staff has shown a great dedication to helping Veterans and ending homelessness. More than 170 Veterans Affairs Housing Vouchers have been provided in Kent County in recent years. I'm proud of the work they've done to help reach Functional Zero."

Northwest & West Central Minnesota Continuum of Care Coordinator Carla Solem, Aug. 24, 2017

"The plans ensure that when homelessness does occur, it is rare, brief, and non-recurring," said Carla Solem, Continuum of Care Coordinator. "[I]t is evidence that the CoCs have plans in place to assure Veteran[s] is sheltered immediately, housed rapidly and supported in a manner that reduces the likelihood that he or she will ever become homeless again."

Lowell, MA, Mayor Edward Kennedy, Aug. 23, 2017

"Lowell has identified every homeless Veteran by name and has a support system in place to ensure, whenever possible, that no Veterans are sleeping on the streets.... Every Veteran has access to permanent housing, and the community has a capacity to ensure that Veteran homelessness when it occurs is rare, brief and nonrecurring."

Allentown, PA, Mayor Ed Pawlowski, July 10, 2017

"[T]he idea that anyone who has worn our country's uniform spends their nights sleeping on the ground should horrify us. Our veterans fought for our freedom and they deserve our help when they need it most."

Akron, OH, Mayor Daniel Horrigan, May 26, 2017

"This designation is a significant achievement for the city of Akron and the Continuum of Care, and a milestone in our fight to end Veterans' homelessness in this community."

Charlotte County, FL, Homeless Coalition's CEO Angela Hogan, Mar. 30, 2017

"We have made homelessness in our community rare, brief and non-reoccurring."

Nashua, NH, Mayor Jim Donchess, Mar. 24, 2017

"The Nashua community takes care of our people, and the elimination of Veteran homelessness is an example of that caretaking."

Minnesota State Director to Prevent and End Homelessness Cathy ten Broeke, Mar. 23, 2017

"[W]hat has been so powerful about the work of ending Veteran homelessness, and the reason we're actually seeing the end of it here in Minnesota and other places around the country, is that they set this goal at the federal level, and it was a bipartisan goal."

Chattanooga, TN, Mayor Andy Berke, Feb. 9, 2017

"Veterans who have served our country should not ... be forced to sleep in parking garages, shelters, cars, or on street corners—unfortunately, that is a reality in too many cities across the country. But over the last two years, Chattanoogans have banded together to say 'Not in our city.'"

Shreveport, LA, Mayor Ollie Tyler, Jan. 5, 2017

"It is my prayer that all that we accomplish in working to eradicate homelessness for Veterans, would be transformational in their lives and allow them to transition into society as productive citizens who enjoy a good quality of life."

La Crosse, WI, Mayor Tim Kabat, Dec 19, 2016

"La Crosse signed on to the national effort, as part of the Mayor's Challenge, to work together and provide permanent housing for our homeless Veterans and it is awe-inspiring to see this dream realized. We are so fortunate to live in such a caring, compassionate, and hard-working community."

Hales, Multnomah County, OR, Chair Deborah Kafoury, Dec. 10, 2016

"This is what it looks like when a community comes together to get things done. We can change lives."

Portland, OR, Mayor Charlie Hales, Dec. 10, 2016

"I'm proud today, that Portland is the first West Coast city to receive official designation in meeting the.... Mayors Challenge to End Veterans Homelessness. This would not have been possible without our government, nonprofit, faith and private sector partners' complete dedication to this work. With continued commitment, I know our community can reach our goal to provide permanent, affordable housing to every Portlander who needs it."

DeKalb County, GA, iCEO Lee May, Dec. 9, 2016

"If you are a veteran in DeKalb County and need a place to live, we will help you."

Dayton, OH, Mayor Nan Whaley, Nov. 28, 2016

"Together, the City of Dayton, Montgomery County, and our community partners have worked to ensure that every veteran has access to permanent housing. Targeted collaboration among our partners has streamlined a community process that ensures that any veteran in the Dayton community, who needs assistance, receives a rapid connection to housing resources."

Governor's Weekly Message: Ending Veteran Homelessness in Delaware, Nov. 16, 2016

"Even one homeless veteran is one too many. That's why this week I was thrilled to announce that—after more than a year's work with our local, state and federal partners—we have effectively ended veteran homelessness in our state. Thank you to everyone who has made it possible to get our veterans the help they need and deserve. Showing them the same level of commitment they made to our country will help keep Delaware moving forward."

Middlesex County, NJ, Middlesex County Freeholder Director Ronald G. Rios, Nov. 4, 2016

"This is the story of many hands and heads working together to achieve a common goal. I thank and commend our County staff and our community partners for sharing my passion and my vision for ending Veterans Homelessness. We did it. And we did it together."

Volusia County/Daytona Beach, FL, Executive Director of the Office on Homelessness with Florida Department of Children and Families Erik Braun, Nov. 4, 2016

"All cities in Volusia County need to come together and collaborate with the county…. If you rapidly house people … we see stability over the long term. About 85 percent don't return to homelessness."

Buffalo, NY, Mayor Byron Brown, Nov. 4, 2016

"We accepted that challenge, we delivered, and I can announce proudly today that we have essentially ended veteran homelessness in our community."

Adviser to the Mayor for the Initiative to End Chronic Homelessness, Boston, MA, Laila Bernstein, Oct. 5, 2016

"In most cases, folks who've been homeless make tremendous tenants. They're very grateful for the housing and they take care of their apartments very well."

Orlando, FL, Mayor Buddy Dyer, Sept. 23, 2016

"It's important that we reflect on victories when we have them and our victory on effectively reaching the end of chronic Veteran homelessness … is a cause for celebration."

Austin, TX, Mayor Steve Adler, Aug. 19, 2016

"We got to this community win today in a classic Austin way. We were innovative, creative and determined. There was great work already being done when this initiative started, but these efforts weren't quite getting the job done all the way. We needed a new way, new partners, and a wider and renewed commitment."

Bergen County, NJ, Executive, James J. Tedesco III, Aug. 4, 2016

"The men and women who have so bravely served our country deserve more than just our deepest gratitude. They deserve to live securely and prosperously in our communities. That security starts with a roof over their heads."

Nassau County (Long Island, NY) Executive Edward P. Mangano, July 15, 2016

"Along with my partners in government, we have ensured that every homeless Veteran seeking shelter on Long Island has been housed, and that any Veteran or active-duty military personnel who may be in need in the future will receive immediate shelter."

Hattiesburg, MS, Mayor Johnny DuPree, June 15, 2016

"Our community is one that stands with one another, especially those who sacrifice their lives for the very freedoms we enjoy today."

Terrebonne Parish, LA, President Gordon Dove, June 3, 2016

"This is an important victory in our ongoing efforts to make our Parish the best place for veterans to live, work and raise a family. However, we must remain committed to keeping homelessness among veterans rare, brief and non-recurring."

Rochester, NY, Mayor Lovely Warren, May 18, 2016

"Our Veterans fought for us, and now it's time to fight for them."

San Antonio, TX, Mayor Ivy R. Taylor, May 13, 2016

"In January 2015, I pledged my commitment to the Mayors Challenge to End Veteran Homelessness. Together, the City of San Antonio, our business sector led by USAA, and our non-profit partners have achieved the goal of effectively ending veteran homelessness in our community."

Lynn, MA, Mayor Judith Flanagan Kennedy, Mar. 17, 2016

"We embrace our responsibility to provide our Veterans with the services and supports they need, with housing at the top of that list."

Supervisor for Central Iowa's Department of Veteran Affairs Jennifer Miner, Mar. 17, 2016

"Any veteran who is experiencing or is at risk of homelessness in Des Moines and Polk County has access to a safety net of resources and services."

Executive director of the Berks Coalition, PA, Sharon Parker, Feb. 18, 2016

"We work[ed] really hard to achieve this goal."

Fayetteville, NC, Mayor Nat Robertson, Jan. 16, 2016

"You need someplace to brush your teeth and clean your clothes and bathe, so you can look presentable when you're out interviewing for a job."

Riverside, CA, Mayor Rusty Bailey, Jan. 7, 2016

"I am so proud of our City staff and immensely grateful for their efforts in combating homelessness among Veterans in Riverside."

Biloxi, MS, Mayor Andrew Gilich, Dec. 31, 2015

"This effort has been a team effort. Biloxi and Gulfport are receiving this designation because of strong partnerships with the Biloxi Veterans Administration, the Biloxi Housing Authority, the Mississippi Housing Authority Region VIII in Gulfport, and community partners that include Oak Arbor, Hancock Resource Center, and Voices of Calvary Ministries who have received federal funds to assist veterans and their families across the Coast."

Gulfport, MS, Mayor Billy Hewes, Dec. 31, 2015

"As the lead agency for the Harrison County HOME Consortium, Gulfport has partnered with Biloxi, Back Bay Mission and Gulf Coast Housing Initiative in the construction of eight new apartments designated for our veterans. This benchmark for veterans is crucial, however, we must build on this work to create solutions for the overall problem and causes of homelessness which persists in our communities."

New York City Mayor Bill de Blasio, Dec. 30, 2015

"The brave women and men who valiantly protected our nation abroad should never be left without a home. Today, we have ensured that those in the veteran community who have struggled to find and remain in housing time and time again will have a stable place to call home. I'm grateful to the city agencies, federal partners and the City Council, who all worked tirelessly together to make this pledge a reality."

Albany, NY, Mayor Kathy Sheehan, Dec. 22, 2015

"We are proud of this recognition and the work we have done, yet we know that our efforts to end homelessness among veterans will continue in the days and years ahead.

We are resolved to make sure that homelessness among veterans will remain infrequent and short-lived."

Montgomery County, MD, Councilman George Leventhal, Dec. 18, 2015

"Montgomery County now has a coordinated and efficient system, which has been developed with our community partners to ensure that every veteran in our County has access to the supports needed to move quickly from homelessness to permanent housing. Providing a stable home for our veterans is simply the right thing to do for those who have sacrificed so much for our country."

Philadelphia, PA, Mayor Michael Nutter, Dec. 17, 2015

"Too often, veterans find themselves struggling with issues like homelessness and poverty and that is a shame. For those who gave so much of themselves to this Nation, there is no reason why they should be left out in the cold. Today, I am happy to report that homelessness among veterans in Philadelphia is now rare, brief and non-recurring. In other words, Philadelphia has effectively ended veteran homelessness for those who want a home."

Rockford, IL, Mayor Larry Morrissey, Dec. 15, 2015

"Every Veteran has a name. Every person has a story. When we make their story part of our story and our life and our work, we're able to get people housed, we're able to manage that list, we're able to make the connections to solve that problem."

Chief of Social Work Service at the VA Southern Nevada Healthcare System Josh Brown, Dec. 8, 2015

"I'm excited that the [mayors] have supported and stood behind this, and as a community, we all can achieve this. Does that mean that we still have some work to do down the road? Absolutely."

Santa Fe, NM, Mayor Javier M. Gonzales, Nov. 12, 2015

"The problem of Veteran homelessness has been a shadow hanging over our country and our community for far too long. But we can finally say that, working with this coalition, we have built a collaborative system that within 30 days will enable us to house the few remaining homeless Veterans in Santa Fe, and, moving forward, any Veteran who becomes homeless in the future will be housed within 30 days."

Virginia Gov. Terry McAuliffe, Nov. 11, 2015 (Veterans Day)

"On a day when we remember those who fought and died for our nation, I am proud to proclaim that Virginia is leading the way in the fight to end veteran homelessness. This is an important victory in our ongoing efforts to make our Commonwealth the best place on earth for veterans to live, work and raise a family. However, we must remain committed to keeping homelessness among veterans, and, all Virginians, rare, brief and non-recurring. This successful effort will serve as the launching pad for our next goal of functionally ending chronic homelessness among all Virginians by the end of 2017."

Schenectady, NY, Mayor Gary McCarthy, Nov. 11, 2015 (Veterans Day)

"It's the nature of it where you have to go through each individual and see what their unique features are and then work through issues like housing, drugs and mental health problems."

Syracuse, NY, Mayor Stephanie Miner, Nov. 11, 2015 (Veterans Day)

"It means we have a process put in place to identify and find services for Veterans to make sure they are not homeless, or slip into homelessness."

Winston-Salem, NC, Mayor Allen Joines, Oct. 27, 2015

"Achieving this milestone is a testimony to the hard work of the people and organizations that have been working tirelessly to house our homeless veterans. Given this success, I have no doubt that we will succeed in meeting our ultimate goal of ending chronic homelessness for all in our community."

Troy, NY, Mayor Lou Rosamilia, Sept. 26, 2015

"Providing homeless veterans a path to proper housing opportunities is a fulfillment of a responsibility to those who answered the call to defend our freedoms. I am incredibly proud of the effort undertaken by our city and our community partners in assisting veterans here in the City of Troy and I look forward to our continued efforts to provide these important services to those who served our country."

Connecticut Gov. Dannel P. Malloy, Aug. 27, 2015

"We established this bold goal to end homelessness among our veterans, not because it's good for our economy and makes communities stronger, but because it's morally right. Ending chronic veteran homelessness is just another step forward and another marker of progress towards reaching our goal of ending all veteran homelessness by the end of this year."

Saratoga Springs, NY, Mayor Joanne Yepsen, July 29, 2015

"Our pledge is that if a Veteran presents as homeless, they do not spend a single night on the street."

Las Cruces, NM, Mayor Ken Miyagishima, July 2015

"Ending veteran homelessness is important for one simple reason: Veterans fought for our freedom and our way of life, and it is now our turn to fight for them."

Houston Mayor Annise Parker, June 1, 2015

"Houston is there for our heroes, and just like on the battlefield, we will leave no one behind. From regular provider coordination meetings and aligning local and federal resources, to dedicated street outreach teams and a coordinated assessment system that identifies, assesses, refers and navigates homeless veterans to housing, the Houston region has come together as a team to transform our homeless response system to effectively end veteran homelessness."

New Orleans Mayor Mitch Landrieu, Jan. 7, 2015

"New Orleans is now the first major city in the nation to answer the call … to end Veteran homelessness—and we did so one year earlier than the federal goal. We owe our Veterans our eternal gratitude for their service and sacrifice to this nation, and making sure they have a place to call home is a small but powerful way we can show our appreciation."

36. Monterey Programs Focused on Supporting Homeless Veterans and Their Families[*]

KURT SCHAKE *and* MICKEY P. MCGEE

The U.S. Department of Housing and Urban Development–VA Supportive Housing (HUD–VASH), a collaborative program between HUD and VA, combines HUD housing vouchers with VA supportive services to help Veterans who are homeless and their families find and sustain permanent housing. Through public housing authorities, HUD provides rental assistance vouchers for privately owned housing to Veterans who are eligible for VA health care services and are experiencing homelessness. VA case managers may connect these Veterans with support services such as health care, mental health treatment and substance use counseling to help them in their recovery process and with their ability to maintain housing in the community. Among VA homeless continuum of care programs, HUD-VASH enrolls the largest number and largest percentage of Veterans who have experienced long-term or repeated homelessness. As of April 8, 2018, HUD has allocated more than 87,000 vouchers to help house Veterans across the country.

The Homeless Providers Grant and Per Diem (GPD) Program supports state, local and tribal governments and nonprofit organizations. These organizations receive capital grants and per diem payments to develop and operate transitional housing and/or service centers for Veterans who are homeless. VA funds an estimated 600 agencies that provide over 14,500 beds for eligible Veterans. Grantees work closely with an assigned liaison from the local VAMC. The VA GPD liaison monitors the services the grantees offer to Veterans and provides direct assistance to them. Grantees also collaborate with community-based organizations to connect Veterans with employment, housing and additional social services to promote housing stability. The maximum stay in this housing is up to 24 months, with the goal of moving Veterans into permanent housing.

Supportive Services for Veteran Families (SSVF) is aimed at supporting very low-income Veterans who are homeless or at imminent risk of becoming homeless. Services may include deposit assistance, rental assistance, veteran outreach, transportation assistance, case management services, assistance obtaining VA and other benefits. SSVF provides case management and supportive services to prevent the imminent loss of a Veteran's

---

*Published with permission of the authors.

home or identify a new, more suitable housing situation for the individual and his or her family or to rapidly re-house Veterans and their families who are homeless and might remain homeless without this assistance. Through referrals and direct outreach, nonprofit agencies and community cooperatives use SSVF funding to quickly house Veterans and their families who are homeless and keep others from slipping into homelessness by providing time-limited supportive services that promote housing stability. Case management includes help securing VA and other benefits such as educational aid and financial planning.

The Monterey County Veterans Transition Center (VTC)

The mission of the VTC is to provide services for homeless Veterans and their families in the Monterey Bay Area. By providing Veterans with transitional housing and case management programs, VTC creates short- and long-terms solutions to homelessness and gives them the tools they need to help themselves become employable, productive members of the community. VTC has a 19-year record of success and continues to achieve the VA's Service Intensive Model Required Minimum Performance Metrics/Targets. VTC seeks to exceed those targets as follows: Service-Intensive Transitional Housing Planned Performance Matrix: Discharge to permanent housing 75 percent; employment of individuals at discharge 60 percent; and negative exits less than 20 percent.

The VTC has provided Transitional Housing since 1998 when it received 23 buildings via the Fort Ord Reuse Authority (FORA) via the McKinney Act. It took about five years to rehabilitate the buildings. Currently there are 20 buildings dedicated to housing Veterans and in some cases family members. VTC is able to walk each client through the process of securing permanent housing through the Housing and Urban Housing Urban Development–VA Supporting Housing (HUD–VASH) office and referrals to Supportive Services for Veteran Families (SSVF). The VTC provides beds for 70 veterans and, in some cases, their family members. Funding for housing comes from the following programs (number of beds provided in parenthesis): VA Grant Per Diem Program, Veterans who are currently homeless, often find themselves on the street, living in their cars or in other areas not meant for human habitation (4); VA Emergency Rapid Rehousing (4); Residential Services; and Permanent Supportive Non–HUD–VSH Vouchers (4); HUD–VSH Permanent and/or until they exceed income qualifications, homeless Veterans and their families (8); VA Transitional Housing/Clinical (14); VA Service Intensive Transitional Housing (30); VA Transitional Housing Bridge (14).

Case Managers evaluate the benefits a Veteran is receiving when they enter into a VTC program and make sure that all earned benefits are being collected. If there is a deficiency, the Veteran and Case Manager work together for the Veteran to start receiving all unpaid earned benefits. VTC Case Managers provide formerly homeless Veterans the tools necessary to achieve successful independence in society. The program is designed to place an emphasis on Veteran accountability through a strong partnership between a client and their Case Manager. Veterans enrolled in VTC programs work to establish short-term goals that accumulate to reach larger program goals. Clients also work with their Case Managers to address any employment barriers and have the opportunity to improve their marketable job skills at VTC's Job Development and Education Center (JDEC), work one-on-one on their resume and job interview skills and take advantage of VTC partnerships with multiple employment agencies.

The Veterans Transition Center can refer Veterans to an agency that can assist with short-term temporary financial assistance with rent, moving expenses, security and utility deposits, child care, transportation, utility costs, and emergency expenses. Agencies may also provide a variety of services including housing and credit counseling, housing advocacy, legal assistance, moving assistance, and representative payee services.

Job Development Center

- Increasing skills and helping Veterans become employment-ready is crucial to become active members of the community. The newly expanded JDC can assist 100 Veterans per year, provide training areas, classes, skills assessments, and other tools that will help a Veteran succeed. Through the VET+PREP! program, VTC currently offers assistance with job placement, quarterly job fairs, job skills training, and skills assessment.
- Upon entering the program, all Veterans are assessed and are provided with an Individualized Service Plan, taking into consideration their specific skill set, interests, and past employment experience. From there, they are provided with assistance in job interview training, resume writing, and job skills classes. Other services provided by VET+PREP! include basic skills and literacy workshops; remedial education and GED assistance; life skills and financial literacy workshops; classroom and vocational workshops; employment uniform and equipment subsidies; specialized and/or certification courses, and other formal training programs deemed appropriate to benefit the Veteran.

Public-private partnership has worked very well. Key stakeholders in the region to include the National Coalition of Homeless Veterans, the Federal Government Departments (HUD, HHS, VA), the State of California, the County of Monterey, the Cities of the Monterey Bay Area and many others contribute funding and serve on local committees to raise and donate money to help solve problems (See the VTC website for a full listing of community supported and sponsors, https://www.vtcmonterey.org/.)

Community supporters and sponsors work together to collaborate and communicate on how best to serve and solve the problems faced by the homeless vet population and their families in Monterey County.

There is a need for a common definition of homelessness was needed to help decipher the various federal, state and local funding application requirements. The biggest challenge for the VTC is operating funds, especially to pay for case work staffing. Funding by supporting sponsors provides specific dollars for the homeless vets and their families however, other grants do not cover much of the labor costs for staff support to assist an ever-growing homeless veteran population.

37. Veteran Homelessness in Monterey County[*]

WILLIAM BARE *and* MICKEY P. McGEE

There are a disproportionately large number of homeless Veterans in the United States. Homelessness levels among our Veteran population are three times more than the rate among non–veteran homeless. On a single night in January 2018, just over 37,800 veterans were experiencing homelessness. On the same night, just over 23,300 of the Veterans counted were unsheltered or living on the street. Between 2017 and 2018, there was a 5.4 percent decrease in the estimated number of homeless veterans nationwide. This number is a significant decrease from the estimated 107,000 in 2010, but nonetheless begs the question: Why does the United States allow *any* veteran to be homeless?

Compounding the problem, on any given day, almost 1.5 million veterans are at— or below—the poverty level (National Veterans Foundation, Sept. 10, 2015). After pledging to give their lives in defense of the nation, don't we owe it to each veteran to keep them from living on the streets, in vehicles, encampments, and shelters? (*Veterans Today*, Sep 2, 2013). Many believe our nation should to do more to help Veterans in their post-military lives. Attending to the veteran homeless is an important moral issue. This chapter provides recommendations on what and how our government and populace should address and resolve it.

In 2010, then-President Barack Obama made a promise and put in place programs to reduce Veteran homelessness to zero in five years (USICH, Sep 7, 2017). That ambitious goal was unmet in 2015, but renewed and re-focused initiatives continue, with $188 million of VA grants recently announced to aid hundreds of programs across the country to provide daily housing for veterans (National Coalition for Homeless Veterans [NCHV], Sep 13, 2017). Since 1994, approximately $2 billion has been awarded to private organizations to realize housing solutions that get veterans off the street and geared towards productive, self-sustaining lives. Another $1 billion has been issued in the last 5 years towards Veteran homelessness prevention (U.S Department of Veteran Affairs [VA], May 3, 2017). The public should continue to take responsibility for sustaining this substantial commitment.

During his Second Inaugural Address in the final months of the Civil War, President Abraham Lincoln proclaimed, "let us strive on to finish the work we are in, to bind up

---

[*]Published with permission of the authors.

the nation's wounds, to care for him who shall have borne the battle and for his widow, and his orphan." These words are a call-to-arms and are etched on plaques outside the entrance of the Department of Veterans Affairs. Their credo, "To care for him who shall have borne the battle and for his widow, and his orphan," has stood the test of time and is a strong reminder of the national commitment to assist our veterans (VA, Origin of the VA Motto, n.d.). Consequently, having a homeless veteran problem in the USA in 2017 is a point of public shame to many. However, many programs and resources are being devoted to tackle the issue, and success is being realized in Monterey County through a combination of public and private collaborations.

Recent developments reveal the homeless veteran problem is being reduced across the board at national, state, and local levels, but—much work remains. Although progress is being broadly realized, challenges remain daunting for further reducing the problem:

1. **Specific challenges for individual homeless veterans**. What makes the situation for homeless veterans different than that of other homeless? Many have regular income, have had job experience and training, and have a higher level of education that their age peers. However, one glaring statistic offers a likely explanation: over 80 percent of homeless veterans suffer from some form of mental illness (VA, Homeless Veterans: Mental Illness, n.d.). Affordable housing is the big issue for most homeless, and for veterans is no exception. In the 2017 Monterey homeless census, the largest obstacle to permanent housing was by far affordability (as per 73 percent of responders) (Coalition of Homeless Service Providers [CHSP], 2017 Homeless Census). Communities can do better to provide affordable housing, especially for low-income individuals, especially veterans who have guaranteed income. Other factors that need to be addressed to ensure transitional or permanent housing include sobriety. employment, medical support, and secured benefits.

2. **Measuring the effectiveness of national, state, and local programs**. Recent measures are showing positive results from a national-level prioritization on ending veteran homelessness. Since 2010, In fact, 3 states and 51 communities have already declared victory in erasing Veteran homelessness to the extent possible (VA, Ending Veteran Homelessness, n.d.). From 2015 to 2017, homelessness in Monterey County increased by 23 percent; however, the Coalition of Homeless Service Providers reported a 22 percent decrease in the number of homeless Veterans in the County (CHSP, 2015 PIT Census & Survey, 2015; and CHSP 2017 Survey). The agency attributes that to a national effort to help veterans through the Supportive Services for Veteran Families rapid re-housing and homeless prevention funding, as well as the joint HUD-VA Supportive Housing program.

3. **Ineffectiveness of state programs.** Part of the problem to assist homeless veterans is the lack of affordable housing in most parts of California. Monterey County is no exception. In addition to a lack of affordable housing, many landlords are reluctant to rent to homeless or even low-income veterans on subsidies, for fear those subsidies will end. However, in the last 3 years there have been promising developments that have trickled down to Monterey County.

- **California Veterans (CalVet) leadership, and California Housing and Community Development (HCD) funding opportunities.** In 2014, California redirected $600,000,000 of bond monies previously identified for veterans mortgage payments, to go to new construction and housing rehab of Veteran communities. Monterey County was able to get $5.9 million of that to build a singular project for affordable housing for veteran families (personal communication, November, 2015).

- **Economic development at the state and municipal levels is key for solving Veteran homelessness.** The development of affordable housing has become a priority in Sacramento. More than 130 bills were introduced into the Legislature in 2017, with major success—several bills were passed that are already having significant impact to the Central Coast and Monterey County (Marino, 2017). California Senate Bill (SB) 3 in particular will be a boost to Veteran housing. SB3, the Veterans and Affordable Housing Bond Act of 2018, seeks to direct $1 billion for affordable housing directly for Veterans, which will benefit the large Veteran population of Monterey County (Marino, 2017). According to Jan Lindenthal of MidPenn Housing, these bills could "double the number of [affordable housing] projects MidPenn is doing in the region" (Marino, 2017).

Recommendations. The United States sent Americans to war. In return, it is only fitting that it should also provide permanent housing for homeless veterans. The U.S. government is rightly contributing an enormous amount of resources into ending Veteran homelessness. Monterey County also needs to strongly echo and support this effort. Some community-level successes have occurred but the problem remains. At the local level, there may not be an official mandate to address this issue; it is a moral one. Veterans who pledged their lives and fortunes to defend this country must certainly be cared for with same amount of devotion, no matter the sacrifice. Monterey County is working to help the large homeless veteran population. The large Monterey County veteran population is committed and encouraging local governments for solutions. Solving the homeless Veteran problem in Monterey County includes:

1. Remain engaged with US Congressman Panetta (D-20), US Senators Harris and Feinstein, California State Assemblyman Mark Stone and other local elected officials of Monterey County to push for continued initiatives to support homeless veterans and affordable housing.

2. Remain engaged with the VA at District and Federal levels to ensure existing and potential programs are in compliance and focused on same goals as ever-changing national efforts.

3. Remain engaged with HUD at District and Federal levels to ensure existing and potential programs are in compliance and focused on same goals as national efforts.

4. Remain engaged with NCHV to promote funding/solutions in Central California.

5. Remain engaged with California CalVet leadership, and Cal Housing and Community Development (HCD) funding opportunities.

6. Remain engaged with Monterey County Veteran Affairs Office and ensure non-profit/community/municipal efforts are tied into County goals and initiatives.

7. Ensure CHSP is at forefront of developing opportunities at State and Federal level to support affordable housing and VA/Federal funding which also requires municipal-level support.

8. Establish independent council of Trustees for Veteran Affairs made up of

senior retired military officials that can espouse need for attention to important Veteran issues (such as homelessness).

9. United Veterans Center of Monterey County take the lead for homeless Veteran issues and provide regular updates to cities and county. Provide leadership to various non-profits with recommended COAs.

Conclusion. As a society, we should be doing all we can to assist veterans who come upon difficult times in their post-military lives. It is debatable whether veteran homelessness is self-inflicted or is a result of their military service. No matter—this is a solvable problem. Millions of dollars are coming into Monterey County to address the issue. The concern is two-fold: Clarify a need and justify federal and state support, and apply those resources in an effective manner and make a difference. This is the issue for public administrators in the county.

Public administrators should consider there are many initiatives in place to address the matter of homelessness in their area of jurisdiction. Progress is being made in Monterey County through a vast collaborative effort that includes the federal, state, county, and city governments, and an array of non-profits and concerned citizens who are motivated to ensure Veterans in need are taken care of. Even though the homeless veteran population can be a geographical-transitory issue on this peninsula and within Monterey County, there are appropriate steps that can be taken by elected and non-elected officials at the county, city, and non-profit levels. It is possible to make a difference. The lives that pledged to defend this nation are depending on us.

REFERENCES

Broom, C.A., Jackson, M., Harris, J.L. *Performance Measurement: Concepts and Techniques*. Washington, DC: American Society for Public Administration, 2012.
Denhardt, J.V., & Denhardt, R.B. (2015). *The New Public Service: Serving, Not Steering*. Ann Arbor, MI: Taylor & Francis.
Herrera, James (Nov. 13, 2015). "Patriot Housing Program in Seaside Providing Affordable Housing for Veterans," *Monterey Herald*; retrieved from http://www.montereyherald.com/article/NF/20151113/NEWS/151119901, 28 Sep 2017.
National Coalition for Homeless Veterans. 2015 Annual Report.
2013 Monterey County Homeless Point-in-Time Census & Survey (Final). http://www.chspmontereycounty.org/CensusPage/2013%20Monterey%20County%20Homeless%20Report_FINAL3_7.3.13.pdf.
2015 Monterey County Homeless Point-in-Time Census & Survey—Comprehensive Report. http://www.chspmontereycounty.org/wp-content/themes/chsp/img/Final-MC-2015-Census-Report.pdf.
2017 Monterey County Homeless Census & Survey—Comprehensive Report. http://www.chspmontereycounty.org/wp-content/themes/chsp/img/2017-Monterey-County-Census-Report.pdf.
U.S. Department of Veteran Affairs; https://www.va.gov/homeless/.
United States Interagency Council on Homelessness. "Ending Veteran Homelessness." 4/8/17.
United States Interagency Council on Homelessness. https://www.usich.gov/.

38. An Assessment of Homeless Veteran Programs in Sacramento County*

BENEDICT SERAFICA *and* MICKEY P. McGEE

Veteran homelessness is an ongoing problem in the United States. Veterans were among the general homeless population as early as the Reconstruction Era. At the end of the Civil War, thousands of veterans wandered the country and some went homeless. In 1932, approximately 15,000 homeless and disabled veterans barricaded Washington, D.C., demanding benefits. It was during that time that homeless veterans were considered to be part of the so called "Bonus Army" (Block, 2007). In 1987, the number of homeless veterans increased rapidly to approximately 300,000. In 2007, Iraq and Afghanistan combat veterans started to be recognized in homeless shelters. And by 2009, the Department of Veterans Affairs reported that about 154,000 veterans were homeless, and about "one-third of all homeless adults are veterans … nearly half of homeless veterans (47 percent) served in Vietnam and one third were stationed in a war zone" (Jannson, 2010, p. 72).

A 2009 Point-in-Time survey conducted by the U.S. Department of Housing and Urban Development predicted that more than 634,000 individuals were either in a sheltered or unsheltered homeless state, and around 111,000 of these individuals were chronically homeless (U.S. Department of Housing and Urban Development, 2010). Schinka et al. (2013) wrote that more than "15% of the homeless population are 51 years of age and older, and the numbers of homeless over the age of 65 are expected to increase dramatically, doubling by 2050."

In 2011, the VA also reported that of the nation's homeless population, 14 percent of adult males and 2 percent of adult females were veterans, and "both groups were over represented within the homeless population compared to the general population" (Metraux et al., 2013, p. 4). From 2012 to 2016, the overall population of homeless veterans in the United States was over 39,000. Homelessness among female veterans is also a nationwide dilemma. Women who have served in the United States military are "three to four times more likely to become homeless than are non-veteran women, though the reasons for this are not clearly understood" (Gamache, Rosenheck, & Tessler, 2003). A study conducted by Dr. Donna Washington and colleagues from Women's Health and

---

*Published with permission of the authors.

Equity at the VA Greater Los Angeles Health Services Research and Development Center of Excellence (2010) indicated that women are considered to be at a high risk among the homeless population (Washington, Yano, McGuire, Hines, Lee, & Gelberg, 2010, p. 82). They also noted that "homeless women veterans likely present different needs with respect to privacy, gender related care, treatment for physical and sexual trauma, housing support, and care for dependent children" (p. 82).

There are numerous reasons or risk factors explaining veteran homelessness and non-veterans. Service members who served in the conflicts in Iraq and Afghanistan for more than ten years expressed concern with regards to their well-being when they returned back to the society (Metraux et al., 2013, p. 255). Some of these factors concern personal issues and unavailability of secured and affordable housing. According to Cunningham, et al., almost "half a million veterans pay more than half their income for rent and more than half of them have incomes below the federal poverty level" (Cunningham, Henry, & Lyons, 2007). The HUD emphasized that, "for every one hundred men living by themselves with incomes below the federal poverty level, twelve are likely to be in the sheltered homeless population over the course of a year compared to four of every one hundred women living alone in poverty" (Department of Housing and Urban Development, 2009).

There are 113,000 homeless individuals living in California, the highest number of homeless veterans of any state and is "home to nearly 26 percent of all homeless veterans in the United States" (Blanton, 2013, p. 1). The City of Sacramento is second only to the City of Los Angeles for highest homeless population in California (Sacramento Steps Forward, 2015). Rebecca Blanton, a Senior Policy Analyst from the California Research Bureau, specified that the County of Los Angeles alone accounts for 10 percent of homeless veterans in America (2013, p. 11). The HUD 2012 Continuum of Care Homeless Population Sub-count revealed, "California is home to 4,512 veterans living in temporary housing or shelters and 11,949 veterans living on the streets or in places unintended for human habitation" (Blanton, 2013, p. 11). In Sacramento County, over 2,659 individuals experience homelessness, and approximately 5,200 individuals will eventually become homeless in a year (Sacramento Steps Forward, 2015). The Sacramento County & Incorporated Cities Homeless Count reported that "roughly one third of Sacramento County's homeless population is unsheltered" (Sacramento Steps Forward, 2015, p. 3).

In 2012, the departments of Veterans Affairs (VA) and Housing and Urban Development (HUD) projected that the growing number of homeless veterans in the United States was around 62,619. Approximately 25 percent of homeless veterans were located in California. California is home to more homeless veterans than any other state. The Housing Unit and Development 2012 Continuum of Care Homeless Population Sub-count revealed, "California is home to 4,512 veterans living in temporary housing or shelters and 11,949 veterans living on the streets or in places unintended for human habitation" (Blanton, 2013, p. 11). Service members who have transitioned from military to civilian life find it difficult to secure employment and housing.

There are programs and services provided to support veterans, programs such as housing assistance, health care, employment services, etc. However, "many of our nation's veterans particularly those with low incomes still face challenges finding affordable and stable housing and supportive services" (Sturtevant, Brennan, Viveiros, Handelman, 2015, p. 1). HUD and VA joined forces to create a housing program that would help veterans and their families find secure housing—the HUD and VA Supportive Housing (HUD–VASH). HUD–VASH has been "an effective tool for combating veteran homelessness and affordability challenges" (Sturtevant et al., 2015, p. 4). The HUD–VASH program provides housing assistance through HUD Section 8 Housing Choice Vouchers along with case management with the help of the Department of Veterans Affairs.

According to the National Alliance to End Homelessness, approximately 70,000 HUD–VASH certificates have been allocated to Public Housing Authorities across the country since 2008 (2015). An assessment regarding the effectiveness of the HUD–VASH program reveals an increase in employment and income and the total amount of days to house a homeless person. Moreover, the HUD–VASH program "has been found to have a one-year cost savings of approximately on $6,000 per participant on health services" (Byrne, Roberts, Culhane, & Kane, 2014).

The presence of strong leadership, sheer-determination, and partnership among federal, state and local programs were vital in the development of key strategies used to help end veteran homelessness in their community. Some of these key strategies are described below:

Mayors Challenge to End Veteran Homelessness. This program was initiated by former First Lady Michelle Obama as a challenge for all mayors and other state and local leaders across the country to help ensure every veteran is provided a house they can call home (USICH, 2016, p. 1). The goal of this strategy was to enlist every mayor in the country to set a deadline for his/her community, designate an effective leader, organize weekly meeting with major agencies such as the Department of Veterans Affairs, and other key financial contributors with the goal of "developing an integrated landlord strategy, and addressing current state/city laws and regulations that are barriers towards housing Veterans" (Bond, 2016, p. 3).

Implementing a Housing First System Orientation and Response (USICH, 2016, p. 1). Communities were encouraged to consider a Housing First System orientation and response to guarantee homeless veterans that are relocating into permanent housing get the proper treatment they deserved. The United States Interagency Council on Homelessness stated that not all veterans have great credit, are substance free or are clear of a criminal record (2016, p. 1). These past faults should not be deterrents in helping place the homeless veterans. Those working with the different programs should be adequately trained to deal with people of different backgrounds, including those with substance abuse, criminal records, and the like. It is vital that these past faults not be hindrances in helping veterans get out of homelessness (USICH, 2016, p. 1).

The City of Philadelphia's 2013 initiative Rapid Results Veteran Bootcamp gave veterans a goal of obtaining housing within 100 days as well as bettering the efforts for other additional housing options. This campaign was funded by the HUD and focused on streamlining the process from identifying homeless veterans to getting them placed in proper housing. The cooperation between the Philadelphia Housing Authority and the VA staff was successful and became an example to other communities. The early success showed that housing homeless veterans in a timely and efficient manner was possible with the right amount of cooperation and team effort (Culbertson et al., 2015, p. 2).

The analysis of data collected for this article reveals the following findings:

- Programs such as permanent housing must be implemented in Sacramento County to house veterans that are experiencing homelessness and at the same time keep them off the streets;

- Programs created to support and reduce the veteran homelessness population are not supported by the homeless individuals;
- Most homeless veterans who seek services such as food vouchers, medical health care, and bus passes from the VA were only there for that type of services only. Many of the homeless veterans do not choose to pursue housing and prefer to remain on the streets.
- Most homeless veterans prefer to stay homeless;
- Most homeless veterans with pets would rather live in a homeless camp than settle in housing where their pets are not allowed, such as housing provided by the VA and other housing agencies;
- Many of the homeless veterans prefer to keep things as status quo because that is the life that they know and are accustomed to;
- Some of the homeless veterans prostitute themselves for food.

The County of Sacramento was provided with recommendations based on best practices from homelessness programs from other cities and regions to help reduce the population of homeless veterans.

Encourage Public/Private Landlords as Partners. The Department of Housing and Urban Development, public and private sector housing industries, as well as rental property owners should collaborate to collectively reduce veteran homelessness.

Develop and Increase Connections to Employment and Education Services. The County of Sacramento, the Department of Veterans Affairs, Volunteers of America and other homeless agencies that provide support to homeless individuals in general must organize, promote and administer additional stand-downs in the form of job training and educational programs. Stand-downs provide homeless veterans with opportunities for skill and job training and educational programs, food, clothing and other resources to come off the streets.

REFERENCES

Blanton, R. (2013) "Overview of Veterans in California." California State Library. Retrieved from: https://www.library.ca.gov/crb/13/13-020.pdf.
Byrne, T., Roberts, C., Culhane, D., & Kane, V. "Estimating Cost Savings Associated with HUD–VASH Placement." 2014. http://www.endhomelessness.org/library/entry/fact-sheet-veteran-homelessness.
Cunningham, M., Henry, M., & Lyons, W. (2007) "Vital Mission." https://www.usich.gov/resources/uploads/asset_library/BkgrdPap_Veterans.pdf.
Gamache, G., Rosenheck, R., Tessler, R. "Overrepresentation of Women Veterans among Homeless Women." *Am J Public Health*. 2003 Jul; 93(7):1132–6.
Jansson, Bruce S. (15 March 2010). *Becoming an Effective Policy Advocate*. Boston: Cengage Learning, p. 72.
Metraux, S., Clegg, L., Daigh, J., Culhane, D., & Kane, V. (2013) "Risk Factors for Becoming Homeless Among a Cohort of Veterans Who Served in the Era of the Iraq and Afghanistan Conflicts." U.S. National Library of Medicine. National Institutes of Health. PubMED.Gov Retrieved from: https://www.ncbi.nlm.nih.gov/pubmed/24148066.
Sacramento Steps Forward. (2015). "2015 Point-in-Time Homeless count Report." Sacramento County & Incorporated Cities. Retrieved from: http://sacramentostepsforward.org/wp-content/uploads/2015/07/SSF2015PITReport-July162015_CoverMemo.pdf.
U.S. Department of Housing and Urban Development. The 2009 Annual Homeless, Assessment Report to congress. Washington, DC: Office of Community Planning and Development, 2010. Available at: http://www.hudhre.info/documents/5thHomelessAssessmentReport.pdf.
Washington, Donna L., M.D., M.P.H., Yano, Elizabeth M., PhD., M.S.P.H., McGuire, James, PhD., M.S.W., Hines, Vivian, M.S.W., A.C.S.W., Lee, M., PhD., & Gelberg, Lillian, M.D., M.S.P.H. (2010). "Risk Factors for Homelessness Among Women Veterans." *Journal of Health Care for the Poor and Underserved*, 21(1), 81–91. Retrieved from http://0-search.proquest.com.library.ggu.edu/docview/220588734?accountid=25283.

39. A Place to Call Home
for U.S. Veterans
in Rancho Cordova, CA*

SAMANTHA WAGNER

In August [2016], Rancho Cordova, California, made regional history by opening the doors of the new Mather Veterans Village—the first permanent supportive housing facility for homeless and disabled veterans in the Sacramento region. The Village includes 50 permanent supportive homes and supportive services that range from counseling to job training. And this is just Phase I—Phases II and III of the project will result in an additional 50 permanent-supportive homes and as many as 50 transitional units for our veterans. This is an interview with Mayor David Sander.

Tell us about how this project came about.

A: The City of Rancho Cordova incorporated in 2003, which included the former Mather Air Force Base and a Veterans Administration (VA) hospital. With our city's strong military heritage, the continued medical services to veterans, and space available at the former base, it made sense to pursue a project that would honor veterans and provide them with a place to call home.

We started creating the vision for Mather Veterans Village almost 10 years ago, and moving the project forward has had its challenges. In a Veterans Affairs meeting in Washington, D.C., HUD and the VA agreed that Rancho Cordova would be an ideal community to provide this type of facility. While on the journey to completion of the project, we often had conflicting tasks which caused us to go back and forth between a number of federal, state and local agencies. This was the first time our city found itself entangled with the complexities involved in a multi-agency, multi-level government project of this type.

Thankfully, we are a young, nimble, risk-taking and aggressive city organization and were able to find solutions to the various hurdles we faced. We believed in this project, so we and our partners—the County of Sacramento, Mercy Housing California and Vet-

*Samantha Wagner, "A Place to Call Home for U.S. Veterans in Rancho Cordova, CA," October 10, 2016, https://icma.org/articles/article/place-call-home-us-veterans-rancho-cordova-ca. Originally published in *Leadership Matters*, October 10, 2016, by ICMA, the International City/County Management Association (icma.org); reprinted with permission.

erans Resource Centers of America—went to great lengths to ensure it came to fruition. We wouldn't take "no" for an answer.

What types of hurdles did you face during the project?

A: One specific hurdle included issues with regional allocation of the Veterans Supportive Housing Credit, which is sort of like the more well-known Section 8 program, only the VA commits credits to a region to help veterans get housing. We had a great project but because we are smaller city in size, and the new kid on the block, it was politically difficult for us to get the attention of the awarding agency, which was a Sacramento-based housing authority. Historically the housing authority hadn't worked with cities of our size.

And even within our partnership, Sacramento County as a land owner did not want to give up the targeted land for the site for free—many within the agency were focused on earning a high return for the county on the development of this site. However, because of the end goal, and the fact that the main focus of the project was about veterans, and our proposal truly outperformed others—those barriers were overcome. In addition, we possessed a trump card. As a young fiscally healthy city we were prepared and ready with cash to contribute to the completion of the project. We were also very ready to partner which was unique for a city of our size and this put us at an advantage with these agencies and partners.

What are some of the primary benefits of the project?

A: Mather Veterans Village provides a sense of community for veterans who have served and have faced homelessness. A place like Mather Veterans Village capitalizes on the camaraderie between veterans, providing supportive services unique to the veteran homeless population, along with a safe and vibrant setting in a welcoming community. This, combined with the VA hospital which is a block away, job training, transportation assistance and other pertinent services means the residents of Mather Veterans Village have easy access to virtually whatever support they need.

Advice to other cities?

A: I would encourage cities that wish to provide this level of service to veterans to think long term. This is not something you can complete quickly and a lot of money is involved. Also think in-depth—our first phase is for 50 veterans, and the next phase is for transitional services that provides more aid to another 50 vets in the community. Phase III of the project is permanent housing for yet another 50 veterans, and Phase IV will pursue the Ronald McDonald House model for the support of the families of veterans seeking care at the VA Hospital.

We have thought beyond today and created a holistic approach which will take time to complete. With each phase comes a sense of hope and accomplishment for how far we've come, but also a sense of how much more there is to do for our veterans. Despite this, our organization chose to take a risk and to get involved because without risk there is no real reward. So we will move to completion of each phase with the intention of doing the best job we can.

Describe the impact the project had on your team:

A: During the opening ceremony of Phase I, I saw the tears from our employees. The stories the vets shared during the ceremony and privately were that moving. Many of these staff have literally worked on this project for ten years, and we are all so grateful to our partners for their help in making this endeavor possible. As a city we are making a statement that is far better than saying "thank you for your service" to the vets we meet in the streets. We still say that, by the way. But now we can also say, "Here is a place you can call home." That is the ultimate thank you.

What is it like to work at a city like Rancho Cordova?

A: The way we are organized as a city is designed to spur innovation. Most agencies have flow charts and org charts—here at Rancho Cordova we are team focused and goal oriented. Anyone can pitch in on projects from any department. Our Economic Development Director headed up this project, and staff members from our building inspectors to finance to marketing all contributed their gifts to the successful completion of Phase I of this project! That's our secret to success—promote individual initiative, long-term vision, healthy risk taking and innovation to accomplish some audacious goals.

40. Three Ways This State Is Housing All Homeless Veterans[*]

ELISHA HARIG-BLAINE

On a day when the nation pauses to give thanks for the sacrifices made by veterans and their families, Virginians are celebrating that all of their veterans have access to the basic dignity of a place to call home.

Today, Governor Terry McAuliffe, U.S. Department of Housing and Urban Development (HUD) Secretary Julián Castro, and U.S. Interagency Council on Homelessness (USICH) Executive Director Matthew Doherty announced that the Commonwealth of Virginia had achieved the historic accomplishment of ensuring all veterans are on the path to a safe, stable place to call home by housing more veterans than are being identified as homeless each month.

Since October 2014, the Commonwealth has housed 1,432 Veterans and their families. Earlier this year, an estimated 605 Veterans were homeless.

"Even in declaring our victory with this battle, the war is still not over," said Governor McAuliffe. "We must remain committed to keeping homelessness among veterans, and, all Virginians, to being rare, brief and non-recurring."

The progress made by Virginia has come as the result of an unprecedented focus on the issue by all levels of government. But local, state and federal officials were not alone. They were joined by the non-profit and business communities, which recognized the need to transform the systems that serve veterans. For the first time, Virginia has shown how an entire state can implement data-driven best practices that ensure available resources are used effectively and efficiently.

The Path to Success

Local Leadership. Since June 2014, after more than 30 years of being viewed as an unsolvable fixture of modern life, 854 local leaders have stepped forward to give their commitment to housing all Veterans through the Mayors Challenge to End Veteran

*Originally published Elisha Harig-Blaine, "Three Ways This State Is Housing All Homeless Veterans," https://citiesspeak.org/2015/11/11/three-ways-this-state-is-housing-all-homeless-veterans/#_ga=2.15625 6120.29049585.1553888189-259213687.1553888189 (November 11, 2015). Reprinted with permission of the publisher and author.

Homelessness. The National League of Cities is proud to be the lead partner with the Administration in this effort.

Across Virginia, 18 mayors and two county executives joined with Gov. McAuliffe on the Mayors Challenge. Their leadership has brought attention and focus to homeless veterans in their city and across the state in ways never seen before.

The Governor's commitment resulted a redoubling of efforts guided by the Governor's Coordinating Council on Homelessness, the Virginia Department of Veterans Services and the Virginia Coalition to End Homelessness.

Systems Coordination. With high-level support from state and local leaders, non-profits in communities such as Richmond, Roanoke, South Hampton Roads and the Peninsula area, as well as other cities across the commonwealth, joined with experts from Community Solutions and the Rapid Results Institute. Together with representatives from area public housing authorities, HUD and U.S. Department of Veterans Affairs (VA) medical centers, these stakeholders began communicating and coordinating in a variety of new ways.

Importantly, all of the partners agreed on the principal of Housing First. Recognizing that the solution to homelessness is housing, Housing First puts housing and the services needed to successfully maintain a home as the first line of treatment.

In the past, homeless individuals and families were regularly required to go through shelters and/or transitional housing programs, which may require lengths of sobriety or participation in other programs prior to placement into housing. This line of treatment is both expensive and prolongs a person's instability, which can perpetuate problems at the core of an individual's homelessness.

In addition to using the Housing First model, community partners began coordinating their assessment processes and prioritizing clients for placement into housing. This coordination allows VA staff and non-profit partners to consolidate their lists of individuals and families coming to them for assistance. Beyond the consolidation of lists, the coordination has allowed communities to develop a by name list of people experiencing homelessness and understand which person needs to access housing most urgently to avoid death.

No longer are homeless veterans known as "that guy by the I-95 underpass."

Instead, "that guy" is James, a 64-year-old Vietnam veteran with diabetes who has previously been treated for mental illness and substance abuse and has lived on the street for more than 15 years.

Community partners not only know James by name, but they know which organization has an available housing voucher. They have a deeper sense of his medical and mental health needs. They know which organization can work with James to find a home. They know which organization can develop and implement a treatment plan that will allow him to keep his home and transition to a new chapter of life.

Available Resources. For the first time since modern homelessness has emerged, cities and community partners have been given the resources they need to tackle the issue. The focus on the veteran subpopulation has generated bi-partisan support for programs such as the HUD–VA Supportive Housing (HUD–VASH) voucher program and the Supportive Services for Veteran Families (SSVF) program.

Since fiscal year 2008, more than 1,260 HUD–VASH vouchers have been made available in Virginia. In the past three years, the VA's SSVF program has provided communities in the commonwealth with more than $5.1 million for homelessness prevention and rapid-rehousing efforts.

The availability of these resources in the commonwealth and across the country has been the difference between the rhetoric of supporting our veterans and making a meaningful, lasting impact on the lives of tens of thousands of men, women and children nationwide.

In Virginia, Gov. McAuliffe recognized the need to supplement these federal investments. He designated $500,000 of a new $1 million program to help veterans access housing through the state's Department of Housing and Community Development. He also proposed increasing the number of housing resource specialists working as part of Virginia's Veteran and Family Support program under the Virginia Department of Veterans Services. The specialists support veterans as they navigate the housing process and connect them with needed services.

These new levels of partnership, coordination and investment inspired the engagement of businesses to also make contributions. Dominion Virginia Power and Appalachian Power Company have made commitments to help veterans meet their energy needs in their new homes.

Parades and proclamations are laudable ways to honor our Veterans. But the true measure of our appreciation is shown in the lives of our veterans.

Virginia's achievement brings the progress already seen in cities across the country to a new level. Communities such as New Orleans, Houston, Winston-Salem and Mobile have made similar announcements this year. As the first state in the nation to make this announcement, Virginia is showing that large-scale success can be achieved when local leaders commit to a bold goal and do not relent.

41. Homeless Vets with Families: An Untold Part of Veterans' Struggles*

Roya Ijadi-Maghsoodi

In 2010, the Obama administration announced the ambitious goal of ending homelessness among veterans. Over the last year, the number of veterans who are homeless dropped 30 percent in Los Angeles County. Nationwide, veteran homelessness fell by almost 50 percent since 2009.

Yet statistics are only part of the story. What is missing from federal and state statistics, the media and the minds of many Americans, is the story of homeless veteran families.

Through my work as a researcher and physician caring for women and homeless veterans, I see these families. I hear about their struggles to find housing in safe neighborhoods instead of Skid Row, where their children are exposed to violence and drug use.

Overlooking Veterans with Families

Families are often missed when volunteers head out to count homeless individuals. Veterans with families often stay with friends, known as "doubling up." Or, forced to fragment, parents send kids to stay with family while they go to a shelter.

Plus, some females who are homeless and the head of their household don't identify as veterans. They may not be eligible for Veterans Affairs (VA) benefits or are unclear about available services. Some may not seek care at the VA due to mistrust, harassment or past military sexual trauma.

Providers, policymakers and the public need to understand that homelessness among the families of men and women who have served our nation may be invisible. But it is significant.

Limited studies point to higher rates of veteran family homelessness than expected from the counts. Nineteen percent of families served by Supportive Services for Veteran Families in the FY 2015 had at least one child. A study of veterans receiving VA homeless

***

*Originally published as Roya Ijadi-Maghsoodi, "Homeless Vets with Families: An Untold Part of Veterans' Struggles," *The Conversation*, May 26, 2017. Reprinted with permission of the publisher.

services by Tsai and colleagues showed that nine percent of literally homeless male veterans—those living on the streets or uninhabitable locations—and 18 percent of unstably housed male veterans had children in their custody.

A striking 30 percent of literally homeless female veterans, as well as 45 percent of unstably housed female veterans, had children in their custody.

Causes of Homelessness

What contributes to homelessness among veteran families?

First, homelessness among women veterans is rising. Eleven percent of military personnel who served in Operation Iraqi Freedom/Operation Enduring Freedom (OIF/OEF) were women, the largest number involved in combat operations in U.S. history.

Women veterans are more likely to be mothers and mothers at a younger age than civilians, and more likely to receive lower income than male veterans.

They face high rates of trauma, especially military sexual trauma, a known risk for homelessness.

And, strikingly, women veterans are up to four times more likely to be homeless than civilian women.

Male veterans returning from OIF/OEF tend to be younger and may have young families. As of 2010, 49 percent of deployed service members had children. They also have a higher prevalence of PTSD, compared to veterans of other wars. This is thought to be associated with an increased risk for homelessness.

To make matters worse, our country is in the grips of an affordable housing crisis. In California, we have only 21 homes available for every 100 extremely low-income households. And every day, families face discrimination searching for housing due to their race or ethnicity, being a veteran or using a voucher.

What Homeless Veteran Families Need

These families are at high risk. Decades of research show that children in homeless families are at risk for physical and mental health problems, academic delay and of becoming homeless themselves as adults—creating a second generation of homelessness. Many homeless veteran families are resilient but face additional stressors of reintegrating into civilian society and coping with parents who may have PTSD and traumatic brain injuries.

Our team has been conducting interviews to understand the needs of veteran families who are homeless. We also formed a work group of recently homeless veteran parents.

We are finding that, although veterans are often satisfied with their own health and mental health services at the VA, many parents feel alone when it comes to their family.

Many veterans are overwhelmed by PTSD and depression, as well as the search to find housing and a job. They worry about the toll on their family. Yet they find few resources for their family within the VA, such as family therapy, and need help finding needed health and mental health care for their spouse and children in the community.

Parents need more help connecting to resources for their families in the community, clearer information about the social services available to veteran families and more emotional support as parents.

Moving Forward

We need to change the conversation when we talk about homeless veterans. We need to talk about homeless veteran families.

These families are in our communities, the children are attending public schools, their parents are trying to work multiple jobs or attend college and many receive care in our VA and community clinics.

Within the VA, we need to consider the whole family and provide more connection to the community to help families succeed. At the VA Greater Los Angeles Healthcare System West Los Angeles Medical Center, a new family wellness center will open as a collaborative effort between UCLA and the VA. The center will serve as a hub to strengthen veteran families, through services such as family and couple resilience programs, parenting skills workshops and connection to community services. More efforts are needed to engage families who may need it most.

Beyond the VA, we need enhanced understanding and empathy for veteran families with homelessness within the community. This involves greater understanding of the needs of these children in schools. We should also find ways to help veteran families dealing with PTSD integrate into the community after being homeless.

And most of all, we need to increase access to affordable housing in safe neighborhoods for these families.

The recent wars may seem over for many Americans, but they are far from over for our homeless veteran families. We owe it to them to do better.

42. "They Deserve It": In Foster Homes, Veterans Are Cared for Like Family*

PATRICIA KIME

With the motto "Where Heroes Meet Angels," a small Veterans Affairs effort pairs vets in need of nursing home care with caregivers willing to share their homes.

Ralph Stepney's home on a quiet street in north Baltimore has a welcoming front porch and large rooms, with plenty of space for his comfortable recliner and vast collection of action movies. The house is owned by Joann West, a licensed caregiver who shares it with Stepney and his fellow Vietnam War veteran Frank Hundt.

"There is no place that I'd rather be. … I love the quiet of living here, the help we get. I thank the Lord every year that I am here," Stepney, 73, said.

It's a far cry from a decade ago, when Stepney was homeless and "didn't care about anything." His diabetes went unchecked and he had suffered a stroke—a medical event that landed him at the Baltimore Veterans Affairs Medical Center.

After having part of his foot amputated, Stepney moved into long-term nursing home care at a VA medical facility, where he thought he'd remain—until he became a candidate for a small VA effort that puts aging veterans in private homes: the Medical Foster Home program.

The $20.7 million-per-year program provides housing and care for more than 1,000 veterans in 42 states and Puerto Rico, serving as an alternative to nursing home care for those who cannot live safely on their own. Veterans pay their caregivers $1,500 to $3,000 a month, depending on location, saving the government about $10,000 a month in nursing home care. It has been difficult to scale up, though, because the VA accepts only foster homes that meet strict qualifications.

For the veterans, it's a chance to live in a home setting with caregivers who treat them like family. For the Department of Veterans Affairs, the program provides an option for meeting its legal obligation to care for ailing, aging patients at significantly reduced costs, since the veterans pay room and board directly to their caregivers.

Cost-effectiveness is but one of the program's benefits. Stepney and Hundt, 67, are

*Originally published as Patricia Kime, "'They Deserve It': In Foster Homes, Veterans Are Cared for Like Family," *Kaiser Health News*, May 30, 2018. KHN's coverage of these topics is supported by the SCAN Foundation and John A. Hartford Foundation.

in good hands with West, who previously ran a home health care services company. And they're in good company, watching television together in the main living room, going to elder care twice a week and sitting on West's porch chatting with neighbors.

West, who considers caring for older adults "her calling," also savors the companionship and finds satisfaction in giving back to those who spent their young lives in military service to the U.S.

"I took care of my mother when she got cancer and I found that I really had a passion for it. I took classes and ran an in-home nursing care business for years. But my dream was always to get my own place and do what I am doing now," West said. "God worked it out."

The Medical Foster Home program has slightly more than 700 licensed caregivers who live full time with no more than three veterans and provide round-the-clock supervision and care, according to the VA. Akin to a community residential care facility, each foster home must be state-licensed as an assisted living facility and submit to frequent inspections by the VA as well as state inspectors, nutritionists, pharmacists and nurses.

Unlike typical community care facilities, foster home caregivers are required to live on-site and tend to the needs of their patients themselves 24/7—or supply relief staff.

"It's a lot of work, but I have support," West says. "I try to make all my personal appointments on days when Mr. Ralph and Mr. Frank are out, but if I can't, someone comes in to be here when I'm gone."

VA medical foster home providers also must pass a federal background check, complete 80 hours of training before they can accept patients, plus 20 hours of additional training each year, and allow the VA to make announced and unannounced home visits. They cannot work outside the home and must maintain certification in first aid, CPR and medicine administration.

But one prerequisite cannot be taught—the ability to make a veteran feel at home. West has grown children serving in the military and takes pride in contributing to the well-being of veterans.

"It's a lot of joy taking care of them," she said of Stepney and Hundt. "They deserve it."

To be considered for the program, veterans must be enrolled in VA health care; have a serious, chronic disabling medical condition that requires a nursing home level of care; and need care coordination and access to VA services. It can take up to a month to place a veteran in a home once they are found eligible, according to the VA.

The veterans also must be able to cover their costs. Because medical foster homes are not considered institutional care, the VA is not allowed to pay for it directly. The average monthly fee, according to the VA, is $2,300, which most veterans cover with their VA compensation, Social Security and savings, said Nicole Trimble, Medical Foster Home coordinator at the Perry Point VA Medical Center in Maryland.

Pilot Program Takes Off

Since 1999, the Department of Veterans Affairs has been required to provide nursing home services to veterans who qualify for VA health care and have a service-connected disability rating of 70 percent or higher, or are considered unemployable and have a disability rating of 60 percent or higher.

The VA provides this care through short- or long-term nursing home facilities, respite care, community living centers on VA hospital grounds, private assisted living facilities and state veterans' homes.

Shortly after, the VA Medical Center in Little Rock, Ark., launched an alternative—a pilot program that placed veterans in individual homes, at an average cost to the VA of roughly $60 a day, including administration and health care expenses, compared with upward of $500 a day for nursing home care.

And because veterans who are enrolled in the Medical Foster Care program must use the VA's Home-Based Primary Care program, which provides an interdisciplinary team of health professionals for in-home medical treatment, the program saves the VA even more. One study showed that the home-based care has yielded a 59 percent drop in VA hospital inpatient days and a 31 percent reduction in admissions among those who participate.

More than 120 VA medical centers now oversee a Medical Foster Home program in their regions, and the VA has actively promoted the program within its health system.

It also has attracted bipartisan congressional support. In 2013, Sen. Bernie Sanders (I–Vt.) introduced a bill to allow the VA to pay for medical foster homes directly.

In 2015, former House Veterans Affairs Committee chairman Rep. Jeff Miller (R–Fla.) introduced similar legislation that would have allowed the VA to pay for up to 900 veterans under the program.

And in May, Rep. Clay Higgins (R–La.) raised the issue again, sponsoring a bill similar to Miller's. "Allowing veterans to exercise greater flexibility over their benefits ensures that their individual needs are best met," Higgins said in support of the program.

A Guardian "Angel"

Foster care has been a blessing for the family of Hundt, who suffered a stroke shortly after his wife died and was unable to care for himself. Hundt's daughter, Kimberly Malczewski, lives nearby and often stops in to visit her dad, sometimes with her 2-year-old son.

"I'm not sure where my father would be if he didn't have this," she said. "With my life situation—my husband and I both work full time, we have no extra room in our house, and we have a small child—I can't take care of him the way Miss Joann does."

Trimble, whose program started in 2012 and has five homes, said she hopes to expand by two to three homes a year. The VA will remain meticulous about selecting homes.

"There is a strict inspection and vetting process to be a medical foster home," Trimble said. "We only will accept the best."

It also takes a special person to be an "angel," as the caregivers are referred to in the program's motto, "Where Heroes Meet Angels."

Stepney and Hundt agree West has earned her wings. On a recent cruise to Bermuda, she brought Stepney and Hundt along.

For Hundt, it was the first time he'd been on a boat. And Stepney said it was nothing like the transport ships he and his fellow troops used in the late 1960s: "Well, I've gotten to travel, but it was mainly two years in Vietnam, and there weren't any women around."

When asked why she brought the pair along, West said caregiving is "a ministry, something you really have to like to do."

"And you know how the saying goes," she said. "When you like what you do, you never work a day in your life."

43. At Some Veterans Homes, Aid-in-Dying Is Not an Option[*]

JoNel Aleccia

California voters passed a law two years ago that allows terminally ill people to take lethal drugs to end their lives, but controversy is growing over a newer rule that effectively bans that option in the state's eight veterans homes.

Proponents of medical aid-in-dying and residents of the Veterans Home of California–Yountville—the largest in the nation—are protesting a regulation passed last year by the California Department of Veterans Affairs, or CalVet, that requires that anyone living in the facilities must be discharged if they intend to use the law.

That's a position shared by most—but not all—states where aid-in-dying is allowed. As more U.S. jurisdictions consider whether to legalize the practice, the status of terminally ill veterans living in state-run homes will loom large.

"It would be a terrible hardship, because I have no place to go," said Bob Sloan, 73, who suffers from congestive heart failure and other serious cardiac problems. He said he intends to seek medical aid-in-dying if doctors certify he has six months or less to live.

"I'm not going to be a vegetable," said Sloan, a Vietnam War–era veteran who moved into the Yountville center five years ago. "I'm not going to end up living in so much pain it's unbearable."

A CalVet official said the agency adopted the rule to avoid violating a federal statute that prohibits using U.S. government resources for physician-assisted death. Otherwise, the agency would jeopardize nearly $68 million in federal funds that helps run the facilities, said June Iljana, CalVet's deputy secretary of communications.

California is not alone. Three other states where aid-in-dying is legal—Oregon, Colorado and Vermont—all prohibit use of lethal medications in state-run veterans homes.

In Montana, where aid-in-dying is allowed under a state Supreme Court ruling, officials didn't respond to multiple requests about whether veterans would be able to use the law in the residences. However, Dr. Eric Kress, a Missoula physician who prescribes the lethal medication, says he has transferred patients to hospice, to relatives' homes, even to extended-stay hotels to avoid conflict.

In Washington, D.C., where an aid-in-dying law took effect last summer, the Armed

*Originally published as JoNel Aleccia, "At Some Veterans Homes, Aid-in-Dying Is Not an Option," *Kaiser Health News*, February 13, 2018. KHN's coverage of these topics is supported by the John A. Hartford Foundation and the SCAN Foundation.

Forces Retirement Home won't assist patients in any way. Those who wish to use the law would be referred to an ethics committee for individual consideration, spokesman Christopher Kelly said in an email.

Only Washington state has a policy that allows veterans to remain in government-run residences if they intend to ingest lethal medications. At least one veteran has died in a state-run home using that law, said Heidi Audette, a spokeswoman for the state's Department of Veterans Affairs.

Paul Sherbo, a spokesman for the U.S. Department of Veterans Affairs, said the choice is up to the states.

"VA does not mandate how states comply with federal law," Sherbo said in an email. "There are a number of ways individual states can choose to handle such situations and still be in compliance."

To date, none of the 2,400 residents of California's veterans homes has formally requested medical aid-in-dying, said Iljana. That includes the more than 900 residents of the Yountville center, located about 60 miles north of San Francisco.

"We would respectfully and compassionately assist them in transferring to a hospice, family home or other location," Iljana said in an email. "We will readmit them immediately if they change their minds."

But Kathryn Tucker, executive director of the End of Life Liberty Project, an advocacy group that supports aid-in-dying, said that CalVet is interpreting the federal regulations too broadly and denying terminally ill veterans the right to choose a "peaceful death" through medical assistance.

"Nothing exists in the federal statute's language that would prohibit a resident from receiving aid-in-dying services at state homes, so long as they are not provided using federal funds or employees," she said.

Ed Warren, head of the Allied Council, a group representing veterans at the Yountville site, co-signed a letter to CalVet officials protesting the ruling.

"My point of view is that it is inhumane to expect people in the last stages of dying to go through the hullabaloo of leaving their homes," he said.

In Washington state, a 60-year-old man diagnosed with terminal chronic obstructive pulmonary disease, or COPD, died in June 2015 after ingesting lethal drugs at the Washington Soldiers Home in Orting, where he lived.

"It was all done very much in the open," said Chris Fruitrich, a volunteer with the group End of Life Washington, which assisted the man.

There has been no indication that the policy jeopardizes the nearly $47 million the agency receives each year in federal funds, said Audette, the state VA spokeswoman.

In California, additional protests have centered on allegations that CalVet suppressed information about the aid-in-dying law.

Critics at the Yountville home contend that CalVet passed the discharge rule quietly, with little public input. Then the agency refused to broadcast a public meeting about medical aid-in-dying on KVET, the center's state-run, closed-circuit television station.

Iljana said the broadcast of the Aug. 21 meeting, led by Tucker and Dr. Robert Brody, also a supporter of aid-in-dying, violated state rules that prohibit using public resources to promote political causes.

"Free speech is great and criticizing the government is great, but not using the government's own resources and paid staff to advocate for a change in the law," Iljana wrote in an email to prohibit the broadcast.

That decision, however, prompted Jac Warren, 81, who has been KVET's station manager for eight years, to resign in protest, citing censorship.

"What is at issue is whether a state may completely suppress the dissemination of concededly truthful information about entirely lawful activity," Warren wrote in an email to CalVet.

The hour-long meeting, attended by about 50 people, was not propaganda, Tucker said, but "an educational event with information provided by an attorney and a physician who both specialize in their respective fields in end-of-life care."

Bob Sloan, who works as an engineer at KVET for a $400 monthly stipend, disagreed with the decision not to broadcast the meeting on the system that serves residents of the Yountville home.

Sloan said he knows other residents who would like to be able to use California's aid-in-dying law if their illnesses progress.

"The only other option that people have in this state is committing suicide," he said. "If I can't find some way of doing it legally, I'll do it illegally."

44. Supporting Our Veterans Isn't Just the Right Thing, It's the Smart Thing[*]

Elisha Harig-Blaine

Two or three times each year, our attention turns toward veterans and the sacrifices they have made for the United States. Yet sustaining that focus beyond Memorial Day, the Fourth of July and Veterans Day has been essential to creating meaningful and lasting change, especially when it comes to ensuring that veterans have a safe place to call home.

Notwithstanding the fact that homelessness continues to be a seemingly intractable public policy challenge, significant inroads have been made with regard to veterans. Overall homelessness for this population has plummeted by 47 percent since 2010, with the number of veterans on our streets falling by 57 percent. This progress has not been happenstance. It is the result of planning, dedicated resources, collaboration and local leadership.

In 2010, the U.S. Interagency Council on Homelessness released Opening Doors, a first-time strategic approach to ending homelessness by prioritizing specified subpopulations, starting with veterans. Federal officials recognized that focusing on them initially presented numerous advantages. First, veterans have unique access to such services and benefits as health care, education and employment.

Beyond access to resources, policymakers understood that reducing homelessness required the support of public and private partners at every level. Recognizing the "sea of goodwill" for veterans, federal officials began to target housing resources to homeless ones with the HUD-VA Supportive Housing voucher program, a partnership of the U.S. Department of Housing and Urban Development (HUD) and U.S. Department of Veterans Affairs (VA). HUD provides a Housing Choice Voucher—Section 8 voucher—for veterans and VA provides case management services.

In addition to longer-term housing subsidies, VA launched a shorter-term program, the Supportive Services for Veteran Families (SSVF) program, in 2009. One year later, Congress authorized and appropriated historic levels of funding to support local efforts to end veteran homelessness.

*Originally published as Elisha Harig-Blaine, "Supporting Our Veterans Isn't Just the Right Thing ... It's the Smart Thing," *PA Times,* October 30, 2017. Reprinted with permission of the publisher and author.

The private sector matched this unprecedented level of congressional support. Businesses and philanthropies joined federal partners to accelerate veteran hiring and fill gaps in services. One example: Since 2011, the Home Depot Foundation has focused on veterans and built or improved more than 30,000 homes in nearly 2,000 cities. Its commitment to veteran-related causes will grow to a quarter of a billion dollars by 2020.

Taken together, communities for the first time had the resources needed to significantly reduce—even end—veteran homelessness. The challenge: Develop the systems and sustainable structures required to effectively and efficiently use those resources. To support these community-based systems, federal partners funded technical assistance initiatives to provide guidance, working with stakeholders to implement best practices like the by-name lists of homeless veterans and common assessment tools to prioritize veterans for assistance based on need.

A final component has been the active engagement of local elected officials through the Mayors Challenge to End Veteran Homelessness, led by federal agencies and supported by the National League of Cities (NLC) and other national organizations. Launched in 2014, the challenge is a network of 611 elected officials—521 mayors, 83 county and city officials and seven governors—who have made the permanent commitment to ensure homelessness is rare, brief and non-recurring, starting with veterans.

The Mayors Challenge has been a mechanism for local elected officials to demonstrate their support for ending veteran homelessness. It also has provided homeless service providers a platform to engage public officials around specific actions they can take to help accelerate community-based efforts. That said, it was not until more than one year after the challenge's launch that federal officials announced the definition of what it actually means to "end" veteran homelessness. The groundswell of support for the goal itself, enabled by the prioritization of the veteran subpopulation, led the officials to take this historic step. Since 2015, more than 50 communities and three states have announced the functional end of veteran homelessness.

As this number grows, the collaborative systems developed to achieve this shared goal must not only be maintained but be strengthened and enhanced to end homelessness for other subpopulations. Beyond veterans, the chronically homeless are men, women and children who are highly likely to use these services. By stabilizing this subpopulation, communities can minimize homelessness' fiscal impact on limited resources.

Beyond Homelessness

A focus on veterans is most visible through the lens of veteran homelessness and specifying them as a subpopulation. Still, communities nationwide are exploring how they can make similar improvements in other areas. With support from The Home Depot Foundation, NLC is partnering with Purple Heart Homes (PHH) to improve how cities can address the home modification needs of senior and disabled veterans.

Federal resources, especially the Community Development Block Grant (CDBG) program, have funded home modification programs in many cities. Yet the level of CDBG resources has plateaued or declined, notwithstanding increasing numbers of residents turning 65 or having some form of a disability. To help communities target resources more effectively, NLC and PHH are working with credit unions, aging agencies, local VA medical centers, United Ways and other stakeholders in eight cities to identify veterans in need of home modifications. These modifications range from installing or repairing grab bars, to lowering counter tops to widening doorways. The key is to connect veterans to appropriate community resources so cities can ensure effective and efficient use of limited resources, while building or expanding collaborative systems to leverage public-private partnerships.

Nearly 8 percent of the U.S. adult population are veterans and an increasing number of military personnel serve multiple overseas tours as part of the nation's longest period of continuous conflict. Supporting veterans and their families is not only a matter of patriotism; it is a matter of national security.

To be sure, VA has a significant role to play in meeting veteran needs, but it cannot be the only one. More and more, communities see the ancillary benefits that come from focusing on veterans. In an ever-present environment of limited resources, we must illustrate—in both words and deeds—that we truly understand the words of President Lincoln and will "care for him who shall have borne the battle and for his widow, and his orphan."

45. Minority Veteran Services and Outreach[*]

Barbara Ward

There are approximately 21 million veterans who have served in various capacities in one of the U.S. military branches of service. Per the March 2017 Minority Veterans Report, minority veterans comprise 23 percent of the veteran population which is equivalent to 5 million veterans. Minority veteran groups were defined by Congress in Public Law 103-446 on November 2, 1994, as: African American, Hispanic, Asian Pacific Islander, American Indian and Alaska Native, and Native Hawaiian. According to the Minority Veterans Report published in March 2017, the minority veteran population will increase from 23 percent to 37 percent of the total veteran population by 2040. During this same time period, the total veteran population is projected to decrease from 22 million in 2014 to 14.5 million in 2043. Therefore, the veteran population will become more diverse in future years.

As the VA continues with his transformation plans and makes progress in serving all veterans, targeted outreach becomes more important in meeting its mission, "To care for him who shall have borne the battle, and for his widow, and his orphan." Today, approximately 9 million veterans of the 22 million veterans utilize VA benefits and services. However, there is a tremendous need to ensure that minority veterans are well informed about their earned benefits, VA services and how to access care when indicated.

Minority veterans are eligible for the same VA services and benefits as are non-minority veterans. The one exception is the Native American Direct Home Loan Program which provides loans to eligible Native American Veterans to finance the purchase, construction, or improvement of homes on Federal Trust Land, or to refinance a prior direct home loan to reduce the interest rate. The tribal government must have a signed Memorandum of Understanding with the Secretary of Veterans Affairs to acquire such a loan. Minority Veterans tend to have a much lower utilization rates of benefit programs and VA services when compared to non-minority veterans. In order to successfully meet the needs of minority veterans, cultural competency of VA providers, employees and community care providers is key.

Due to cultural differences, geographic locations, age, gender, language barriers and

---

[*]Published with permission of the author.

trust issues, effective outreach strategies to minority veterans can prove to be extremely challenging. Culture is defined as a set of values, practices, traditions or beliefs that a group shares due to age, race or ethnicity, religion or gender and attributes to the need for the development and implementation of targeted outreach strategies that address differences in outreaching to minority Veterans groups. Geographic locations can serve as a barrier for Native American Veterans who live in rural areas on reservations.

Often times, there is no broadband wireless service, thus decreasing opportunities to access online information or software applications aimed at keeping veterans informed on available services and earned benefits. Their native traditions are vastly different from the cultural backgrounds and traditions of other minority veteran groups. Many tribes believe that they were gravely wronged by the U.S. government and therefore, deserve equal, if not, greater access to VA services and benefits in return for their military service. According to the Department of Defense, American Indians and Alaska Natives have one of the highest representations in the armed forces. As with many veterans, family members become their biggest advocate for accessing VA services and benefits. Language barriers for non–English speaking family members can serve as a deterrent to an advocacy role. Cultural stereotypes and associated stigmas also play a significant role in the distrust of minority veterans when deciding whether or not to access VA services and benefits.

Historically, distrust is prevalent in African American communities and is a result of past practices where they were used as test subjects, without their consent, in medical research studies. The Tuskegee Syphilis Study which was conducted by the United States Public Health Service on black males from 1932 to 1972. The knowledge of such past experiences among minority groups fosters ongoing distrust in the VA and other health care systems. Older minority veterans are less likely to seek information online, use different forms of social media or online applications such as appointment scheduling, PTSD coach or ask a Pharmacist.

As a result of cultural differences and diverse backgrounds, various outreach approaches are required to successfully inform and increase the awareness level of all minority veterans. The number of minority veterans who are enrolled in VA health care as of 2014 is 1,261,559 out of 5 million minority veterans. 1.9 million minority veterans used at least one benefit or service during the same time period. Chapter 63 of Title 38, U.S.C. clearly defines the outreach mission for VA as to provide information and awareness to Veterans and family members so they have the proper tools to access VA benefits and services. According to the 2016 Biennial Report to Congress: Veterans Outreach Activities, a first step is acknowledging and understanding that "veterans" are not a monolithic group but rather a highly diverse population of more than 22 million people. Recognizing the diversity of the veteran population, VA has strengthened its outreach to specific populations such as women veterans, Native American veterans and other minority groups.

Cultural differences and the increasing diversity of the veteran population demands strategic outreach plans that include a combination of traditional and non-traditional approaches, collaborative strategies with partners and appropriate tools and people resources. The success of such plans can be measured in terms of their capacity to successfully target outreach activities to communities where minority veterans live and by the increased utilization of VA services and benefits. Examples of traditional outreach approaches involve advertising and public service announcements, websites that are routinely updated with current information, distribution of outreach brochures and other relevant materials, videos, storytelling by veterans, outreach forums and meetings, stand downs, and social media sources.

As technology advances have occurred, ongoing communication processes have been tremendously enhanced. This has produced what some may consider as non-traditional targeted outreach approaches. Virtual town hall meetings, twitter town halls, Facebook pages and online blogs are a few examples of how targeted outreach can be effectively used to disseminate information to large veteran populations, including women and minority veteran groups. There are two versions of town hall meetings that are very effective in communicating with veterans. A face-to-face town hall meeting at a specific location allows for that personal exchange of information. A virtual town hall meeting is not as personal, requires more advance planning and coordination. This outreach activity provides easy access to information simply by dialing in to a designated number from the comfort of the veteran's home. If the town hall meeting is coordinated with a veteran service organization, space may be provided for a group of veterans to engage in the discussion with fellow minority veterans. In this environment, relevant information can be presented by subject matter experts and questions can be readily answered. Another example of a successful targeted outreach tool is conducting Lunch and Learn workshops at federal and/or state agencies where minority veterans work. These workshops can also be held in community locations such as churches, public libraries and selected centers located in minority community.

In many instances, the lack of transportation may be a deterrent for minority veterans, therefore, taking the information to veterans where they live can enhance the opportunity to reach more veterans and their support group. Establishing strong working relationships with collaborative partners offer numerous opportunities to participate in job fairs, community health fairs, training programs, conferences and large annual outreach events where minority veterans can receive valuable information regarding services and benefits that are available to them. Many local churches have established a military or veterans ministry whose mission is to provide assistance to veterans and their families. Based upon the experience of the Center for Minority Veterans, these ministries are very prevalent in churches where African American and Hispanic veterans attend services. Additionally, many homeless minority veterans receive ongoing support such as housing assistance, financial aid, clothes closets and food shelters.

Collaborating with church representatives by disseminating outreach materials, presenting benefit workshops, hosting job fairs and participating in special programs that recognize veterans provide a great ongoing targeted outreach opportunity. Since many Native Indians and tribal members reside in rural communities and on reservations, the most effective way to conduct targeted outreach activities to their communities is engaging with them where they live whenever possible. It is also highly recommended that you build a relationship with tribal members in advance and if possible, identify a Native Indian veteran who shares an interest in ensuring that fellow veterans know how to access VA services and benefits.

Successful outreach to Natives is highly dependent on conducting outreach in conjunction with such traditions as powwow events or special gatherings. There is a need to engage individual minority veteran groups to determine what type of outreach has the greatest appeal thus producing the desired outreach outcomes. Staying abreast of current issues that impact individual minority veteran groups and providing assistance through outreach activities is also a key to targeted outreach.

Since many Native American veterans reside in rural areas on tribal lands, the use of a Tribal Veteran Representative (TVR) in planning outreach activities is highly recommended. A TVR can play a major role in determining the success of outreach efforts to this rural veteran population by serving as a liaison between veterans, state, local and federal organizations. These representatives are usually appointed and supported by tribal governments which means they are trusted by Native American veterans who live on tribal lands. TVRs are trained, by the Department of Veterans Affairs, to help veterans access VA benefits, assist with filing claims and gaining access to various VA services. More information regarding the TVR program can be found at: www.ruralhealth.va.gov/native/programs/tribal-veterans.asp. In addition to collaborating with TVRs, outreach campaigns can be planned and coordinated by tribal leaders who are interested in partnering with VA's Office of Tribal Government Relations.

Today, Hispanic veterans fear being deported and losing the ability to access VA services and benefits. Many of them assumed that they were automatically granted citizenship after serving on active duty and failed to apply for citizenship through the approved process. Future targeted outreach activities to Hispanic veterans and family members could include information packets on applying for citizenship or including representatives who can best provide assistance and address their concerns. Since family members are frequently the biggest advocate for minority veterans, language barriers can serve as a deterrent to receptiveness to attend organized outreach activities and events. This issue can easily be addressed by having a Spanish speaking interpreter onsite at outreach events and making certain that outreach brochures and materials are available in Spanish versions. It is so important to take all of these factors into consideration when planning targeted outreach strategies for minority veterans.

In conclusion, as the veteran population becomes more diverse, the need for targeted outreach becomes even greater. In conclusion, the success of targeted outreach programs depends on the ability to: identify the targeted minority veteran group, recognize cultural differences, prepare by planning in advance, consider transportation issues, have appropriate materials and adequate resources, and collaborate with community partners who share a common goal in reaching out to minority veterans. The purpose of targeted outreach to minority veterans is to inform them and increase their awareness level of VA services and benefits, thus increasing utilization of earned benefits.

REFERENCES

Minority Veterans Report: "Military Service History and VA Benefit Utilization Statistics." National Center for Veterans Analysis and Statistics, March 2017.
2016 Biennial Report to Congress Veteran Outreach Activities. U.S. Department of Veterans Affairs.

46. Homeless Women Veterans*

ALEXANDRA LOGSDON *and* KAYLA M. WILLIAMS

When asked where she is from, Tracey Staff answers, "everywhere, and nowhere." Following in her mother's footsteps, who served 15 years in the Army, Tracey enlisted in the U.S. Air Force before graduating high school. She served for six years but struggled to find a place for her and her son to call home after being discharged in 2002. She bounced from city to city, spending no more than a couple of years in each location. Finally, she landed in Houston and knew she wanted to stay, however she found it difficult to secure a job that offered the right combination of income and schedule for her lifestyle. Without steady employment, Tracey and her son found themselves living in low-rate motels and couch-surfing at friends' houses.

A woman's face may not be the image that springs to mind when someone mentions homeless veterans, but Tracey's story is similar to those of other female veterans who bravely served our country. For instance, Krystal Ridley grew up in New York City before joining the Army. After being discharged with a service-connected disability, Krystal and her four young children found themselves couch surfing at the houses of various family members.

Though it is often unrecognized in national discussions, these women are part of a proud legacy of military service: American women have fought in every conflict since the Revolutionary War, but their military participation was originally informal and later limited by law: not only were they barred from certain jobs and units, but women's enlistment was capped at 2 percent of the military until 1967. Their representation in the military increased to roughly 15 percent by the early 1990s, where it remains today. Accordingly, women made up a small fraction of the population of veterans through much of U.S. history. Women now make up about 9.5 percent of veterans, which will climb to 10.5 percent by 2020 and nearly 16 percent by 2040, making them one of the fastest growing subgroups of veterans (Aponte, 2017).

Compared to men veterans, women are younger (with a median age of 50, compared to a median age of 65 for men veterans), more ethnically diverse, less likely to be married, and more highly educated; compared to women who have never served, women veterans have higher median household incomes, and are less likely to live in poverty or have no health insurance ("Profile of Women Veterans," 2016). Differences between men and women veterans—and between women who have and have not served in the military— are also reflected in the homeless population.

---

*Published with permission of the authors.

Homeless Women Veterans

Historical Data. Women veterans are estimated to make up a relatively small, but growing, proportion of the homeless veteran population (Perl, 2015). The U.S. Department of Housing and Urban Development (HUD) began identifying veterans in its annual Point-in-Time count in 2009. Point-in-Time (PIT) Counts are unduplicated one-night estimates of both sheltered and unsheltered homeless populations. The one-night counts are conducted by Continuums of Care nationwide and occur during the last week in January of each year. Continuums of Care (CoC) are local planning bodies responsible for coordinating the full range of homelessness services in a geographic area, which may cover a city, county, metropolitan area, or an entire state. For PIT Count purposes, a veteran refers to any person who served on active duty in the armed forces of the United States. This includes Reserves and National Guard members who were called up to active duty (Henry, 2017).

In 2010, female veterans comprised eight percent (8 percent) or 5,926 of the 74,087 total homeless veterans. Between 2010 and 2017, the number of homeless female veterans has decreased by a total of forty percent (40 percent), though the numbers fluctuated year-to-year during this period (Abt Associates, Inc., 2010).

Data Trends. In 2017, there were a total of 215,709 women identified as homeless in the U.S. Department of Housing and Urban Development (HUD) Point-in-Time Count. Of these women, 3,571 were veterans. Of the homeless female veterans, 2,071 were sheltered and 1,500 were unsheltered. Female veterans represent 8.9 percent of the 40,056 total veterans identified in the 2017 Point-in-Time Count. Since 2016, the number of homeless veterans who were women increased by seven percent (7 percent) or 243 additional female veterans (Henry, 2017).

Risk and Protective Factors. Research indicates that characteristics associated with homelessness among women veterans include "sexual assault during military service, being unemployed, being disabled, having worse overall health," and certain mental health conditions; protective factors were having graduated college or being married (Washington, 2010). Women veterans are more likely to have experienced many of those risk factors than civilian women and/or male veterans. Before, during, and after their military service, women veterans may be more likely to have faced certain challenges than men. Adverse Childhood Experiences (ACEs) are known to have an impact on lifelong outcomes; women with military backgrounds are more likely to have experienced the Adverse Childhood Experiences of physical abuse, household alcohol abuse, exposure to domestic violence, and emotional abuse than nonmilitary women (Blosnich, 2014).

While serving, women are more likely than men to experience military sexual harassment and assault, collectively referred to as Military Sexual Trauma (MST); in addition, women veterans who were sexually assaulted are significantly more likely to develop post-traumatic stress disorder (PTSD) and substance abuse disorders (Hamilton, 2015; Hyun, 2009). Intimate partner violence (including psychological, physical, or sexual violence from a current or former intimate partner; IPV) is also a major contributor to housing instability among women in general, and women veterans in particular (Hamilton, 2011). Overall, women are also more likely to experience wage disparities, domestic violence, and gender discrimination. Women veterans are, however, more likely to have graduated from college than either civilian women or male veterans.

Unmet Needs. Since its launch in 1994, the Department of Veterans Affairs has administered Project CHALENG (Community Homelessness Assessment, Local Education, and Networking Groups) each year to bring together homeless providers, advocates, veterans, and other concerned citizens to identify the needs of homeless veterans. Project CHALENG has two components: A CHALENG survey, in which participants rate the needs of homeless veterans in their local communities, and CHALENG meetings, which encourage partnership development between VA and community service providers ("Community Homelessness Assessment, Local Education and Networking Groups", 2017).

In 2016, 5,280 individuals completed a CHALENG Participant survey. This included 3,191 homeless veterans and 2,089 non-homeless veterans (VA staff, state and public officials, community leaders, volunteers). Twelve percent (12 percent) of the homeless veteran survey participants were women. Over fifty percent (50 percent) of the female veterans surveyed were between the ages of 45 and 60, and eight-four percent (84 percent) were of non–Hispanic/non–Latino decent. At the time of the survey, thirty-two percent (32 percent) of the women surveyed were living in permanent subsidized housing, such as HUD–VASH, and twenty-five percent (25 percent) were literally homeless.

The Top Ten Highest Unmet Needs of Female Veterans Surveyed were as follows (in order descending from highest unmet need): Registered Sex Offender Housing, Child Care, Family Reconciliation Assistance, Dental Care, Credit Counseling, Financial Guardianship, Legal Assistance for Child Support Issues, Legal Assistance to Prevent Eviction and Foreclosure, Legal Assistance to Help Restore a Driver's License, and Discharge Upgrade. The Top Ten Highest Met Needs of Female Veterans Surveyed were as follows (in order descending from highest met need): Medical Services, TB testing and Treatment, Case Management, HIV/AIDS Testing and Treatment, Food, Services for Emotional or Psychiatric Problems, Hepatitis C Testing and Treatment, Clothing, Substance Abuse Treatment, and Medication Management.

VA Progress

VA Homeless Programs. The VA takes a three-pronged approach to ending veteran homelessness: (1) Conducting coordinated outreach to proactively seek out veterans in need of assistance; (2) Connecting homeless and at-risk veterans with housing solutions, health care, community employment services, and other required supports; and (3) Collaborating with federal, state, and local agencies, housing providers, faith-based and community nonprofits, and others to expand employment and affordable housing options for veterans exiting homelessness. The VA provides key health care, housing assistance, mental health, and employment/job training resources for homeless and at-risk veterans ("Homeless Veterans," 2018). Through coordinated efforts, a growing list of 57 communities, including the entire states of Connecticut, Delaware, and Virginia, have effectively ended veteran homelessness as of the end of 2017, while also building and sustaining systems that can effectively and efficiently address veterans' housing crises in the future ("Ending Veteran Homelessness," 2017).

VA Services for Women Veterans. HA now provides health care to over 500,000 women veterans at 151 medical centers and 985 outpatient clinics nationwide ("Women Veterans Health Care," 2018). VHA out-performs all other sectors of care in providing gender-specific care for women veterans, including cervical cancer and breast cancer screening rates. All VA Medical Centers (VAMCs) have at least one Dedicated Women's Health Provider (DWHP) since VA has trained over 3,000 providers in women's health and continues to train hundreds more annually. VA provides prenatal and preconception care, maternity care services, and seven days of newborn care for women veterans, all managed by dedicated Maternity Care Coordinators. To continually improve our ability to provide high-quality evidence-based, culturally competent mental health care to women, VA held a National Women's Mental Health Mini-Residency at which approximately 200 participants from across the country were trained on gender-specific aspects of psychotherapies and psychiatric medications, trauma, integrating peer counselors, and more (Williams, 2016). VA provides all care related to military sexual trauma (MST) free of charge; all veterans are screened and each VAMC has an MST Coordinator. VBA benefits can be a vital part of veterans' economic stability, and outreach efforts to women veterans have worked: women veterans now access disability compensation at rates equal to men, and utilize other benefits at equal or higher rates. Over 26,000 women have accessed their Post–9/11 GI Bill education benefits so far, and women veterans graduate at higher rates than all other groups. In FY15, nearly 66,000 women veterans (10 percent of Veterans served) were guaranteed home loans totaling $16 billion.

Partnerships. Though their paths to permanent housing may have diverged, both Tracey and Krystal relied on vital resources from the Department of Veterans Affairs and other community and government partners to secure stability for their families. Tracey's path to success started with a referral to a VA community partner that helps Veterans transition from service to civilian life. VA facilities nationwide rely on critical community and inter-governmental partnerships to fill in the gaps and provide wrap-around services where VA programs and resources fall short. Tracey became an active participant in her local Supportive Services for Veteran Families (SSVF) program. The SSVF program awards grants to private nonprofit organizations and consumer cooperatives who provide a range supportive services to very low-income veterans and their families residing in or transitioning to permanent housing to promote housing stability. (Williams, 2016). SSVF offered Tracey employment services, referrals to housing, case management, and temporary financial assistance while she applied for VA benefits. Tracey gained a renewed sense of confidence and determination. Through SSVF, she found meaningful employment with a community partner to not only provide for her family, but to also support local veterans like herself. Most importantly, Tracey was able to secure permanent housing for her and her son.

Along with SSVF, VA maintains other important partnerships including programs such as HUD–VASH Program (U.S. Dept. of Housing & Urban Development—VA Supportive Housing), Grant and Per Diem (GPD) Program, Health Care for Homeless Veterans, Homeless Veteran Community Employment Services, Veteran Justice Outreach, and many more. The most heavily utilized of these programs is HUD–VASH. HUD–VASH is a partnership between the U.S. Department of Housing and Urban Development and VA Supportive Housing Program to provide permanent, supportive housing and treatment services for homeless veterans.

Krystal consulted with her local VA medical center in New York City to determine a path to permanent housing. Due to unavailability of child care, Krystal brought her kids along to her meeting with her case manager. Understanding the great need of putting this family in housing immediately, Krystal's case manager contacted the HUD–VASH coordinator at the facility. Coincidentally, a HUD–VASH voucher had just come available for Krystal and her kids. The case manager performed a warm hand-off to the HUD-VASH team who were able to secure a residence for the family within a few days of Krystal's initial meeting at the VA Medical Center. As of Sept. 30, 2015, HUD had allocated more than 78,000 vouchers to help house veterans across the country. The HUD-VASH Program is for the most vulnerable veterans, and provides special services for women veterans, those recently returning from combat zones, and veterans with disabilities.

References

Abt Associates, Inc. (2010). "Veteran Homelessness: A Supplemental Report to the 2010 Annual Homeless Assessment Report to Congress." Retrieved January 11, 2018, from https://www.va.gov/HOMELESS/docs/Center/AHAR_Veterans_Report_2010.pdf.

Aponte, M., Balfour, F., Garin, T., Glasgow, D., Lee, T., Thomas, E., & Williams, K. (2017, February). "Women Veterans Report: The Past, Present, and Future of Women Veterans." National Center for Veterans Analysis and Statistics, Department of Veterans Affairs, Washington, DC. Retrieved from https://www.va.gov/vetdata/docs/SpecialReports/Women_Veterans_2015_Final.pdf.

Blosnich, J., Dichter, M., Cerulli, C., Batten, S., & Bossarte, R. (2014). "Disparities in Adverse Childhood Experiences Among Individuals with a History of Military Service." *JAMA Psychiatry.* doi: 10.1001/jamapsychiatry.2014.724.

"Community Homelessness Assessment, Local Education and Networking Groups." (2017, June). Retrieved January 11, 2018, from https://www.va.gov/HOMELESS/docs/CHALENG-2016-factsheet-508-2017-07-29.pdf.

"Ending Veteran Homelessness." (2017, August 4). Retrieved January 11, 2018, from https://www.usich.gov/goals/veterans.

Hamilton, A. (2015, November 3). "Military Sexual Trauma: Prevalent and Under Treated." Retrieved January 11, 2018, from http://www.apa.org/news/press/releases/2015/11/military-sexual-trauma.aspx.

Hamilton A.V., Poza I., Washington D.L. (2011). "Homelessness and Trauma Go Hand-in-Hand: Pathways to Homelessness Among Women Veterans." *Women's Health Issues*, 21(4):S203-S209.

Henry, M., Watt, R., Rosenthal, L., & Shivji, A. (2017, December). "The 2017 Annual Homeless Assessment Report (AHAR) to Congress." Retrieved January 11, 2018, from https://www.hudexchange.info/resources/documents/2017-AHAR-Part-1.pdf.

"Homeless Veterans." (n.d.). Retrieved January 11, 2018, from https://www.va.gov/homeless/.

Hyun, J.K., Pavao, J., Kimerling, R. (2009). "Military Sexual Trauma." *PTSD Research Quarterly, 20* (2). Retrieved January 11, 2018, from http://www.ncdsv.org/images/NCPTSD_MilitarySexualTrauma_Spring2009.pdf.

Perl, L. (2015, November 6). "Veterans and Homelessness." Retrieved January 11, 2018, from https://fas.org/sgp/crs/misc/RL34024.pdf.

Profile of Women Veterans: 2015. (2016, December). Retrieved January 11, 2018, from https://www.va.gov/vetdata/docs/SpecialReports/Women_Veterans_Profile_12_22_2016.pdf.

"VA Programs to End Homelessness Among Women Veterans." (n.d.). Retrieved January 11, 2018, from https://www.va.gov/homeless/for_women_veterans.asp.

Washington, D.L., Yano, E.M., McGuire, J., Hine, V., Gelberg, L. (2010, February). "Risk Factors for Homelessness among Women Veterans." *Journal of Health Care for the Poor and Underserved, 21* (1): 82–91. doi: 10.1353/hpu.0.0237.

Williams, K. (2016, July 15). "VHA Mini-Residency Program Focuses on Providing Mental Health Services for Women Veterans." Retrieved January 11, 2018, from https://www.blogs.va.gov/VAntage/29140/.

Women Veterans Health Care. (n.d.). Retrieved January 11, 2018, from https://www.womenshealth.va.gov/WOMENSHEALTH/womenshealthservices/healthcare_about.asp.

47. Veteran, Minority, Woman and Homeless[*]

GINGER MILLER

My upbringing was simple. I grew up in Hempstead, New York, with my two brothers and one sister. Our parents were immigrants from Honduras, so my culture was different from most of my friends' and that always made me feel a little different, a little awkward. My mother and father were both proud Hondurans and they both spoke Spanish, but my mother didn't want to teach us Spanish for fear of us getting confused in school. Things were a lot different during the '70s for bilingual students, and she didn't want us to be singled out by teachers, or laughed at by the other kids.

I watched my parents do the best with what they had, which was not a lot, and no matter the situation they found themselves in, they always appreciated the smaller things in life. If we had breakfast for dinner it was not frowned upon because it was food and at least we had something to eat and a roof over our heads. I remember my mother getting used clothes from one of our neighbors who would get clothes from a wealthy client, and while most people would frown upon used clothes, I was simply grateful. It was times like this that instilled lessons in my heart that would carry me through some of the worst times in my life.

When it came time for me to go to college, I would have been the first one in my immediate family to attend and I was excited. Initially I had dreams of attending the Katherine Gibbs Secretarial School on Long Island, New York, and then I decided that I wanted to be a flashy accountant on Wall Street, but all of that was just a dream. Unfortunately for me, my parents did not have money for me to go to college, and that's when I made the decision to go into the Navy to get the GI Bill so that I could have the money to pay for college.

That was an exciting time for me. Here I was, a young girl about to see the world and embark on an entirely different life. I was both excited, but afraid at the same time. I was about to leave the only world I had ever known. It wasn't filled with lots of money, status, or luxury, but it was mine. It's where I felt safe. It's what I called home and it belonged to me.

But because I was always a dreamer, I knew that I had to go. I had to go because of the experiences that I would have. I also had to do it for my mom and dad who sacrificed

*Published with permission of the author.

so much for me and my siblings to have a better life. I knew that even though I was a little scared, I had what it took deep down inside of me to do the job.

In life you never know what's going to happen. You set out to do one thing and everything else happens besides that one thing. I had no idea what would be waiting for me, but I knew that I always wanted to see the world and enjoy my life, never get married and probably never have kids. But when I got to my first duty station in Annapolis, Maryland, all that wishful thinking went right out of the window. I met and fell in love with a young lance corporal. We got married after dating for six months of courtship, and shortly after were shipped off to Camp Lejeune, North Carolina.

While at Camp Lejeune, I was stationed with a Navy boat crew and my husband was stationed with a Marine Corps expeditionary unit that deployed often. My husband's unit served in Operation Sharp Edge and Operation Desert Storm.

When he came back off his last deployment he was different. He was quieter, drank more than usually and he was somewhat explosive. I didn't think much of it and I just thought it was a little stress. Boy, was I wrong.

After serving five years in the Marine Corps, my husband got out and I planned to stay in the Navy for twenty years. That plan derailed when I got a medical discharge in 1992 due to injuries from the car accident and two boat accidents I had while on duty. All the accidents left me with physical pain and a decrease in my physical abilities. I had a broken back and suffered from severe migraines. I was hurt that my dream of serving in the military had now taken a cruel turn. It seemed like for every step forward, there were three steps backwards. I was pregnant with our first son, and I had no idea what we were going to do next, but I knew we had to think fast.

When you're living the military life, it's different from the civilian life. While being enlisted in the military the government makes sure all your needs, housing, shelter and healthcare are taken care of. I was being faced with having to leave this security blanket behind, and now having to take care of these things with a baby on the way. My only skill set was driving boats. How were we going to do this?

We decided to put our furniture in storage and went to stay with my family in New York for one year until we could move to Pennsylvania where my husband had secured a job at a correctional facility that was being built.

Everything was planned out nicely. So we thought. It may not have been a big deal to most, but that job in Pennsylvania that we were depending on didn't happen. They canceled his assignment due to lack of funding and my husband's PTSD kicked into high gear, because we had a lot riding on that job.

My husband's mood swings came more and more and would elevate beyond my understanding. It was always like sitting on a firecracker, and never knowing when it would explode. I did everything I could to try and keep him calm. I would reassure him that we would be ok. Even when I wasn't sure, I knew that I couldn't make things worse by being upset with him for yelling at me. I knew what he was dealing with was real. Maybe because I was in the military as well, I have seen the effects of others with this diagnosis. If you are not faced with this, you can't fully understand what people are going through. It's like suffering inside of your very own skin, and you can't get out.

When I tried to get him help from the local veteran and VSO support groups it wouldn't last long. My husband could not relate to the support group because most of the members were not his age and were mostly Vietnam veterans, so my husband stopped going and his PTSD just seemed to escalate.

I don't come from a military town or a military family so my family we were staying with in New York could not comprehend nor sympathize with what my husband was going through. The mood swings, anxiety, depression were just too much, and they told us that we had to find someplace else to stay.

Where do you go with no formal training and an associate's degree, a husband suffering from PTSD and a toddler? I was afraid to ask for help and we ultimately became homeless. My world as I had known it and the one that I imagined were all gone in the blink of an eye! I served my country, got a medical discharge, never had time to prepare for the civilian world, and like a lot of veterans we went back home to stay with family and it didn't work out according to plan.

Every ounce of pride and patriotism had left my body! How could this be happening? I felt alone and too ashamed and even if I knew where to reach out to for help, there was no way I could bring the words "I'm a homeless veteran" out of the pit of my stomach through my mouth. Unfortunately, in the early '90s there were not any major efforts under way to support younger veterans, homeless veterans or women veterans and the outreach to our population was almost nonexistence.

I packed my family up along with my pride and jumped into a world that no person who has served their country should ever have to experience, a world of uncertainty, darkness, desperation and despair. I felt isolated, scared, depressed, anxious, alone, confused and desperate but I thank God that my will to survive was strong enough to override all those emotions!

There were times when we had to sleep in our car or make a choice to eat little and stay in a hotel. I thought to myself, You are still the same Ginger Miller with drive, hopes and ambitions with a few major setbacks, and rather than succumbing to my situation, I decided to take matters into my own hands.

It was exhausting hiding that secret from everyone. There were so many times I just wanted to scream out to my friends and my family and tell them that I needed help. So many times, I wanted to share it with my counselor, but I was too afraid of how she and everyone else would look at me. I was embarrassed, and I felt like a failure as if I had let everyone down. They all believed that I was living the American Dream, but I was living the American Nightmare.

I worked three jobs and went to school full time to pull us out of our homeless state. As an unskilled worker, I had to take whatever jobs would bring in money to support my family and I worked during peak hours as a bank teller, as a nighttime cashier at a gas station and a work study job at the university I attended.

It wasn't easy at all. I remember going from house to house, hotels, our car, and when I think about it sometimes it just leaves me speechless. When you're living in that type of fear, you are on heightened alert all the time. But I had to just keep going anyway so that we could eventually do better and get our own place. I often look back and think to myself, how did we ever make it out of hell alive and intact as a family?

I was in a confused state: My God, I just must survive, and then I looked at our son every night, and would think, okay, he doesn't deserve this, this is not why you brought him into this world. And then I would look at my husband and think, okay he really can't help because he's off the charts right now. I remember thinking to myself, okay Ginger Miller, either you take control of the ship, or you're going to go down with it.

As a woman veteran who was previously homeless, I consider myself to be one of the lucky ones because I made an incredible comeback and I am grateful to God!

I was homeless in the early '90s and here we are well into the twenty-first century and women veterans are the fastest growing segment of the homeless population and this should not be! Homelessness should never be an option and can be prevented with proper outreach, training, education and resources. Anyone who served their country should never ever become homeless and it is because of my experience with homelessness that I have dedicated my life's work to serving and supporting women veterans.

48. After Sexual Trauma, Soldiers Search for Better Care, Peace[*]

CAITLIN CRUZ *and* ASHA ANCHAN

At least one in five female veterans of the wars in Iraq and Afghanistan has screened positive for military sexual trauma (MST) once back home, Department of Veterans Affairs records show. And this may understate the crisis, experts say, because this number only counts women who go to the VA for help.

Young female veterans—those returning from the wars in Iraq and Afghanistan—often don't show up for their first VA appointments, if they show up at all, said Ann LeFevre, MST coordinator at the VA Palo Alto Health Care System in California. "They think they're alone and they don't want to talk about it," LeFevre said. "Especially with new returners, it takes a lot to get them on the VA campus. It can remind them of their base where the assault occurred."

The assault itself defies the discipline and values of the armed forces, but the problem is exacerbated, experts say, when victims report an assault and their allegations are met with skepticism and possible retaliation.

Even after their military service is over, many sexual assault victims are reluctant to approach the VA, a system intertwined with the military and perceived at times as prescribing drugs instead of meeting their treatment needs.

"There's a disconnect between what survivors believe they need and the educated treatment community as to what is necessary and helpful," said Mylea Charvat, a fellow in clinical neuroscience with the Stanford School of Medicine.

Charvat, who worked in the VA system for about 10 years, starting shortly after 9/11, described the department as "slow to respond" to the broad needs of women. "Historically, it's not a highly responsive system. It's huge, it's bureaucratic," she said. "I can understand women being hesitant to seek care, and frankly, a lot of men, too."

In 2012, the Department of Defense's Sexual Assault Prevention and Response Office estimated that 26,000 cases of "unwanted sexual contact" occurred. Of these, only about 13 percent of service members reported their assault.

Now, Charvat is working to develop a new model for effectively treating military

*Originally published as Caitlin Cruz and Asha Anchan, "After Sexual Trauma, Soldiers Search for Better Care, Peace," *Kaiser Health News*, October 30, 2013. News21 Fellow Mary Shinn contributed to this article.

sexual trauma and the resulting post-traumatic stress disorder with the Artemis Rising Invisible War Recovery Program, a treatment program inspired by the documentary *The Invisible War.*

"We need to attack this on a multi-faceted approach," she said. "It's a complex problem."

The burden of the problem falls on the Department of Defense—which consistently states it has a zero-tolerance policy for sexual assault—and on the VA—which has been charged since 1992 with addressing the failures of that policy. In 2010, the VA spent $872 million on sexual-assault-related health care, records show.

But many veterans feel lost in the void between these two large bureaucracies.

Women like Jessie de Leon and Corey Barrows are veterans who feel the military failed them—not only because the assaults occurred, but also because of what they consider inadequate responses once they returned from their deployments. As a result, they sought their own means of treatment.

"For a while it's just like I was numb to the world. Just fake happiness, drug-induced happiness," said de Leon, who was raped while serving as an Army medic in Bamberg, Germany, from 2007 to 2009. "I didn't realize that this process was going to be more hindering to me in trying to recover from it than it was helping me."

As a medic, she examined soldiers and their families at the health clinic in Germany and prepared soldiers to be deployed to Iraq and Afghanistan. She also comforted families who lost soldiers in the war.

But back home in Florida, de Leon found no comfort with therapists at the West Palm Beach VA. They didn't seem to understand the impact of her rape. Their recommended treatment consisted of prescription drugs for sleeping, anxiety and depression.

Harvard psychologist Paula Caplan has talked with hundreds of veterans, many of whom told her the VA pushed prescription drugs instead of examining the impact of the assaults.

"Women already, so often, feel that they don't belong in the military, either they're not wanted or they have to prove to other people or themselves that they deserve to be there," Caplan said. "When you are traumatized and you're devastated … then you think, 'But I have military training, I'm supposed to be tough, I'm supposed to be resilient.'"

De Leon had a young son, she was going to nursing school and she decided to leave the VA. Eventually, de Leon ended up at Healing Horse Therapy Center with other female veterans, located in Loxahatchee, Fla., 15 minutes from her home.

"No one was forcing you to talk, nobody was saying you had to do anything," de Leon said of the therapy center. "I didn't realize you could gain so much confidence, gain so much self-motivation, get back your self-esteem, just by working with a horse, who never said a word to you."

In October, she will graduate from nursing school and she and her 5-year-old son will move to North Carolina to be with her fiancé.

"From going through years of a lot of people not caring about what you went through and how you felt about things, and to finally come to a place where you felt safe, it was, it was very wonderful," she said. "It validates your pain."

The VA defines military sexual trauma, or MST, as the "psychological trauma, which in the judgment of a VA mental health professional, resulted from a physical assault of a sexual nature, battery of a sexual nature, or sexual harassment which occurred while the veteran was serving on active duty or active duty for training."

Veterans can seek a disability compensation rating for MST and the related effects. According to the VA, the necessary documentation has been reduced. Despite this, Amanda Schroeder, a union president for employees of the Veterans Benefits Administration in Portland, Ore., said MST claims are complicated and time-consuming to complete because many people do not report their assault.

"Men and women alike are already completely disabused, disempowered and often completely disenfranchised by the time they get to us and so a lot of times the sexual trauma cases take a lot of time because we have to seek so much additional evidence and it's not all maintained in one place," Schroeder said.

Because of this, Rep. Chellie Pingree, D–Maine, introduced the 2013 Ruth Moore Act, which aims to make it easier for service members to receive benefits for military-related sexual assaults.

"Most people are just shocked to think that we would ask someone to serve in the military and they would be more likely to be sexually assaulted than blown up by an IED (improvised explosive device)," she said. Her bill passed the House but never passed the Senate.

In January, Army Gen. Martin Dempsey, the chairman of the Joint Chiefs of Staff, said he believes sexual assault and harassment continue "because we've had separate classes of military personnel." Identifying men as "warriors" and women as "something else" breeds an environment that can lead to sexual crimes, he said.

A 2013 Institute of Medicine report found a link between MST and long-term poor mental and physical health. Moreover, the Independent Budget, a policy evaluation created by various veteran service organizations about, but independent of, the VA, found that women with MST had a 59 percent higher risk for mental health problems.

Common conditions linked to MST range from PTSD and anxiety to eating disorders, hypervigilance and insomnia. More specifically, LaFevre said the women she works with often show signs of stomach problems, experience weight gain—"They don't want to get attention from men in any way, so they emotionally eat"—and have a hard time maintaining a job, leading to homelessness. The Independent Budget reported that of homeless female veterans using VA health care, 39 percent screened positive for MST.

These side effects remain wide-ranging and lifelong and the resources for treatment vary across the country.

"The assault itself is very traumatizing," said Jennifer Norris, an advocate with the Military Rape Crisis Center who was assaulted while serving with the Air Force and Air National Guard. "That trauma, you're going to have it no matter what, for the rest of your life."

Marine Corps veteran Corey Barrows was raped by a fellow service member while off-post in September 2006, near Marine Corps Air Station Cherry Point, N.C. When she reported her assault, her master sergeant told her she must have been too drunk—even though she doesn't drink. "Nobody believed me," she said.

She deployed in July 2007 to Iraq, where she was coping with her trauma—until her old unit, which included friends of her attacker, deployed to the same installation. Barrows, unable to manage the stress, took a handful of Percocet in an attempt to kill herself.

"We talk so much about unit cohesion being critically important in the military, just how well people work together when they're serving, and it's hard to imagine that anything does more damage to that than a sexual assault within a unit," said Pingree, the congresswoman from Maine. "It's not good policy to let it happen."

Barrows was honorably discharged in November 2008. After enrolling in VA health care in early 2009, she was prescribed numerous medications for anxiety and depression. She then went to a civilian therapist because she had lost faith in the VA system. Her therapist suggested activities such as yoga and talking with other survivors to aid Barrows's recovery. Barrows now uses fewer medications.

After her husband was discharged from the Marine Corps, they moved to his hometown of Bozeman, Mont.

"It's just therapeutic out here. I'm out of the military bubble," she said. "I still have horrible anxiety, especially with crowds, but in Montana you tend to have less of that."

49. Years After Silently Combating Sexual Trauma, Female Veterans Seek Help*

ANNA CASEY

Sheila Procella joined the Air Force in 1974 to "see the Earth," she said. She enlisted at the tail end of the Vietnam War, shortly after graduating from high school. Although she never left her home state of Texas during eight years of service, her office job proved to be its own battlefield.

"Some of us actually went to war, some of us had war right here in the States, going to work every day knowing we are going to be harassed," said Procella, now 62 and living in Plano, Texas.

At the time, fewer than 3 percent of service members were women. Procella recalled the daily barrage of sexual comments, gestures and men grabbing her inappropriately. And one of her superiors made it clear that her hopes of moving up the career ladder were dependent on having sex with him. "He was kind of discreet about the way he put it, but his one advance and my one acceptance of his advance led to my promotion," Procella said.

At the time, Procella, who served in the Air Force until 1979 and then went on to the Texas Air National Guard until 1982, accepted the common belief that reporting the incidents would be bad for her career. "It definitely wasn't talked about, you definitely did not report your superiors for any kind of harassment," she explained. "At the time that it happens you sweep it away like you're going to be OK."

But it wasn't OK, and after her military career, Procella found herself dependent on alcohol and drugs to cope.

Eventually, she came to associate her deep depression, anxiety and panic attacks with the harassment and assaults during her military service. Procella, who had also experienced childhood sexual abuse, was diagnosed with military sexual trauma and post-traumatic stress disorder (PTSD) in 2014, nearly three decades after her service. Today she has a 70 percent disability rating from the Department of Veterans Affairs.

---

*Originally published as Anna Casey, "Years After Silently Combating Sexual Trauma, Female Veterans Seek Help," *Kaiser Health News*, September 29, 2017. KHN's coverage of women's health care issues is supported in part by the David and Lucile Packard Foundation.

There are many others like Procella, who served decades ago, but are just coming to terms with their experience.

Midlife Awareness

A 2015 study published by the American Psychological Association asked 327 female veterans in Southern California about their experiences with sexual trauma. They divided the respondents into two groups—those who served before the terrorist attack on Sept. 11, 2001, and those in uniform afterward. Nearly half of those in the earlier group reported sexual contact against their will during their military service. In the later group, reports of unwanted sexual contact dropped to 30 percent.

A majority of those who reported sexual abuse met the criteria for a PTSD diagnosis, the researchers said.

And a study published last year in the journal Women's Health Issues found that women ages 45 to 54 reported more sexual harassment and assault while in the military than other age groups.

"I was struck by the idea that it wasn't just younger women," said Carolyn Gibson, a women's health research fellow at the San Francisco VA Medical Center and co-author of that study.

The research also found that the association between sexual trauma and its negative effects on health—such as cardiovascular disease, substance abuse and other physical and mental illnesses—was most pronounced among female veterans ages 45 to 64.

Gibson said these effects may be exacerbated among women in midlife because there was less awareness around the issue when they were in uniform and they felt compelled to bear the stress alone.

Midlife is also a time of great change for women, Gibson explained, both physically and emotionally, which could lead them to come forward about sexual trauma after their service ended.

"As people go through periods of transition, then those symptoms tend to pick up a lot more," she said. More of the veterans who are younger now, she added, may go public about their struggles with sexual trauma when they enter this phase of life 10 to 15 years down the road.

Battle for Recognition

The Veterans Health Administration coined the term "military sexual trauma" in 2004, and today about 25 percent of women and 1.5 percent of men who use VA health services have the diagnosis, according to the VA. The symptoms are closely associated with PTSD and put individuals at an increased risk for other mental health conditions, including anxiety, depression and eating disorders.

But getting a disability claim based on military sexual trauma can be a long and complicated battle. A 2014 Government Accountability Office report found that disability claims related to sexual trauma during military service used to be far less likely to be approved than PTSD claims from other sources. In 2010, 46 percent of all claims related to non-sexual trauma were approved by the Veterans Benefits Administration, while 28 percent of those related to military sexual trauma were, GAO said. By 2013, half of the sexual abuse claims and 55 percent of PTSD claims were approved.

The GAO and veterans groups say the increase came after the VA mandated training on military sexual trauma for employees processing claims at regional centers and for health professionals providing the veterans' evaluations.

The VA has added resources specifically for women in recent years, even separate entrances for women at some counseling facilities. Still, it's a challenge to get women through the door to receive help. According to a 2015 VA report on barriers to women's health care, only 19 percent of female veterans used VA services.

"During the Vietnam era, a lot of veterans who came back had a hard time getting into the VA, especially women—they were put off by the VA for several years," said Pam Maercklein, who coordinates women's health care for the Texas Veterans Commission and is an Air Force veteran. "Now the VA, especially here in Texas, is doing a fairly good job of gender-specific treatment."

Anna Baker, the manager of the commission's women's program, said women who are now middle-aged were forgotten when it came to treatment for sexual trauma at the time of their service and afterward.

"We've had several nurses who served in Vietnam who are just now coming out, who are saying that for so many years they just suppressed it," Baker said, "and they're just now starting to have those conversations and deal with those issues that are causing them anguish."

While there's a tendency to associate PTSD with military combat, a 2015 study published in JAMA Psychiatry found that women who served in Vietnam had increased odds of PTSD. The effect, the report found, "appears to be associated with wartime exposures, especially sexual discrimination or harassment and job performance pressures."

Delia Esparza, a psychiatric mental health nurse with the Vet Center in Austin, Texas, has been helping veterans—women and men—deal with sexual trauma for more than 22 years.

The Austin Vet Center is one of 300 community facilities across the country that provide veterans (and family members) with free individual and group counseling, in addition to other readjustment services.

Esparza said that even with increased attention to military sexual trauma, many of the problems that Procella and other veterans experienced persist. Among them: Women especially feel stigmatized for speaking out.

She recalled that when she first started practicing she had a female client who was a veteran from World War II.

"She was very troubled by this whole thing," Esparza said of the veteran, who was then in her 70s, "and when she talked about it she became very tearful.

"It stays with you."

50. African American GIs of World War II: Fighting for Democracy Abroad and at Home*

MARIA HÖHN

Until the 21st century, the contributions of African American soldiers in World War II barely registered in America's collective memory of that war.

The "tan soldiers," as the black press affectionately called them, were also for the most part left out of the triumphant narrative of America's "Greatest Generation." In order to tell their story of helping defeat Nazi Germany in my 2010 book, *Breath of Freedom*, I had to conduct research in more than 40 different archives in the U.S. and Germany.

When a German TV production company, together with Smithsonian TV, turned that book into a documentary, the filmmakers searched U.S. media and military archives for two years for footage of black GIs in the final push into Germany and during the occupation of post-war Germany.

They watched hundreds of hours of film and discovered less than 10 minutes of footage. This despite the fact that among the 16 million U.S. soldiers who fought in World War II, there were about one million African American soldiers.

They fought in the Pacific, and they were part of the victorious army that liberated Europe from Nazi rule. Black soldiers were also part of the U.S. Army of occupation in Germany after the war. Still serving in strictly segregated units, they were sent to democratize the Germans and expunge all forms of racism.

It was that experience that convinced many of these veterans to continue their struggle for equality when they returned home to the U.S. They were to become the foot soldiers of the civil rights movement—a movement that changed the face of our nation and inspired millions of repressed people across the globe.

As a scholar of German history and of the more than 70-year U.S. military presence in Germany, I have marveled at the men and women of that generation. They were willing to fight for democracy abroad, while being denied democratic rights at home in the U.S. Because of their belief in America's "democratic promise" and their sacrifices on behalf

---

*Originally published as Maria Höhn, "African American GIs of WWII: Fighting for Democracy Abroad and at Home," *The Conversation*, February 9, 2017. Reprinted with permission of the publisher.

of those ideals, I was born into a free and democratic West Germany, just 10 years after that horrific war.

Fighting Racism at Home and Abroad

By deploying troops abroad as warriors for and emissaries of American democracy, the military literally exported the African American freedom struggle.

Beginning in 1933, when Adolf Hitler came to power, African American activists and the black press used white America's condemnation of Nazi racism to expose and indict the abuses of Jim Crow at home. America's entry into the war and the struggle against Nazi Germany allowed civil rights activists to significantly step up their rhetoric.

Believing that fighting for American democracy abroad would finally grant African-Americans full citizenship at home, civil rights activists put pressure on the U.S. government to allow African American soldiers to "fight like men," side by side with white troops.

The military brass, disproportionately dominated by white Southern officers, refused. They argued that such a step would undermine military efficiency and negatively impact the morale of white soldiers. In an integrated military, black officers or NCOs might also end up commanding white troops. Such a challenge to the Jim Crow racial order based on white supremacy was seen as unacceptable.

The manpower of black soldiers was needed in order to win the war, but the military brass got its way; America's Jim Crow order was to be upheld. African-Americans were allowed to train as pilots in the segregated Tuskegee Airmen. The 92nd Buffalo Soldiers and 93rd Blue Helmets all-black divisions were activated and sent abroad under the command of white officers.

Despite these concessions, 90 percent of black troops were forced to serve in labor and supply units, rather than the more prestigious combat units. Except for a few short weeks during the Battle of the Bulge in the winter of 1944 when commanders were desperate for manpower, all U.S. soldiers served in strictly segregated units. Even the blood banks were segregated.

"A Breath of Freedom"

After the defeat of the Nazi regime, an Army manual instructed U.S. occupation soldiers that America was the "living denial of Hitler's absurd theories of a superior race," and that it was up to them to teach the Germans "that the whole concept of superiority and intolerance of others is evil." There was an obvious, deep gulf between this soaring rhetoric of democracy and racial harmony, and the stark reality of the Jim Crow army of occupation. It was also not lost on the black soldiers.

Post-Nazi Germany was hardly a country free of racism. But for the black soldiers, it was their first experience of a society without a formal Jim Crow color line. Their uniform identified them as victorious warriors and as Americans, rather than "Negroes."

Serving in labor and supply units, they had access to all the goods and provisions starving Germans living in the ruins of their country yearned for. African American cultural expressions such as jazz, defamed and banned by the Nazis, were another reason so many Germans were drawn to their black liberators. White America was stunned to see how much black GIs enjoyed their time abroad, and how much they dreaded their return home to the U.S.

By 1947, when the Cold War was heating up, the reality of the segregated Jim Crow Army in Germany was becoming a major embarrassment for the U.S. government. The Soviet Union and East German communist propaganda relentlessly attacked the U.S. and challenged its claim to be the leader of the "free world." Again and again, they would point to the segregated military in West Germany, and to Jim Crow segregation in the U.S. to make their case.

Coming "Home"

Newly returned veterans, civil rights advocates and the black press took advantage of that Cold War constellation. They evoked America's mission of democracy in Germany to push for change at home. Responding to that pressure, the first institution of the U.S. to integrate was the U.S. military, made possible by Truman's 1948 Executive Order 9981. That monumental step, in turn, paved the way for the 1954 Supreme Court decision in *Brown v. Board of Education.*

The veterans who had been abroad electrified and energized the larger struggle to make America live up to its promise of democracy and justice. They joined the NAACP in record numbers and founded new chapters of that organization in the South, despite a wave of violence against returning veterans. The veterans of World War II and the Korean War became the foot soldiers of the civil rights movement in the 1950s and 1960s. Medgar Evers, Amzie Moore, Hosea Williams and Aaron Henry are some of the better-known names, but countless others helped advance the struggle.

About one-third of the leaders in the civil rights movement were veterans of World War II.

They fought for a better America in the streets of the South, at their workplaces in the North, as leaders in the NAACP, as plaintiffs before the Supreme Court and also within the U.S. military to make it a more inclusive institution. They were also the men of the hour at the 1963 March on Washington, when their military training and expertise was crucial to ensure that the day would not be marred by agitators opposed to civil rights.

"We structured the March on Washington like an army formation," recalled veteran Joe Hairston.

For these veterans, the 2009 and 2013 inaugurations of President Barack Obama were triumphant moments in their long struggle for a better America and a more just world. Many never thought they would live to see the day that an African American would lead their country.

To learn more about the contributions of African American GIs, visit "The Civil Rights Struggle, African-American GIs, and Germany" digital archive.

51. Dallas and Baton Rouge Shooters: A Reminder of the Troubled History of Black Veterans in America*

CHAD WILLIAMS

The shooting deaths of eight police officers in two separate incidents in 2016 shocked the nation and left us searching for answers.

One Sunday morning, Gavin Long engaged in a shootout with police in Baton Rouge that left three officers dead and three injured. Long was also killed.

Just 10 days earlier, on the night of July 7, Micah Xavier Johnson drove to a Black Lives Matter protest in downtown Dallas, Texas, determined to kill white police officers. He killed five policemen and wounded seven others before he was killed after a long standoff with law enforcement.

While we may never fully know what caused Johnson and Long to commit such horrific crimes, the fact that they were both African Americans and served in the military has received significant attention.

Johnson has been variously described as "demented," a "disgrace" and filled with hatred. Initial reports suspect Long suffered from "paranoia" and "mental instability."

African Americans have a long and proud history of participation in the United States armed forces. Black soldiers have fought in every war from the American Revolution to the present. I have written about their important role in World War I. They are powerful symbols of black patriotism and respectability, and demonstrate how in spite of slavery, Jim Crow and institutionalized discrimination, African-Americans have been willing to fight for their country and die for its ideals.

Micah Johnson and Gavin Long violently disrupt this narrative. Their actions speak to a rarely acknowledged aspect of the history of African American veterans—one of injustice, disillusionment, trauma, racial militancy and undignified death. Johnson, Long and their troubled humanity remind us that the history of black servicemen and women has been fraught with tension.

---

*Originally published as Chad Williams, "Dallas and Baton Rouge Shooters: A Reminder of the Troubled History of Black Veterans in America," *The Conversation*, July 18, 2016. Reprinted with permission of the publisher.

The Meaning of Service

Johnson and Long were dedicated soldiers. Johnson's mother, Delphine Johnson, said that her son, like so many black servicemen before him, "loved his country" and wanted to protect it. Johnson served in the United States Army Reserves for six years, enlisting out of high school in 2009. He completed a tour of duty in Afghanistan with the 420th Engineer Brigade before receiving an honorable discharge in 2015.

Long was a former U.S. Marine who served for five years—including one year in Iraq as a data specialist. He achieved the rank of sergeant until his discharge in 2010. He received several awards during his time in the Marines, including a good conduct medal.

Like Long and Johnson, black men and women have joined the military for various reasons throughout American history. While love of country has been an important motivation, other factors such as the opportunity for freedom, the desire for adventure and the promise of gainful employment have also been meaningful. More than just patriotic symbols, black servicemen and women, like all individuals, possess complex identities that have shaped their military experiences.

Disillusionment and Trauma

These experiences have not always been positive.

According to his family, Johnson returned home from Afghanistan a different person. "The military was not what Micah thought it would be," Johnson's mother has stated, adding, "He was very disappointed, very disappointed." In her words, he became "a hermit" and resentful toward the government.

After his discharge, Long also seems to have become isolated and aggrieved. He divorced his wife, changed his name to "Cosmo Setepenra," accused the government of placing him under surveillance and in numerous online videos decried systematic racism against African Americans, including the July 5 police killing of Alton Sterling in Baton Rouge.

Johnson's mother said that "it may be that the ideal that he thought of our government, of what he thought the military represented, it just didn't live up to his expectation."

In the longer historical context of African Americans in the armed forces, Johnson would not be alone. For much of its history, the military has been a deeply racist institution. Black soldiers, having to endure often virulent discrimination and abuse, naturally questioned the value of risking their life for a nation that refused to respect both their American identity and basic humanity.

Studies have shown that black soldiers suffer from higher rates of Post-Traumatic Stress Disorder (PTSD) than their white counterparts. However, many black veterans suffer the added trauma of their disillusioning experiences in the armed forces and the cognitive dissonance between the ideals and reality of the United States, especially in regard to race. African American veterans have often questioned how they could fight for freedom and democracy abroad while still confronting racism at home.

It is fair to ask: How did serving in Iraq and Afghanistan, and then seeing videos of police killing unarmed black people, possibly affect Long and Johnson's respective psyches? Both men may not have served in combat, but they would not be immune from the psychological traumas of being black soldiers and the need to make sense of this conflicted identity at a time of heightened racial tensions.

Black Radicalism and the Specter of Violence

That Long and Johnson apparently exhibited a stronger sense of racial militancy following their discharge should not be surprising.

Black veterans constitute an important part of the history of black radicalism in the United States. While Long and Johnson appear to have had no formal affiliations and likely acted alone, examples abound of African American veterans participating in and leading militant organizations committed to black freedom and racial justice.

Following World War I, many disillusioned black veterans joined groups such as the African Blood Brotherhood and, most notably, Marcus Garvey's Universal Negro Improvement Association. Former soldiers played a significant role in the civil rights and black power movements of the 1960s. Ernest Thomas, a veteran of World War II, founded the Deacons of Defense that provided armed protection for southern civil rights activists. The Black Panther Party was cofounded by Bobby Seale, who served three years in the United States Air Force until he was dishonorably discharged for fighting.

The connection among African American veterans, black militancy and the specter of violence is also not new. Historical fears of radicalized black soldiers and veterans sparking racial conflict—especially in the South—and killing white people date back to the Reconstruction era and continued following World War I and World War II.

The Dallas and Baton Rouge shootings also invoke memories of more modern incidents. In 1973, a disgruntled black Navy veteran, Mark Essex, murdered nine people, including five police officers, in New Orleans. Essex's rampage ended when law enforcement trapped him on a hotel roof and filled his body with over 200 bullets. Micah Johnson met a similarly grisly fate when he was cornered by Dallas police in a parking garage and killed by a robot-delivered bomb.

Should we mourn for Micah Johnson and Gavin Long? Did their lives matter? Do their violent actions erase the meaning of their years of military service? Do we ignore their humanity?

The actions of Micah Johnson and Gavin Long are inexcusable. They do not represent the Black Lives Matter movement. They certainly do not represent the millions of black veterans, past and present, who served their country and as civilians have made valuable contributions to society.

But there is also no denying that Johnson and Long speak to a more unsettling historical reality, that for many black veterans the nation they swore to protect and defend has ultimately failed them by not sufficiently protecting and defending black people.

This makes them American tragedies.

52. Promises Made and Promises Broken

Joaquin Jay Gonzalez III

I witnessed an emotional encounter with an elderly veteran who had lived through so much: heavy enemy fire and labor camp as a prisoner of war in his early twenties, and now, in his seventies, he was coping with cancer alone and in a "foreign land." Yet, Idelfonso "Tatang Floro" Bagasala seemed undaunted by the many challenges he had been through. Smiling, he began his conversation with the audience, saying, "I feel blessed to be with you tonight." The 76-year-old Filipino American World War II veteran then proceeded to tell bittersweet life stories which, ironically, were highlighted not by his exploits on the battlefields of Luzon, but instead, the perilous streets of San Francisco's low-income Tenderloin and South of Market neighborhoods.

Tatang Floro told the audience how he earned a living shoulder-to-shoulder with homeless people, pimps, prostitutes, street entertainers, petty thieves, gang members, as well as drug dealers and users. As a former U.S. Commonwealth Army regular, Tatang Floro explained to the attentive crowd, "We were promised U.S. citizenship by General Douglas MacArthur for fighting under his USAFFE [U.S. Armed Forces of the Far East] command." After waiting more than 40 years to be naturalized at the U.S. Embassy in Manila, it became clear that he could no longer count on receiving the veterans' benefits promised to him years earlier. So the aging veteran left his wife, children, and grandchildren in the Philippines to come to the U.S. and earn money to support them. When he arrived in San Francisco, Tatang Floro had no income, so he supplemented his welfare checks doing odd jobs along downtown Market Street.

A few feet away from San Francisco's famous cable cars and trendy shops, he rented out chess tables. "After I was diagnosed with cancer at San Francisco General Hospital, I lay in the hospital begging for an interpreter," he said. The gray-haired Tatang Floro admitted that he did not even understand some of the questions on the forms he was asked to sign, since he barely knew how to read English and did not know how to write. A devout Christian, Tatang Floro credits the power of prayer for what he calls his "miraculous recovery." Having no relatives in the United States, he added that his strong faith in God is what keeps him going from day to day. Many in the dimly lit room became teary-eyed.

The account that Tatang Floro shared with his young audience that evening sums up the fate of many aging Filipino World War II veterans (also referred to as the *veteranos*, *manongs*, or elders), as well as their strong faith, which fosters the belief that with the help of the younger generation of Filipino migrants, their pleas would finally be answered in the halls of the U.S. Congress.

Making a Promise: Veterans' Rights and Benefits

Historically, the Filipino military units that would later be called "the Commonwealth Army of the Philippines" were started in the early 1900s at the same time that the United States assumed formal sovereignty over its prized colony. The Philippine Commonwealth Army was formally established through Philippine Commonwealth Act Number 1, approved by the U.S. Congress on December 1935. As commander-in-chief of the U.S. Armed Forces, President Franklin Delano Roosevelt issued the Presidential Order (6 Federal Register 3825) that required the Philippine Commonwealth Army to respond to the call to military service of a U.S. President (Meixsel 1995). In addition to these recruitment initiatives, the U.S. Army established many military bases throughout the colony's various islands. These included two of the largest outside of the continental United States—heavyweights Clark Air Base and Subic Naval Base—which gave America a formidable presence in the Asia-Pacific region.

On July 26, 1941, sensing a growing threat from Japan, President Roosevelt ordered the Commonwealth Army of the Philippines—then comprised of U.S. nationals—to serve under General Douglas MacArthur's United States Armed Forces of the Far East (USAFFE). At the time of the USAFFE's formation, the unit consisted of 22,532 troops; 11,972 of these were Philippine Scouts and 10,473 were members of the Philippine Division, which consisted of 2,552 Americans and 7,921 Filipinos. All of the division's enlisted men, with the exception of the 31st Infantry Regiment and various military police and headquarters troops, were Philippine Scouts.

Not long afterwards, imperial Japan began plotting takeovers of nations along the Pacific Rim, supposedly to construct a "Greater East Asia Co-Prosperity Sphere"—a group of self-sufficient Asian nations that were free of Western powers, and of course, led by the Japanese. One of the nations targeted was the Philippines; after all, the country was America's Pacific buffer and was only a couple of hours from Tokyo by plane. Hence, Japan made plans to cut off America's ties to its Asian outpost. The Japanese military launched a surprise air raid on the U.S. Navy's Fleet stationed at Pearl Harbor, Hawaii on December 7, 1941, and a subsequent air attack on the following day of key U.S. military targets in the Philippines. Having destroyed parts of Hawaii, Japanese air attacks were conducted against Davao, Baguio and Aparri on the same day in the Philippines, which were all places where American soldiers were stationed. The U.S. and its Asian commonwealth territory had no choice but to defend itself by entering the war against Japan.

President Roosevelt was in desperate need of men and women to serve in the United States military. Fighting a war on both the Asian and European fronts took its toll on the numbers of both active duty and reserve soldiers. To maintain effective air, land, and sea operations, the president and congressional leaders knew that the U.S. Army would need sustained troop replenishments urgently. Understandably, few wanted to enlist during wartime. Since the Philippines was not only an American colony but also under attack by Japan, President Roosevelt turned to Filipinos, who were then U.S. nationals, for help. The Commonwealth Government of the Philippines complied by drafting Filipino males between the ages of 21 and 50.

Taking the president's cue, the U.S. Congress passed the Second War Powers Act (1942), amending the Nationality Act of 1940. This new legislation essentially liberalized "naturalization requirements for alien servicemen in the United States armed forces outside the territory of the continental United States" and eliminated barriers to naturalization. The drafting of regular and non-traditional Filipino combatants into the U.S. Army helped America's war effort tremendously. Nevertheless, the U.S. lost control of the Philippines in April 1942.

The forced departure of General MacArthur from the Philippines, the surrender of the USAFFE forces to the Japanese Imperial Army in Corregidor, and the consequent Bataan Death March, in which 3,000 Americans and 10,000 Filipinos were killed, fueled the United States' resolve to continue fighting. Surviving Filipino soldiers retreated to the mountains and turned to warfare tactics they had used effectively decades earlier during the Philippine revolution and the Philippine-American War. Welcomed by MacArthur and the USAFFE command, Filipino and American soldiers formed guerrilla and underground units that sabotaged Japanese civil and military activities, hindering Japan's full administrative control of the Philippines. Ultimately, only 12 of 48 provinces fell to Japan's imperial flag. From 1942 to 1946, guerrilla and underground resistance units also passed on critical intelligence to the USAFFE chain of command. In return for their loyalty and gallantry, President Roosevelt and General MacArthur reiterated their promise of citizenship and veterans' benefits to Filipino soldiers fighting under the American flag. Many veterans have also recalled that U.S. government and military officials enticed them to serve by saying "Lay your lives on the line for the American ideals … and we will make you Americans." As U.S. nationals, the Filipino soldiers recruited in the Philippines—Old and New Philippine Scouts, Philippine Commonwealth Army regulars, and guerrillas—would never forget these promises. But would they ever be fulfilled?

Close to 100,000 Filipino civilians lost their lives during World War II. In September of 1945, Japan was convinced to surrender to the United States after U.S. Air Force planes dropped two atomic bombs on Hiroshima and Nagasaki. Japan's defeat was a proud moment for the U.S. and the Philippines. A month after Japan's surrender, Congress passed the Armed Forces Voluntary Recruitment Act of 1945 (Public Law 79–190), authorizing the recruitment of 50,000 "new" Philippine Scouts. These New Philippine Scouts served under the U.S. Army from October 6, 1945, to June 30, 1947. In gratitude for their heroism in the defense of America and the Philippines, President Roosevelt in a 1945 White House policy speech reiterated his promise that Filipino soldiers—i.e., Scouts, Commonwealth Army and guerrillas—would be granted U.S. citizenship and receive the same benefits as all other U.S. veterans. Roosevelt's policy pronouncement was received by General Omar Bradley, then Administrator of the U.S. Veterans Administration, who began preparing his VA staff to process the inflow of Filipinos as American veterans. After their wartime service, the Filipino World War II veterans waited.

Breaking the Promise: Truman and the Rescission Acts

As it turned out, those Filipino veterans would have to wait for a long time. The emotional fervor of the war and America's promise died with Roosevelt's death in April 1945. His vice president, Harry S. Truman, ascended to the presidency to complete the unfinished business of World War II. Germany and Japan were defeated. The year 1946 ushered in three major political events that would become embedded in the national histories of both the United States and Philippines. The first event occurred on July 4: the United States granted full independence to the Philippines after 40 years of colonial rule. Having helped save the Philippines on behalf of the United States, the Filipino World War II veterans anxiously anticipated their promised benefits and pensions. However, two succeeding events in Washington, D.C., would bring the veterans only disappointment and frustration.

Democratic President Truman, assisted by a Democratically controlled Senate and House, disregarded President Roosevelt's promise—but even worse, the Filipino veterans' patriotism and loyalty to America—by signing and executing two Rescission Acts, formally breaking America's promise to them. The initial blow was the First Supplemental Surplus Appropriation Rescission Act, or Public Law 79-301, which authorized a $200 million appropriation to the Commonwealth Army of the Philippines, with the provision that those soldiers be deemed to have never been in the U.S. military. Another blow was delivered through Public Law 79-391, the Second Supplemental Surplus Appropriation Rescission Act, enacted in May, which disenfranchised the Filipinos in the New Philippine Scouts of their U.S. military service. Those who fought in USAFFE guerrilla units were also disowned.

Therefore, only the "old" Philippine Scouts, the First and Second Filipino Infantry Regiments, and others who signed up directly with the Army in the United States were acknowledged as having fought for America in World War II. Ironically, before the passage of the 1946 Rescission Acts, Veterans Administration (VA) officials considered all Filipino military service to have met the statutory requirements for U.S. World War II veteran status. But in 1945, the VA was asked by President Truman to determine how much it cost to provide veterans' benefits to the Filipino soldiers. The VA study estimated that it would cost the U.S. $3.2 billion to award them continuing veterans' benefits. In effect, President Truman and Congress connived to craft legislation that would deny the Filipino World War II soldiers naturalization and privileges because the VA report conceded that these benefits would be very costly. Critics therefore contend that the promises to Filipino recruits of naturalization, benefits, and pensions were also disingenuous.

Fifty Years Later: Citizenship and Welfare Benefits

Congressional justifications for cutting back on Roosevelt's promise did not put a halt to the veterans' fight for justice. Many bilateral talks between the Philippine and the United States governments have involved the problematic Rescission Acts. The veterans took a step closer towards realizing their goal of naturalization in 1990. During that year, President George H. Bush enacted a critical second installment to Roosevelt's promise when he signed the Immigration and Naturalization Act of 1990, or Public Law 101-649. After 40 years of advocacy and litigation, "special provisions" on the naturalization of Filipino veterans were finally introduced by their Congressional sympathizers in this comprehensive immigration reform act. Specifically, Section 405 of the law granted U.S. citizenship to Filipino veterans who served honorably in an active duty status under the command of the USAFFE, or within the Philippine Commonwealth Army, the Philippine Scouts, or recognized Guerrilla Units at any time during the period beginning September 1, 1939, and ending December 31, 1946. Further amendments authorized the Immigration and Naturalization Service to naturalize eligible Filipino veterans at the U.S. Embassy in Manila.

This was definitely a gigantic step in the right direction for the veterans. However, there was still one large problem: although the veterans were allowed to become U.S. citizens, they still did not have the same benefits that U.S. veterans enjoyed. All in all, veterans who had been naturalized found themselves in a situation that was far different than they originally expected. That is, before immigrating, many viewed it as the land of opportunity and open doors. However, those same migrants often find later on that those impressions are not quite accurate. Since President George H. Bush passed the Immigration Act, about 28,000 veterans have moved to the United States from the Philippines and been naturalized. Most of them have settled in various parts of California, but many have also found homes in Hawaii, Nebraska, New Jersey, Illinois, Florida, Texas and New York. Many of these veterans were not able to bring their families with them because they simply could not afford the travel costs. Far from home and separated from their families, these men often suffer from depression, poverty and loneliness. Having no family to turn to, many veterans bond together, creating a community amongst themselves. With little money, they often live under impoverished conditions. Some veterans have told of spending "their first months homeless and destitute, in a chilly storage room basement." Others gathered in "groups of four or more and crowded into cheap, single-room apartments." Their living conditions are often unsanitary, overcrowded and unsafe. Nevertheless, many veterans choose to contend with such conditions as they wait for the government to fulfill its promise to them.

53. Advocacy and Actions for World War II Immigrant Veterans

Joaquin Jay Gonzalez III

Most of the World War II Filipino veterans are in their 80s and 90s and too old to work, but they have discovered sources of money to help them survive. For example, they have learned that the government provides welfare. However, this was not the more generous veterans' welfare that would enable them to support their families; instead, the naturalized veterans were only eligible only for the same, lower welfare payments as non-veterans. Veterans also obtain money from organizations and individuals who support their struggle.

As late life migrants, there was no doubt about it—life is hard in extremely expensive San Francisco. Not having enough money to live on their own, many veterans banded together, sharing expenses and small living spaces. But some who did not, ended up on the streets, homeless and penniless. A residential building that housed many of the veterans at rates they could afford was the Delta Hotel. This former hotel had been converted into tiny apartments to accommodate the high demand for living space, primarily from the Filipino veterans. The areas in which they settled, SoMa and the Tenderloin District, are known as neighborhoods where homelessness, drug problems, gang encounters, vehicle break-ins, petty thefts, street harassment, prostitution, sex shops, and violence abound—these are all things that are particularly frightening to lonely, aging men with very little money and who speak little English. Obviously, jobs are extremely hard to find in these areas, but some have managed to find employment as custodians, janitors, security guards, kitchen helpers, and doormen in various San Francisco businesses—essentially, low-paying, undesirable jobs. To supplement their Social Security income, some of them also provide paid childcare services and elderly company to other migrant families and fellow seniors in the area.

Displaced and impoverished, a group of veterans and their family members experienced further devastation when the residential Delta Hotel burned down on August 11, 1997. The four-alarm fire destroyed the five-story hotel and left many people either dead or homeless. The Red Cross came to the aid of the veterans; to some, the Red Cross cots and the gray blankets brought back memories of the war. The veterans were provided with temporary shelter in a gymnasium. One veteran wryly remarked, "This is like the

Army again." A woman—one of the few veterans' wives—tried to put the loss in perspective, adding, "We only lost our means of shelter. We lost everything when we moved here."

Veterans and Youth Advocacy

During the most heated battles with Congress, the aging Filipino World War II veterans staged numerous demonstrations and garnered plenty of public support from private individuals and public officials in San Francisco, most especially the youth in high school and college. Veterans know that city officials are powerless to change the veterans' situation, since theirs is a federal government issue, but this has not stopped San Francisco politicians from declaring their support of the veterans in official terms. For instance, on May 27, 1999, heavy lobbying from Filipino veterans and students convinced the San Francisco Human Rights Commission (SFHRC) to pass a resolution acknowledging and supporting the battle against the "unjust and inequitable treatment" of Filipino veterans who fought under the American flag in World War II. The San Francisco Immigrant Rights Commission (SFIRC) followed with their own resolution. After all, San Francisco government units, like the Departments of Health and Human Services, will essentially have to care for the veterans, whether or not they get their benefits from Congress and the federal agencies concerned.

With Filipino American community organizations and churches lobbying, the San Francisco Mayor's office and Board of Supervisors agreed to budget for social programs that help to fill in the veterans' "equity gap." These include accommodations such as meals, a food bank, and skills enhancement programs to improve their employability. While these programs are helpful, they are ultimately unsatisfying to the veterans and their supporters, as they constitute welfare rather than the well-deserved benefits and pensions they are after. The Veterans Equity Center (VEC), recently renamed Bayanihan Equity Center, was established in the South of Market to implement policies.

In Washington, D.C., besides engaging in meditations, prayers and candlelight vigils, Filipino veterans and members of Student Action for Veterans Equity (SAVE) have risked their health and lives by participating in hunger strikes, chaining themselves to the White House fence, and staging fake deaths (or *die-ins*). But this has only gotten them the minor legislative installments mentioned earlier. Nevertheless, they have earned a good amount of publicity, so much that many more people are acknowledging their struggle and joining them in their fight. As I mentioned in the beginning of this chapter, Filipino American youth have joined the Filipino churches and other Filipino community-based organizations in their support of the veterans. As the next generation of activists, listeners, and leaders, this group of youth has proven its commitment and usefulness in demonstrations, marches, parades, and protests for the veterans' cause. SAVE members come from the San Francisco Bay Area's colleges and universities. They have been politicized by information gathered from the internet, newspapers, their peers, documentaries, Filipino American non-profit organizations, and their teachers.

The Results of Intergenerational Advocacy

The aging World War II veterans and their youth group allies prevailed in the end. In 1999, President Bill Clinton signed Public Law 106-169, which expanded income-based

Social Security disability benefits to certain World War II veterans, including Filipino veterans of World War II who served in the organized military forces of the Philippines. It gave them the opportunity to return to the Philippines to receive a portion of their Social Security income there. In October 2000, a genuine, i.e., non-welfare-based veterans' benefit law was passed (Public Law 106-377). In it, Congress authorized the VA to provide full-dollar rate compensation payments to veterans of the Commonwealth Army or recognized guerrilla forces residing in the U.S. if they were either U.S. citizens or lawfully admitted permanent resident aliens. Public Law 106-377 also requested the VA to provide care at its clinics for any non-service-related conditions of those same veterans. These Filipino veterans benefit provisions were supplemented by Public Law 106-419, which authorized the payment of burial benefits on behalf of veterans in these groups. Only the New Philippines Scouts remained ineligible for burial allowances.

In 2003, Congress passed Public Law 108-170 (Veterans Health Care, Capital Asset, and Business Improvement Act of 2003) and Public Law 108-183 (Veterans Benefits Act of 2003). Signed into law by President George W. Bush in December of 2003, this legislation expanded compensation and burial benefit payments to the full-dollar rate for New Philippine Scouts residing in the U.S. if they were either U.S. citizens or lawfully admitted permanent resident aliens. It also increased Dependency and Indemnity Compensation benefits to the full-dollar rate for survivors of veterans who served in the New Philippine Scouts, Philippine Commonwealth Army or recognized guerrilla forces, if the survivor resided in the U.S. and was either a U.S. citizen or a legally admitted resident alien.

The intergenerational advocacy continued and the results are more executive and congressional actions, which fulfilled MacArthur's promise. In October 2017, 72 years after the war ended, the United States Congress awarded the remaining veterans, who were mostly in their 90s and 100s, the nation's highest civilian honor—Congressional Gold Medal.

Benefits for Filipino World War II Veterans as of August 2018

Which Filipino Veterans are Eligible for Benefits? Filipino Veterans may be eligible for benefits if they served in one of the following:

- Armed Forces of the United States
- Commonwealth Army of the Philippines with service from July 26, 1941 through June 30, 1946
- Regular Philippine Scouts who enlisted prior to Oct. 6, 1945
- Insular Force of the U.S. Navy
- Special Philippine Scouts who enlisted between Oct. 6, 1945 and June 30, 1947
- Guerilla with service prior to July 1, 1946

Three benefits are available to Filipino Veterans:

- Service-connected disability compensation is a monthly payment to veterans disabled by injury or disease occurring or worsening during active service. To be eligible, you must:

- Have been discharged under other than dishonorable conditions
- Currently suffer from disabling symptoms
- Nonservice-connected pension is paid to wartime veterans who:
- Have limited income
- Are permanently and totally disabled or are 65 years or older
- Clothing allowance is an annual payment to a veteran whose service-connected disability requires a prosthetic or orthopedic device that damages clothing.

VA provides hospital, nursing home and outpatient medical care to certain Filipino Veterans. Regular Philippine Scouts are eligible for health care benefits based on their status as U.S. Veterans. The following groups are eligible for health care benefits in the U.S. on the same basis as U.S. Veterans if they are U.S. citizens or lawfully admitted for permanent address:

- Commonwealth Army
- Special Philippine Scouts
- Guerilla Veterans

54. Veterans Equity Center*

Luisa M. Antonio

In 1990, President George H.W. Bush signed the Immigration and Nationality Act that made it possible for Filipino World War II Veterans to become U.S. Citizens. Approximately 30,000 Filipino World War II Veterans came to the United States 50 percent of whom settled in California. Those who came to the Bay Area found their new home in the South of Market and the Tenderloin neighborhood in San Francisco. The concentration of Filipino Veterans in these communities is due to the socio-ethnic network that exists, and because these areas still have some of San Francisco's remaining unsubsidized affordable housing.

On August 11, 1997, a fatal blaze destroyed the Delta Hotel, a residential hotel in the heart of the South of Market neighborhood, displacing almost 100 Filipino World War II Veterans. The Red Cross set up a shelter at the South of Market Recreation Center. Volunteers poured their support for the veterans bringing food and clothing and listening to stories of their experience being denied access to medical services and monetary benefits from the Department of Veterans Affairs (VA).

Shortly after the fire, service providers, individual members of the community, students and a number of Filipino Veterans formed the Veterans Equity Center (VEC) Task Force. The task force aimed to address the multi-faceted needs of the displaced veterans who needed housing, counseling, legal assistance, recreational and social activities, health services and a better understanding of VA benefits. The task force's vision was the establishment of a center capable of addressing the needs of the newly arrived veterans.

VEC was born with the mission to "honor, serve and advocate" for the veterans. In 1999, VEC opened its doors in the South of Market after receiving a grant from the City and County of San Francisco. The center provided a "one-stop-shop" system of care that connected the veterans with the existing programs and services available in the community. VEC provided the following services not only to the veterans, but also to their immediate family members:

- Case Management offered assistance in understanding public benefits including VA benefits, access to health services and food including referral to congregate meal programs, and assistance in completing affordable housing application.

---

*Published with permission of the author.

- Legal clinic *pro bono* lawyers assisted with immigration issues including family petition and naturalization, VA benefit appeals, and tenant's rights.
- Recreational programs gave opportunity for veterans and their family members to socialize with their peers in a safe environment through monthly dances, birthday celebrations, and weekly arts and crafts.
- Educational and informational workshops gave updates on legislations and information on issues that affect Filipino World War II Veterans and older adults in general (e.g., Equity Bill Legislation, Medicare/MediCal, housing opportunities, etc.).
- Immigrant food assistance program, in partnership with the San Francisco Food Bank, VEC distributed produce and non-perishable groceries to augment the food that low income seniors were able to buy from their meager Supplemental Security Income (SSI).
- Advocacy was centered around the unfair treatment of Filipino World War II Veterans. VEC understood that the root of inequity can only be addressed by rescinding the 1946 Rescission Act—a law that declassified the Filipino Veterans' service in the United States Army as inactive making them ineligible to receive monetary benefits from the VA. Only Filipino Veterans with service-connected disability received some compensation from the VA, 50 cents for every $1.00 given to a US Veteran. In 1993, the first Filipino Veterans Equity Act was introduced. The legislation was introduced several times in succeeding congress; however, the bill never passed. Fair and just treatment of the Filipino Veterans remains an issue and the only issue in Congress that directly affects the Filipino community.

Educating and uniting the community behind the aging veterans was not easy. In 2000, the VEC was instrumental in organizing and establishing the National Network for Veterans Equity (NNVE)—the first coalition with a sole mission to advocate for the passage of the Equity Bill. VEC actively participated in shaping the public education campaign for the network. VEC believed that grassroots support can only be achieved through education with the goal of engaging the community to participate in the campaign. In addition, VEC played a major role in enlisting national organizations (i.e., National Coalition of Asian Pacific Americans for Community Development, Japanese-American Citizens League, Organization of Chinese Americans, and Labor Unions) to support the network's efforts by including the Filipino Veterans issue in their advocacy platform. Local governments joined the network of Filipino Veterans' supporters; the City and County of San Francisco and the Alameda County Board of Supervisors passed resolutions in support of the Equity Bill and encouraged congressional representatives to co-sponsor the Filipino Veterans Equity legislations. VEC increased public awareness about the Filipino Veterans issue beyond the Filipino community.

Since 1999, a number of legislations passed giving certain Filipino Veterans certain benefits such as Special Veterans Benefits, access to the VA healthcare system, burial in national cemeteries and a dollar-for-dollar service-connected disability compensation while Filipino Veterans reside in the United States. However, Filipino Veterans remain ineligible to receive pension from the VA.

In 2001, California Governor Arnold Schwarzenegger attempted to balance the state budget by cutting the California Veterans Cash Benefits (CVCB)—the State Supplemental

Payment given to an eligible veteran who permanently resides in the Philippines. The Governor's proposal takes away payments to about 1,700 Filipino Veterans. The VEC responded by working with the Asian Pacific Islander Legislative Caucus and the Asian Americans for Civil Rights and Equality in rejecting the Governor's proposal. In addition, the VEC mobilized two busloads of supporters, majority of whom were Filipino Veterans, to attend hearings at the State Capitol. As a result, the legislators rejected the proposed cut and today, Philippine-based veterans continue to receive their CVCB.

On February 17, 2009, President Barack Obama signed the American Recovery and Reinvestment Act, authorizing the creation of the Filipino Veterans Equity Compensation Fund (FVEC) and the release of a one-time, lump-sum payment to Filipino Veterans—$15,000 to U.S. Citizens and $9,000 to non-citizens. A total of $226,000,000 has been awarded to eligible Filipino Veterans.

VEC assisted hundreds of Filipino World War II Veterans in completing applications for FVEC. According to the Department of Veterans Affairs (DVA), as of January 1, 2019, 42,755 applications were processed; 9,313 applications were approved for $15,000 compensation and 9,670 were approved for $9,000. 23,772 or about 55 percent of the applications received were disapproved.

In the administration of FVEC, the VA disbursed payments to certain veterans deemed qualified—veterans whose names appeared on documents and records available at the National Personnel Records Center (NPRC) in St. Louis, Missouri (a.k.a. Missouri List). The VA, however, admitted that in 1972, a fire destroyed about 80 percent of the military service records of U.S. soldiers who served between 1912 and 1959. In October 2010, the VEC joined a number of Filipino World War II Veterans in a lawsuit challenging VA's implementation of the FVEC. VEC felt that the veterans who were denied the FVEC were unfairly treated because they served and were honorably discharged from the United States Army, some were decorated war heroes and prisoners of war.

In an effort to gain recognition for their service in the U.S. Armed Forces, VEC joined a national effort to advocate for the passage of a legislation to award the Congressional Gold Medal to Filipino World War II Veterans. The Filipino Veterans Recognition and Education Project—a national organization established for the purpose of recognizing the veterans and educating the community about the contributions of the veterans spearheaded the campaign. VEC played a major role in garnering the support of 47 out of 53 congressional representatives from California—a major contribution in the passage of the Congressional Gold Medal Legislation.

The United States Congress passed S1555—Filipino Veterans of World War II Congressional Gold Medal in November 2016 and signed into law in December 2016. The Filipino Veterans are among recipients of the highest honor bestowed by the United States Congress for their contribution in the United States military's successful campaign in the Pacific Theater during the Second World War. The Speaker of the House of Representatives presented the Congressional Gold Medal (CGM) to the Filipino Veterans on October 25, 2017.

In June 2016, the United States Citizenship and Immigration Services (USCIS) started implementing the Filipino World War II Veterans Parole Program (FWVP) which enables the Filipino Veterans to bring previously petitioned children to the United States under humanitarian parole. The program was part of President Obama's efforts to "Modernize the Immigration System for the 21st Century." A majority of veterans who came to the United States in the '90s petitioned for their children to come to the U.S.; however, because of the backlog in the immigration system, it takes two decades for the children to come to the U.S. Some veterans are opting to go home to the Philippines. With the implementation of FWVP, veterans are rethinking their options and sees the program as an opportunity to have their children take care of them in the U.S. while waiting for their priority date to become current and their visas available. FWVP is also extended to surviving spouses of Filipino Veterans who are in the United States. The center provides assistance to eligible veterans and survivors to apply for FWVP. The FWVP has an impact on the housing needs of veterans and their survivors increasing the demand for family housing to accommodate family member arriving from the Philippines.

From the 30,000 veterans who emigrated from the Philippines, there are approximately 5,000 remaining Filipino Veterans in the United States. In order to remain relevant in the community and to allow for expansion in services, the Veterans Equity Center changed its name and brand to the Bayanihan Equity Center (BEC). Although the center expanded its services to the low-income immigrants, older adults, adults with disability, and LGBTQ communities, BEC remains to be a staunch advocate for Filipino Veterans. In years ahead BEC will continue to advocate for the just and fair treatment of Filipino World War II Veterans.

55. Veterans Day Offers Opportunity to Honor Service of Immigrants in the Military*

GRANT RISSLER

In February 2008, more than 65,000, or 4.8 percent, of the 1.36 million active duty personnel in the U.S. military were foreign born. Recent choices by the Trump administration have altered incentives for immigrants to enlist.

With annual Veterans Day remembrances just around the corner (November 11), communities across the country will be organizing activities to thank veterans for their service in the U.S. military, past and present. If this Veterans Day is like those of the past decade, the day will also be marked by a number of naturalization ceremonies held in the U.S. and at military outposts around the world for active duty U.S. military becoming U.S. citizens.

Though military service is often thought of as a high calling for U.S. citizens, non-citizens with valid immigration status have long been able to serve as enlisted personnel in the U.S. military (officer ranks are restricted to U.S. citizens). The Migration Policy Institute cites USCIS statistics that the "foreign born composed half of all military recruits by the 1840s and 20 percent of the 1.5 million service members in the Union Army during the Civil War."

A fact sheet from the National Immigration Forum further notes that over our history as a country, one in five Medal of Honor recipients have been immigrants and that in 2016, about three percent of the living veteran population were immigrants. The 2008 MPI report also noted that almost five percent (approximately 65,000) of active duty military in that year were foreign born, with just over 20,300 of those not yet naturalized. Since then, the average number of non-citizens on active duty has declined somewhat, to an average of 18,700 (based on 2010 to 2016) as the number of active duty immigrants who naturalized while in service grew significantly due to several policy changes.

The policy changes that sped up naturalization options are:

- After September 11, a presidential executive order allowed non-citizens with honorable service after that date to naturalize in expedited fashion.

*Originally published as Grant Rissler, "Veterans Day Offers Opportunity to Honor Service of Immigrants in the Military," PA Times, October 26, 2017. Reprinted with permission of the publisher.

- A 2009 policy shift set up opportunities for naturalization when a non-citizen completed basic training.
- In the same year, the Military Accessions Vital to the National Interest (MAVNI) program was set up, allowing non-citizens to fast track their path to citizenship if they enlisted for several years and possessed certain skills in short supply (often linguistic or medical skills). In 2014, MAVNI was briefly opened up to Deferred Action for Childhood Arrival (DACA) recipients.</BUL>

As a result, from 2001 to 2015, 109,321 immigrant military service members became U.S. citizens, including more than 11,000 in ceremonies around the world. Unsurprisingly, the large majority of naturalizations for fiscal years 2008 to 2015 took place in either areas of significant ongoing conflict (Iraq, Afghanistan) or places with large and long-standing U.S. military bases (Japan, South Korea, Germany, Italy).

Certain policy changes by the Trump administration could further curtail future numbers. In April 2017, President Trump and the Department of Defense announced they would continue to recruit non-citizens and to offer those troops who enlisted an expedited pathway to naturalization. However recent reporting this month suggests because of the Trump administrations concerns over immigrants as potential security threats, legal permanent residents will no longer be able to enlist in the Army Reserve or National Guard and will have to delay entry into basic training for active duty service until more stringent security checks can be completed on them (which can take up to a year).

New regulations also instituted at 180 day waiting period in the program that gave green-card holders the ability to naturalize during basic training. Despite some successes, the MAVNI program, suspended in 2016 to allow the security checks that were part of the program to be reviewed, reportedly also may be discontinued. This could leave some DACA beneficiary recruits and others with lapsed or expired visas who are already in the enlistment pipeline to face deportation.

These changes are causing some experts to worry about the impact this will have on overall recruitment of non-citizens as a small but vital portion of enlisted military personnel. *The Washington Post* quotes Margaret Stock, a retired Army officer who led the effort to create MAVNI, as saying the following: "It looks like we're now afraid of foreigners in the military. And that means mission failure. If you're going to be deployed in more than 100 countries to fight a global war, you can't be afraid of foreigners."

For more information on the details of military naturalization processes, see the USCIS fact sheet on the topic.

56. PTSD Basics[*]

U.S. Department of Veterans Affairs

PTSD (posttraumatic stress disorder) is a mental health problem that some people develop after experiencing or witnessing a life-threatening event, like combat, a natural disaster, a car accident, or sexual assault.

It's normal to have upsetting memories, feel on edge, or have trouble sleeping after a traumatic event. At first, it may be hard to do normal daily activities, like go to work, go to school, or spend time with people you care about. But most people start to feel better after a few weeks or months. If it's been longer than a few months and you're still having symptoms, you may have PTSD. For some people, PTSD symptoms may start later on, or they may come and go over time.

Anyone can develop PTSD at any age. A number of factors can increase the chance that someone will have PTSD, many of which are not under that person's control. For example, having a very intense or long-lasting traumatic event or getting injured during the event can make it more likely that a person will develop PTSD. PTSD is also more common after certain types of trauma, like combat and sexual assault.

Personal factors, like previous traumatic exposure, age, and gender, can affect whether or not a person will develop PTSD. What happens after the traumatic event is also important. Stress can make PTSD more likely, while social support can make it less likely.

What Are the Symptoms?

PTSD symptoms usually start soon after the traumatic event, but they may not appear until months or years later. They also may come and go over many years. If the symptoms last longer than four weeks, cause you great distress, or interfere with your work or home life, you might have PTSD

There are four types of PTSD symptoms, but they may not be exactly the same for everyone. Each person experiences symptoms in their own way.

1. **Reliving the event (also called re-experiencing symptoms).** Memories of the traumatic event can come back at any time. You may feel the same fear and horror you did when the event took place. For example:

---

[*]Public document originally published as U.S. Department of Veterans Affairs, "PTSD Basics," https://www.ptsd.va.gov/understand/what/ptsd_basics.asp (January 22, 2019).

- You may have nightmares.
- You may feel like you are going through the event again. This is called a flashback.
- You may see, hear, or smell something that causes you to relive the event. This is called a trigger. News reports, seeing an accident, or hearing a car backfire are examples of triggers.

2. **Avoiding situations that remind you of the event.** You may try to avoid situations or people that trigger memories of the traumatic event. You may even avoid talking or thinking about the event. For example:

- You may avoid crowds, because they feel dangerous.
- You may avoid driving if you were in a car accident or if your military convoy was bombed.
- If you were in an earthquake, you may avoid watching movies about earthquakes.
- You may keep very busy or avoid seeking help because it keeps you from having to think or talk about the event.

3. **Negative changes in beliefs and feelings.** The way you think about yourself and others changes because of the trauma. This symptom has many aspects, including the following:

- You may not have positive or loving feelings toward other people and may stay away from relationships.
- You may forget about parts of the traumatic event or not be able to talk about them.
- You may think the world is completely dangerous, and no one can be trusted.

4. **Feeling keyed up (also called hyperarousal).** You may be jittery, or always alert and on the lookout for danger. You might suddenly become angry or irritable. This is known as hyperarousal. For example:

- You may have a hard time sleeping.
- You may have trouble concentrating.
- You may be startled by a loud noise or surprise.
- You might want to have your back to a wall in a restaurant or waiting room.

What Are the Symptoms in Children?

Children may have symptoms described above or other symptoms depending on how old they are. As children get older, their symptoms are more like those of adults. Here are some examples of PTSD symptoms in children:

- Children under 6 may get upset if their parents are not close by, have trouble sleeping, or act out the trauma through play.
- Children age 7 to 11 may also act out the trauma through play, drawings, or stories. Some have nightmares or become more irritable or aggressive. They may also want to avoid school or have trouble with schoolwork or friends.

- Children age 12 to 18 have symptoms more similar to adults: depression, anxiety, withdrawal, or reckless behavior like substance abuse or running away.

Will People with PTSD Get Better?

After a traumatic event, it's normal to think, act, and feel differently than usual—but most people start to feel better after a few weeks or months. Talk to a doctor or mental health care provider (like a psychiatrist, psychologist, or social worker) if your symptoms:

- Last longer than a few months
- Are very upsetting
- Disrupt your daily life

"Getting better" means different things for different people. There are many different treatment options for PTSD. For many people, these treatments can get rid of symptoms altogether. Others find they have fewer symptoms or feel that their symptoms are less intense. Your symptoms don't have to interfere with your everyday activities, work, and relationships.

What Treatments Are Available?

There are two main types of treatment, psychotherapy (sometimes called counseling or talk therapy) and medication. Sometimes people combine psychotherapy and medication.

Psychotherapy for PTSD
Psychotherapy, or counseling, involves meeting with a therapist.

Trauma-focused psychotherapy, which focuses on the memory of the traumatic event or its meaning, is the most effective treatment for PTSD. There are different types of trauma-focused psychotherapy, such as:

- **Cognitive Processing Therapy (CPT)** where you learn skills to understand how trauma changed your thoughts and feelings. Changing how you think about the trauma can change how you feel.
- **Prolonged Exposure (PE)** where you talk about your trauma repeatedly until memories are no longer upsetting. This will help you get more control over your thoughts and feelings about the trauma. You also go to places or do things that are safe, but that you have been staying away from because they remind you of the trauma.
- **Eye Movement Desensitization and Reprocessing (EMDR)**, which involves focusing on sounds or hand movements while you talk about the trauma. This helps your brain work through the traumatic memories.

Medications

Medications can be effective too. Some specific SSRIs (selective serotonin reuptake inhibitors) and SNRIs (serotonin-norepinephrine reuptake inhibitors), which are used for depression, also work for PTSD. These include sertraline, paroxetine, fluoxetine, and venlafaxine.

57. Understanding PTSD: A Guide for Family and Friends*

U.S. Department of Veterans Affairs

PTSD is a mental health problem that some people develop after a trauma, or life-threatening event. A traumatic event could be something that happened to your loved one, or something they saw happen to someone else.

Types of traumatic events that can cause PTSD include:

- Combat and other military experiences
- Sexual or physical assault
- Child sexual or physical abuse
- Learning about the violent or accidental death or injury of a loved one
- Serious accidents, like a car wreck
- Natural disasters, like fire, tornado, hurricane, food, or earthquake
- Terrorist attacks

If you're concerned about a loved one who has experienced trauma, it's important to learn about PTSD. Knowing how PTSD can affect people will help you understand what your loved one is going through—and how you can support them.

Support Your Loved One

It's normal to feel like you don't know how to support your loved one. You may feel helpless when they're upset or in crisis. But support from family and friends is important for people with PTSD—and there's a lot you can do to help them.

- Plan enjoyable activities with friends and family. Encourage your loved one to get out and do things, but go at their pace. For example, if they find it hard to leave the house, a small get-together at a neighbor's house may be less stressful than going to a crowded restaurant.
- Offer to go to the doctor with them. This is especially helpful if your loved one

---

*Public document originally published as U.S. Department of Veterans Affairs, "Understanding PTSD: A Guide for Family and Friends," https://www.ptsd.va.gov/publications/print/understandingptsd_booklet.pdf (April 2018).

is having a hard time focusing and remembering details. You can take notes on what the doctor says, and keep track of recommended medicines and treatments.

- Make a crisis plan—together. You can't always prevent a crisis, but you can learn to recognize triggers and take steps to help your loved one cope.
- Talk with your loved one ahead of time about what to do during a nightmare, flashback, or panic attack. They may be able to share things that have helped them in the past.
- Check in with your loved one often. This can help you and your loved one figure out which support strategies are working, so you can focus on what's most helpful to them. You can also talk about different strategies to try if something isn't working well.

Talking to Kids About PTSD

If you have kids, they may notice the changes in your loved one, too. And if they don't understand what's going on, they may be scared or confused. You and your loved one can help by talking to them about PTSD.

- Share age-appropriate information. Tell them what PTSD is and the challenges it's causing, but avoid any details that might be too graphic or scary. Older kids may also want to know what they can do to support your loved one.
- Tell them it's not their fault. Make sure your kids know that they didn't cause your loved one's PTSD—and it's not their job to fix it.
- Encourage them to share their feelings. Check that your kids understand what you've told them, and ask if they have any questions. Make sure they know they can talk with you about their own worries and fears.
- Express hope for the future. It's important for your kids to know that there are treatments for PTSD that work—and that you believe things will get better. Let them know that your family will work together to support your loved one.

If your family is having a hard time talking, consider seeing a family therapist. They can help you and your family learn how to share tough emotions, support each other, and cope with PTSD. To find a family therapist who specializes in PTSD, talk to your doctor, or contact a religious or social services organization.

Talking to Friends About PTSD

Your friends and neighbors may also notice changes in your loved one. They may have questions about what's going on. And, like you, they'll want to know how they can help.

Talk with your loved one first. Before you talk with friends, ask your loved one how they want you to handle those questions. For example, they may not want you to share any details about their trauma. They may also have ideas for how friends can support them.

Share what you've learned. Your friends may also be struggling to connect with your loved one. You can help by sharing tips about how to communicate—and how to be sensitive and patient as your loved one works through their symptoms.

Here are some examples of how friends can support you and your loved one:

- Learning about PTSD and its symptoms
- Inviting you and your loved one to do things
- Listening, if you or your loved one want to talk
- Helping with everyday tasks, like babysitting or grocery shopping

Communicate with Your Loved One

When a loved one is dealing with PTSD, it may be hard to communicate with them, but it's important to try. Sharing feelings and everyday challenges with each other can strengthen your relationship—and help you learn how to better support your loved one. Here are some tips that can help:

- Let your loved one share at their own pace. It can be hard for people with PTSD to talk about their trauma, even with people they love. Let your loved one know that you understand if they don't want to share everything—and that you'll be there to listen when they're ready.
- Be a good listener. Your loved one may talk about things that are hard for you to hear—especially if they do open up about their trauma. It can be tempting to offer advice or say it's going to be okay, but it's important to listen without judging, interrupting, or trying to fix things.
- To support your loved one and show that you're listening, you can make eye contact and repeat back what they've told you to make sure you understand. You can also ask open-ended questions, like "how do you feel?" or "how can I help?"
- Share your feelings, too. Your loved one may not know you're sad, frustrated, or worried if you don't tell them. Choose a time that feels comfortable, and try not to blame them or their PTSD for your feelings.

And remember, you can also talk to friends, family, or a therapist about how you're feeling—especially if it will help you to be calm and clear with your loved one.

Take Care of Yourself

Supporting someone with PTSD can take a lot of time and energy—and it can be stressful. It's common to feel that taking care of yourself is selfish, or that you don't have time. But taking care of yourself is actually an important part of caring for your loved one. If your needs are met, you'll be a stronger source of support for them.

- Take care of your own health. Getting plenty of sleep, exercising regularly, and eating well will help you manage stress and stay healthy. Make sure you're staying on top of your own doctor's appointments, too.

- Keep doing the things you like to do. It's important to recharge—and to have things to look forward to, like spending time with friends.
- Set boundaries for yourself. Be realistic about how much you can do. Talk with your loved one about how you'll let them know if you need a break, and make a plan for how they can get support during those times—like calling a friend or texting a hotline.
- Talk about what you're going through. Your close family and friends can be a good place to start. You may also want to check out support groups, where you can talk with people who are having similar experiences.
- Consider seeing a counselor or therapist. They can help you deal with emotions that might be hard to discuss with friends, including sadness and anger. They can also help you work on other things, like communicating with your loved one.

Learn About PTSD Treatment

Treatment works. For some people, treatment can get rid of PTSD altogether. Others may have fewer symptoms or find that their symptoms are less intense. After treatment, most people say they have a better quality of life.

There are many treatments for PTSD that have been proven to work, including different types of talk therapy and medication.

- Talk Therapy. Some types of talk therapy focus on thinking or talking about the trauma in a way that helps people change how they react to their memories. Others focus on challenging negative or unhelpful thoughts about the trauma. Therapy can also help your loved one learn how to manage symptoms, deal with stress, and communicate better.
- Medication. If your loved one has PTSD, they may not have enough of certain chemicals in their brain that help them manage stress and anxiety. There are medications that can help raise the level of these chemicals in their brain so they feel better.

Help Your Loved One Through Treatment

It's common to think that your loved one's PTSD symptoms will just go away with time. But if PTSD isn't treated, it usually doesn't get better—and it may even get worse. That's why encouraging your loved one to get treatment is one of the most important things you can do to support them. Here are some tips that can help:

- Be patient. For most people, it takes more than one conversation to accept that they may need to seek treatment. Express your support and concern, and remind your loved one that going to get help is their choice.
- Share information about treatment. Many people have misconceptions about what PTSD treatment is like. Share resources to help your loved one learn about their options—like the AboutFace website (www.ptsd.va.gov/aboutface),

where they can hear stories about PTSD and treatment from people who have been there.

- Offer practical help. You can't make your loved one get treatment if they're not ready, but there are things you can do to make it easier. For example, you could offer to research PTSD services and therapists in your area. You can also help with logistics, like calling to schedule an appointment.

58. PTSD and DSM-5: Provider Version*

U.S. DEPARTMENT OF VETERANS AFFAIRS

In 2013, the American Psychiatric Association revised the PTSD diagnostic criteria in the fifth edition of its *Diagnostic and Statistical Manual of Mental Disorders* (DSM-5). PTSD is included in a new category in DSM-5, Trauma- and Stressor-Related Disorders. All of the conditions included in this classification require exposure to a traumatic or stressful event as a diagnostic criterion. For a review of the DSM-5 changes to the criteria for PTSD, see the American Psychiatric Association website on Posttraumatic Stress Disorder.

Full copyrighted criteria are available from the American Psychiatric Association. All of the criteria are required for the diagnosis of PTSD. The following text summarizes the diagnostic criteria:

Criterion A (one required): The person was exposed to: death, threatened death, actual or threatened serious injury, or actual or threatened sexual violence, in the following way(s):

- Direct exposure
- Witnessing the trauma
- Learning that a relative or close friend was exposed to a trauma
- Indirect exposure to aversive details of the trauma, usually in the course of professional duties (e.g., first responders, medics)

Criterion B (one required): The traumatic event is persistently re-experienced, in the following way(s):

- Unwanted upsetting memories
- Nightmares
- Flashbacks
- Emotional distress after exposure to traumatic reminders
- Physical reactivity after exposure to traumatic reminders

---

*Public document originally published as U.S. Department of Veterans Affairs, "PTSD and DSM-5: Provider Version," https://www.ptsd.va.gov/professional/treat/essentials/dsm5_ptsd.asp (September 28, 2018).

Criterion C (one required): Avoidance of trauma-related stimuli after the trauma, in the following way(s):

- Trauma-related thoughts or feelings
- Trauma-related reminders

Criterion D (two required): Negative thoughts or feelings that began or worsened after the trauma, in the following way(s):

- Inability to recall key features of the trauma
- Overly negative thoughts and assumptions about oneself or the world
- Exaggerated blame of self or others for causing the trauma
- Negative affect
- Decreased interest in activities
- Feeling isolated
- Difficulty experiencing positive affect

Criterion E (two required): Trauma-related arousal and reactivity that began or worsened after the trauma, in the following way(s):

- Irritability or aggression
- Risky or destructive behavior
- Hypervigilance
- Heightened startle reaction
- Difficulty concentrating
- Difficulty sleeping

Criterion F (required): Symptoms last for more than 1 month.

Criterion G (required): Symptoms create distress or functional impairment (e.g., social, occupational).

Criterion H (required): Symptoms are not due to medication, substance use, or other illness.

Two specifications:

- Dissociative Specification. In addition to meeting criteria for diagnosis, an individual experiences high levels of either of the following in reaction to trauma-related stimuli:
- Depersonalization. Experience of being an outside observer of or detached from oneself (e.g., feeling as if "this is not happening to me" or one were in a dream).
- Derealization. Experience of unreality, distance, or distortion (e.g., "things are not real").
- **Delayed Specification.** Full diagnostic criteria are not met until at least six months after the trauma(s), although onset of symptoms may occur immediately.

Note: *DSM-5* introduced a preschool subtype of PTSD for children ages six years and younger.

How Do the DSM-5 PTSD Symptoms Compare to DSM-IV Symptoms?

Overall, the symptoms of PTSD are generally comparable between *DSM-5* and *DSM-IV*. A few key alterations include:

- The revision of Criterion A1 in *DSM-5* narrowed qualifying traumatic events such that the unexpected death of family or a close friend due to natural causes is no longer included.
- Criterion A2, requiring that the response to a traumatic event involved intense fear, hopelessness, or horror, was removed from *DSM-5*. Research suggests that Criterion A2 did not improve diagnostic accuracy.
- The avoidance and numbing cluster (Criterion C) in *DSM-IV* was separated into two criteria in *DSM-5*: Criterion C (avoidance) and Criterion D (negative alterations in cognitions and mood). This results in a requirement that a PTSD diagnosis includes at least one avoidance symptom.
- Three new symptoms were added:
- Criterion D (Negative thoughts or feelings that began or worsened after the trauma): Overly negative thoughts and assumptions about oneself or the world; and, negative affect
- Criterion E (Trauma-related arousal and reactivity that began or worsened after the trauma): Reckless or destructive behavior

What Are the Implications of the DSM-5 Revisions on PTSD Prevalence?

Changes in the diagnostic criteria have minimal impact on prevalence. National estimates of PTSD prevalence suggest that *DSM-5* rates were only slightly lower (typically about 1 percent) than *DSM-IV* for both lifetime and past-12 month. When cases met criteria for *DSM-IV*, but not *DSM-5*, this was primarily due the revision excluding sudden unexpected death of a loved one from Criterion A in the *DSM-5*. The other reason was a failure to have one avoidance symptom. When cases met criteria for *DSM-5*, but not *DSM-IV*, this was primarily due to not meeting *DSM-IV* avoidance/numbing and/or arousal criteria. Research also suggests that similarly to *DSM-IV*, prevalence of PTSD for *DSM-5* was higher among women than men, and increased with multiple traumatic event exposure.

REFERENCES

American Psychiatric Association. (2013) *Diagnostic and Statistical Manual of Mental Disorders*, 5th ed. Washington, DC: American Psychiatric Association.
Friedman, M.J., Resick, P.A., Bryant, R.A., & Brewin, C.R. (2011). "Considering PTSD for *DSM-5*." *Depression & Anxiety, 28*, 750–769. doi:10.1002/da.20767.
Kilpatrick, D.G., Resnick, H.S., Milanak, M.E., Miller, M.W., Keyes, K.M., & Friedman, M.J. (2013). "National Estimates of Exposure to Traumatic Events and PTSD Prevalence Using *DSM-IV* and *DSM-5* Criteria." *Journal of Traumatic Stress, 26*, 537–547. doi:10.1002/jts.21848.

59. Military Health System's Care for PTSD, Depression Falls Short, Report Finds[*]

Shefali Luthra

The military's health program falls significantly short in providing mental health care to active service members, according to a RAND Corp. study.

The study focuses on post-traumatic stress disorder and depression, the two most common mental health conditions experienced in the armed services.

It finds some good news: The Military Health Services—which is operated by the U.S. Department of Defense and provides care to active soldiers—is effective at contacting soldiers diagnosed with one of the conditions. In addition, a vast majority of soldiers who get diagnosed with PTSD or depression receive at least one talk therapy session, the study finds. In that regard, it outperforms civilian health services.

But the system faces difficulties ensuring that patients continue with treatment—either by continuing to see a psychotherapist or following up with a doctor after being prescribed medication.

"It's essential to provide excellent care for these service members because of how much we ask of them," said Kimberly Hepner, the study's lead author and a senior behavioral scientist at RAND.

The study examined medical records for close to 40,000 soldiers diagnosed with one of the two conditions between January and June 2012. It's the largest ever assessment of mental health in the military, according to RAND, a nonpartisan research institute based in California. Of those, about 15,000 had PTSD, and about 30,000 had depression. About 6,000 had both.

After soldiers get their initial mental health visit, the next treatment steps are a different story, the study found. About one in three patients newly diagnosed with PTSD got the appropriate follow-up care after starting treatment—typically, that's at least four visits to a psychotherapist within two months of being diagnosed. For soldiers with depression, less than a quarter of them completed those four visits.

Meanwhile, only about 40 percent of patients who were prescribed medication for

*Originally published as Shefali Luthra, "Military Health System's Care for PTSD, Depression Falls Short, Report Finds," *Kaiser Health News*, February 19, 2016.

one of those conditions followed up with a doctor afterward. Those visits are essential, Hepner said, because the physician can make sure patients take their medication and help them manage side effects. A physician's involvement also ensures that medication doesn't counteract any other prescription drugs the soldiers take.

"Service members received a tremendous amount of medical treatment," she said. "That's why it's even more critical to make sure that it's a successful experience."

Because other studies use different metrics for diagnosing and treating mental health conditions, it's hard to compare these results to those of civilian health systems, Hepner said.

Depending on the experiences soldiers have, military combat can contribute to mental health problems, according to the Department of Veterans Affairs. Meanwhile, research has found suicide attempts seem to be more common in soldiers than in civilians, though it can be difficult to compare. A 2015 study found about 377 out of an estimated 10,000 enlisted soldiers attempted suicide.

The RAND study, which was commissioned by the DOD, is only the first part of an overarching project to assess the quality of mental health care for soldiers. It doesn't yet delve into questions like why these soldier-patients stop their therapy and medication—considering, for instance, that about 90 percent of those who are diagnosed with PTSD get at least one follow-up visit to therapy, and about 80 percent with depression do.

Potential explanations could include insufficient access to mental health professionals, said Joe Davis, a spokesman for Veterans of Foreign Wars. Many soldiers might also fear judgment from their peers for asking for help.

"It's very easy for senior leaders to say there is no stigma, but far different on the ground at the small-unit level, where everyone relies on their buddy … and vice versa," he said in an email.

Soldiers might also have been unhappy with the mental health care they got, he added, and therefore not return.

The shortage of mental health professionals is one of the biggest barriers to continuous mental health care, said Elspeth Cameron Ritchie, a former military psychiatrist. Since more soldiers have been deployed to Iraq and Afghanistan, the need for doctors has grown, she added.

Beyond questions of stigma and a shortage of providers, there could be an issue of appointments not being available at convenient times, Hepner said. "We ask a lot of service members, and they have a lot of demands on their jobs."

Because soldiers travel a lot, it can be difficult for them to keep up good, continuous access to care, Ritchie said. That difficulty in finding time and flexibility can compound many soldiers' reluctance to keep up with mental health care. Many, she added, worry about others' perception if they are seen regularly visiting a psychiatrist.

"If you need to go to the doctor all the time, people will think, 'Oh what's wrong with that person?'" Ritchie said. "There's a lot of talk about how we should treat this as a broken leg, and there shouldn't be a stigma. But there is a stigma."

The Defense Department's action in commissioning RAND's study is encouraging, Hepner said, because it suggests an active interest in trying to improve mental health care and access to it. DOD could build on efforts to publicly measure how good military, mental health providers are, she said. The department's begun doing that, but Hepner said the public needs more information about quality of care. The RAND findings could have understated the difficulty of obtaining mental health care, Hepner added. RAND focused on patients who had been diagnosed with mental health problems, but it likely missed soldiers who either hadn't seen a doctor at all or who had but hadn't been diagnosed.

Even when they go to the best doctors, soldiers must ask for help, which can be difficult, Davis noted.

For instance, all the soldiers in RAND's study had been identified as needing help. That makes it easier to connect them with care—which could have influenced the high proportion of soldiers who had their initial visit, Hepner said.

"The real risk here is the people we are not addressing," she added.

60. Reverberations from War Complicate Vietnam Veterans' End-of-Life Care[*]

April Dembosky

Many of Ron Fleming's fellow soldiers have spent the past five decades trying to forget what they saw—and did—in Vietnam.

But Fleming, now 74, has spent most of that time trying to hold on to it. He's never been as proud as he was when he was 21.

Fleming was a door gunner in the war, hanging out of a helicopter on a strap with a machine gun in his hands. He fought in the Tet Offensive of 1968, sometimes for 40 hours straight, firing 6,000 rounds a minute. But he never gave much thought to catching a bullet himself.

"At 21, you're bulletproof," he said, as he sat on the edge of his hospital bed at the San Francisco VA Medical Center. "Dying wasn't on the agenda."

Now it is. Fleming has congestive heart failure and arthritis, and his asthma attacks often land him in the hospital. Ten years ago, he was diagnosed with post-traumatic stress disorder (PTSD), which makes him quick to anger and hypervigilant, as if he's still in that helicopter.

Fleming's physical and mental health symptoms, combined with his military history, are a challenge to the VA's palliative care team, which is coordinating his care as his health deteriorates. It is a challenge they are facing more often as Vietnam veterans age and develop life-threatening illnesses.

For some veterans, the stoicism they honed on the battlefield often returns full-force as they confront a new battlefront in the hospital, making them less willing to admit they are afraid or in pain, and less willing to accept treatment. Other vets, with PTSD, are even more reluctant to take pain-relieving opioids because the drugs can actually make their symptoms worse, triggering frightening flashbacks.

About 30 percent of Vietnam vets have had PTSD in their lifetime, the highest rate

*Originally published as April Dembosky, "Reverberations from War Complicate Vietnam Veterans' End-of-Life Care," *Kaiser Health News*, January 4, 2018. This story is part of a partnership that includes KQED, NPR and Kaiser Health News, an editorially independent program of the Kaiser Family Foundation. KHN's coverage of these topics is supported by the Gordon and Betty Moore Foundation and the John A. Hartford Foundation.

among veteran groups, according to the U.S. Department of Veterans Affairs' National Center for PTSD. Their rate is higher because of the unique combat conditions they faced and the negative reception many of them received when they returned home, according to numerous studies.

Since the war, many vets have developed coping strategies to keep disturbing memories and other PTSD symptoms at bay. But facing a terminal illness—the severe pain of cancer, the nausea of chemotherapy or the breathlessness of heart failure—can drain their energy so much that they're unable to maintain their mental defenses. Vets previously diagnosed with PTSD can slip out of remission, and some may experience it for the first time.

"They're so distracted trying to cope with their physical symptoms that they might have flashbacks," said VJ Periyakoil, a palliative care physician at the VA Palo Alto Health Care Center and director of palliative care education at Stanford University. "War memories start coming back; they start having nightmares."

Gasping for breath can induce panic for anyone, but it can make vets feel as threatened as they did in a combat zone, said Eric Widera, director of hospice and palliative care at the San Francisco VA and professor of geriatrics at the University of California–San Francisco.

That's what happens to navy vet Earl Borges, who logged 240 24-hour river patrols in Vietnam with three other men on a plastic boat, constantly looking for enemy soldiers in the brush.

Since then, he's been startled by loud noises and fast-moving shadows. Now, at age 70, Borges has amyotrophic lateral sclerosis (ALS) and chronic obstructive pulmonary disease, or COPD, which can intensify the anxiety from his PTSD.

If he lies down without his breathing machine, he panics, then hyperventilates.

"I have to talk him through it, tell him he's OK, 'just breathe,'" said his wife, Shirley Borges, 67.

They both say Earl's PTSD is under control—as long as he doesn't talk about the war—and his ALS is progressing very slowly, without pain.

But for patients who are in severe pain, the go-to treatment is opioids, which can also make PTSD symptoms worse. This forces vets to choose between physical pain and mental anguish.

"Oftentimes, pain medications like morphine or oxycodone make some people feel a little bit fuzzy," Widera said. "That may contribute to that feeling of loss of control."

That's why Periyakoil isn't surprised when vets refuse pain medications.

"'Don't you try and give me none of those narc pills, doc,'" she recalled one of her patients saying while he grimaced in pain.

Some vets also refuse medication because they feel as if they deserve the pain.

"We see a lot of feelings of guilt over what they've seen and done during their experience in Vietnam," Widera said, "and they don't want to blunt that."

At the end of life, this sense of guilt is amplified as vets look back and review their lives and, perhaps, contemplate the consequences of their actions in the line of duty. This is even true for vets like Fleming, whose overriding feeling about his service is pride.

"Sometimes I think that now I'm being paid back for all the men I killed. And I killed a lot of them," said Fleming, who has not required opioids for his condition, but has declined other medications.

"If there is a judge, I figure I'm going to hell in a handbasket," he said.

Watching vets choose to endure their pain can be hard for families, as well as for palliative care doctors and nurses. Just like soldiers, doctors hate doing nothing.

"Staff suffer terribly because they feel like, 'What good are the hospice experts if we can't take care of patients' pain?'" Periyakoil said.

Often, the only thing they can do is stand back and respect the vets' choice to bear their pain, she said.

Once, when Periyakoil was dressing the ulcer wounds of the patient who refused "narc pills," he began talking about the war. She didn't press, just kept working quietly on the wounds. As he stared at the ceiling, wincing, he confided in her about a time he was forced to kill a pregnant teenager.

But this kind of revelation is unusual. With weeks or months left to live, after a lifetime of silence about their most horrifying memories, there often isn't enough time for vets to talk about them at all.

That's one reason the VA has been trying to start end-of-life care earlier—to address vets' moral distress or PTSD years before they land in hospice, Widera said.

Fleming's doctors, for instance, have urged him to consider mental health counseling or antidepressants. He refuses.

"I don't want to take psychiatric drugs," he said. "The vets call them the happy pills. I don't want any of those, because they change you. I don't want to change."

The emotional pain connects Fleming to his past.

He was awarded 18 Air Medals for meritorious acts and heroism in flight. The loss and grief he experienced in Vietnam are woven into those memories of victory and glory.

"You see all the combat. There's a charge to it," he said. "And after a while, it bites you right in the ass. And once you've been bit, you're bit for life. Nothing else works."

61. Purple Heart or Scarlet Letter: PTSD-Stigmatization of War Veterans[*]

RACHEL ROBINSON

Veterans deserve to enjoy the freedoms they fought for. Unfortunately, due to the stereotype that they all suffer from post-traumatic stress disorder that PTSD makes them inherently dangerous (at worst) or unreliable (at best), veterans are sometimes unable to fully reintegrate into the society they served. Not all veterans suffer long-term PTSD effects, but for those that do, this social stigma imposes personal shame and can prevent them from obtaining the care they need.

When veterans cannot find employment, they may not have the financial resources to cover the costs of their medical care. The VA reports that there are currently 20 million veterans in the United States spanning four wars: World War II, Korea, Vietnam and the Gulf Wars. The Department of Defense calculates over two million current active duty and reserve service members. This segment of the population cannot be ignored, not only because of their number but also because of their military contribution and potential to contribute in civilian life.

From Homer's *Iliad* to Hollywood, society has glamourized war and acknowledged the mental effects it can have on its heroes. In real life, when these heroes return to civilian life, they may be forced to contend with an even more difficult and insidious enemy than the one they were trained to face on the battle field: the stigmatization associated with PTSD.

To properly train and prepare soldiers for battle, the military accentuates and rewards strength and stoicism while eschewing any perceived physical, mental or moral weakness. This focus on personal strength fuels the concept that mental disorders are a result of personal weakness rather than symptoms of personal trauma. Interestingly, in its attempt to treat veterans' mental disorders and ameliorate the social stigma, the medical community has inadvertently contributed to it.

Nash writes that Hippocrates, known as the Father of Modern Medicine, may have been the first to propose that mental disorders could be caused by a diseased mind rather than by direct intervention by the gods. Hippocrates' theory was mostly ignored, however, until the Age of Enlightenment, when the scientific method was used to assess the

*Originally published as Rachel Robinson, "Purple Heart or Scarlet Letter: PTSD-Stigmatization of War Veterans," *PA Times,* August 1, 2017. Reprinted with permission of the publisher.

behavior of humans under stress. During this era, military surgeons documented the disabling mood and anxiety symptoms of soldiers at war and named it "nostalgia." This led to soldiers obtaining treatment rather than being shamed, exiled or even executed for cowardice. Since then, PTSD has been known by many names.

Nash continues that during the bloody American Civil War, PTSD was diagnosed as "soldier's heart," "irritable heart" and "sunstroke." In World War I, doctors believed physical brain trauma from nearby artillery blasts caused PTSD and, accordingly, renamed the disorder "shell shock" or "nervenshock" among the Germans. In 1916, the German Association for Psychiatry proclaimed that PTSD only occurred in individuals with "hysteria." Although blatantly stigmatizing, the term persisted until the third edition of the Diagnostic and Statistical Manual of Mental Disorders ("DSM") removed it in 1980 and replaced it with PTSD. Since then, PTSD has been defined as the result of a stressor "that would evoke significant symptoms of distress in almost everyone." Plainly stated, "a normal reaction to an abnormal event."

While this definition seeks to normalize PTSD and thus reduce the accompanying social and personal stigma, only a minority of veterans suffer from long-term PTSD even when exposed to the same stressor events as their comrades. Thus, personal weakness has persisted as the default explanation. In response, the fourth edition of the DSM added a person's preexisting vulnerabilities contribute to the effect of a stressor event. This can be construed, however, as simply a more neutral way of attributing long-term PTSD to a personal weakness.

Nash's proposed "Stress Injury Model" attributes stressor events to physical changes in the brain that result in PTSD symptoms. This model seeks to neutralize the negative effects of PTSD stigmatization by proving that PTSD is not the result of personal weakness. However, while this model will likely lead to better medical care, it does not account for the societal and personal shame that prevents veterans from seeking that care in the first place. It will not assuage employers' concerns or encourage them to hire veterans. The issue is not why some veterans suffer from PTSD but rather why society is so afraid of those who do.

The National Institute of Mental Health estimates about 18 percent of the U.S. population suffers a mental disorder. Yet, most people live fulfilling lives whether they seek treatment or not because they are not presumed to be mentally ill in the same way veterans are presumed to have PTSD. The irony is reintegration and access to proper medical care will ameliorate symptoms of PTSD and allow our soldiers to regain their rightful place in society so they can again enjoy the freedoms they fought for.

62. A Therapeutic Photography Program to Enhance PTSD Mental Health Services[*]

Jeanne DeLaney *and* Mickey P. McGee

The women's movement and child advocacy groups in the 1970s broadened our understanding of post-traumatic syndrome disorder (PTSD). "What had been previously contextualized primarily as a problem among military personnel and veterans was broadened to include battered women, rape victims and child abuse" (Stein, et al., 2011, p. 3). The *Diagnostic and Statistical Manual of Mental Disorders-3* (DSM-III) process acknowledged that "these various syndromes (e.g., combat-related syndrome, battered women syndrome, rape trauma syndrome and child abuse syndrome) had very similar patterns of symptoms that became embodied within the PTSD diagnostic criteria" (Stein, et al., 2011, p. 3). Hence, there was no longer a focus on the different causes for the disorder but a focus on the similar behavior characteristics shared among the various groups. So in regard to treatment, therapeutic photography would be appropriate for the different syndromes of individuals who share similar characteristic of PTSD.

The symptoms of PTSD range in degrees, mild to severe, and greatly diminish the quality of a person's life. The National Center for PTSD (Understanding PTSD Treatment, 2011, p. 2) states that there are four types of symptoms. The first one is reliving the event or having nightmares of the past trauma. The second form is avoiding situations that remind the person of the event by remaining isolated from people in normal day-to-day activities. A third symptom is a feeling of numbness, finding it hard to express your feelings and hard to remember or talk about parts of the trauma. Finally, there is the symptom of feeling hyper-aroused, suddenly becoming angry or irritable.

Key Survey Data Findings—Group A (General Population): Survey data shows that 25 of 45 respondents (56 percent) consider therapeutic photography as an effective option to reduce PTSD symptoms. The "yes" responses for therapeutic photography are slightly greater than the "no" responses against therapeutic photography. However, there is a significant preference for left cerebral therapy. There is a high rate of left cerebral therapy for each PTSD category, yet there is a slight decreasing trend as the severity of PTSD increases. In other words, there is a noticeable increase in the right cerebral therapy

---

*Published with permission of the authors.

category as the severity of PTSD increases. My assumption is that the more severe the disorder, the more intuitive the need for the individual to balance his/her brain. Another key finding for this study is that within this small sampling, 78 of 110 respondents (69 percent) have PTSD.

Key Interview Findings—Group B (Clinicians): Interview data findings for clinicians revealed that they had a strong preference for left hemisphere therapies such as Cognitive Processing Therapy (CPT), Cognitive Behavioral Therapy (CBT) and Prolonged Exposure (P.E). Only 1 out of 5 clinicians thought therapeutic photography would reduce anxiety. However, it was viewed favorably as a treatment similar to art therapy and as an avenue to positively express one's experience. There is consensus among the clinicians that there should not be a set time to begin a therapeutic photography program because every person has a different recovery process. Beginning a program when a client is not emotionally ready can possibly re-traumatize the individual.

Interview Data Results and Findings–Group C (Art Instructors): Interview data confirms a consensus among the instructors that therapeutic photography was an effective treatment to reduce PTSD symptoms for students. The symptoms most effectively treated using therapeutic photography are fear, anxiety, stress and the inability to cope and lack of ability to communicate. They also gave insight and meaningful components to fit in the technical, aesthetic, and emotional categories for a successful therapeutic photography program. However, there was no consensus regarding the time frame for when therapy should begin.

Overall Significant Findings: The literature review affirms the main question that therapeutic photography can reduce symptoms of anxiety, however there is no data to affirm that a photography program taken within twelve months of a trauma would reduce anxiety. The review indicates that photographs offer a therapeutic dialogue in a visual language for those who are emotionally unable to express or are disabled in verbal communication, because they contain psychologically and emotional information about an individual. Additionally, both CPT (left hemisphere) therapy and therapeutic photography (right hemisphere) therapy allows an individual to process one's trauma experience and to identify thoughts that are obstacles to their recovery. The review identifies three obstacles that prevent our American culture from choosing right brain therapies. The biases include cultural, socio-economics and structural elements. It also indicates a critical component for a photography program is to have no restrictions on the type of camera used or the type of processing or post-processing used to transform pictures. Lastly, there are measures that can be taken to add a sense of safety for PTSD participants in a program. Threatening attitudes, actions, or words should not be allowed in the program

Jeanne DeLaney's Story Regarding PTSD

In January 2010, I was a victim of a crime and developed significant PTSD symptoms. Even though I was not diagnosed or treated by a medical physician, I recognized the classic symptoms of the disorder: flashbacks of the trauma, difficulty concentrating, feeling emotionally cut off and extremely anxious. My PTSD symptoms interrupted my daily living activities. In addition, my symptoms prevented me from gainful employment.

In April 2010, I began a self-therapeutic photography program three months after my trauma. "Therapeutic photography is photo-based activities conducted by oneself or as part of an organized group where no formal professionalized therapy is taking place" (Therapeutic Photography, 2014). After participating for five months, I noticed an increase in my sense of wellness by my ability to sleep through the night, and a slight decrease in my anxiety level particularly when I was driving my car *out* of the garage after dark. Nevertheless, it would be an entire year before I was able to return to work because I still experienced panic attacks just from my thoughts of driving my car *into* my garage at night.

In June 2010, I began cognitive processing therapy. The therapist provided emotional support by validating my traumatic experience and allowing me to speak about it without judgment. It gave me relief to know that someone else knew my story. At one point, during a particular CPT counseling session, my therapist used Eye Movement Desensitization and Reprocessing (EMDR) when I became noticeably distressed from re-experiencing my trauma. The therapist controlled my eye movements by directing them with the movement of her hand. Even though, I have not been in a formal EMDR therapy, I experienced an immediate calming and was able to continue my therapy session. CPT, a left hemisphere therapy, was helpful to me; however, I didn't feel like the cognitive therapy had the strength to move me from point A to point B of my recovery process. From my perspective, both treatments, the right and left hemisphere therapies, collectively helped to relieved my anxiety symptoms.

In August 2010, to advance my healing process, I expanded my right cerebral therapy experience by taking two classes at Access Sacramento, a public television station, so that I could be certified to produce television programs at the station: a digital production class and a multi camera studio operations class. In my opinion, the photography therapy and digital camera classes taken within twelve months of my trauma provided a swifter recovery time. The right brain therapy of photography was more effective than the left brain therapy in giving me a sense of empowerment and positive mental arrangement. I was able to focus my energy as a camera person for the show "The Forgotten Warrior," a half hour segment that showcased speakers and provided information to assist military veterans to live productive lives. During that season, my anxiety level decreased considerably and I was able to drive my car *into* my garage at night without a panic attack. Subsequently, I returned to work in the summer of 2011. In my opinion, therapeutic photography was effective in reducing my anxiety which had become a physical and emotional obstacle.

Beginning a therapeutic photography program within twelve months of a trauma was very beneficial to me. The right cerebral therapy helped to decrease my panic attacks so that I could return to work after over a year of absence. Initially, CPT, a left cerebral therapy, was important because having someone to talk to helped me to validate my trauma and to not feel emotional isolated in my trauma experience. Therapeutic photography was more effective for me than CPT in reducing my anxiety. Nevertheless, I believe that participating in both right and left cerebral therapy provided for a swifter recovery process for me.

Therapeutic photography is an effective way to treat individuals with PTSD by reducing the anxiety level for the individuals. In addition, my study supports that therapeutic photography is a treatment which should not be considered better or worse than other types of PTSD treatments.

The validity of this study is strengthened by the convergence of multiple sources of data. Survey data, Group C's key informants' interview data, and literature review findings collectively support the hypothesis of this study that therapeutic photography is an effective option to reduce PTSD symptoms. From the survey data, 25 out of 45 respondents considered therapeutic photography as an effective option to reduce PTSD symptoms, which includes anxiety symptoms, Interview data from Group C also leads to a similar conclusion. This group of artistic informants, who access their right hemisphere on a regular basis, were in agreement that therapeutic photography is an effective treatment to reduce PTSD symptoms in students. The symptoms most effectively treated using therapeutic photography are fear, anxiety, stress and the inability to cope and lack of ability to communicate. The findings from the literature review also supports the research hypothesis. Several articles and authors such as Hunsberger (1984), Natoli (2011), Ramsey (2008), Rubin (2005), and Suler (2003), affirm a direct correlation between the therapeutic properties of therapeutic photography and its ability to reduce anxiety individuals with PTSD. Lastly, my personal observations and experiences affirm the entire research question; therapeutic photography can reduce anxiety if a therapeutic photography program is taken within 12 months of the trauma.

On the other hand, a second research hypothesis that the therapeutic program should be taken within 12 months of the trauma was not supported by the literature nor by the clinicians. However, there is a consensus among the clinicians in Group B that there should not be a set time to begin a therapeutic photography program because every person has a different recovery process. Beginning a program when a client is not emotionally ready can possibly re-traumatize the individual. There was no consensus, nor support from the art instructors in Group C regarding the time frame for taking a therapeutic photography program. Lastly, the literature review offers no reference in regards to when a therapeutic photography program should begin. In sum, my research question was only partially affirmed; therapeutic photography reduces anxiety in individuals with PTSD.

REFERENCES

Hunsberger, P. (1984). "Uses of Instant-Print Photography in Psychotherapy." *The American Psychological Association*, Vol. 15, No. 6, pp. 884–890

Natoli, A. (2011). "The Psychologically Beneficial Aspect of Photography." Independent Study. Rider University. (pp. 1–25).

Ramsay, G.G.; Sweet, H.B. (2008). *Creative Guide to Exploring Your Life Self-Reflection Using Photography, Art, and Writing*. London: Jessica Kingsley, 2008.

Rubin, J.A. (2005). *Artful Therapy*. Hoboken, NJ: Wiley. Retrieved on February 2, 2014, from http://site.ebrary.com/lib/gguu/Doc?id=10114183&ppg=71.

Stein, D.J., Friedman, M.J. & Blanco, C. (2011). *Post-Traumatic Stress Disorder*. Chichester, West Sussex, U.K.: John Wiley & Sons. Retrieved on January 22, 2014, from http://0-site.ebrary.com.library.ggu.edu/lib/gguu/docDetail.action?docID=10575453.

Suler, J. (2003). *Photographic Psychology: Image and Psyche*. Doylestown, PA: True Center Publishing.

"Understanding PTSD Treatment." (2011). U.S. Department of Veteran Affairs. Produced by the National Center for PTSD. Retrieved on December 4, 2013, from http://www.ptsd.va.gov/public/page/treatment-ptsd.asp.

63. To Treat Pain, PTSD and Other Ills, Tennessee Vets Try Tai Chi*

Blake Farmer

Every week in Murfreesboro, Tenn., Zibin Guo guides veterans in wheelchairs through slow-motion tai chi poses as a Bluetooth speaker plays soothing instrumental music.

"Cloudy hands to the right, cloudy hands to the left," he tells them, referring to the move traditionally known as "cloud hands." "Now we're going to open your arms, grab the wheels and 180-degree turn."

The participants swivel about-face and continue to the next pose. Guo modified the ancient Chinese martial art to work from a seated position. Even though many of those in his class don't rely on wheelchairs for mobility, using the mobile chairs makes it easier for them to get through a half-hour of movement.

The Department of Veterans Affairs has given $120,000 in grant money to Guo to spread his special wheelchair tai chi course. He started in Chattanooga, Tenn., and has expanded his classes to Murfreesboro.

This idea of going beyond prescriptions—and especially beyond opioid painkillers—has been a key focus of the VA nationally.

In Tennessee, nearly a quarter of all VA patients with an active medical prescription were on opioids in 2012. That number has dropped to 15 percent, but that's still higher than in most other parts of the country.

According to a national survey from 2015, nearly every VA hospital now offers some kind of alternative health treatment—like yoga, mindfulness and art therapy.

Guo is teaching people in a half-dozen VA hospitals in Florida, Texas, Utah and Arizona to use his version of tai chi. He believes the focus on breathing and mindfulness—paired with manageable physical activity—can help ease a variety of ailments.

"When you have a good amount of body harmony, people tend to engage in proactive life," he says, "so that helps with all kinds of symptoms."

While wheelchair tai chi would provide activity for those who've lost some use of their legs, the exercise program is also geared toward helping vets who have mental health issues, including post-traumatic stress disorder.

*Originally published as Blake Farmer, "To Treat Pain, PTSD and Other Ills, Tennessee Vets Try Tai Chi," *Kaiser Health News*, April 6, 2018. This story is part of a partnership that includes Nashville Public Radio, NPR and Kaiser Health News.

Thomas Sales of Nashville, Tenn., recalls his most recent panic attack: "Night before last, when we had the thunderstorm," he said. "The thunder is a big trigger for some people."

Sales still has panic attacks regularly—25 years after he fought in the first Gulf War with the Navy Special Warfare Command.

"You'll find yourself flashing back to being out there with the fellas, and you'll just kind of snap," he said. "And I found myself, for some reason, thinking about doing the breathing techniques [from tai chi], and doing the 'heaven and earth,' and then breathing deep and slow."

Sales said he knows it must look crazy to some people when he reaches to the sky and then sweeps his arms to the ground. There was a time when he would have agreed. Most of the patients in this class had some skepticism going into the tai chi program. But Vietnam veteran Jim Berry of Spring Hill, Tenn., says he's now convinced.

"My daughter sent me a T-shirt that sums it up," he said. "Tai chi is more than old folks chasing trees."

Berry credits meditation and tai chi with helping him quit smoking. "No cigarettes for three months now," he said.

Zarita Croney, a veteran with the National Guard, said tai chi has helped her, too, with chemical dependence. She now makes the nearly-two-hour drive from Hopkinsville, Ky., to Murfreesboro each week, and has reduced her use of opioids for pain.

"My whole life ... revolved around, 'Oh shoot, when can I take my next pill? When can I take my next pill?'" Croney recalled. "I've gone from about 90 percent of my day being on my bed to being able to come out and be social."

The Department of Veterans Affairs has been aggressively trying to wean vets from reliance on strong narcotics—partly by using prescription data as a key measurement to judge VA hospitals across the country—while trying to make sure alternatives don't cause their own harmful side effects.

The VA acknowledges that there's very little evidence at this point that tai chi or mindfulness therapy or acupuncture will do any good for PTSD or addiction, though recently there has been research into the quality of life benefits of tai chi among the older adults.

But these alternative therapies have been in use by the department long enough that the VA aims to more closely track the treatments' effectiveness. It is especially targeting people for alternative treatment who have only recently completed their military service.

The goal, proponents say, is to have veterans incorporate these techniques into their weekly routine, not just rely on a drug prescription to ease pain or anxiety.

"Whole health, along with how many opiates are being prescribed—we're going to look at how does this impact that," said Aaron Grobengieser, who oversees alternative medicine for VA hospitals in Tennessee.

"I believe this is going to be an avenue," he said, "to really help address that group of folks that are really looking for ways to manage those types of conditions without popping another pill."

64. Marijuana Use and PTSD Among Veterans[*]

Marcel O. Bonn-Miller *and* Glenna S. Rousseau

Marijuana use for medical conditions is an issue of growing concern. Some veterans use marijuana to relieve symptoms of PTSD and several states specifically approve the use of medical marijuana for PTSD. However, controlled studies have not been conducted to evaluate the safety or effectiveness of medical marijuana for PTSD. Thus, there is no evidence at this time that marijuana is an effective treatment for PTSD. In fact, research suggests that marijuana can be harmful to individuals with PTSD.

Marijuana use has increased over the past decade. In 2013, a study found that 19.8 million people reported using marijuana in the past month, with 8.1 million using almost every day. Daily use has increased 60 percent in the prior decade.[1] A number of factors are associated with increased risk of marijuana use, including diagnosis of PTSD,[2] social anxiety disorder,[3] other substance use, particularly during youth,[4] and peer substance use.[5]

Cannabis Use Disorder Among Veterans Using VA Health Care

There has been no study of marijuana use in the overall veteran population. What we do know comes from looking at data of veterans using VA health care, who may not be representative of veterans overall. When considering the subset of veterans seen in VA health care with co-occurring PTSD and substance use disorders (SUD), cannabis use disorder has been the most diagnosed SUD since 2009. The percentage of veterans in VA with PTSD and SUD who were diagnosed with cannabis use disorder increased from 13.0 percent in fiscal year (FY) 2002 to 22.7 percent in FY 2014. As of FY 2014, there are more than 40,000 veterans with PTSD and SUD seen in VA diagnosed with cannabis use disorder.[6]

Rates of cannabis use disorder diagnoses grew from 13.0 percent in FY02 to 22.7

---

[*]Public document originally published as Marcel O. Bonn-Miller and Glenna S. Rousseau, "Marijuana Use and PTSD Among Veterans," https://www.ptsd.va.gov/professional/co-occurring/marijuana_use_ptsd_veterans.asp (September 24, 2018).

percent in FY14. Cocaine use disorder was the most diagnosed SUD among veterans with PTSD in FY02, at 18.9 percent. In FY09, cocaine became less common than cannabis use disorder (15.4 percent and 15.9 percent respectively), and as of FY14, cocaine use disorder is the second most common SUD diagnosis among veterans with PTSD, at 14.8 percent. Among this subset of veterans, opioid use disorder was diagnosed at a rate of 9.9 percent in FY02, rising to 12.5 percent in FY14. Amphetamine use disorder was diagnosed at a rate of 2.6 percent in FY02 and rose to 4.4 percent in FY14.

Problems Associated with Marijuana Use

Marijuana use is associated with medical and psychiatric problems. These problems may be caused by using, but they also may reflect the characteristics of the people who use marijuana. Medical problems include chronic bronchitis, abnormal brain development among early adolescent initiators, and impairment in short-term memory, motor coordination and the ability to perform complex psychomotor tasks such as driving. Psychiatric problems include psychosis and impairment in cognitive ability. Quality of life can also be affected through poor life satisfaction, decreased educational attainment, and increased sexual risk-taking behavior.[7] Chronic marijuana use also can lead to addiction, with an established and clinically significant withdrawal syndrome.[8]

Active Ingredients and Route of Administration

Marijuana contains a variety of components (cannabinoids), most notably delta-9-tetrahydrocannabinol (THC) the primary psychoactive compound in the marijuana plant. There are a number of other cannabinoids, such as cannabidiol (CBD), cannabinol (CBN), and cannabigerol (CBG). Marijuana can vary in cannabinoid concentration, such as in the ratio of THC to other cannabinoids (CBD in particular). Therefore, the effects of marijuana use (e.g., experience of a high, anxiety, sleep) vary as a function of the concentration of cannabinoids (e.g., THC/CBD).

In addition, the potency of cannabinoids can vary. For example, the concentration of THC in the marijuana plant can range in strength from less than 1 percent to 30 percent based upon strain and cultivation methods. In general, the potency of THC in the marijuana plant has increased as much as tenfold over the past 40 years.[9] Recently, cannabis extract products, such as waxes and oils, have been produced and sold in which the concentration of THC can be as high as 90 percent. Thus, an individual could unknowingly consume a very high dose of THC in one administration, which increases the risk of an adverse reaction.

Marijuana can be consumed in many different forms (e.g., flower, hash, oil, wax, food products, tinctures). Administration of these forms also can take different routes: inhalation (smoking or vaporizing), ingestion, and topical application. Given the same concentration/ratio of marijuana, smoking or vaporizing marijuana produces similar effects[10]; however, ingesting the same dose results in a delayed onset and longer duration of effect.[11] Not all marijuana users may be aware of the delayed effect caused by ingestion, which may result in greater consumption and a stronger effect than intended.

Neurobiology

Research has consistently demonstrated that the human endocannabinoid system plays a significant role in PTSD. People with PTSD have greater availability of cannabinoid type 1 (CB1) receptors as compared to trauma-exposed or healthy controls.[12] As a result, marijuana use by individuals with PTSD may result in short-term reduction of PTSD symptoms. However, data suggest that continued use of marijuana among individuals with PTSD may lead to a number of negative consequences, including marijuana tolerance (via reductions in CB1 receptor density and/or efficiency) and addiction.[13] Though recent work has shown that CB1 receptors may return after periods of marijuana abstinence,[14] individuals with PTSD may have particular difficulty quitting.[15]

Marijuana, Treatment and Clinical Recommendations

The belief that marijuana can be used to treat PTSD is limited to anecdotal reports from individuals with PTSD who say that the drug helps with their symptoms. There have been no randomized controlled trials, a necessary "gold standard" for determining efficacy. Administration of oral CBD has been shown to decrease anxiety in those with and without clinical anxiety.[16] This work has led to the development and testing of CBD treatments for individuals with social anxiety,[17] but not yet among individuals with PTSD. With respect to THC, one open trial of 10 participants with PTSD showed THC was safe and well tolerated and resulted in decreases in hyperarousal symptoms.[18]

People with PTSD have particular difficulty stopping their use of marijuana and responding to treatment for marijuana addiction. They have greater craving and withdrawal than those without PTSD,[19] and greater likelihood of marijuana use during the six months following a quit attempt. However, these individuals can benefit from the many evidence-based treatments for marijuana addiction, including cognitive behavioral therapy, motivational enhancement, and contingency management.[20] Thus, providers should still utilize these options to support reduction/abstinence.

Treatment providers should not ignore marijuana use in their PTSD patients. The VA/DoD PTSD Clinical Practice Guideline (2010) recommends providing evidence-based treatments for the individual disorders concurrently. PTSD providers should offer education about problems associated with long-term marijuana use and make a referral to a substance use disorder (SUD) specialist if they do not feel they have expertise in treating substance use.

Individuals with comorbid PTSD and SUD do not need to wait for a period of abstinence before addressing their PTSD. A growing number of studies demonstrate that that these patients can tolerate trauma-focused treatment and that these treatments do not worsen substance use outcomes. Therefore, providers have a range of options to help improve the lives of patients with the co-occurring disorders. For more information, see Treatment of Co-Occurring PTSD and Substance Use Disorder in VA.

NOTES

1. SAMHSA. (2014). Results from the 2013 National Survey on Drug Use and Health: Summary of National Findings. (Vol. NSDUH Series H-48, HHS Publication No. (SMA) 13-4795). Rockville, MD: Substance Abuse and Mental Health Services Administration.

2. Cougle, J.R., Bonn-Miller, M.O., Vujanovic, A.A., Zvolensky, M.J., & Hawkins, K.A. (2011). "Post-

traumatic Stress Disorder and Cannabis Use in a Nationally Representative Sample." *Psychology of Addictive Behaviors*, 25, 554–558.

3. Buckner, J.D., Schmidt, N.B., Lang, A.R., Small, J.W., Schluach, R.C., & Lewinsohn, P.M. (2008). "Specificity of Social Anxiety Disorder as a Risk Factor for Alcohol and Cannabis Dependence." *Journal of Psychiatric Research*, 42, 230–239.

4. Butterworth, P., Slade, T. & Degenhardt, L. (2014). "Factors Associated with the Timing and Onset of Cannabis Use and Cannabis Use Disorder: Results from the 2007 Australian National Survey of Mental Health and Well-Being." *Drug and Alcohol Review*, 33, 555–564.

5. Von Sydow, K., Lieb, R., Pfister, H., Höefler, M., & Wittchen, H.U. (2002). "What Predicts Incident Use of Cannabis and Progression to Abuse and Dependence? A 4-Year Prospective Examination of Risk Factors in a Community Sample of Adolescents and Young Adults." *Drug and Alcohol Dependence*, 68, 49–64.

6. Program Evaluation and Resource Center, VA, 2015.

7. Volkow, N.D., Baler, R.D., Compton, W.M., & Weiss, S.R.B. (2014). "Adverse Health Effects of Marijuana Use." *New England Journal of Medicine*, 370, 2219–2227.

8. Budney, A.J., Hughes, J.R., Moore, B.A., & Vandrey, R. (2004). "Review of the Validity and Significance of Cannabis Withdrawal Syndrome." *American Journal of Psychiatry*, 161, 1967–1977.

9. Mehmedic, Z., Chandra, S., Slade, D., Denham, H., Foster, S., Patel, A.S., Ross, S.A., Khan, I.A., & ElSohly, M.A. (2010). "Potency Trends of Δ9-THC and Other Cannabinoids in Confiscated Cannabis Preparations from 1993 to 2008." *Journal of Forensic Sciences*, 55, 1209–1217; Sevigny, E.L., Pacula, R.L., & Heaton, P. (2014). "The Effects of Medical Marijuana Laws on Potency." *International Journal of Drug Policy*, 25, 308–319.

10. Abrams, D.I., Vizoso, H.P., Shade, S.B., Jay, C., Kelly, M.E., & Benowitz, N.L. (2007). "Vaporization as a Smokeless Cannabis Delivery System: A Pilot Study." *Clinical Pharmacology & Therapeutics*, 82, 572–578.

11. Grotenhermen, F. (2003). "Pharmacokinetics and Pharmacodynamics of Cannabinoids." *Clinical Pharmacokinetics*, 42, 327–360.

12. Neumeister, A., Normandin, M.D., Pietrzak, R.H., Piomelli, D., Zheng, M.Q., Gujarro-Anton, A., Potenza, M.N., Bailey, C.R., Lin, S.F., Najafzaden, S., Ropchan, J., Henry, S., Corsi-Travali, S., Carson, R.E., & Huang, Y. (2013). "Elevated Brain Cannabinoid CB1 Receptor Availability in Post-Traumatic Stress Disorder: A Positron Emission Tomography Study." *Molecular Psychiatry*, 18, 1034–1040; Passie, T., Emrich, H.M., Brandt, S.D., & Halpern, J.H. (2012). "Mitigation of Post-Traumatic Stress Symptoms by Cannabis Resin: A Review of the Clinical and Neurobiological Evidence." *Drug Testing and Analysis*, 4, 649–659.

13. Kendall, D.A. & Alexander, S.P.H. (2009). *Behavioral Neurobiology of the Endocannabinoid System: Current Topics in Behavioral Neurosciences*. Heidelberg: Springer-Verlag.

14. Hirvonen, J., Goodwin, R.S., Li, C-T., Terry, G.E., Zoghbi, S.S., Morse, C., Pike, V.W., Volkow, N.D., Huestis, M.A., & Innis, R.B. (2012). "Reversible and Regionally Selective Downregulation of Brain Cannabinoid CB1 Receptors in Chronic Daily Cannabis Smokers." *Molecular Psychiatry*, 17, 642–649.

15. Bonn-Miller, M.O., Moos, R.H., Boden, M.T., Long, W.R., Kimerling, R., & Trafton, J.A. (2015). "The Impact of Posttraumatic Stress Disorder on Cannabis Quit Success." *The American Journal of Drug and Alcohol Abuse* 41(4): 3239–44.

16. Crippa, J.A., Zuardi, A.W., Martín-Santos, R., Bhattacharyya, S., Atakan, Z., McGuire, P., & Fusar-Poli, P. (2009). "Cannabis and Anxiety: A Critical Review of the Evidence." *Human Psychopharmacology*, 24, 515–523.

17. Bergamaschi, M.M., Queiroz, R.H.C., Hortes, M., Chagas, N., de Oliveira, C.G., De Martinis, B.S., Kapczinski, F., Quevedo, J., Roesler, R., Schröder, N., Nardi, A.E., Martín-Santos, R., Hallak, J.E.C., Zuardi, A.W., & Crippa, J.A.S. (2011). "Cannabidiol Reduces the Anxiety Induced by Simulated Public Speaking in Treatment-Naïve Social Phobia Patients." *Neuropsychopharmacology*, 36, 1219–1226.

18. Roitman, P., Mechoulam, R., Cooper-Kazaz, R., & Shalev, A. (2014). "Preliminary, Open-Label, Pilot Study of Add-On Oral Δ9-Tetrahydrocannabinol in Chronic Post-Traumatic Stress Disorder." *Clinical Drug Investigation*, 34, 587–591.

19. Boden, M.T., Babson, K.A., Vujanovic, A.A., Short, N.A., & Bonn-Miller, M. (2013). "Posttraumatic Stress Disorder and Cannabis Use Characteristics Among Military Veterans with Cannabis Dependence." *The American Journal on Addictions*, 22, 277–284.

20. Roffman, R.A. & Stephens, R.S. (2006). *Cannabis Dependence: Its Nature, Consequences, and Treatment: International Research Monographs in the Addictions*. Cambridge, UK; New York: Cambridge University Press.

65. VA and Marijuana—
What Veterans Need to Know*

U.S. Department of Veterans Affairs

Several states have approved the use of marijuana for medical and/or recreational use. Veterans should know that federal law classifies marijuana—including all derivative products—as a Schedule One controlled substance. This makes it illegal in the eyes of the federal government.

The U.S. Department of Veterans Affairs is required to follow all federal laws including those regarding marijuana. As long as the Food and Drug Administration classifies marijuana as Schedule One VA health care providers may not recommend it or assist veterans to obtain it.

Veteran participation in state marijuana programs does not affect eligibility for VA care and services. VA providers can and do discuss marijuana use with veterans as part of comprehensive care planning, and adjust treatment plans as necessary.

Some things veteran need to know about marijuana and the VA:

- Veterans will not be denied VA benefits because of marijuana use.
- Veterans are encouraged to discuss marijuana use with their VA providers.
- VA health care providers will record marijuana use in the veteran's VA medical record in order to have the information available in treatment planning. As with all clinical information, this is part of the confidential medical record and protected under patient privacy and confidentiality laws and regulations.
- VA clinicians may not recommend medical marijuana.
- VA clinicians may only prescribe medications that have been approved by the U.S. Food and Drug Administration for medical use. At present most products containing tetrahydrocannabinol (THC), cannabidiol (CBD), or other cannabinoids are not approved for this purpose.
- VA clinicians may not complete paperwork/forms required for veteran patients to participate in state-approved marijuana programs.
- VA pharmacies may not fill prescriptions for medical marijuana.
- VA will not pay for medical marijuana prescriptions from any source.

*Public document originally published as U.S. Department of Veterans Affairs, "VA and Marijuana—What Veterans Need to Know," https://www.publichealth.va.gov/marijuana.asp (January 7, 2019).

- VA scientists may conduct research on marijuana benefits and risks, and potential for abuse, under regulatory approval.
- The use or possession of marijuana is prohibited at all VA medical centers, locations and grounds. When you are on VA grounds it is federal law that is in force, not the laws of the state.
- Veterans who are VA employees are subject to drug testing under the terms of employment.

VHA Directive 1315 (below) "Access to VHA Clinical Programs for Veterans Participating in State-Approved Marijuana Programs" provides more guidelines.

If you have questions regarding VA's marijuana policy please contact: population. health@va.gov.

VHA Directive 1315

Access to Veterans Health Administration Clinical Programs for Veterans Participating in State-Approved Marijuana Programs

1. Purpose

This Veterans Health Administration (VHA) directive provides policy regarding access to VHA clinical programs for Veterans participating in a State-approved marijuana program.

2. Definitions

a. **Controlled Substance.** A drug or other substance included in Schedule I, II, III, IV, or V established by section 202 of the Controlled Substances Act of 1970 (84 Stat.

b. 1236), as updated and republished under the provisions of that Act (21 United States. Code [U.S.C] 812). Schedule I includes drugs or other substances with a high potential for abuse, without a currently acceptable medical use in treatment in the United States, and lacking accepted safety for use under medical supervision. Marijuana is classified as a Schedule I.

c. **Marijuana:** All parts of the plant Cannabis sativa L., whether growing or not; the seeds thereof; the resin extracted from any part of such plant; and every compound, manufacture, salt, derivative, mixture, or preparation of such plant, its seeds or resin. Such term does not include the mature stalks of such plant, fiber produced from such stalks, oil or cake made from the seeds of such plant, any other compound, manufacture, salt, derivative, mixture, or preparation of such mature stalks (except the resin extracted therefrom), fiber, oil, or cake, or the sterilized seed of such plant which is incapable of germination.

3. Policy

It is VHA policy that:

a. VHA providers and/or pharmacists discuss with the Veteran marijuana use, due to its clinical relevance to patient care, and discuss marijuana use with any Veterans requesting information about marijuana;

b. To comply with Federal laws such as the Controlled Substances Act (Title 21

c. United States Code [U.S.C.] 801 et al.), VHA providers are prohibited from completing forms or registering Veterans for participation in a State-approved marijuana program; and,

d. VHA providers and/or pharmacists should discuss with patients how their use of State-approved medical marijuana to treat medical or psychiatric symptoms or conditions may relate to the Veterans participation in other clinical activities, (e.g.,

e. discuss how marijuana may impact other aspects of the overall care of the Veteran such as how marijuana may interact with other medications the Veteran is taking, or how the use of marijuana may impact other aspects of the overall care of the Veteran such as pain management, Post-Traumatic Stress Disorder [PTSD], or substance use disorder treatment).

4. Responsibilities

a. **Under Secretary for Health.** The Under Secretary for Health is responsible for ensuring VHA compliance with this directive.

b. **Deputy Under Secretary for Health for Operations and Management.** The Deputy Under Secretary for Health for Operations and Management, or designee, is responsible for ensuring that the Department of Veterans Affairs (VA) medical facility Directors are aware that it is VHA policy for providers to assess Veteran use of marijuana but providers are prohibited from recommending, making referrals to or completing paperwork for Veteran participation in State marijuana programs.

c. **Deputy Under Secretary for Health for Policy and Services.** The Deputy Under Secretary for Health for Policy and Services, or designee, is responsible for assuring that all policies are aligned with the content of this directive.

d. **Assistant Deputy Under Secretary for Health for Policy and Services, Patient Care Services.** The Assistant Deputy under Secretary for Policy and Services, Patient Care Services, or designee, is responsible for assuring that VA providers receive

e. current information regarding known/potential impact of participation in State marijuana program on clinical care and treatment planning.

f. **Chief Consultant, Population Health Services.** The Chief Consultant, Population Health Services is responsible for the content of this directive and development of strategies to educate Veterans and VHA staff regarding this directive.

g. **Veterans Integrated Service Network (VISN) Director.** The VISN Director, or designee, is responsible for assuring that this policy is disseminated and implemented at all facilities in the VISN.

h. **VA Medical Facility Director.** Each VA medical facility Director, or designee, is responsible for ensuring VA facility staff are aware of the following:

(1) Clinical staff may discuss with veterans relevant clinical information regarding marijuana and when this is discussed it must be documented in the veteran's medical record. Veterans must not be denied VHA services solely because they are participating in State-approved marijuana programs. Providers need to make decisions to modify treatment plans based on marijuana use on a case-by-case basis, such decisions need to be made in partnership with the veteran and must be based on concerns regarding veteran health and safety.

(2) The prohibition on recommending, making referrals to or completing forms and registering veterans for participation in State-approved marijuana program.

(3) If a Veteran presents an authorization for marijuana to a VHA provider or pharmacist, VA will not provide marijuana nor will VA pay for marijuana to be provided by a non–VA entity.

(4) Possession of marijuana, even for authorized medical reasons, by veterans while on VA property is in violation of 38 CFR 1.218(a)(7) and places them at risk for prosecution under the Controlled Substances Act, 21 U.S.C 801 et al.

(5) Employees of VA, including those who are veterans receiving care through VHA, are prohibited from using a Schedule 1 drug, including marijuana, by the Mandatory Guidelines for Federal Workplace Drug Testing Programs published by the Department of Health and Human Services and VA Handbook 5383.2, VA Drug-Free Workplace Program.

(6) If a veteran reports marijuana use and/or participation in a state-approved marijuana program to a member of the clinical staff, that information is entered into the "non–VA/herbal/Over the Counter (OTC) medication section" of the veteran's electronic medical record following established procedures for recording non–VA medication use (see VHA Directive 2011–012, Medication Reconciliation, or subsequent policy document, VHA Directive 1108.08, VHA Formulary Management Process). If a provider discusses marijuana with a veteran, relevant information must be documented in progress notes, and considered in the development or modification of the treatment plan.

5. References

a. 21 U.S.C. 801 et al, the Controlled Substances Act. 38 CFR 1.218(a)(7).
b. VA Handbook 5383.2, VA Drug-Free Workplace Plan, dated April 11, 1997, or subsequent policy.
c. VHA Directive 1108.08, VHA Formulary Management Process, dated November 2, 2016, or subsequent policy.
d. VHA Directive 2011–012, Medication Reconciliation, dated March 9, 2011, or subsequent policy.
e. Department of Human Health Services, Federal Register 73, Number 228. https://www.gpo.gov/fdsys/pkg/FR-2008-11-25/html/E8–26726.htm.
f. Office of General Counsel (OCG) opinion on State Marijuana Registration Forms—VAOPGCADV 9–2008.

66. VA Clears the Air on Talking to Patients About Marijuana Use[*]

MICHELLE ANDREWS

"Don't ask, don't tell" is how many veterans have approached health care conversations about marijuana use with the doctors they see from the Department of Veterans Affairs.

Worried that owning up to using the drug could jeopardize their VA benefits—even if they're participating in a medical marijuana program approved by their state—veterans have often kept mum. That may be changing under a new directive from the Veterans Health Administration urging vets and their physicians to open up on the subject.

The new guidance directs VA clinical staff and pharmacists to discuss with veterans how their use of medical marijuana could interact with other medications or aspects of their care, including treatment for pain management or post-traumatic stress disorder.

The directive leaves in place a key prohibition: VA providers are still not permitted to refer veterans to state-approved medical marijuana programs, since the drug is illegal under federal law, with no accepted medical use.

That disconnect makes veterans wary, said Michael Krawitz, a disabled Air Force veteran in Ironto, Va., who takes oxycodone and marijuana to treat extensive injuries he suffered in a non-combat-related motorcycle accident while stationed in Guam in 1984.

"Vets are happy that there's a policy, but they're unnerved by that prohibition," he said.

Krawitz, 55, is the executive director of Veterans for Medical Cannabis Access, an advocacy group. He has always been open with his VA doctors about his medical marijuana use and hasn't suffered any negative consequences. But Krawitz said he has worked with veterans who have been kicked out of their VA pain management program after a positive drug test and told they couldn't continue until they stopped using cannabis.

Such actions are usually misunderstandings that can be corrected, he said, but he suggests that the Veterans Health Administration should provide clear guidance to its staff about the new directive so veterans aren't harmed if they admit to using marijuana.

Although the new guidance encourages communication about veterans' use of mar-

*Originally published as Michelle Andrews, "VA Clears the Air on Talking to Patients About Marijuana Use," *Kaiser Health News*, January 9, 2018.

ijuana, the agency's position on the drug hasn't changed, said Curtis Cashour, a VA spokesman.

Cashour referred to a quote from Veterans Affairs Secretary David Shulkin at a White House briefing last May, who said he thought that among "some of the states that have put in appropriate controls [on the use of medical marijuana], there may be some evidence that this is beginning to be helpful. And we're interested in looking at that and learning from that." But until federal law changes, the VA is not "able to prescribe medical marijuana."

Cashour declined to provide further information about the new directive.

Under federal law, marijuana is classified as a Schedule 1 drug, meaning it has no accepted medical use and a high potential for abuse. Heroin and LSD are other Schedule 1 drugs. Doctors aren't permitted to prescribe marijuana. Instead, in states that have legalized the use of medical marijuana, doctors may refer patients to state-approved programs that allow marijuana use in certain circumstances. (Doctors can, however, prescribe three drugs approved by the Food and Drug Administration that are made of or similar to a synthetic form of THC, a chemical in marijuana.)

Twenty-nine states and the District of Columbia have laws that allow people to use marijuana legally for medical purposes. Patients who have a disease or condition that's approved for treatment with marijuana under the law are generally registered with the state and receive marijuana through state-regulated dispensaries or other facilities.

Moves by states to legalize marijuana for medical or recreational use have created a confusing landscape for patients to navigate. Attorney General Jeff Sessions announced he would rescind an Obama-era policy that discouraged federal prosecution for marijuana use in states where it is legal. That action has further clouded the issue.

Some consider caution a good thing. The accelerating trend of states approving marijuana for medical and recreational purposes may be getting ahead of the science to support it, they say.

A report released last January by the National Academies of Sciences, Engineering and Medicine examined more than 10,000 scientific abstracts about the health effects of marijuana and its chemical compounds on conditions ranging from epilepsy to glaucoma. The experts found conclusive evidence for a relatively limited number of conditions, including relief of chronic pain, nausea and vomiting associated with chemotherapy and muscle spasms associated with multiple sclerosis.

"I believe that there are chemicals in marijuana that have medicinal properties," said Dr. Otis Brawley, chief medical officer at the American Cancer Society. "I would love to know what those are, what their medicinal properties are and what the dose should be." But, he said, studies are extremely challenging to do because of restrictions in the United States on conducting research on Schedule 1 drugs.

No matter where the research stands, getting a complete medication or drug history should be standard procedure at any medical appointment, say medical providers.

In that respect, the guidance from the VA is a positive development.

"It's absolutely critical that you know what your patients are taking, if only to be better able to assess what is going on," said Dr. J. Michael Bostwick, a psychiatrist at Mayo Clinic in Rochester, Minn., who has written on medical marijuana use.

PART III

The Future

67. Veterans Have Fought in Wars—And Fought Against Them[*]

Michael Messner

If President Donald Trump had his way, the nation would be celebrating the centennial of the World War I armistice on Nov. 11 with a massive military parade in Washington, D.C.

But that won't be happening. When the Pentagon announced the president's decision to cancel the parade, they blamed local politicians for driving up the cost of the proposed event.

There may have been other reasons.

Veterans were especially outspoken in their opposition. Retired generals and admirals feared such a demonstration would embarrass the U.S., placing the nation in the company of small-time authoritarian regimes that regularly parade their tanks and missiles as demonstrations of their military might. And some veterans' organizations opposed the parade because they saw it as a celebration of militarism and war.

Veterans of past wars, as I document in my book *Guys Like Me: Five Wars, Five Veterans for Peace* have long been at the forefront of peace advocacy in the United States.

Politicians' Betrayal?

Over the past year, the advocacy group Veterans for Peace joined a coalition of 187 organizations that sought to "Stop the Military Parade; Reclaim Armistice Day." There is a deep history to veterans' peace advocacy.

As a young boy, I got my first hint of veterans' aversion to war from my grandfather, a World War I Army veteran. Just the mention of Veterans Day could trigger a burst of anger that "the damned politicians" had betrayed veterans of "The Great War."

In 1954 Armistice Day was renamed as Veterans Day. In previous years, citizens in the U.S. and around the world celebrated the 11th hour of the 11th day of the 11th month of 1918 not simply as the moment that war ended, but also as the dawning of a lasting peace.

---

*Originally published as Michael Messner, "Veterans Have Fought in Wars—And Fought Against Them," *The Conversation*, November 8, 2018. Reprinted with permission of the publisher.

"They told us it was 'The War to End All Wars,'" my grandfather said to me. "And we believed that."

Veterans for Peace

What my grandfather spoke about so forcefully was not an idle dream. In fact, a mass movement for peace had pressed the U.S. government, in 1928, to sign the Kellogg-Briand Pact, an international "Treaty for the Renunciation of War," sponsored by the United States and France and subsequently signed by most of the nations of the world.

A State Department historian described the agreement this way: "In the final version of the pact, they agreed upon two clauses: the first outlawed war as an instrument of national policy and the second called upon signatories to settle their disputes by peaceful means."

The pact did not end war, of course. Within a decade, another global war would erupt. But at the time, the pact articulated the sentiments of ordinary citizens, including World War I veterans and organizations like the Veterans of Foreign Wars, who during the late 1930s opposed U.S. entry into the deepening European conflicts.

In 1954, President Dwight D. Eisenhower signed the law changing the name of the holiday to Veterans Day, to include veterans of World War II and Korea.

For my grandfather, the name change symbolically punctuated the repudiation of the dream of lasting peace. Hope evaporated, replaced with the ugly reality that politicians would continue to find reasons to send American boys—"guys like me," as he put it—to fight and die in wars.

World War I, like subsequent wars, incubated a generation of veterans committed to preventing such future horrors for their sons.

From working-class army combat veterans like my grandfather to retired generals like Smedley Butler—who wrote and delivered public speeches arguing that "war is a racket," benefiting only the economic interests of ruling-class industrialists—World War I veterans spoke out to prevent future wars. And veterans of subsequent wars continue speaking out today.

There have been six U.S. presidents since my grandfather's death in early 1981—Presidents Ronald Reagan, George H.W. Bush, Bill Clinton, George W. Bush, Barack Obama and Donald Trump—and each committed U.S. military forces to overt or covert wars around the world.

Most of these wars, large or small, have been met with opposition from veterans' peace groups. In the 1960s and early 1970s, Vietnam Veterans Against the War was a powerful force in the popular opposition to the American war in Vietnam. And Veterans for Peace, along with About Face: Veterans Against the War remain outspoken against America's militarism and participation in wars in the Middle East and elsewhere.

Were he alive today, I believe my grandfather would surely express indignation that American leaders continue to send the young to fight and die in wars throughout the world.

Still, I like to imagine my grandfather smiling had he lived to witness some of the activities that will take place this Nov. 11: Veterans for Peace joins other peace organizations in Washington, D.C., and in cities around the U.S. and the world, marching behind banners that read "Observe Armistice Day, Wage Peace!"

68. What Is Moral Injury in Veterans?*

HOLLY ARROW *and* WILLIAM M. SCHUMACHER

On Nov. 11 each year, Americans honor military veterans who have transitioned to civilian status from active duty.

The cultural transition back to civilian life goes smoothly for some, but for others it is a challenging and sometimes lengthy process. Those who have deployed overseas or spent a substantial amount of time in the military may even deal with "reverse culture shock"—that is, upon return, their home culture can feel distant and disorienting.

Along with the cultural transition, veterans may be coping with post-traumatic stress disorder. More recently, clinicians who work with veterans have identified an additional cluster of symptoms that are related to military deployment but do not fit the criteria for PTSD.

These symptoms fit with what has been called "moral injury."

What Is Moral Injury?

Moral injury can occur when a personal moral code—one's understanding of "what's right"—is violated. Most individuals develop this code in childhood based on instructions from parents, teachers and religious leaders.

This sense of morality can incorporate fundamental values of religious and legal doctrines such as "Thou shalt not kill" and "Do unto others as you would have them do unto you." Most of us occasionally stray from what our code says is right, but military service—especially in combat zones—can expose people to situations in which every available choice has morally fraught results.

One combat veteran who served in Afghanistan, for example, told my psychology of war class that he had shot and killed a child soldier who was about to fire on his men. He knew he had made the "right" choice, but the responsibility for a child's death was still a heavy moral burden.

The moral conflict created by the violations of "what's right" generates moral injury when the inability to reconcile wartime actions with a personal moral code creates lasting psychological consequences.

---

*Originally published as Holly Arrow and William M. Schumacher, "What Is Moral Injury in Veterans?" *The Conversation*, May 21, 2017. Reprinted with permission of the publisher.

Psychiatrist Jonathan Shay, in his work with Vietnam veterans, defined moral injury as the psychological, social and physiological results of a betrayal of "what's right" by an authority in a high-stakes situation. In "Achilles in Vietnam," a book that examines the psychological devastation of war, a Vietnam veteran described a situation in which his commanding officers used tear gas on a village after his unit had their gas masks rendered ineffective due to water damage. The veteran stated, "They gassed us almost to death." This type of "friendly fire" incident is morally wounding in a way that attacks by an enemy are not.

Psychologist Brett Litz and his colleagues expanded this to include self-betrayal and identified "perpetrating, failing to prevent, bearing witness to, or learning about acts that transgress deeply held moral beliefs and expectations" as the cause of moral injury.

Guilt and Moral Injury

A research study published in 1991 identified combat-related guilt as the best predictor of suicide attempts among a sample of Vietnam veterans with PTSD. Details of the veterans' experiences connected that guilt to morally injurious events. As the authors noted,

"One man, for example, shot and killed a woman who was advancing toward his patrol and did not heed his order to stop. She turned out to be wired with explosives, but the veteran ruminated about whether he could have stopped her by firing a warning shot or wounding her in the legs."

A more recent study of active duty service members found that the connection between guilt and suicidal thoughts was strongest among those with combat exposure. Another review of research concluded that service members who committed acts that violated accepted bounds of behavior were more prone to substance abuse and suicidal behavior.

Can Moral Injury Be Healed?

The truth is that military engagement will always involve morally problematic actions. However, healing from moral injury is possible.

Mental health treatment can help. Preliminary evidence suggests that cognitive-behavioral therapy modified to treat issues related to moral injury can reduce depression as well as guilt- and shame-related thoughts. Treatment can come in other forms as well. Psychotherapist Edward Tick, for example, organizes trips to Vietnam for U.S. veterans to meet their Vietnamese counterparts, for the healing of decades-long wounds.

However, we don't need to be trained therapists to make a difference. Everyday social connections can also help the morally injured heal. For his dissertation, an author of this article (William M. Schumacher), conducted a series of interviews with veterans exposed to potentially morally injurious events and found consistent differences between those with higher levels of depression and suicidal thoughts and those with fewer symptoms. Veterans who weren't doing so well felt isolated and lacked support by friends, family and peers. Veterans with few symptoms felt supported by family, friends, peers and by their community. That's the rest of us.

When we discover that someone has a military background, replacing the perfunctory "Thank you for your service"—which rarely leads to a meaningful exchange—with questions that start a conversation can create a new connection. The hopes, dreams, insecurities and mistakes of those who have served may be somewhat different based on their military background; many won't be different at all.

More positive social connections aren't just psychologically healthy for veterans and their families. They are good for all of us, on Veterans Day and every other day of the year.

69. Veteran Teaches Therapists How to Talk About Gun Safety When Suicide's a Risk*

APRIL DEMBOSKY

Jay Zimmerman got his first BB gun when he was 7, and his first shotgun when he was 10.

"Growing up in Appalachia, you look forward to getting your first firearm," he said, "probably more so than your first car."

His grandfather taught him to hunt squirrels and quail. Zimmerman, who lives in Elizabethton, Tenn., said pretty much everyone he knows has a gun. It's just part of the culture.

"When I went into the military, that culture was reinforced," he said. "Your weapon is almost another appendage. It's part of who you are."

Zimmerman served as a medic in the Army in the late 1990s and early 2000s, with stints in Bosnia, Africa and the Middle East. Since he came home, he's struggled with PTSD and depression. It reached a crisis point a few years ago, when his best friend—the guy who had saved his life in a combat zone—killed himself. Zimmerman decided his time was up, too.

"I decided that I would have one more birthday with my daughter, one more Christmas with my daughter," he said. "I had devised my own exit strategy for 16 February 2013."

But then he bumped into a woman who used to ride the same school bus when they were kids. His exit date came and went. They're married now.

Zimmerman still gets depressed, but now he's a peer counselor at the Mountain Home VA Medical Center in Johnson City, Tenn. He also travels to conferences all over the country, sharing his story with therapists and with other vets, encouraging them to ask for help when they need it.

Even today, he explains at these conferences, if he's not doing well, he disassembles

---

*Originally published as April Dembosky, "Veteran Teaches Therapists How to Talk About Gun Safety When Suicide's a Risk," *Kaiser Health News*, February 17, 2017. Kaiser Health News is a nonprofit news service covering health issues. It is an editorially independent program of the Kaiser Family Foundation that is not affiliated with Kaiser Permanente. This story is part of a partnership that includes KQED, NPR and Kaiser Health News.

his guns and stores them separately from ammunition, so he can't make any rash decisions. And if things get really bad, Zimmerman has a special arrangement with a few friends.

"I call them and say, 'Look, I'm feeling like it's not safe for me to have firearms in my home. Can you store them for me for a couple days till I feel like I'm OK to have them back?'"

Suicide is often an impulsive act. Nearly half the people who survive an attempt say the time between their first thought of suicide and the attempt itself was less than 10 minutes. But the method can mean the difference between life and death: People who take pills have time to change their minds or may still be alive when discovered. That's not the case with guns.

Almost 70 percent of veterans who commit suicide do so with a gun, which prompted President Barack Obama to order the VA to talk to vets about gun safety and storage options like the ones Zimmerman uses.

But here's the trouble: Most therapists aren't gun people. They don't know how to talk about guns and so they don't.

"One obvious reason for that is that no one has taught them how," explained Megan McCarthy, a psychologist and National Deputy Director in the Office for Suicide Prevention in the U.S. Department of Veterans Affairs.

McCarthy was invited to speak recently at a suicide prevention conference in San Francisco, aimed at therapists who work with vets.

"How many of you would say you feel really comfortable having a conversation with any of the people you work with about limiting access to all lethal means?" she asked the roomful of therapists.

Hardly anyone raised their hand.

"OK, so that's why we're here today," she said.

Researchers recommend starting with a field trip to a shooting range. There, therapists can learn about different kinds of firearms, as well as gun locks, and get an introduction to gun culture.

When counseling vets, therapists have to ask more questions and be less directive, McCarthy said.

"We often conceive of ourselves as experts—as people who impart information to clients," she said. But with vets, "it may take time to build trust. Telling them what to do the first time you've met them is probably not going to be a very effective approach."

McCarthy presented a case study at the conference: A 28-year old, unmarried Army veteran who fought in Iraq told his VA psychiatrist that he had an argument with his girlfriend last week. He drove to an empty parking lot and sat with his loaded handgun in his lap, intending to kill himself.

He didn't do it. A week later, the man told his psychiatrist things were still tense with his girlfriend. But he didn't want to talk about suicide or storing his gun.

McCarthy asked the clinicians in the audience what they would do next, if they were this man's psychiatrist.

"Why did he not do it? That would be my question," one therapist said.

"I would want to see this individual again, within the same week," said another. "I believe in strong intervention."

Jay Zimmerman, the former army medic and peer counselor, stood up and explained his different perspective.

"Chances are the reason he's not talking to you is because he's afraid he's going to lose his gun that he carries pretty much all the time," Zimmerman said. "My buddies are the same way. We all carry—all the time."

A lot of veterans would sometimes rather confide in a fellow vet than someone in a white coat, Zimmerman said. And that was an unusual takeaway for the professional counselors: Sometimes their role is not to intervene at all, but to be a facilitator. To make sure vets have someone to talk to outside the therapy office.

70. Why Privatizing the VA or Other Essential Health Services Is a Bad Idea[*]

Sebastian Jilke *and* Wouter Van Dooren

The Trump administration wants to shift billions of dollars from government-run veterans' hospitals to private health care providers. That's true even though earlier this year the administration vehemently denied it would privatize any part of the Department of Veterans Affairs.

The privatization of essential government services is nothing new, of course. Over the years, countries have privatized dozens of services and activities that were once the sole domain of governments, such as the provision of electricity and water, road operations and prisons and even health care, with the ostensible aim of making them more efficient.

But before going down that road, the question needs to be asked whether privatizing essential human services such as those for military veterans serves the public interest. New research we recently published suggests that privatization may come at a social cost.

Economic Incentives of Privatization

Privatization theory assumes that organizations, including those that deliver social services, thrive on competition and monetary gain.

Supporters of privatization argue that companies can perform government functions more efficiently. More competition and more choice for clients are expected to put pressure on providers to be more innovative and aware of financial costs.

In the public sector, however, competition is almost by definition absent, either because users of services cannot be excluded from the service—breathing clean air, for example—or because there is little monetary gain to be made—such as with services to the homeless.

So in situations where there is no real market, governments have attempted to mimic

*Originally published as Sebastian Jilke and Wouter Van Dooren, "Why Privatizing the VA or Other Essential Health Services Is a Bad Idea," *The Conversation*, January 15, 2019. Reprinted with permission of the publisher.

their conditions, such as by giving citizens the freedom to choose a public service provider or negotiating contracts that include certain performance incentives.

But this reliance on performance contracts can lead business providers to focus on short-term financial targets—such as the number of people processed per dollar spent—often at the expense of long-term outcomes for those served.

This gives business providers a strong incentive to concentrate on serving people who are most likely to help them achieve these goals by either focusing on those clients who are most likely to succeed or disregarding the ones that are harder to serve. By focusing on easier-to-serve clients and shunning the ones who are costly, service providers are more likely to make a profit.

However, it's often difficult to know in advance who's going to cost more than someone else. As a result, many service providers end up relying on imperfect, discriminatory cues to help them weed out potential cost burdens. Companies do something similar when they use stereotypes about race or ethnicity as discriminatory proxies for unobserved characteristics in job applicants.

Kenny and Mohammed

To learn more about whether for-profit service providers treat people of marginalized ethnic backgrounds differently, we ran a field experiment in the Belgian elderly care sector. We chose Belgium because the industry includes both public and private homes, and one of us is based there.

We sent basic information requests to all public and for-profit nursing homes in Flanders, the Dutch-speaking part of Belgium. Half of the requests, randomly assigned, appeared to come from a Belgian citizen (Kenny Maes), while the rest bore the signature of someone with a North African name (Mohammed El Makrini). The names were chosen based on the results of a separate survey we sent out to 2,000 Belgians asking them to rate several names on their perceived ethnicity, age, level of education and wealth.

In the requests, we asked nursing homes for advice on how to subscribe for a place in their facility. Withholding such information would make it harder for a prospective client to apply for a spot.

Of the 223 nursing homes we contacted, 71 percent responded, with public facilities being a little more likely than for-profit ones to get back to us. In general, each type of home responded to our two senders at similar rates. For example, 76 percent of public facilities replied to "Kenny," compared with 79 percent for "Mohammed." The response rate of for-profit homes was a bit more lopsided, but it was not what we'd consider a significant difference given the sample size: 66 percent for Kenny and 57 percent for Mohammed.

The really interesting finding was when we analyzed the actual responses. Upon closer inspection, we found that for-profit nursing homes were significantly less likely to provide information to Mohammed on how to enroll. Only about 43 percent of the for-profit homes that responded offered him the info, compared with 63 percent for Kenny. There was basically no difference among public facilities.

This is direct proof of for-profit providers discriminating against prospective clients based on their perceived ethnicity. But they're not doing it simply out of ethnic animus. If it was, we'd have seen the same discrimination at the public facilities as well.

Rather, the motivation seems to be primarily economic. This is what economists call "statistical discrimination." In other words, average characteristics of the minority group—such as language barriers and having different cultural needs and habits that make them more difficult to serve—are used to stereotype individuals who belong to that particular group.

Unintended Consequences

The public debate about privatization tends to almost exclusively focus on its supposed financial and managerial advantages—which are hardly clear cut. Meanwhile, the potential social costs of privatization are commonly neglected.

Our research suggests that privatizing human services such as health care can result in less access for groups perceived as harder to serve because of language barriers and cultural differences.

Unfortunately, they also happen to be the groups that need such services the most.

71. Veterans and the California Courts[*]

Ruth Astle Samas

There are several programs available to veterans who find themselves involved with the criminal justice system in California. The San Francisco Veterans Justice Court was established in 2013 pursuant to Penal Code section 1170.9 to provide an alternative for veterans involved in the criminal justice system. The San Francisco Veterans Justice Court is a collaboration with the San Francisco Superior Court, District Attorney's office, Public Defender's office, Probation Department and the U.S. Department of Veterans Affairs.

According to the Veterans Justice Court, many veterans return from military service and find themselves facing unique personal challenges, including mental health problems or substance abuse, that they would not have faced but for their military service. Criminal behavior, mental health problems and substance abuse often are a direct result of service in combat zones and may be amplified by reentry into home life (see McMichael, 2011). A key finding of a RAND 2008 study identified that nearly 20 percent of soldiers involved in the wars in Iraq and Afghanistan have a current mental health condition (Tanielian and Jaycox, 2008).

Many counties in California have established Veterans Treatment Courts. The goals of the SF Veterans Justice Court are to reduce veteran contact with the criminal justice system; reduce costs associated with criminal cases; ongoing recovery for the participant; and an increase in public safety. San Francisco Veterans Justice Court will take veterans regardless of their discharge status. They serve approximately 60 to 65 veterans each month.

Pursuant to Penal Code section 1001.80, California has created a military diversion program for misdemeanor offenses. This section can only be used for misdemeanor offenses. It requires the defendant (1) To have been or currently be, a member of the United States military. This includes the reserves and National Guard; and (2) The defendant may be suffering from sexual trauma, traumatic brain injury, post-traumatic stress disorder, substance abuse, or mental health problems as a result of his or her military service. The court may request, using existing resources, an assessment to aid in the determination that this applies to a defendant.

With the consent of the defendant and a speedy trial waiver, the court can place the defendant in a pretrial diversion program, if the court determines the defendant is eligible. This procedure is used most successfully for Driving Under the Influence cases.

---

[*]Published with permission of the author.

Under Penal Code section 1001.36, a veteran may be eligible for a Mental Health Diversion. This can be used to grant pretrial diversion on any charge, whether or not the defendant is competent. The court must be satisfied of the following: (1) The defendant has a mental disorder in the current Diagnostic and Statistical Manual (DMS) (except antisocial personality disorder, borderline personality disorder, or pedophilia) diagnosed by a qualified mental health expert; (2) The mental health disorder played a significant role in the commission of the charged offense; (3) The defendant is not at unreasonable risk to commit a new "superstrike" offense (violent sex offenses, child molest, homicide or attempted homicide, solicitation of murder, any life without parole or death-penalty eligible offense, weapon of mass destruction possession, machine gun assault no police or firefighters); (4) The recommended outpatient or inpatient program meets the defendant's needs; (5) A qualified mental health expert opinion that symptoms motivating the criminal behavior would respond to mental health treatment; (6) A time waiver; and (7) Defendant's agreement to diversion and treatment

Once diversion is granted the program shall provide regular reports to the court on the progress of treatment. Diversion may last no longer than two years.

Upon successful completion of diversion, the charges are dismissed. Successful completion requires the defendant to substantially comply with the requirements of diversion; avoid significant new violations unrelated to the mental health condition; and there is a plan in place for long-term mental health care.

Unsuccessful diversion can result in reinstatement of the criminal charges; modification of the treatment plan; or conservatorship if the defendant is gravely disabled.

The San Francisco Veterans Justice Court has mentors available for defendants who act as peer support. Participants are better served by having support from other veterans who understand combat experience and the different aspects of military service. Mentors participate in a supportive relationship to increase the likelihood that the veterans in the program will remain in treatment, attain and manage sobriety, maintain law-abiding behavior and successfully readjust to civilian life. The mentors are asked to motivate participants utilizing a strengths-based approach. Mentors provide encouragement by highlighting strengths, including talent, skills and knowledge; encouraging the participants to learn and grow. Confidentiality is an essential piece of successful mentoring.

Collaborative Justice Approach

Veteran Treatment Courts follow the Drug Treatment model, in that it is a collaborative justice court. The court offers alternatives to case proceedings that address underlying problems which contribute to criminal activity or other court involvement. Veteran Treatment Courts lead to the placement of as many mentally ill offenders who are veterans of the U.S. military, including those with PTSD, TBI and MST, substance abuse, or any mental health problem, in VA counseling and treatment programs. In many cases, counseling is required and incorporated into the treatment programs that are designed to treat the underlying psychological disorders. Participating veterans are ordered to complete the recommended treatment plan and comply with any other terms and conditions of probation imposed by the court (https://www.calvet.ca.gov/VetServices/Pages/Veterans-Treatment-Court.aspx).

The best argument for veterans courts, advocates said, is that they seem to work: 70

percent of defendants finish the programs and 75 percent are not rearrested for at least two years after, according to the National Association of Drug Court Professionals. Moreover, these courts have resulted in programs that have reduced recidivism, lowered crime and rebuilt lives among the courts' participants (https://www.calvet.ca.gov/VetServices/Pages/Veterans-Treatment-Court.aspx).

There are a few differences that exist among various states and within the veterans court community. For example, some feel that all vets should be accepted, including those who never deployed to a war zone. Others believe the courts should admit only combat veterans with mental health issues associated with their wartime experiences. Some courts don't hear cases where veterans have been charged with violent crimes, others do, with stipulations.

Keep in mind: Even if you don't have a lawyer or don't have all the paperwork, it is critical to attend all hearings on time. The court's first impression is important.

1. You may have to request a continuance in order to finalize your legal representation and review your situation with Veterans Court—don't rush into anything or plead guilty to anything just to get into a particular program or court.

2. Inform your Public Defender or Attorney that you are a veteran. They will, in turn, present the information to the judge and the judge will make the decision to transfer your case to a veteran court.

3. The VTC continually promotes education and job placement, and access to services for medical; mental health; dental; homelessness; unemployment; family counseling; employment; etc. are offered/provided.

4. Remember, Veteran Treatment Courts are very involved and often times, the treatment plan can be very intense. You will have regular contact with the Judge, Public Defender/Attorney, VA Case Managers, Mentors, etc. Rules are based on your performance, which are directly communicated to the Judge, who rewards progress or penalizes noncompliance. (https://www.calvet.ca.gov/VetServices/Pages/Veterans-Treatment-Court.aspx).

This approach to helping veterans who have encountered the criminal justice system is worth the time and expense to help those who have served our country. The San Francisco Justice Court is hoping to commission a study on recidivism. An informal study indicated that there was only a 7 percent recidivism rate for those that completed the program. This is remarkable. The success of this program is worthy of our support.

REFERENCES

McMichael, William H. (2011). "The Battle on the Home Front." *ABA Journal*, November 2011.
Psychological and Cognitive Injuries, Their Consequences, and Services to Assist Recovery. Santa Monica, CA: RAND Corporation.
Tanielian, Terri, and Jaycox, Lisa H. (2008). *Invisible Wounds of War*. Santa Monica, CA: Rand Center for Military Health Policy.

72. Evaluation Principles for Veteran-Serving Agencies and Veterans Treatment Courts[*]

SIDNEY GARDNER *and* LARISA OWEN

The good news is many programs for veterans are proliferating, as the VA and state and local agencies respond to the needs of veterans.

The other news is many of these programs are only measuring enrollment numbers, rather than the program outcomes. We would suggest a common-sense evaluation principle: if reports talk about what agencies are doing, rather than how well the clients are doing, the evaluation may be missing the point. The point is the program is supposed to improve the well-being of its customers. In veterans' programs, those customers include not only the veteran, but also their kids.

Of the more than 1 million veterans who have served since 9/11 and then were discharged from active duty, more than 40 percent have children—an average of two each. These children are sometimes affected by their parents' deployment, and making sure they are doing OK is, in part, an evaluation task. But too many programs aren't yet meeting that standard.

One example: The VA and other federal agencies don't use the same evaluation outcomes in measuring the effectiveness of programs that treat substance use disorders, which affect a sizable segment of veterans. We once asked a thoughtful VA official why that happens, and his answer was "because each agency has its own programs and its own standards for evaluating them." Another part of the answer, we found, is when many funders make grants, whether public agencies or private foundations, they only include funding for services, with little set aside to evaluate the impact of those services.

A rule of thumb is that with hard work 10 percent of a total grant budget can support an adequate evaluation, while it takes 15 to 20 percent of the budget to do a first-rate evaluation. A lot of funders seem to operate on the principle that funding should go for services, rather than evaluation, which seems to some of them like "overhead."

Three types of evaluation plans can be described: basic, intermediate and intensive. Depending on the level of evaluation, different data collection methods are used, such

*Originally published as Sidney Gardner and Larisa Owen, "Evaluation Principles for Veteran-Serving Agencies and Veterans Treatment Courts," *PA Times,* September 22, 2017. Reprinted with permission of the publisher.

as surveys, focus groups, observations, case management notes and screening and assessment tools. Basic evaluation establishes accountability and focuses on evaluation readiness and program processes.

This includes preparing for the process evaluation, identifying measurable objectives (such as numbers assessed, number treated, court attendance, peer mentor/participant interactions), examining program implementation, comparing proposed plans to the project in operation, integration of evidence-based standards, identifying challenges and successes, documenting output (units of service) and counting participants and their family members.

An intermediate evaluation incudes all of the basic evaluation components but adds a more intensive process evaluation that includes a detailed review of program coverage, establishing client attributes at intake, conducting drop-off analysis to identify the points of client attrition, analysis of implementation fidelity, performance measurement, preparing the program for outcome evaluation, identification of the instruments, methods, and data sources used, project database development and implementation, project performance measurement and analysis and identification of the project's short term and intermediate outcomes.

An intensive evaluation includes all of the basic and intermediate evaluation in addition to the impact (long term effects) of the program, measurement and analysis of the project's long-term outcomes with outcome objectives (results you hope the project will achieve such as sobriety, employment, reduced recidivism), experimental or quasi-experimental designs, and cost studies.

But arguing that funding for services shouldn't be devoted to evaluating those services is like saying we don't care if the road takes us where we want to go—we just enjoy the trip. That's a good principle for random exploring of the countryside, but not so good for evaluating whether a program really makes a difference in the lives of its clients.

Another part of the problem is that there are no baselines. Even if validated assessment tools are used, and even if there are good pre- and post-measures being used, the big question in evaluation sooner or later comes down to the punch line of an old joke. Woman asks her friend "How's your husband?" Second woman answers, "Compared to what?" Without a baseline measure of how well an agency performs for veteran clients, a new program has no standard to compare how well it is doing.

In an earlier article in this series, we discussed the invisibility of veterans and, even more often, the children of veterans in the intake data of most agencies. If there is no box on the intake form asking about the children of the veterans, you can't evaluate the effectiveness of child welfare agencies or treatment agencies when they serve veterans and their family members—because they're not identified in the caseload.

Ideally, an evaluation answers questions about which clients with what characteristics received which services and achieved which specific outcomes. It asks whether the program is reaching the veterans that most need the programs services, and whether veterans' family members are screened and served. These are the evaluation questions that veterans' programs should be asking and answering, as they ensure that the needs of those who served their country are met by the programs that are funded to help them.

73. Preventing Burnout Among Veterans Affairs Social Workers and Mental Health Providers: A Case Study[*]

KIRA SERNA *and* MICKEY P. McGEE

The basis for this chapter was a research project completed by the first named author for Golden Gate University's Executive Master's of Public Administration course. This research study addressed the problem of burnout among mental health providers and social workers in the VA. Thirty participants completed the 19-question Quality of Life Survey for Social Workers and Mental Health Workers and their answers were analyzed to determine the degree of association between the quality of life factors and burnout. A final interview question was examined to determine if other factors besides the independent variables may be correlated with burnout as well.

Social workers and mental health workers work very closely with their patients to solve highly complex psychosocial problems. Many health service providers have very high caseloads and are exposed to traumatic stories, resulting in vicarious traumatization. Constraints of the system can lead to increased frustration and feelings of helplessness among clinicians and result in case workers' feelings of exhaustion, amotivation, depression, and ineffectiveness. This impacts provider quality of life and leads to lower job satisfaction and higher turnover.

Social workers and other mental health providers are highly prone to experiencing burnout (Evans, et al., 2006). Burnout among mental health care workers leads to lower job satisfaction, poor quality of life, and lower effectiveness on the job. It also leads to depersonalization, psychological distress, and physical disorders. Burnout is more prevalent among those in the helping profession due to the nature of the work. Department of Veterans Affairs (VA) providers are especially vulnerable to developing burnout due to high caseloads, complexity of patient issues, and the characteristics of the population being served.

Burnout among social workers and mental health providers within the Veterans Health Administration has been a growing concern and is worthy of attention of administrators

---

*Published with permission of the authors.

as the population of veterans continues to grow. Prior research has shown that burnout is linked to consumer outcomes in the healthcare industry. Specifically, burnout has been linked to lower patient satisfaction, lower quality of care, and higher occurrences of mistakes made in the healthcare setting and mental health profession (Garman, Corriga, & Morris, 2002). A variety of complicated factors contribute to burnout. Several sociodemographic factors have been studied and have been found to be associated with burnout. Past studies link age to burnout levels (Maslac, 2001). Younger workers typically report higher rates of burnout, which may perhaps be due to lack of experience. Providers over 40 years of age typically experience lower rates of burnout, which may be due to role familiarity and workload expectations. In general, older workers take fewer sick days and report higher job satisfaction (Thomas, Kohli, & Choi, 2014). Gender is also correlated with burnout. Women overall report higher rates of compassion fatigue and burnout (Thomas, Kohli, & Choi, 2014).

There are two client populations that have been identified as significantly contributing to burnout: trauma victims and clients diagnosed with personality disorders (Ben-Porat, & Itzhaky, 2015). Therapists who work with these populations are more likely to suffer from burnout than those who work with other populations. In addition, providers who do not feel like they do not have a positive impact on clients have been linked to increased job absenteeism (Thomas, Kohli, & Choi, 2014). A study of 137 VA therapists exposed to secondary trauma found that patient characteristics such as trauma content, patient malingering, and patient personality disorders contribute to provider burnout (Garcia, et al., 2016).

Changes in public administration, such as lack of promotion opportunities, cutbacks, reduction in funding, reduction in resources, and policy changes create a source of stress for practitioners and social workers (Lloyd, et al., 2011). Competing values between administrators and social workers lead to conflict in the workplace and creates an increase in stress. This can also lead to low decision-making power among social workers (Lloyd, et al., 2011). Within the helping profession, there has been a shift of focus from the patient to outcomes and metrics.

There have been several interventions that have been identified to help reduce burnout among healthcare providers within the VA. Research led to the development and testing of an intervention named BREATHE, Burnout Reduction: Enhanced Awareness, Tools, Handouts, and Education (Rollins & Roudebush, 2015). The program aimed to produce a user-friendly program that improves organizational/system outcomes, improves veteran quality of care outcomes, and reduces provider burnout. The study revealed that most of the interventions had little impact, but the BREATHE education component was found to show small improvements in burnout reduction.

Research by the VA has shown that burnout decreases quality of care and patient satisfaction (Edwards, Kim, & Stockdale, 2017). To address this, the VA implemented patient aligned care teams (PACT). PACT was implemented in more than 900 clinics throughout the nation (Rose, 2015). The implementation of PACT aims to improve team communication, clinical efficiency, cohesiveness, and staff autonomy (Rose, 2015). Preliminary studies on the PACT model have shown mixed results. Some studies show that the PACT model can actually increase the rate of provider burnout.

Social workers and mental health providers are the subjects of the study and all the providers are full-time employees of the VA. These clinicians provide individual, couples, family, and group therapy and case management services, or they provide supervision services to other social workers and mental health providers. The mental health providers consist of psychologists, social workers, and marriage and family therapists. The providers serve veterans of all ages who experience a variety of psychosocial issues, such as post-traumatic stress disorder, major depressive disorder, generalized anxiety disorder, pain disorder, various personality disorders, substance abuse disorders, homelessness, unemployment, and traumatic brain injury.

The main research question examined in this author's study was: what can help prevent provider burnout among VA social workers and mental health workers? The following sub-question was also investigated. What programs/policies can VA administrators create and implement to decrease burnout, reduce sick days taken, reduce turnover, and improve quality of care? The researcher's hypotheses were (1) more professional training, lower case-loads, less paperwork, more time for self-care, and flexible work schedules can lower rates of burnout among mental health providers within the Department of Veterans Affairs *and* (2) positive relationships with coworkers and supervisors can be a protective factor against burnout.

Almost 45 percent of the survey respondents reported that they are either moderately or severely burned out. Respondents who spend between 31 to 41 or more hours on work-related tasks are more than three times as likely to experience burnout symptoms. This indicates that the workload for some providers is too high and that they are not able to take breaks at work. The data show that those who spend 16 or more hours on administrative tasks are more likely to suffer from burnout. Respondents with the lowest levels of burnout spend under three hours per week in staff meetings, while those who spend over four hours per week in staff meetings suffer from higher levels of burnout.

One of the strongest findings of this study is the correlation between positive relationships with coworkers and supervisors and levels of burnout. The majority of respondents indicated that they enjoy working with their coworkers and supervisors. One-fourth of the respondents suggested that more teambuilding activities would help to connect coworkers and their supervisors. Respondents reflected that they spend little time exercising and little time with friends. Both of these areas are important for stress-management and wellbeing. The lack of time spent on these positive activities is likely due to other demands placed on the provider. Those who commuted more, spend less time exercising overall. Furthermore, the data show that higher commute times are correlated with higher levels of burnout.. Participants who work alternative work schedules report lower levels of burnout overall.

The data from the survey results suggest that the following factors are correlated with burnout:

- Amount of time spent on work-related tasks
- Amount of time spent on administrative tasks
- Amount of time spent in staff meetings
- Time spent commuting
- Time spent on self-care
- Positive feelings toward coworkers
- Alternative/ flexible work schedules
- Positive feelings toward supervisor
- Organizational strategies to prevent burnout

Based on this study, the following policy recommendations were provided:

1. VA administrators should create and implement organizational strategies that create awareness of ways to prevent burnout and offer trainings to teach self-care and stress management techniques.

2. Increase access to alternative work schedules by either offering compressed or flexible schedules or by offering telework opportunities. Alternative work schedules can reduce the amount of time spent commuting and leave more time for other activities.

3. Streamline administrative tasks and reduce the workload by eliminating duplicate documentation and by creating templates to record progress notes and assessments.

4. Implement teambuilding events throughout the year. These events should focus on facilitating positive interactions between coworkers and between supervisees and supervisors.

5. VA supervisors of social workers and mental health professionals should aim for their supervisees to spend no more than three hours per week in staff meetings overall.

6. Reduce the amount of time spent on work-related tasks. Two ways to reduce the amount of time spent on work-related tasks is to reduce time spent on administrative tasks and time spent in staff meetings. Both of these variables are correlated with burnout.

7. Determine the reasons that social workers and mental health providers spend little time with friends and whether or not they are relying on their coworkers for this social support.

8. Determine why many social workers and mental health workers reporting spending over 41 hours per week on work-related tasks. Find ways to prevent providers from being overworked.

References

Ben-Porat, A., & Itzhaky, H. (2015). "Burnout Among Trauma Social Workers: The Contribution of Personal and Environmental Resources." *Journal of Social Work*, 15(6), 606–620.

Edwards, S., Kim, L., & Stockdale, S. (2017) "The Role of Practice Environment on PACT Provider and Staff Burnout." Retrieved on January 20, 2019 from https://www.hsrd.research.va.gov/for_researchers/cyber_seminars/archives/2333-notes.pdf.

Evans, S., Huxley, P., Gately, C., Webber, M., Mears, A., Pajak, S., … & Katona, C. (2006). "Mental Health, Burnout and Job Satisfaction Among Mental Health Social Workers in England and Wales." *The British Journal of Psychiatry*, 188(1), 75–80.

Garcia, H.A., McGeary, C.A., Finley, E.P., McGeary, D.D., Ketchum, N.S., & Peterson, A.L. (2016). "The Influence of Trauma and Patient Characteristics on Provider Burnout in VA Post-Traumatic Stress Disorder Specialty Programmes." *Psychology and Psychotherapy: Theory, Research and Practice*, 89(1), 66–81.

Garman, A.N., Corrigan, P.W., Morris, S. (2002) "Staff Burnout and Patient Satisfaction: Evidence of Relationships at the Care Unit Level." *Journal of Occupational Health Psychology* 7:235–241.

Lloyd, Chris, King, Robert, & Chenoweth, Lesley. (2011). "Social Work, Stress and Burnout: A Review." 11. 10.1080/09638230020023642.

Maslach, C., Schaufeli, W.B., & Leiter, P.P. (2001). "Job Burnout." *Annual Review of Psychology*, 52, 397–422.

Rollins, A., & Roudebush, R. (2015) "BREATHE in the VA." Retrieved on January 20, 2019 from https://www.hsrd.research.va.gov/research/abstracts.cfm?Project_ID=2141702498.

Thomas, M., Kohli, V., & Choi, J. (2014). "Correlates of Job Burnout Among Human Services Workers: Implications for Workforce Retention." *J. Soc. & Soc. Welfare*, 41, 69.

74. World War II in the Philippines in California's History Curriculum*

Cecilia I. Gaerlan

History was made on July 14, 2016, when the California State Board of Education (SBE) approved the inclusion of World War II in the Philippines in the revised history curriculum framework for the state after almost 75 years since the bombing of Pearl Harbor on December 7, 1941, and the subsequent attack on the Philippines several hours later on December 8. This seminal part of World War II history has been included in the Grade 11 U.S. history (part of Chapter 16) curriculum framework. This is the first time that World War II in the Philippines will be mandated in high schools in the United States. The Bataan Legacy Historical Society (BLHS) worked closely with the California Department of Education to achieve this milestone.

The roots of BLHS can be traced to a theater group, Artis Mundi, which I founded in the 1990s. In 2011, Artis Mundi presented staged readings of *In Her Mother's Image*, an adaptation of a historical fiction book that I wrote, based upon stories that I heard as a child while growing up in the Philippines. My father, Luis Gaerlan, Jr., was a survivor of the Bataan Death March during World War II in the Philippines. During the staged readings, I realized that not too many people had heard about the Bataan Death March. Moreover, not only was there a huge lack of information about the role of the Filipinos during World War II, which made up seven-eighths of the main line of resistance of the U.S. Army Forces in the Far East, there were also sources that denigrated the Filipino soldiers.

BLHS was founded in 2012 for these underlying reasons and it organized the first mainstream commemoration of the Bataan Death March in the Bay Area in April of the same year at California State University East Bay sponsored by the Theater Department. The program (Rediscovering the Role of Filipinos thorough Literature and Theater) was an amalgamation of theater, film and an homage to several Bataan Death March survivors as well as World War II in the Philippines survivors.

I also created a PowerPoint presentation on World War II in the Philippines based on my research using primary documents, interviews with military and civilian survivors and other visual materials. A compelling narrative has emerged on how the Philippine Commonwealth soldiers were called to serve in the newly-created U.S. Army Forces in

---

*Published with permission of the author.

263

the Far East (USAFFE) on July 26, 1941, to "perform a sacrificial delaying action on the mouth of Manila Bay" (in accordance with War Plan Orange 3 in Rainbow Plan 5). However, their fate was already sealed long before the first bomb hit Pearl Harbor. In November 1940, Admiral Harold R. Stark, Chief of Naval Operations, wrote Plan Dog Memo which became the basis for the Europe First Policy.

Based on this policy, the American-British-Dutch-Australian (ABDA) conversations took place between January and April 1941 resulting in Rainbow Plan 5. There was no plan to send reinforcements to the USAFFE troops until the war in Europe was over. But despite suffering from massive disease, starvation and fighting without any reinforcement or air support, the USAFFE troops were able to disrupt the 50-day timetable of the Imperial Japanese Army by holding on to Bataan for 99 days. After their surrender, they were forced to march approximately 65 miles away to their prison camp without any provisions for food, water, shelter or medicine. Those who could no longer go on were beaten, bayoneted, shot, some were even beheaded. This became known as the infamous Bataan Death March where roughly 5,000–10,000 Filipino and 250–650 American soldiers died along the way.

Another 20,000 Filipinos and 1,600 Americans died inside the prison camp at Camp O'Donnell. The Filipinos and some Americans banded into guerrilla groups and worked to pave the way for the liberation of the Philippines. Five months after the end of World War II, the Rescission Act was passed in the United States in 1946 which deemed the service of the Filipino soldiers of USAFFE as not active, thereby depriving them of their rightful veterans' benefits. This law has never been repealed.

Starting in 2012, this powerful story has been presented to universities, high schools, veterans' groups, civic organizations, teachers' groups, churches, military events, etc., in California, Virginia, New Mexico, Hawaii, Iowa, Illinois, Washington, Kansas and the Philippines.

Since 2012, BLHS has continued to organize an annual commemoration of the Bataan Death March around April 9 as part of its mission to educate the public about World War II in the Philippines. These events have taken place at the San Francisco Public Library, the Philippine Consulate, the Presidio, the American Battle Monuments Commission World War II West Coast Memorial, the San Francisco National Cemetery and the Golden Gate National Cemetery. Only a handful of Bataan Death March survivors are still alive but a growing number of active duty soldiers as well as students from the San Francisco Unified School District Junior Reserve Officers' Training Corps (JROTC) have participated through the years. In addition, it has also organized the World War II in the Philippines Conferences starting in 2015. Presenters have included veterans, survivors, academics and students from the U.S., Canada and the Philippines. BLHS has also organized exhibitions and other events pertaining to World War II in the Philippines.

In 2014, BLHS became a 501(c)(3) non-profit organization with an Educational Advisory Group mainly composed of Filipino-Americans from academia and the military.

That same year, BLHS became aware of Legislation AB199, which was sponsored in the California Legislature by Fiona Ma and Leland Yee and was passed in 2011. AB199 "encourages for the inclusion of the role of the Filipinos during WWII in the history/social sciences curriculum framework for Grades 7–12." However, from 2011 to 2014, the legislation was not acted upon mainly because it was not a strong mandate. BLHS requested several legislators to sponsor an amendment to make it a requirement but it did not come to fruition. Instead, BLHS started a change.org campaign which garnered numerous signatures and caught the attention of the State Superintendent.

By the end of 2014, the California Department of Education started the state's curriculum revision process which only takes place every ten years or so. It is a democratic process that involves a series of public meetings wherein anyone can address the proposed curriculum framework. The History Social Sciences Committee (HSSC) of the Instructional Quality Commission (IQC) of the California Department of Education oversaw the history/social sciences curriculum framework revision. Even though it is a democratic process, we secured support from community leaders, government and military officials, veterans' groups, Philippine Consular officers and civic groups and some of them spoke on behalf of our petition during the public comments of the IQC public meetings.

We also communicated and met with the State Superintendent's Office including the State Superintendent himself, Tom Torlakson, the Chair of HSSC-IQC, Bill Honig, the Executive Director of IQC Tom Adams and State Board of Education Executive Director Karen Stapf Walters. Most of all, we put out press releases which caught the attention of the mainstream press. In May of 2016, the HSSC-IQC approved all of our recommendations. The final approval of the revised California curriculum framework was made by the State Board of Education on July 14, 2016. From the initial proposal of two events (Bataan Death March and Battle of Manila), we were able to expand it to several seminal events which are now part of Chapter 16 of the Grade 11 U.S. History: The Philippine Commonwealth; the creation of the United States Army Forces in the Far East (USAFFE) comprised of Americans and a majority of Filipinos; the disruption of the timetable of the Imperial Japanese Army by the USAFFE Forces despite suffering from massive disease and starvation and fighting without any air support; the Bataan Death March and the thousands of casualties; the role of the Filipino and American guerrillas during the liberation; the American soldiers who were transported in hell ships to labor camps in Asia; the Leyte Landing; the Battles of Leyte Gulf and the destruction of Manila.

In 2017, BLHS organized two teachers' workshops to create sample lesson plans in accordance with California's common core standards to help implement the World War II in the Philippines history curriculum framework. These lesson plans, including primary documents, are now available for free through the BLHS website. Some of the teachers have presented the process of creating the lesson plans as well as the results of their implementation in national conferences as well as the BLHS conferences on World War II in the Philippines in 2017 and 2018.

BLHS also collaborated with the National Park Service (NPS) and the Asian Art Museum of San Francisco in October of 2017 during the NPS teachers' workshop "Dissonant Voices," a professional development workshop for secondary social studies educators. The workshop, "Speaking to the Filipino American Experience," concentrated on World War II in the Philippines.

California's new history curriculum framework can become the model for teaching this seminal point of World War II history in the United States. Since the 2016 approval, BLHS' mission has evolved to instilling civic pride and engagement in young adults through the lessons of World War II in the Philippines from the perspectives of Filipino and American military and civilians. During the BLHS Conference in September 2018, a high school teacher from Tallahassee, Florida, who adapted one of our sample lesson plans presented the results of her implementation. A junior high school student from Milwaukee, Wisconsin, presented her project on the Rescission Act.

In early 2016, BLHS organized several events in California to introduce the public to the Filipino Veterans Recognition and Education Project which spearheaded the Congressional Gold Medal Act for the Filipino veterans of World War II. This was finally passed by both the U.S. Congress and the Senate and signed into law by President Obama in December 2016. The first Award Ceremony took place in Washington in October 2017.

What started as an homage to my father, Luis Gaerlan, Jr., whose stories inspired me to write *In Her Mother's Image*, has become an organization dedicated to honoring the legacy of all the Filipino and American soldiers and civilians of World War II in the Philippines. After seventy-five years, their stories of sacrifice and heroism are now being learned. Their legacy has been secured. They have finally taken their rightful place in history.

REFERENCES

Arcadia-Proceedings of the American-British Joint Chiefs of Staff Conference, Washington, D.C. December 24, 1941–January 14, 1942.

California Department of Education (2017). "History Social Science Framework for California Public Schools, Kindergarten to Grade 12." Pages 402–403.

Matloff, Maurice, & Snell, Edwin (1980). "Strategic Planning for Coalition Warfare 1941–1942." Center for Military History.

Miller, Edward S. (1991). *War Plan Orange: The U.S. Strategy to Defeat Japan 1897–1945*. Annapolis, MD: Naval Institute Press.

Morton, Louis (Editor). (1953). "The Fall of the Philippines, WWII in the Pacific." Dept. of History, US Military Academy.

Office of the Chief of Military History, Department of the Army, Washington, D.C. (1959). "Order of Battle of the United States Army Ground Forces in World War II, Pacific Theater of Operations."

Parker, George, Maj. General. "Report of Operations of South Luzon Force, Bataan Defense Force & II Philippine Corps in the Defense of South Luzon and Bataan." 8 December 1942 to 9 April 1942.

Stark, Harold R., Admiral. Plan Dog Memo. (November 12, 1940). Office of the Chief of Naval Operations.

Appendices

A. Glossary of U.S. Veteran Care and Services Terms and Acronyms*

BARBARA WARD *and* ALAN ROPER

1151 Benefits: VA awarded monthly compensation benefits for disability or death incurred as the result of VA hospital care, medical or surgical treatment or examination, but only if the disability or death was proximately caused by negligence or an unforeseen event.

Access: Access is the veteran's ability to obtain medical care at his/her desired location. The ease of access is determined by components, such as availability of health care services, location of health care facilities, transportation, hours of operation, and cost-effective delivery of health care. Efforts to improve access often focus on improving efficiency of health care delivery processes.

Active Service: Full time military service that qualifies a veteran to be eligible to receive benefits. Active service includes service:

- In one of the five branches of the military
- As a commissioned officer for the Public Health Service or other federal service administrative organizations
- As a cadet or midshipman at a military academy

- In attendance at a military academy preparatory school, if the person had an active duty commitment
- During authorized travel to or from any of the above listed types of active service

Adjunct Condition: An adjunct condition, for medical treatment purposes, is a non service-connected condition that may be associated with and held to be aggravating an adjudicated service-connected condition. VA bills health insurance plans for treatment of an adjunct condition and as applicable, may charge a copay for treatment of the adjunct condition.

Adult Day Health Care: Adult Day Health Care is a therapeutic day care program which provides medical and rehabilitation services to disabled veterans in a congregate setting.

Affordable Housing: Defined as costing 30 percent or less of an individual's income.

Aid and Attendance (A&A): A VA compensation or pension benefit awarded to a veteran determined to be in need of the regular aid and attendance of another person to perform basic functions of

*Published with permission of the authors.

everyday life. A veteran may qualify for aid and attendance benefits if he or she:

- Is blind or so nearly blind as to have corrected visual acuity of 5/200 or less, in both eyes, or concentric contraction of the visual field to 5 degrees or less; or
- Is a patient in a nursing home because of mental or physical incapacity; or
- Proves a need for aid and attendance under established criteria

Allowable Deductions: Allowable deductions are those payments made by veterans for certain non-reimbursed medical expenses, funeral and burial expenses and educational expenses. Veterans are able to exclude allowable deductions from their total gross household income in determining their eligibility for VA health care benefits.

Anxiety: A habitual, heightened level of worry or nervousness that negatively affects the individual's day to day activities.

Armed Forces: United States Army, Navy, Marine Corps, Air Force and Coast Guard.

Bereavement Counseling: Bereavement counseling is assistance and support to people with emotional and psychological stress after the death of a loved one. Bereavement counseling includes a broad range of transition services, including outreach, counseling, and referral services to family members.

Board of Veterans' Appeals (BVA): If a claim was denied by the Regional Office, the BVA is the section of the VA that reviews disability benefits and claims appeals with the purpose of issuing decisions on those appeals. The BVA consists of attorney board members. One of the members will act as an administrative judge in an appeal. The BVA can consider new evidence and even look for medical opinions on its own before making a decision

on an appeal. This process averages two to two-and-a-half years.

Case Management Supportive Services: Supportive case management services are services or activities for the arrangement, coordination, monitoring, and delivery of services to meet the needs of individuals and families who experience homelessness. Component services and activities may include individual service plan development; counseling; monitoring, developing, securing, and coordinating services; monitoring and evaluating client progress; and assuring that clients' rights are protected.

Catastrophically Disabled: A veteran who has a permanent, severely disabling injury, disorder, or disease that compromises the ability to carry out the activities of daily living to such a degree that he/she requires personal or mechanical assistance to leave home or bed, or requires constant supervision to avoid physical harm to self or others.

C-file: A claims file. VA creates a hard copy paper file for each claimant that contains all the documents related to that claimant since the first application for benefits. C-files can contain thousands of pages of documents and must be physically shipped between offices when claims are reviewed by different VA groups or the Veterans Court.

Chronic Care: Long-term care of individuals with long-standing, persistent diseases or conditions. Chronic care includes care specific to the problem, as well as other measures to encourage self-care, promote health, and prevent loss of function.

Chronically Homeless Individual: The Department of Housing and Urban Development (HUD) adopted the federal definition which defines a chronically homeless person as either (1) an unaccompanied homeless individual with a disabling condition who has been continuously homeless for a year or more, OR (2) an unaccompanied individual with a disabling condition who has had at least four episodes of homelessness in the past three years. Families can now be considered chronically homeless. Disabling condition is defined as "a diagnosable substance use disorder, serious mental illness, developmental disability, or chronic physical illness or disability, including the co-occurrence of two or more of these conditions." A disabling condition limits an individual's ability to work or perform one or more activities of daily living.

To be considered chronically homeless, persons must have been sleeping in a place not meant for human habitation (e.g., living on the streets) and/or in an emergency homeless shelter. An episode is an event that is distinct and separate, although part of a larger series, occurring at usually irregular intervals. A chronically homeless family is a household with at least one adult member who meets the definition of chronic homelessness.

Claim: A request for veterans' benefits.

Cognitive Behavioral Therapy (CBT): It became popular in the 1960s and was originated by Albert Ellis, Ph.D. and Aaron Beck, M.D. Beck's approach became known for its effective treatment of depression (Stevens, 2008).

Cognitive Processing Therapy (CPT): Developed by Resick and Schnicke in the 90s as a therapy that combines exposure and restructuring of the beliefs and schemas that were developed as after a traumatic event and developed into PTSD (Resick & Schnicke, 1996).

Combat Service: A status applied for a veteran who served on active duty in a theater of combat operations during a period of war recognized by the VA.

Commonwealth Army Veterans: The term "Commonwealth Army veterans" refers to persons who served before July 1, 1946, in the organized military forces of the Government of the Philippines. These Fil-ipino forces were made a part of the U.S. Armed Forces by a military order of the President dated July 26, 1941.

Community Residential Care: Community Residential Care provides health care supervision to eligible veterans not in need of hospital or nursing home care but who, because of medical and/or psychosocial health conditions as determined through a statement of needed care, are not able to live independently and have no suitable family or significant others to provide the needed supervision and supportive care. The veteran must be capable of self-preservation with minimal assistance and exhibit socially acceptable behavior.

Compensable Disabilities: A VA rated service-connected disability for which monetary compensation is authorized for payment. You might even be entitled to compensation when your disabilities are rated 0 percent disabling.

Compensation: A monetary benefit awarded based on the degree of disability caused by a service-connected condition.

Congressional Appropriation: The funding allocated by Congress to VA for providing benefits and medical services to eligible VA beneficiaries.

Continuum of Care: An approach that helps communities plan for and provide a full range of emergency, transitional, and permanent housing and service resources to address the various needs of homeless persons.

Contract Provider: Any hospital, skilled nursing facility, extended care facility, individual, organization, or agency that has a contractual agreement with VA for providing medical services to veterans.

Copay: A specific monetary charge for either medical services or outpatient medications provided by VA to veterans whose financial assessment determines they are able to pay.

Court of Appeals for the Federal Circuit (CAFC): This court has jurisdiction over VA regulations, and reviews CAVC decisions. If the CAFC denies a claim, the final step in the process is to appeal to the U.S. Supreme Court.

Court of Appeals for Veterans Claims (CAVC): The seven-member administrative court whose sole responsibility is to deal with appeals from the BVA. If your VA claim is denied here, the next step in the appeals process is the Court of Appeals for the Federal Court.

Covered Benefit: Medically necessary care and services included in the Medical Benefits Package as defined within 38 Code of Federal Regulation (CFR) 17.38.

Critical Time Intervention (CTI): A time-limited case management model designed to prevent homelessness and other adverse outcomes in people with mental illness following discharge from hospitals, shelters, prisons, and other institutions.

Decision Review Officer (DRO): Decision Review Officers are senior technical experts authorized by the VA to uphold or overturn the original decision of a claim, based on the same evidence used during the initial review. DROs review the evidence "de novo"—meaning with fresh eyes and without deference to the previous decision makers' determination of the claim. Additional evidence may also be considered necessary by the DRO to resolve a claim.

Deductible: An amount that a veteran must pay for covered services in a specified time period before VA benefits begin.

Department of Veterans Affairs (VA): The Department of Veterans Affairs has two main roles:

1. Providing medical care for veterans, and
2. Paying benefits to veterans.

The veterans' benefits the VA handles include:

- Compensation for service-related disabilities,
- Pensions to veterans or their widows, and
- Compensation to widows and families of veterans.

These responsibilities are divided between the Veterans Benefits Administration (VBA) and the Veterans Health Administration (VHA). Veterans who need to process a claim for Veterans Benefits would deal only with the VBA.

Dependent: Spouse or unmarried child (to include a biological, legally adopted, or step child under the age of 18, or between the ages of 18 and 23 and attending school, or a child who was permanently and totally disabled before the age of 18).

Diagnosis: The identity of a medical condition, cause or disease.

Disability Compensation: Tax-free benefits paid on a monthly basis to a veteran by the VA due to service-connected disability.

Disenrollment: The discontinuation of a veteran's enrolled status. Disenrollment may result because the veteran requests not to participate in VA enrollment, or when VA determines that certain priority groups will no longer be provided services. Requests to dis-enroll must be in writing.

Domiciliary: A VA facility that provides care on an ambulatory self-care basis for veterans disabled by age or disease who are not in need of acute hospitalization and who do not need the skilled nursing services provided in a nursing home.

Durable Medical Equipment: Equipment intended for frequent use in the treatment of a medical condition or injury. Examples include wheelchairs, hospital beds, walkers, etc.

Earned Income: Money you receive from working

eBenefits: VA online portal that allows veterans to manage their benefits and personal information.

Emergency: An emergency medical condition is a medical condition manifesting itself by acute symptoms of sufficient severity such that a prudent layperson, who possesses an average knowledge of heath and medicine, could reasonably expect the absence of immediate medical attention to result in (1) placing the health of the individual in serious jeopardy, (2) serious impairment to bodily functions, or (3) serious dysfunction of any bodily organ or part.

Emergency Shelter Programs: These programs provide short-term housing on a first-come, first-served basis where clients must leave in the morning and have no guaranteed bed for the next night OR provide beds for a specified period of time, regardless of whether or not clients leave the building. Facilities that provide temporary shelter during extremely cold weather (such as churches) and emergency shelters or host homes for victims of domestic violence and runaway or neglected children and youth are also included.

Enrollee: A veteran who has applied for VA medical services under 38 United States Code (U.S.C.) 1710 and 38 CFR 17.36, has been accepted for such care, and who has received confirmation of enrollment in the VA health care system.

Environmental Contaminants/Gulf War Illness: Gulf War veterans were exposed to a wide variety of environmental hazards and potential harmful substances during their service in Southwest Asia. These include depleted uranium, pesticides, the anti-nerve gas pill pyridostigmine bromide, infectious diseases, chemical and biological warfare agents, and vaccinations (including anthrax and botulinum toxoid), and oil well free smoke and petroleum products. VA recognizes that there are other health risk factors encountered by Gulf War veterans. Veterans with service during the Gulf War are eligible to receive treatment for conditions related to this service.

Eye Movement Desensitization and Reprocessing (EMDR): developed in 1987 by Francine Shapiro. She discovered that eye movements decreased the intensity of negative thoughts. She believed the EMDR procedure would decrease the anxiety level a person would experience (Shapiro, 1995).

Filipino World War II Veterans: Filipinos who served under the United States Armed Forces of the Far East (USAFFE). They may be eligible for benefits if they served in one of the following:

- Armed Forces of the United States
- Commonwealth Army of the Philippines with service from July 26, 1941, through June 30, 1946
- Regular Philippine Scouts who enlisted prior to Oct. 6, 1945
- Insular Force of the U.S. Navy
- Special Philippine Scouts who enlisted between Oct. 6, 1945 and June 30, 1947
- Guerilla with service prior to July 1, 1946

Financial Assessment: A means of collecting income and asset information used to determine a veteran's eligibility for health care benefits.

Forever GI Bill: Legislation, also known as the Harry W. Colmery Veterans Education Assistance Act, passed by Congress and signed into law in August 2017. The Forever GI Bill expands education benefits for some members of the Reserve effective August 1, 2018.

Form 9: The VA form that must be submitted after receipt of a Statement of the Case to perfect an appeal to the Board of Veterans Appeals.

Geriatric Evaluation: Geriatric evaluation, which is part of the basic benefits package, is the comprehensive assessment of a veteran's ability to care for him/herself, physical health, and social environment, which leads to a plan of care. The plan could include treatment, rehabilitation, health promotion, and social services.

GI Bill: The Servicemen's Readjustment Act of 1944—commonly known as the GI Bill of Rights. President Franklin D. Roosevelt signed the GI Bill into law on June 22, 1944. The Veterans Administration (VA) was responsible for carrying out the law's key provisions: education and training, loan guaranty for homes, farms or businesses, and unemployment pay.

Gross Household Income: Generally, gross income of the veteran, spouse and dependent children is counted for determining a veteran's eligibility for VA health care benefits. This includes earned and unearned income but excludes most need-based payments such as welfare, Supplemental Security Income (SSI).

Gross Income: Income before allowable expenses are subtracted.

Hardship: A "hardship" exists when there is a significant reduction in your family income and net worth from the previous calendar year to the present year. You could have been working in the previous year and due to a recent disability are no longer able to work. Chances are this type of situation would create a significant change in your family's income.

Health Insurance Portability and Accountability Act (HIPAA): HIPAA is a federal law enacted in 1996. It was designated to improve availability and portability of health coverage and the efficiency of the health care system by standardizing the electronic exchange of health information and protecting the security and privacy of member-identifiable health information.

Home Health Care: Skilled nursing and other therapeutic services provided by VA or a home health care agency in a home setting as an alternative to confinement in a hospital or skilled nursing facility.

Homeless Emergency Assistance and Rapid Transition to Housing (HEARTH): The Act of 2009 that includes Emergency Solutions Grant (ESG) and Continuum of Care (CoC) grants.

Homeless Management Information System (HMIS): A computerized data collection application designed to capture client-level information over time on the characteristics and service needs of men, women, and children experiencing homelessness. It is designed to aggregate client-level data to generate an unduplicated count of clients served within a community's system of homeless services. The HMIS can provide data on client characteristics and service utilization. In Nashville, the HMIS is being developed by the Metro Public Health Department.

Homemaker/Home Health Aide Services: The Homemaker/Home Health Aide (H/HHA) Program provides services as an "alternative" to nursing home care. The H/HHA Coordinator along with the interdisciplinary team makes a clinical judgment that the veteran would, in the absence of H/HHA services, require nursing home equivalent care.

Hospice/Palliative Care: Hospice/Palliative Care programs offer pain management, symptom control, and other medical services to terminally ill veterans or veterans in the late stages of the chronic disease process.

Hostilities: Any armed conflict in which the members of the Armed Forces are subjected to combat conditions comparable to a period of war. The periods of armed conflict are determined by the Secretary of VA in consultation with the Secretary of Defense.

Housebound Benefit: The VA's Housebound benefit is an additional amount available to eligible veterans and dependents who are entitled to VA pension or VA compensation. The housebound allowance may be paid to veterans, dependent spouses, or surviving spouses who because of their physical limitations, are unable to walk or travel beyond their home and are reasonably certain the disabilities or confinement will continue throughout his or her lifetime. Certain restrictions apply.

Housing and Urban Development (HUD): A federal department whose mission is to create strong, sustainable, inclusive communities and quality affordable homes for all. HUD is working to strengthen the housing market to bolster the economy and protect consumers; meet the need for quality affordable rental homes: utilize housing as a platform for improving quality of life; build inclusive and sustainable communities free from discrimination; and transform the way HUD does business.

Housing and Urban Development Geographic Index: Congress wanted to grant relief from making VA copay for some veterans with marginal incomes, recognizing that income alone is not always a fair measure of one's standard of living because of sometimes large differences in the cost of living in different areas of the country. Congress modified VA's system of determining veterans' ability to pay for health care by creating a geographically based income limit and reducing inpatient copay for those veterans whose income falls below these new geographic income thresholds. The new geographic income thresholds are adjusted for all standard metropolitan statistical areas (SMSAs) and are updated periodically to reflect economic changes within the SMSAs. The geographic means test thresholds are based upon the geographically based low-income threshold set by the U.S. Department of Housing and Urban Development (HUD) for public housing benefits.

Housing Choice Voucher (HCV): Formerly known as Section 8 Vouchers. Federally funded housing voucher for low-income individuals and families. Usually administered by a Housing Authority.

Housing First: The Housing First model was developed by Dr. Sam Tsemberis of Pathways to Housing in the 1990s. The concept is simple: Offer a person housing first, then connect the housed person with supportive treatment services. This approach is called permanent supportive housing.

Low-Income Threshold: Veterans with gross household income under the "low income threshold" are eligible to receive certain health related benefits at no cost to the veteran. The low-income threshold is set by law and varies according to the veteran's family size and benefit applied for.

McKinney-Vento Act: Major federal legislative response to homelessness that consists of fifteen programs providing a range of services to homeless people, including emergency shelter, transitional housing, job training, primary health care, education, and some permanent housing.

Medicaid: A jointly funded federal and state program that provides hospital expense and medical expense coverage to persons with low-income and certain aged and disabled individuals.

Medical Benefits Package: The term "Medical Benefits Package" refers to a group of health care services that are provided to all enrolled veterans.

Medical Need: The determination that care or service(s) are required to promote, preserve, or restore a veteran's health as specified within 38 CFR 17.38(b). A treatment, procedure, supply, or service is considered medically necessary as determined by the patient's care provider and in accordance with generally accepted standards of clinical practice.

Medicare: A federal program that provides health care coverage for people aged 65 and older, as well as some younger individuals with specific health problems. Medicare Part A covers hospitalization, extended care and nursing home care; Medicare Part B covers outpatient services, and is subject to a monthly premium.

Military Sexual Trauma (MST): Sexual trauma experienced while on active duty in the military. Sexual trauma is defined as sexual harassment, sexual assault, rape and other acts of violence. Sexual harassment is further defined as repeated unsolicited, verbal or physical contact of a sexual nature, which is threatening in nature. If the veteran is being treated for any condition during this episode of care that the provider believes is related to MST; the veteran does not have to pay a copay for the visit or the medication.

Noncompensable: Awards of service-connection which VA determines do not warrant the award of monetary compensation.

Nonservice-Connected Pension: A monetary support benefit awarded to permanently and totally disabled, low-income veterans with 90 days or more of active military service, of which at least one day was during wartime. Veterans of a period of war who are age 65 or older and meet service and income requirements are also eligible to receive a pension, regardless of current physical condition. Payments are made to qualified veterans to bring their total income, including other retirement or social security income, to a level set by Congress.

Nonservice-Connected Veteran: An eligible veteran who has been discharged from active military duty, and does not have a VA adjudicated illness or injury incurred in or aggravated by military service.

Other than dishonorable conditions: All veterans are potentially eligible for most veterans' health care benefits are based solely on active military service in the Army, Navy, Air Force, Marines, or Coast Guard (or Merchant Marines during World War II), and discharged under other than dishonorable conditions

Pension Benefit: VA pension is a monetary award paid on a monthly basis to veterans with low income who are permanently and totally disabled, or are age 65 and older, may be eligible for monetary support if they have 90 days or more of active military service, at least one day of which was during a period or war. Payments are made to qualified veterans to bring their total income, including other retirement or social security income, to a level set by Congress annually. Veterans of a period of war who are age 65 or older and meet service and income requirements are also eligible to receive a pension, regardless of current physical condition.

Permanent Supportive Housing: Safe, decent, affordable housing that provides the necessary support services to enable formerly homeless persons with special needs to live independently. Permanent supportive housing options are designed to meet the specific needs of clients based on the client's level of functioning.

Philippine Scouts: Philippine Scouts guerrilla forces were considered part of the Commonwealth Army of the Philippines. They were organized under commanders appointed, designated, or later recognized by the U.S. Army.

Post–9/11 GI Bill: Pays up to all public in-state tuition and fees. If a recipient attends a private or out-of-state school, tuition rates may be more than the covered amount. However, if the school participates in the Yellow Ribbon Program, additional funds may be available to the student. Institutions that voluntarily enter into a Yellow Ribbon Program Agreement with VA choose the amount of tuition and feeds to contribute. VA will match that amount and directly pay the institution.

Post-Traumatic Stress Disorder (PTSD): Severe anxiety disorder associated with significant traumatic events; such as being hurt or losing a loved one, being physically close to the traumatic event, feelings of not being in control, and having a lack of support after the event. The symptoms of PTSD are nightmares of the events, anxiety, reoccurring nightmares, loss of interest for previous hobbies, substance abuse, and hyper-vigilance.

Preferred Facility: The veteran identified VA health care location where the veteran prefers to receive care. A preferred facility may be any VA health care location, for example, VA health care facility, independent clinic, or community based outpatient clinic. If VA is unable to provide your needed health care, that facility will make arrangements to refer you to another VA health care facility or to one of VA's private sector affiliates to provide the required care.

Primary Care Provider: The clinician who is responsible for the supervision, coordination, and provision of the veteran's medical care. This clinician provides routine health services and is the veteran's first point of contact when the veteran becomes sick. The primary care provider can easily refer patients to a specialist (such as a surgeon) should they require care outside the scope of his or her expertise.

Prolonged Exposure (P.E.): Evidence-based, manualized protocol effective for the treatment of posttraumatic stress disorder (PTSD).

Prosthetic Devices: A device which replaces all or a portion of a part of the human body. A prosthetic device can be used when a part of the body is permanently damaged, is absent, or is malfunctioning.

Public Law (PL) 104–262: The public law passed by Congress in October 1996, also known as the *Veteran's Health Care Eligibility Reform Act of 1996*. This law established national standards of access and equitable health care services to veterans and required that most veterans be enrolled to receive care.

Public Law (PL) 107–135: "Department of Veterans Affairs Health Care Programs Enhancement Act of 2001" provides for chiropractic care and services for veterans through Department of Veterans Affairs medical centers and clinics.

Purple Heart: A medal given by the military to a service person injured as a direct result of combat.

Rating Decision: The initial VA decision on a claim which either grants or denies an award or "continues" the claim for further development.

Rating Schedule: The table of medical conditions and disabilities established by law that VA raters use to determine the degree of disability for compensation purposes.

Rescission Acts: Congressional bills signed into law by President Harry Truman which removed Filipino World War II Veterans from VA benefit eligibility. The First Supplemental Surplus Appropriation Rescission Act, or Public Law 79-301, which authorized a $200 million appropriation to the Commonwealth Army of the Philippines, with the provision that those soldiers be deemed to have never been in the U.S. military. Public Law 79-391, the Second Supplemental Surplus Appropriation Rescission Act, which disenfranchised the Filipinos in the New Philippine Scouts of their U.S. military service. Those who fought in USAFFE guerrilla units were also disowned.

Referral: The process of referring a veteran from one practitioner to another for health care services.

Remand: Return of a decision to the organization that made it for additional review and revision. The Board remands rating decisions to the originating regional office. The Veterans Court remands Board decisions back to the Board.

Respite care: Respite care gives the caregiver of a veteran a planned period of relief from the physical and emotional demands associated with providing care.

Restore Health: The process of improving a veteran's quality of life or daily function level that has been lost due to illness or injury.

Secondary Condition: A secondary condition, for medical treatment purposes, may be the result of an adjudicated service-connected condition. Veterans are encouraged to file compensation claims for non-rated secondary conditions. Non-rated secondary conditions are billable as a non-service-connected condition. If awarded service-connection for the secondary condition, VA may reimburse all copays related to such service-connection retroactive to the date of the original claim filing.

Service-connected: Generally, a service-connected disability is a disability that VA determines was incurred or aggravated while on active duty in the military and in the line of duty. A service-connected rating is an official ruling by VA that your illness/condition is directly related to your active military service. Service-connected ratings are established by VA Regional Offices located throughout the country.

Service-Connected Veteran: A veteran who has an illness or injury incurred in or aggravated by military service as determined by VA.

Sexual Trauma: Sexual Harassment, Sexual Assault, Rape and other acts of violence. Repeated unsolicited, verbal or physical contact of a sexual nature, which is threatening in nature.

Shelter Plus Care: HUD provides grants for rental assistance to homeless persons with chronic disabilities under the Shelter Plus Care program. Eligible recipients are state and local government units, public housing agencies and Indian tribes. To receive the funds each recipient must provide supportive services at least equal in value to the rental assistance. Supportive services would address mental illness, substance abuse and acquired immunodeficiency syndrome (AIDS) and related diseases.

VA Form 10–10EZ, Application for Health Benefits: The VA form completed by veterans to apply for VA health care benefits. The form includes demographic, military, insurance and financial information

VA Form 10–10EZR, Health Benefits Renewal: The VA Form used by veterans to submit their updated personal, insurance and financial information to VA.

Veteran: The term "veteran" means a person who served in the active military, naval, or air service, and who was discharged or released under conditions other than dishonorable.

Veterans Affairs Supportive Housing (VASH): Combination of Section 8 rental assistance and individualized case management services for homeless veterans.

Yellow Ribbon GI Education Enhancement Program: Or the Yellow Ribbon Program, is a part of the Post-9/11 Veterans Educational Assistance Act of 2008. This program allows U.S. institutions of higher learning to voluntarily enter into an agreement with VA. These degree-granting institutions partner with VA to cover tuition and fee expenses that exceed VA's maximum payable amount. Schools can contribute a specified dollar amount. VA will match the amount, not to exceed 50 percent of the difference.

Abbreviations and Terms Used in VA Benefits Claims and Appeals

A&A   Aid and attendance

AAO   Assistant adjudication officer

ABCMR   Army Board for Correction of Military Records

ACAP   Annual clothing allowance payment

ADA   Americans with Disabilities Act

ADHC   Adult day health care

ADL   Activities of daily living

ADT   Active duty for training

AFB   Air Force Base

AFBCMR   Air Force Board for Correction of Military Records

AFHRA   Air Force Historical Research Agency

AFI   Air Force instruction

AFIP   Armed Forces Institute of Pathology

AGG   Aggravated in service

AHRC   Army Human Resources Command

AL   American Legion

ALJ   Administrative Law Judge

ALS   Amyotrophic lateral sclerosis

AMC   Appeals Management Center

AML   Acute myelogenous leukemia

AMVETS   American Veterans

AO   Agent Orange or adjudication officer

AOCAP   Agent Orange Class Assistance Program

AOJ   Agency of original jurisdiction

AOR   Agent Orange Registry

APA   Administrative Procedures Act

ARBA   Army Review Boards Agency

AVSCM   Assistant Veterans Service Center Manager

AWA   All Writs Act

AWOL   Absent without official leave

BCD   Bad conduct discharge

BCMR   Board for Correction of Military Records

BCNR   Board for Correction of Naval Records

BDD   Benefits Delivery at Discharge

BDN   Benefits Delivery Network

BHL   Bilateral hearing loss

Board   Board of Veterans' Appeals or "BVA"

BVA   Board of Veterans' Appeals. The Board is the organization within VA that reviews initial rating decisions when the claimant files a Notice of Disagreement.

CAAF   Court of Appeals for the Armed Forces

CAVC   United States Court of Appeals for Veterans Claims. The appellate court to which claimants can appeal adverse Board decisions. Also known as the "Veterans Court."

C&P   Compensation and Pension

CARES   Capital Asset Realignment for Enhanced Services

CAVC   Court of Appeals for Veterans Claims

CBO   Chief business office

CBOC   Community Based Outpatient Clinic

CCF   Compound comminuted fracture

CDR   Counter designation of record

CFR   Code of Federal Regulations

CG   Coast Guard

CGBCMR   Coast Guard Board for Correction of Military Records

CHAMPUS   Department of Defense Civilian Health and Medical Program of the Uniformed Service

CHAMPVA   Civilian Health and Medical Program of the Department of Veterans Affairs

CHR   Consolidated health record

CIB   Combat Infantryman Badge

CLC   VA Community Living Center (formerly VA Nursing Home Care Units)

CLL   Chronic lymphocytic leukemia

CMB   Combat Medical Badge

CMD   Chief Medical Director

CMO   Chief Medical Officer

CNHC   Community nursing home care

CO   VA Central Office or commanding officer

COD   Character of discharge

COG   Convenience of the government

COLA   Cost-of-living adjustment

CONUS   The contiguous United States

COVA   Court of Veterans Appeals (Renamed Court of Appeals for Veterans Claims)

COWC   Committee on Waivers and Compromises

CPI   Claims Processing Improvement

CRC   Community residential center

CRDP   Concurrent retirement and disability pay

CRSC   Combat-related special compensation

CUE   Clear and unmistakable error

CURR   Center for Units Records Research

CWT   VA Compensated Work Therapy Program

DAV   Disabled American Veterans

DBQ   Disability Benefits Questionnaire

DC   Diagnostic code

DD   Dishonorable discharge

DD-214   Discharge certificate

DDD   Degenerative disc disease

DEA   Dependent's educational assistance

DES   Disability evaluation system

DFAS   Defense Finance and Accounting Services

DFR   Dropped from the rolls

DIC   Death & Indemnity Compensation. A benefit awarded to surviving spouses and qualifying dependents when a service-connected condition is a cause of a veteran's death.

DM   Diabetes mellitus

DMZ   Demilitarized zone

DOD   Department of Defense

DRB   Discharge Review Board

DRO   Decision Review Officer. Usually an experienced member of a regional office rating team who reviews a rating decision at the request of the claimant after an initial denial. DRO review is optional and cannot change decisions favorable to a claimant.

DSM   American Psychiatric Association's Diagnostic and Statistical Manual for Mental Disorders

DSO   Department service officer

DTR   Deep tendon reflexes

DVA   The Department of Veterans Affairs. A technically more accurate abbreviation than "VA," although not as widely used.

EAD   Entry on active duty

EAJA   Equal Access to Justice Act

ECA   Expedited Claims Adjudication Initiative

ED   Erectile dysfunction

EGC   Electrocardiogram

EKG   Electrocardiogram

1151 Claim   A claim for benefits under 38 U.S.C. Section 1151 as a result of injury caused by VA treatment or rehabilitation services similar to a medical malpractice claim.

EOB   Explanation of benefits

EOD   Entry on Duty or Explosive Ordinance Disposal

EVR   Eligibility verification report

FDC   Fully Developed Claim

FOIA   Freedom of Information Act

FTCA   Federal Tort Claims Act

GAO   Government Accounting Office

GC   General counsel

GPO   Government Printing Office

GSW   Gunshot wound

GWS   Gulf war syndrome

HB   Housebound

HIPAA   Health Insurance Portability and Accountability Act

HISA   Home improvement and structural alterations

HIV   Human immunodeficiency virus

HO   Hearing officer

IED   Improvised explosive device

IG   Inspector general

IME   Independent medical expert or independent medical evaluation

INC   Incurred in service

IOM   Institute of Medicine

IOP   Internal operating procedures

IRIS   Inquiry Routing and Information System

IU   Individual unemployability

IVAP   Income for VA purposes

JAG   Judge Advocate General

JMR   Joint motion for remand

JSRRC   Joint Services Records Research Center

LOD   Line of duty

LOM   Limitation of motion

LSW   Licensed social worker

M21-1MR   Adjudication   Procedures Manual Rewrite

M-1   VA Healthcare Adjudication Manual

M-21   VA Claims Adjudication Manual

MACR   Missing air crew reports

MAPR   Maximum annual pension rate

MGIB   Montgomery GI Bill

MIB   Marine index bureau

MOS   Military occupational specialty

MPR   Military personnel records

MRI   Magnetic resonance imaging

MST   Military Sexual Trauma

NA   National Archives

NARA   National Archives and Record Administration

NAS   National Academy of Sciences

NAUS   National Association for Uniformed Services

NHL   Non-Hodgkins lymphoma

9   VA Form 9, Appeal to the Board of Veterans' Appeals

NMCB   U.S. Navy Mobile Construction Battalion

NOA   Notice of Appeal

NOD   Notice of Disagreement. Claimants must file a written NOD within one year of receiving a rating decision to be able to appeal that decision.

NOS   Not otherwise specified

NPC   Naval Personnel Command

NPRC   National Personnel Records Center

NRPC   Naval Reserve Personnel Command

NSC   Non-service-connected

NSLI   National Service Life Insurance

NSO   National service officer

NVLSP   National Veterans Legal Services Program

OEF   Operation Enduring Freedom

OGC   Office of the General Counsel

OIF   Operation Iraqi Freedom

OIG   Office of Inspector General

OMPF   Official military personnel file

OPC   Outpatient clinic

OPT   Outpatient treatment

OQP   Office of Quality and Performance

OTH   Other than honorable

PDBR   Physical Disability Board of Review

PDR   Physicians Desk Reference

PEB   Physical Evaluation Board

PERMS   Permanent Electronic Records Management System

PG   Persian Gulf

PGW   Persian Gulf War

PIES   Personnel Information Exchange System

PIF   Pending issue file

PMC   Pension Maintenance Center

POA   Power of attorney

POW   Prisoner-of-war

PRC   Polytrauma Rehabilitation Center

PT   Physical therapy or permanent total disability

PTE   Peace time era

PTSD   Posttraumatic stress disorder

PEBLO   Physical Evaluation Board Liaison Officer

RAD   Release from active duty

RMC   Records Management Center

RMO   Records Management Officer

RN   Registered nurse

RO   Regional Office

ROTC   Reserve Officers' Training Corps

RVN   Republic of Vietnam

RVSR   Rating Veterans Service Representative

SBP   Survivor Benefit Plan

SC   Service-connected

SDRP   Special Discharge Review Program

SDVI   Service Disabled Veterans' Insurance

SF   Special forces

SGLI   Service members' Group Life Insurance

SMC   Special Monthly Compensation. Additional compensation available to the most seriously disabled veterans for anatomical loss of limbs or loss of use of body parts, aid and attendance, and other special needs.

SMP   Special monthly pension

SMR   Service medical record

SN   Service number

SOC   Statement of the Case. A document that VA must prepare and provide to a claimant who has submitted a timely Notice of Disagreement. The purpose of an SOC is to identify the facts and law VA used to reach the decision(s) with which the claimant disagrees.

SPD   Separation program designator

SPN   Separation program number

SRD   Schedule for Rating Disabilities

SSA   Social Security Administration

SSB   Special separation benefits

SSDI   Social Security Disability Income

SSI   Supplemental Security Income

SSN   Social Security Number

SSOC   Supplemental Statement of the Case

STR   Service treatment records

STS   Soft tissue sarcoma

TAD   Temporary active duty

TBI   Traumatic brain injury

TDIU   Total Disability based on Individual Unemployability. A special rating that considers whether a claimant who does not meet the rating schedule requirements for 100 percent disability is still unable to work in a substantially gainful occupation. A TDIU award pays benefits at the 100 percent scheduler rate even though the actual rating percentage is less than 100 percent.

10-10EC   VA Form 10–10EC, Application for Extended Care Services

10-10EZ   VA Form 10–10EZ, Application for Health Benefits

10-10EZR   VA Form 10–10EZR, Health Benefits Renewal Form

TRDL   Temporary disabled retirement list

TDY   Temporary duty

UCMJ   Uniform Code of Military Justice

U.S.C.   United States Code

U.S.C.A.   United States Code Annotated

U.S.C.S.   United States Code Service

USGLI   United States Government Life Insurance

USJSRRC   United States Joint Service Records Research Center

VA   The most commonly used acronym for the Department of Veterans Affairs.

VACO   VA Central Office

VAF   VA form

VAGC   VA General Counsel

VAHAC   VA Health Administration Center

VAMC   VA Medical Center

VAOGC   VA Office of the General Counsel

VAOIG   VA Office of the Inspector General

VAOPC   VA outpatient clinic

VAR   VA regulation

VARO   VA Regional Office

VBA   Veterans Benefits Administration

VCAA   Veterans Claims Assistance Act

VEAP   Post-Vietnam Era Veterans' Educational Assistance Program

VFW   Veterans of Foreign Wars

VGLI   Veterans' Group Life Insurance

VHA   Veterans Health Administration

VISN   Veterans Integrated Service Network

VJRA   Veterans Judicial Review Act

VLJ   Veterans Law Judge. A member of the Board of Veterans' Appeals who hears appeals from claimants who disagree with a rating decision.

VMLI   Veterans' Mortgage Life Insurance

VONAPP   Veterans Online Application. A VA website for electronically applying for VA benefits.

VRC   Vocational rehabilitation counseling

VSCM   Veterans Service Center Manager

VSM   Vietnam Service Medal

VSO   Veterans service organization

VSR   Veterans Service Representative

WRIISC   War Related Illness and Injury Center

B. New York City Veterans Advisory Board By-Laws: Draft[*]

Article I—Name

The official name of the board shall be the New York City Veteran's [*sic*] Advisory Board (VAB).

Article II—Definition and Purpose

The New York City Veteran's Advisory Board (VAB) is established pursuant to Section 14 of the New York City Charter. The Veterans Advisory Board is charged with advising the Commissioner of the Department of Veteran Services (DVS) on all matters concerning veterans, Active Duty, Reserve and Guard components of the military services here in New York City.

Pursuant to Chapter 68, Section 2601, Subdivision 1 of the City Charter, the Veterans Advisory Board is an Advisory Committee constituted to: *"provide advice or recommendations to the city and has no authority to take a final action on behalf of the city or take any action which would have the effect of conditioning, limiting or requiring any final action by any other agency, or to take any action which is authorized by law."*

The purpose of the board is to serve as a major link between the administration, the New York City Council, the Department of Veteran Services (DVS) and the veteran's community. To this end, the board will:

1. Serve the best interests of New York City and it's [*sic*] veteran and military communities;

2. Hold at least one (1) public meeting in each borough on an annual basis, keep a record of its deliberations; determine its own rules of procedures; and submit an annual report of its activities to the Mayor and the Council on or before December 31st of each year;

3. Review and consider those matters before them in a wholly non-partisan manner;

4. Promote and encourage the residents and visitors of our city to view and

---

*Public document originally published as "New York City Veterans Advisory Board By-Laws: DRAFT," https://www1.nyc.gov/assets/veterans/downloads/pdf/Charter.pdf (April 21, 2016).

treat veterans and service members with compassion, dignity, respect and the honor they have earned by their service to our country while helping to bridge any civilian-military divide that may exist;

5. Identify and secure resources meant to support the human service and other needs of the veteran and military population operating or residing in New York City;

6. Identify and secure resources meant to encourage the continued service of New York City's veterans to its citizens;

7. Identify and secure resources, processes and procedures meant to encourage veteran employment, entrepreneurship and educational opportunities in New York City;

8. Identify and secure resources intended to connect veterans and their families to cultural institutions and other opportunities New York City has to offer;

9. Formally consider matters by any veteran groups operating within the five (5) boroughs of the City of New York upon a two-thirds vote of the VAB. Once approved, the VAB will issue a formal advisory to the Commissioner. Individual cases will be referred to the appropriate City, State or Federal agency.

10. Make recommendations to the Commissioner in all instances in which it learns of legal, administrative or procedural hurdles which may create an impediment to the quality of service delivery or the status of veterans and military within the five boroughs.

Article III—Membership

As amended by New York City Local Law 113 (2015) the board shall consist of eleven members, all of whom shall be veterans, six (6) of whom shall be appointed by the Mayor and five (5) of whom shall be appointed by the Speaker of the New York City Council.

Of these eleven appointees, there shall be one representative from each of the five boroughs of the City of New York. The Mayor and Speaker shall each consider service in conflicts involving members of the United States armed forces when making such appointments.

All members shall serve for a term of three (3) years and may be removed by the appointing official for cause.

Upon appointment to the board, every member, pursuant to Section 3103 of the City Charter, shall create an electronic mailing address dedicated exclusively to the conduct of the business of the board. Such electronic mailing address may not be commingled with any other personal or professional electronic mail addresses held or maintained by the members of the board.

In the event of a vacancy on the advisory board during the term of office of a member by reason of removal, death, resignation, or otherwise, a successor shall be chosen in the same manner as the original appointment.

A member appointed to fill a vacancy shall serve for the balance of the unexpired term.

No member of the Veterans Advisory Board shall represent him/herself as the spokesperson of the board except its duly elected chairperson unless given an express charge by the chairperson.

Article IV—Officers

The elected officers of the board shall be the Chairperson and Vice-Chairperson, along with Secretary (as needed). These board members will constitute the Executive Committee.

The Executive Committee will make recommendations to the board in the area of policy and operations. The Executive Committee shall be empowered to act on behalf of the full board in emergency circumstances. In the event of such act or such actions, a full report shall be made to the membership at the next regular meeting of the full board.

Any vacancy occurring in an office will be filled for the remainder of the term by appointment of the board from among its current members.

Article V—Nominations and Elections of Officers

Members of the advisory board shall nominate and elect by majority vote one (1) member to serve as chairperson, one (1) member to serve as vice-chairperson, and one (1) member to serve as secretary, to each serve in that capacity for one-year terms.

Announcements for the nominations of officers shall be made one (1) month prior to the first fall public meeting (defined as the first meeting held after July) of the full board. Any member can make nominations from the floor during the private session. Each nominee for office shall be granted two (2) minutes to speak if they so desire. Election of officers shall be held at the public meeting of the full board by ballot.

The candidate who receives a majority of votes cast for such office shall be deemed elected and assumes the office immediately. In the event no candidate receives a majority, the two candidates with the same number of votes shall engage in a runoff election following the prior vote count.

Every member of the board attending shall be entitled to one (1) vote, in person.

Article VI—Duties of Officers

a. Chairperson:

The chairperson shall call for and preside at all meetings of the Veterans Advisory Board and shall appoint all standing committees and such other committees, as s/he deems necessary. The chairperson shall be an ex-officio member of all committees and shall perform all other duties incident to the office.

The chairperson shall have the right to call a special session when deemed necessary and must do so if six (6) members serve written request upon the Secretary of Vice Chair.

The chairperson shall have the right to invite a person to speak at any meeting of the board if deemed necessary to the proper operation of the board.

The chairperson will authenticate all acts, orders, and proceedings of the board and will be the sole spokesperson for the board in relation to the media, agencies, and the public at large, except, as he/she otherwise specifically authorizes.

b. Vice-Chair:

The vice-chairperson shall perform the duties of the chairperson in his/her absence, and shall perform any other duties delegated by the chairperson.

c. Secretary:

The secretary shall keep minutes of all meeting, establish a system for their distribution, notify the membership of all meetings and be responsible for all official correspondence and documents, including a current list of members.

Article VII—Meetings

a. Private Session

There shall be a private meeting of all board members prior to the public session for the purposes of updates, correspondence and training as needed.

b. Public Meeting

Pursuant to Section 14 of the City Charter, the board will hold at least one meeting open to the public in each borough on an annual basis, with notice of each with notice of each public meeting provided in accordance with the public notice requirements of article 7 of the public officers law except with respect to those requirements provided in section 31-105 of the administrative code, and with each public meeting recorded and broadcast in accordance with subdivision d of section 1063 of the charter.

c. Special Session

A special session can be called upon by the chairperson when deemed necessary and must do so if six (6) members serve written request upon the Secretary or Vice Chairperson. A minimum number of seven (7) business days must be given before such meeting takes place.

d. Participation

Except as required otherwise by law, board members may participate in the regular or special meeting through the use of any means of communication by which all members participating may simultaneously hear each other during the meeting, including in person, internet video (if applicable) or telephone conference call.

e. Participation of Agency Representative(s)

The presence and participation of a representative from the Department of Veteran Services at all scheduled meetings of the board shall be considered essential to effective functioning of the board.

Article VIII—Committees

There shall be an Executive Committee to consist of the elected officers of the board. The chairperson, in cooperation with the board, shall create any committees and/or subcommittees in a manner deemed appropriate for the execution of the board's mandated responsibilities.

All committees shall make such investigations as it may deem necessary and report its findings and recommendations by majority vote of said committee, to the full board.

Article IX—Voting

Each duly appointed member of the board shall be entitled to one (1) vote.

Voting shall either be by voice vote or through show of hands unless elections, where ballots will be used.

Proxy voting is prohibited.

Electronic voting (through internet video and/or telephone conference call) is allowed with the exception of voting for officers of the board.

Except as otherwise specifically required by the by-laws herein, all action shall be decided by a majority vote of those voting.

Article X—Removal of Board Members

Board members may be removed by the Mayor or Speaker for substantial neglect of duty, gross misconduct in office or the inability to discharge the powers or duties of the office.

Article XI—Conflict of Interest

No board member shall disclose any confidential information concerning the affairs or government of the city, which is obtained as a result of the individual's official duties on the board, which is not otherwise available to the public, or use any such information to advance any direct or indirect financial or other private interest. Pursuant to Section 68 of the City Charter, violation of this article can lead to removal from the board by the Mayor or Speaker of the City Council.

A board member is deemed to have a conflict of interest if he/she has an existing or potential business, financial or personal interest or holds an elected or appointed position in a corporation or non-profit that could impair or might reasonably appear to impair the exercise of independent, unbiased judgment in the discharge of his or her responsibilities to the board.

Any officer or board member having a personal or financial interest, including a conflicting fiduciary interest (due to status as an officer or director in another organization) shall disclose the interest and provide prompt, full and frank disclosure of such interest to the board. The matter of a conflict of interest shall be decided by a majority of votes from the board.

If a conflict of interest is deemed to exist, such person shall not vote on, or use his or her personal influence on, or be present for or participate in (other than to present factual information or to respond to questions) in the discussions or deliberations with respect to, such contract or transaction.

Article XII—Rule of Order

The board may adopt such rules and regulations, which it deems necessary to its operation except where it conflicts with these by-laws or with City policy and regulations.

Article VIII—Amendments

These by-laws may be amended by a two-thirds vote (7 members) of those present at a meeting of the board provided the proposed amendment has been presented in writing to all board members and was discussed at a prior meeting of the board.

C: City of Worcester Veterans' Services[*]

Veterans' Services Division, City of Worcester, Massachusetts

History

The City of Worcester has a long and rich history of important people, places and events. The Office of the City Clerk is the keeper of many significant historical records, memorabilia and information that is vital to Worcester's heritage.

Worcester, named after Worcester, England, was first established as a town in 1722 and later became a city in 1848. During the past three centuries Worcester has evolved from its modest, but instrumental revolutionary beginnings to a major manufacturing center to its current concentration of world-class colleges and universities, medical facilities and teaching hospitals.

Worcester's history boasts many firsts, inventions and innovations as well as visits from American presidents and significant historical figures.

For more information about Worcester's history we encourage you to visit the Worcester Historical Museum in person or online.

The City of Worcester is a diverse governmental body, consisting of numerous departments, divisions and sections all working together to serve the residents of Worcester. The main goal of each department, division and section is simple: to provide the best services possible each day in order to produce a comfortable environment in which to live, visit and work.

Veterans Services Department

The Veterans' Services Division provides support to residents of Worcester who are veterans, currently serving members of the military and their families. Support services vary based on individual circumstances but may include financial aid, reimbursement of medical costs and referral services for a variety of issues such as housing, employment and education.

---

[*]Public document originally published as Veterans' Services Division, City of Worcester, Massachusetts, "Veteran Services," http://www.worcesterma.gov/veterans-services (2019).

In conjunction with the Massachusetts Department of Veterans' Services, the City of Worcester takes applications and disperses veterans' benefits (also known as "Chapter 115 Benefits") enacted through Chapter 115 of the Massachusetts General Law.

Once benefits are established or if found ineligible, the Veterans' Services Division assists clients in finding more permanent solutions to meet their needs by referring clients to a variety of social service agencies and programs such as Workforce Central, the U.S. Department of Veteran Affairs, and the Worcester Housing Authority.

Additionally, the staff serves as liaison to the Worcester Veterans' Council and the City Council's Subcommittee for Veteran and Military Affairs. The City, through Veterans' Services, also sponsors the Veterans' Day and Memorial Day parades. The Veterans' Services Division and their community partners serve as caretakers of all veterans' memorials and graves.

Top Services: Please contact the Veterans' Services Division for information on the following services:

- Housing allowances for everyday living expenses such as food, rent, heat, etc.
- Payments for medical expenses such as prescriptions, visits to a doctor, dentists or hospital, eyeglasses and existing hospital insurance.
- Additional referrals to other sources of possible income such as the United States Social Security Administration and the Department of Veterans Affairs.

History: The Department of Veterans' Services has been providing services and benefits to veterans since 1861.

From the date of that commitment the Commonwealth of Massachusetts insured that no individual who served his or her state and nation with honor during periods of war or other conflicts, would ever be "pauperized" or forced to turn to public welfare for assistance. The Massachusetts Executive Office and the Massachusetts House and Senate have shown their concern for the welfare of the veteran and his or her dependents. This support has proven to be one of the most comprehensive programs in the country. These services are provided through the Massachusetts Department of Veterans' Services and the local Veterans' Services Office.

- 1888—The Soldiers' Relief Law was enacted, which gave cities and towns the right to support honorably discharged veterans, their spouses, widows and minor children.
- 1945—The Office of Commissioner of Veterans' Services was created.
- 1946—Chapter 115 (Veterans' Services) of the Massachusetts General Laws was reorganized to form the basis of today's benefits and services program.
- 1946—Chapter 599 Acts of 1946 mandated "municipal and district Departments of Veterans' Services." Veterans' Agents and Directors of Veterans' Services have become the first individuals that the veteran will turn to for assistance.

The City of Worcester Veterans' Services is committed to continuing to assist our veterans, and their dependents, with high quality, caring, compassionate, effective and efficient professional service.

Contact Information

Edward O'Connor, Veterans' Services Officer/Director
Veterans' Services
City Hall Room 101
455 Main Street
Worcester, MA 01608
Accessible via WRTA Bus Line
Phone: (508) 799-1041

D. Nevada State Veteran's Benefits & Discounts[*]

STATE OF NEVADA

The state of Nevada provides several veteran benefits. Below is brief description of each of the following benefits.

- Housing Benefits
- Financial Assistance Benefits
- Employment Benefits
- Other State Veteran Benefits

Nevada Veteran Housing Programs

Nevada Veterans' Home: A State-owned and operated veterans' home is located in Boulder City. The 180-bed home consists of an extended care facility for veterans in need of skilled nursing home care. The cost to stay in a semiprivate room is $110 per day— well below the Nevada average of $216 a day.

The cost for a spouse or a Gold Star parent is $187 a day. Refer to http://issuu.com/news_review/docs/rnr_nsvh_022615 for a publication on the home. Future plans call for a Veterans Home in Northern Nevada. Applicants must meet the following requirements:

- Have a military discharge other than dishonorable
- Be a spouse of a veteran who meets the above requirement or a Gold Star parent, (parent whose children all died during war time service in the Armed Forces of the United States)
- Must be a current resident of Nevada or provide verification of Nevada residency at the time of enlistment in the military.
- Not require care the Home is unable to provide.
- Not exhibit traits that may prove dangerous to the applicant, residents, staff, or visitors

---

[*]Public document originally published as State of Nevada, "Nevada State Veteran's Benefits & Discounts," http://www.veteransresources.org/wp-content/uploads/2015/05/Vet-State-Benefits-Discounts-NV-2015.pdf (May 2015).

The first step toward admission is the completion of an application packet, accompanied by appropriate documentation, (when applicable). Additionally, to be admitted, applicants must present a current, signed admission order, from a licensed physician, verifying the need for 24-hour skilled nursing care. Applicants must complete all sections of the admission application and provide accurate and current information. This includes the financial section related to all household income and liabilities. Residents must agree to pay a daily per diem and additional ancillary charges, such as physician visits and medications.

Charges may vary over time and between residents, depending on each resident's situation. Some residents may be eligible for VA benefits, Medicaid, Medicare, military retirement, and/or Social Security. The Home also accepts private insurance. In addition to the information listed above, applicants' scores on screening tools must fall within ranges deemed suitable for placement. The Admissions Application can be downloaded at http://veterans.nv.gov/page/nsvh-admissions-policies.

Visit the Nevada Office of Veterans Services website, http://veterans.nv.gov, for contact information and benefits assistance.

Nevada Financial Assistance Benefits

Veterans Tax Exemption: An annual tax exemption is available to any veteran with wartime service (including in-theater service during the Persian Gulf War, Afghanistan and Iraqi Wars). To obtain this exemption, take a copy of your DD214 or discharge papers to your local County Assessor.

The exemption can be applied to a veteran's vehicle privilege tax or real property tax. The exemption cannot be split between the two. To obtain the exact amount of this benefit, contact your County Assessor. Veterans may also "donate" their exempted tax directly to the Nevada Veterans' Home Account, which will contribute the amount toward the operation of a Veterans' Home in Nevada.

Disabled Veteran Tax Exemption: Nevada offers a property tax exemption to any veteran with a service-connected disability of 60 percent or more.

The amounts of exemption that are or will be available to disabled veterans varies from $6,250 to $20,000 of assessed valuation, depending on the percentage of disability and the year filed. To qualify, the veteran must have an honorable separation from the service and be a resident of Nevada.

The widow or widower of a disabled veteran, who was eligible for this exemption at the time of his or her death, may also be eligible to receive this exemption.

This exemption can be applied to a veteran's vehicle tax or personal property tax. To determine the actual value of this benefit or to obtain further information, contact your local county assessor's office.

Visit the Nevada Office of Veterans Services website http://veterans.nv.gov for contact information and benefits assistance.

Nevada Employment Benefits

Civil Service Preference: Civil service preference is given to veterans applying for State employment in Nevada. Veterans with service-connected disabilities receive additional preference.

Visit the Nevada Office of Veterans Services website http://veterans.nv.gov for contact information and benefits assistance.

Other Nevada State Veteran Benefits

Assistance with Claims: Any veteran family member of a veteran, or Nevada resident on Active Duty can receive free assistance in filing a claim with the U.S. Department of Veterans Affairs for a service-connected disability, pension or other benefit program. Assistance includes help in filing claims, representation at local hearings, appeals and discharge upgrades.

Hunting and Fishing License: The State of Nevada Wildlife Division will issue free hunting fishing licenses to any honorably separated veteran who has a service-connected disability of 50 percent or more.

Guardianship Program: Nevada State Law permits the Nevada Office of Veterans' Services to act as the financial guardian for incompetent veterans, their widows and children.

Veteran Cemetery Plots: Eligible veterans and members of their immediate family may be buried at the Northern Nevada Veterans Memorial Cemetery in Fernley or at the Southern Nevada Veterans Memorial Cemetery in Boulder City.

There is no charge for the plot, vault and opening and closing of a gravesite for a Veteran. A $450 fee (subject to change) is charged for the burial of the spouse or dependent of a veteran. Eligibility criteria for burial at the Northern/Southern Nevada Veterans Memorial Cemetery is the same used by the National Cemetery System and is based on military service. Dependents of a veteran may also be eligible for burial at the cemetery. A columbarium wall is also available for those veterans and dependents that have been cremated.

Both cemeteries are located in quiet, peaceful surroundings, and provide an atmosphere of respect and dignity to those who have served. The cemeteries were established in 1990 and have become the final resting place for over 10,000 veterans and their family members. One plot is allowed for the interment of each eligible veteran and for each member of their immediate family, except where soil conditions or the number of decedents of the family require more than one plot. Specific plots may not be reserved as plots are assigned by the cemetery superintendent. Casket and cremation burials can be accommodated at both cemeteries.

For more information concerning dependent eligibility and pre-registration, contact:

- Northern Nevada Veterans Memorial Cemetery, 14 Veterans Way, Fernley, Nevada 89408. Tel: (775) 575–4441/5713F.
- Southern Nevada Veterans Memorial Cemetery, 1900 Buchanan Blvd, Boulder City, NV, 89005. Tel: (702) 486–5920.

Disabled Parking Privileges: The State of Nevada authorizes special parking permits for physically disabled persons. Applications are available at your local DMV office or can be obtained by contacting the DMV Special Plate Section in Carson City.

Special Veteran License Plates: The Nevada Department of Motor Vehicles offers several distinctive license plates for veterans that include:

- Ex-Prisoner of War
- Disabled Veteran Purple Heart
- Army, Army Airborne, Army National Guard, Navy, Navy Seabee, Air Force National Guard, Marine Corps, or Coast Guard Veteran
- National Guard Active
- Pearl Harbor Survivors & Veterans
- Congressional Medal of Honor

Applications for special plates can be obtained at your local DMV Office. Initial fee is $61 with an annual $30 renewal fee. Personalized plates run $96 with an annual renewal fee of $50. A portion of the fees help subsidize veteran causes.

Documents: Veterans or their dependents filing claims for service-connected disabilities may receive a one-time free copy of their birth, divorce, death or marriage certificate from the appropriate county courthouse.

Recording Fees: Discharge certificates are recorded free of charge to eligible veterans by Nevada Count Recorders.

Visit the Nevada Office of Veterans Services website http://veterans.nv.gov for contact information and benefits assistance.

Veterans Advocacy and Support Team Offices

For information on veterans benefits and services, contact our Veterans Advocacy and Support Teams (VAST) at the following locations:

- VAST Las Vegas: 6900 N. Pecos Rd., Rm. 1C237, North Las Vegas, NV, 89086 (located at the New VA Hospital in North Las Vegas). Tel: (702) 224-6025/ 6927F OR 791-9000, Ext. 46025
- VAST Reno: 5460 Reno Corporate Dr. Suite 131 Reno, NV 89511 (Located in the VA Regional Office). Tel: (775) 321-4880/1656F
- VAST Fallon: 485 W. B Street, Suite 103 Fallon, NV 89406 (located in the Churchill County Offices). Tel: (775) 428-1177/ FAX (775) 423-9371
- VAST Elko: 762 14th Street, Elko, NV 89801. Tel: (775) 777-1000/1055F
- VAST Pahrump: 1981 E Calvada Blvd #110 Pahrump, NV 89048. Tel: (775) 751-6372/6371F
- VAST Rural Outreach Coordinator 5460 Reno Corporate Dr. Suite 131 Reno, NV 89511. Tel: (775) 688-1653/1656F

Rural Outreach/ROVER: Walk-in appointments are welcome, but can only be seen as time permits. To schedule an advanced appointment, contact Josh @ 775 688–1653. Veterans are advised to bring a copy of their DD-214 discharge document, current VA paperwork, medical information and banking account information. If the claim involves dependents, bring birth certificates, current and prior marriage certificates, divorce decrees, and social security numbers. A separate page is available for each month. See the drop down menus above for the month you are looking for at http://veterans.nv.gov/page/rural-outreach-rover [Source: http://www.military.com/benefits/veteran-state-benefits/nevada-state-veterans-benefits.html May 2015 ++]

Military Discounts in Nevada

1. MVDC has close to 2000 business locations in Nevada that have discounts for military personnel and veterans. In addition to businesses providing discounts, the state of Nevada also provides discounts for those that have served. To find business discounts, enter your zip code and category in the search box at http://military andveteransdiscounts.com/location/nevada.html

2. Veterans Designation on driver's license: Honorably-discharged veterans may have a Veteran designator placed on their license. Present your DD-214 at any DMV office. Visit archives.gov to obtain a copy of your DD-214.

3. Discounted Fees and Taxes
   - National Guard members may receive hunting and fishing license permits for free
   - Eligible veterans with a service-connected disability of 50 percent or more may be issued a hunting and fishing license permit for free.
   - Veterans are eligible for special license plates

4. Property tax
   - Any veteran with wartime service can apply an annual tax exemption to the vehicle privilege tax or real property tax. However, the exemption cannot be split between the two. For more information on the exact benefit, contact the county assessor
   - Nevada also offers a property tax exemption to eligible veterans with a service-connected disability of 60 percent or more. The amount varies depending on the percentage of disability and the year filed.
   - The widow or widower of the disabled veteran who was eligible at the time of his or her death, may also be eligible to receive this exemption. It is applicable to either the vehicle tax or personal property tax. More information can be obtained through the local county assessor's office.

5. Education Discounts
   - 100 percent tuition waiver for members of the National Guard for fall and spring semester at state schools (including text books, but excluding tech and lab fees)
   - 100 percent of summer semester costs for members of the National Guard subsidized through the Education Encouragement Fund [Source: http://militaryandveteransdiscounts.com/location/nevada.html May 2015 ++]

E. City of Vallejo Proclamation, October 22, 2013, Proclaiming Veterans Day 11/11/13 to 11/11/14 as "Vietnam War Veterans Year of Commemoration" and Welcome*

Whereas, on August 2, 1964, North Vietnamese torpedo boats attacked the United States Navy destroyer USS *Maddox* and President Lyndon Johnson presented the Tonkin Gulf Resolution to Congress, which voted overwhelmingly in favor on August 7 to take all necessary measures to repel any armed attack against the United States and to prevent further aggression; and

Whereas, we observe the 50th anniversary of the Vietnam War with solemn reverence upon the valor of a generation that served with honor, and we pay tribute to the more than three million Service members who left their families to serve bravely, a world away from everything they knew and everyone they loved; and

Whereas, thousands of Vallejo residents answered our country's call to military or civil service by joining the Armed Forces or by working at Mare Island Naval Shipyard, Travis Air Force Base, and other military bases; and the schools in Vallejo were, and still are, immensely instrumental in preparing our residents to meet the educational requirements of the U.S. Armed Forces; and

Whereas, from Ia Drang to Khe Sanh, from Hue to Saigon, and countless villages in between, our Service members pushed through jungles, rice paddies, punishing heat, and monsoons fighting heroically to protect the ideals we hold dear as Americans; and

Whereas, we draw inspiration from the heroes who suffered unspeakably as prisoners of war, yet who returned home with their heads held high and we pledge to keep faith with those who were wounded and still carry the scars of war, seen and unseen; and with more than 1,600 of our Service members still among the missing, we pledge as a Nation to do everything in our power to bring these patriots home; and

Whereas, through more than a decade of combat, over air, land, and sea, our proud Service members upheld the highest traditions of our Armed Forces, and as a grateful Nation, we honor the more than 58,220 patriots, their names etched forever in black

---

*Public document originally published as City of Vallejo Proclamation, October 22, 2013, Proclaiming Veterans Day 11/11/13 to 11/11/14 as "Vietnam War Veterans Year of Commemoration."

granite at the Vietnam Veterans Memorial, who sacrificed all they had and all they would ever know; and

Whereas, in the reflection of "The Wall," we see the Families and Veterans who carry a pain that may never fade, and that they may they find peace in knowing their loved ones endure, not only in medals and memories, but in the hearts of all Americans, who are forever grateful for their Service, Valor, and Sacrifice; and

Whereas, of the 47,434 battle deaths, 10,786 non-battle deaths, and over 153,300 wounded-in-action, 38 Vallejoans gave the ultimate sacrifice for our great Nation; and of the 10,000 Veterans living in Vallejo, it is estimated that 3,000 are Vietnam Veterans; and

Whereas, while no words will ever be fully worthy of their service, nor any honor truly befitting their sacrifice, let us remember that it is never too late to pay tribute to the men and women who answered the call of duty with courage and valor, and let us renew our commitment to the fullest possible accounting for those who have not returned; and

Whereas, on August 9, 2014, on the 50th Anniversary of the Tonkin Gulf Resolution, the Vallejo Veterans Memorial Building Council will honor the brave men and women who received the Vietnam Service Medal and are residents of Vallejo and will also pay lasting tribute to the missing in action and prisoners of war and to those that gave the last full measure of devotion for our grateful Nation.

Now, Therefore, Be It Resolved, that I, Osby Davis, Mayor of the City of Vallejo, and the Vallejo City Council do hereby proclaim from Veterans Day 2013 to Veterans Day 2014 as Vietnam War Veterans Year of Commemoration to recognize a chapter in our Nation's history that must never be forgotten, and to renew our sacred commitment to the Veterans who answered our country's call to serve in Vietnam and to the Family members who also immensely sacrificed in our homeland; and we call upon all governing bodies, businesses, schools, and organizations to honor our Vietnam Veterans, our fallen, our wounded, those unaccounted for, our former prisoners of war, their families, and all who served with appropriate programs, ceremonies, and activities.

About the Contributors

Katherine **Albertson** is a senior lecturer at the Helena Kennedy Centre for International Justice, Sheffield Hallam University.

JoNel **Aleccia** is a senior correspondent focused on aging and end-of-life issues on the *Kaiser Health News* enterprise team.

The American Legion is the nation's largest wartime veterans service organization.

Asha **Anchan** is with Carnegie-Knight News21, a national reporting initiative headquartered at Arizona State University's Walter Cronkite School of Journalism and Mass Communication.

Michelle **Andrews** is a contributing columnist with *Kaiser Health News*.

Luisa M. **Antonio** is the executive director of the Bayanihan Equity Center (formerly Veterans Equity Center) in San Francisco, California.

Holly **Arrow** is the director, Groups and War Lab, University of Oregon.

William **Bare** retired as a colonel with the Air Force and then became the executive director of a non-profit organization whose mission was to house and assist homeless veterans and their families.

Martha **Bebinger** is a reporter covering health care and other general assignments for WBUR in Boston.

Marcel O. **Bonn-Miller** is a research health science specialist with the National Center for PTSD at the U.S. Department of Veterans Affairs.

Elisa **Borah** is a research associate with University of Texas at Austin.

Willie L. **Britt** is a distinguished adjunct professor of public administration at Golden Gate University and is the business manager of Makati Chiropractic Center, USA, and general manager of United Nations Avenue Chiropractic Center, Philippines.

Anna **Casey** writes for *Kaiser Health News*.

Ann **Cheney** is an assistant professor, Center for Healthy Communities, University of California, Riverside.

Caitlin **Cruz** is with Carnegie-Knight News21, a national reporting initiative headquartered at Arizona State University's Walter Cronkite School of Journalism and Mass Communication.

Terry **Curl** is a senior adjunct professor of public administration at Golden Gate University as well as an army veteran.

Jeanne **DeLaney** is the founding director and art consultant for Cup of Life & Calm.

April **Dembosky** is the health reporter for the California Report and KQED News.

Department of Veterans' Services, City of Cambridge, Massachusetts serves as an advocate for all Cambridge veterans and their dependents.

Daniel **Devoy** is an associate professor of law and director of the Veterans' Legal Advocacy Center, Golden Gate University School of Law.

Blake **Farmer** is a senior health care reporter for Nashville Public Radio.

Cecilia I. **Gaerlan** is the executive director of the Bataan Legacy Historical Society.

Phil **Galewitz** is a senior correspondent covering Medicaid, Medicare, long-term care, hospitals and various state health issues for *Kaiser Health News*.

Glenn J. **Galman** is an alumnus of the Coast Guard Academy and Golden Gate University and provided over 20 years of distinguished service to the nation as an officer in the Coast Guard.

Sidney **Gardner** is the president of Children and Family Futures.

Silvana **Giacalone** has been working to help veterans with their VA benefits for over nine years and plans to continue her work as a public servant for the veterans in her local community.

Joaquin Jay **Gonzalez** III is the Mayor George Christopher Professor of Public Administration at the Edward S. Ageno School of Business at Golden Gate University.

Elisha **Harig-Blaine** is the manager, veterans and special needs, of the Center for City Solutions National League of Cities.

Maria **Höhn** is a professor and chair of history, Vassar College.

Emmarie **Huetteman** is a *Kaiser Health News* correspondent who came to KHN from the *New York Times*.

Roya **Ijadi-Maghsoodi** is an assistant professor of psychiatry and a biobehavioral sciences/investigator at the VA Greater Los Angeles HSR&D Center for the Study of Healthcare Innovation, Implementation & Policy, University of California, Los Angeles.

Sebastian **Jilke** is an assistant professor, Rutgers University, Newark.

Roger L. **Kemp** is a distinguished adjunct professor of public administration at the Department of Public Administration of Golden Gate University.

Patricia **Kime** is a contributor to *Kaiser Health News*.

Quil **Lawrence** is an award-winning correspondent with NPR News.

Gregory B. **Lewis** is a professor of public management and policy, Georgia State University.

Alexandra **Logsdon** is a senior portfolio manager, Secretary's Center for Strategic Partnerships, U.S. Department of Veterans Affairs.

Shefali **Luthra** is a *Kaiser Health News* correspondent covering consumer issues in health care.

Mickey P. **McGee** is an associate professor of public administration at the Edward S. Ageno School of Business at Golden Gate University.

Jonn **Melrose** is a veteran service officer, Placer County, California.

Members of the ICMA Veterans Task Force. The task force was created to examine issues affecting military-community relations and the health and well-being of service members, veterans and their families.

Michael **Messner** is a professor of sociology and gender studies, University of Southern California—Dornsife College of Letters, Arts and Sciences.

Ginger **Miller** is a navy veteran and president and CEO of Women Veterans Interactive Inc.

Brian **Mittendorf** is the Fisher College of Business Distinguished Professor and Chair, Department of Accounting & Management Information Systems (MIS), The Ohio State University.

Stephanie **O'Neill** is an award-winning healthcare journalist with the NPR/KHN Collaboration.

Larisa **Owen** is a program director with the Center for Children and Family Futures (CCFF).

Rachel **Robinson** is an assistant circuit attorney in St. Louis, Missouri.

Grant **Rissler** is an affiliate faculty with L. Douglas Wilder School of Government and Public Affairs, Virginia Commonwealth University.

Alan **Roper** is a senior adjunct professor at Golden Gate University and an instructional designer/curriculum developer for the University of California, Office of the President.

Glenna S. **Rousseau** is a psychologist at the Veterans Health Administration.

Sanjay **Saint** is the George Dock Professor of Medicine, University of Michigan, and works for the VA Ann Arbor Healthcare System, where he serves as chief of medicine.

Ruth Astle **Samas** is a retired California administrative law judge and senior adjunct professor of Public Administration at Golden Gate University.

Kurt **Schake** is the executive director of the Monterey County Veterans Transition Center (VTC) in Marina, California.

William M. **Schumacher** is a PTSD postdoctoral fellow, New Mexico VA HCS, University of Oregon.

Benedict **Serafica** is a navy veteran and is serving with the California Air National Guard and with the California Military Department as an executive NCO to the Command Senior Enlisted Leader.

Kira **Serna** is an air force veteran, owns a small private psychotherapy practice, and works as a Licensed Clinical Therapist for the Department of Veterans Affairs.

Michael **Tomsic** is a reporter with WFAE, Connecticut Public Radio.

Eileen **Trauth** is a professor of information sciences and technology and women's, gender and sexuality studies, Pennsylvania State University.

U.S. Department of Veterans Affairs is a federal Cabinet-level government agency that provides near-comprehensive healthcare services to eligible military veterans.

Laurie **Udesky** is a San Francisco–based independent journalist.

Wouter **Van Dooren** is a professor of public administration at the Department of Political Science of the University of Antwerp, Belgium.

Barbara **Ward** is an adjunct professor of public administration at Golden Gate University and is the former director of the Center for Minority Veterans at the U.S. Department of Veterans Affairs.

Samantha **Wagner** is the senior manager, marketing and content, at the International City/County Management Association, Washington, D.C.

Eric **Whitney** is the news director for Montana Public Radio.

Chad **Williams** is an associate professor of African and Afro-American studies, Brandeis University.

Kayla M. **Williams** is a senior fellow and director of the Military, Veterans, and Society Program at the Center for a New American Security.

Jeffrey R. **Zimmerman** is the director of processing services within the North Carolina Division of Motor Vehicles.

Index